1-E

FOR ESSAY - CHP'S 7 - 8

POSS CHP 5 ?

COMMUNISM AND COLLABORATION

1   The old city of Marseille, *c* 1930

COMMUNISM
AND
COLLABORATION:

*Simon Sabiani and Politics
in Marseille, 1919–1944*

Paul Jankowski

Yale University Press
New Haven and London
1989

Set in Linotron Bembo by Best-set Typesetter Limited, Hong Kong, and printed and bound in Great Britain at the University Printing House, Oxford by David Stanford, printer to the University of Oxford.

Library of Congress CIP Data
Jankowski, Paul, 1950–
   Communism and collaboration: Simon Sabiani and politics in Marseille, 1919–1944 / by Paul Jankowski.
      p.   cm.
   Bibliography: p.
   Includes index.
   ISBN 0-300-04345-7
   1. Sabiani, Simon.   2. Marseille (France)—Politics and government.   3. Marseille (France)—Biography.   4. Politicians—France—Marseille—Biography.   5. Ex-communists—France—Marseille—Biography.   6. Fascists—France—Marseille—Biography.   7. World War, 1939–1945—Collaborationists—France—Marseille—Biography.
8. Parti Populaire Française.   I. Title.
DC801.M37S235   1989
944'.91—dc19
[B]   88-18708
                                                                                                  CIP

11289562

Printed in Great Britain
at the University Printing House, Oxford
by David Stanford
Printer to the University

CONTENTS

LIST OF ILLUSTRATIONS

2 Simon Sabiani and friends, *c* 1936

PREFACE AND ACKNOWLEDGEMENTS

I began work on this book thinking of it as a contribution to the controversy over 'French fascism'. A study of Simon Sabiani and his following in Marseille, from his Communist beginnings to his collaborationist end, would yield some local findings relevant, I thought, to the wider discussion. But I soon found that Sabiani's story had a life of its own and when I looked at the recondite literature about 'French fascism' I began to reconsider my participation. Rather than spend several years of my life and several hundred pages of the reader's time worrying about a hypothetical description for an unknown man, I decided to give the subject whatever treatment it deserved and forget about its assigned pigeonhole. I decided to write a thesis about *Sabianisme* and worry about fascism later.

Sabianisme is a rather tragic story. It began as a typical if noisy prewar *marseillais* political clan and ended in disaster, its members in disgrace, in exile, in prison, or in front of a firing squad. I set out to tell how and why it all happened, taking Sabiani's agitated life as a narrative thread; and then I looked again at the literature about 'French fascism'.

Historians have been arguing about the existence and nature of an indigenous French fascism for over thirty years, so much so that the subject is almost as controversial as Italian fascism or German Nazism. But it is much more limited: the protagonists in the debate have focussed almost obsessively on ideology.

At first they concentrated on the enthusiasms of intellectuals, mostly journalists and men of letters, for a new man and a new élite and a *romantisme d'action* — the enthusiasms of Brasillach for 'fascist joy' and of *Je Suis Partout*:

> French fascism does exist. It's not a party...but above all a state of
> mind, a family of reflexes, a heroic way of seeing life, it's a lot of

hardship and demands, it's a constant will to grandeur and purity...

They recognized some French precursors, variously identified as Péguy and Barrès and Sorel and Hervé, among others, and differed at times over the 'Frenchness' of the tradition they discerned rather than over its intellectual badge.[1]

More controversial were the political and social philosophers. Nolte, but not de Felice, thought Maurras fascist — de Felice found the idea 'absolutely impossible from any point of view'. Grossman, but not Bergounioux, thought Déat close to fascism by the mid-1930s — Bergounioux saw him as a Jacobin republican whose views were never more than reactions to events. For Plumyène and Lasierra he was only fascist after 1940. Most agreed that Georges Valois in his *Faisceau* phase was fascist, but some saw only an aberration in his intellectual development, the opportunistic digression of an ambitious crank whom even Brasillach, in his own day, had called a 'highly suspect lunatic'.[2] The arguments went on: the problem was that no one could agree on definitions, on the ingredients of a 'fascist minimum'.

The problem deepened and the controversy intensified with the appearance of Sternhell's *Ni Droite ni Gauche. l'Idéologie du Fascisme en France*. Now all sorts of thinkers were pre-fascist or fascist without even knowing it — Déat, de Man, Mounier, Maulnier, Sorel, among others — and one of them, unfortunate enough to find himself included within the long arm of the author's law, sued for libel. Sternhell's fascists formed a 'socialisme national' with roots in the late nineteenth century, a union of disaffected left-wing marxists and right-wing nationalists; they marked a synthesis of a certain socialism with a certain nationalism. Their ideological family was the forerunner of other fascist ideologies, and was all the purer in its ancestral French form for escaping the forced miscegenations of political office. They were fascist well before 1940 and if some later joined the resistance they had already flaunted their true ideological colours and their hostility to liberalism, democracy and Marxism alike.[3] Sternhell's work provoked a storm of protest. His critics attacked him for ignoring the context in which his thinkers thought up their theories; for a fallacious fatality, a 'causalité régressive' in which they were pre-fascist in 1930 because they were fascist in 1940; for exaggerating the very limited influence of a very limited number; for imposing an artificial coherence on their views; for ignoring or trivialising their anti-Nazi sentiments; for leaving out the fascists of the right, men like Céline or Brasillach who had never been Marxists, disillusioned or otherwise. Above all they attacked him for wielding the stigma of fascism so freely and flexibly as to threaten almost anyone: it was the problem of definition all over.[4]

The political movements were less controversial, Jacques Doriot's Parti Populaire Français least of all. Most found it fascist. Even sceptics like Plumyène and Lasierra who doubted the Frenchness of French fascism conceded that 'the PPF is the only authentic fascist party that France has produced' and Rémond, who shared their doubts, recognised its fascist characteristics along with them. For Winock the PPF was simply 'the most influential fascist formation'; for Milza it was '[the] only large mass fascist party ever to develop in France'.[5] And most historians found the *Francistes* and the *Solidarité Française* fascist also — small movements, overtly racist and authoritarian, sometimes violent, rich in ritual but bereft of doctrine. Conversely few historians, other than dogmatists of the left, found the *Croix-de-Feu* or the Parti Social Français fascist; Anderson found them pre-fascist, their members threatened socially but not *déclassés*. There was less unanimity over Taittinger's Jeunesses Patriotes. Soucy saw them as the party of 'centrist fascism', Anderson as pre-fascist, like the *Croix-de-Feu*, Plumyène and Lasierra as neither fascist nor a party. But about the PPF there was little disagreement.[6]

Like the historians of political ideas the historians of political organisations tended to rely on public aspect — on declared ideals and affected images. When Rémond recognised the fascist characteristics of the PPF he recognised its cult of the leader, its anticapitalism and revolutionary aspirations, its visceral anticommunism, its ritual; when Milza did so he likewise thought first of ideology and of ritual: 'Fascist, Doriot's party was indeed...in its behaviour — ceremony, flag, insignia, Roman salute, violent methods, etc — as in its ideology.' For hidden aspects, such as social composition and still more the mentalities and motivations of the members, there was, as they recognised, little evidence, and when Brunet or Wolf looked at the prior political antecedents or the social backgrounds of the members of the PPF they had to rely on the party's own claims, based mostly on the delegates at its national congresses.[7] To this extent much of the work on French fascism, and in particular on the PPF, resembles older work on Italian fascism or German Nazism, done before the specialised monographs and sociological analyses of the past 15 years. And on this basis the PPF, a synthesis of extreme left and right in its ideology as in its founders, does bear some resemblance to the first wave of Italian fascism and reflects the very ingredients of Sternhell's recipe.[8]

The PPF was Sabiani's party: he was its south-eastern regional leader and he espoused its ideology, if not its ritual, with energy and enthusiasm. If ideology were all that matters he could be tidily classified, perhaps even subclassified as a regional variant, a 'meridional' fascist. But ideology is not all that matters. I had discovered among Sabiani's following so limited a downward diffusion of fascist doctrines, if that is what they were, that I had forgotten about them altogether. I had asked who the *Sabianistes* were, first in the early 1930s, and then in the mid-1930s, and then at successive points during the occupation, and why they or others joined Sabiani's party, and who collaborated with the Germans during the occupation, and why they did so, and how they did so, and whether the *Sabianistes* differed from them, and a succession of other natural questions: the answers, I thought, would be useful to anyone interested in the recent history of Marseille, or in wartime collaboration, or in the narrower topic of the PPF. But they did not have much to do with fascism. The story that gradually came through was about a freak movement thrown up by the encounter between an archaic form of clan politics and a modern form of mass politics: a political grotesquerie. I still see it as an example of how periods of stress like the mid-1930s or of shock like the early 1940s can produce such an episodic creature, and of how quickly a return to normalcy can suppress it. I am unable to place it in any recognised tradition, fascist or other, and until other local episodes bearing comparison are unearthed I think it is best understood in its own terms.

In the end perhaps the story of *Sabianisme* is a contribution to 'French fascism' nonetheless. Perhaps it will encourage the protagonists in this interminable debate to apply their theories to the unknown thousands supposed to fit them — to ask who they were and what they did and what happened to them, in one place over time and under the stress of events; and if in the process fascism should evaporate of itself, so be it.

I would like to begin my list of acknowledgements by thanking Professor and Madame Pierre Guiral for all their hospitality and help while I was in Marseille. Professor Guiral put his knowledge and his time at my disposal, greatly helping me to understand the subject and the city, and I join countless former students of his in expressing my gratitude to him.

One of them, Jean-André Vaucoret, the author of a fine biography of Sabiani,[9] was equally generous with his knowledge of Sabiani the man and with his acquaintances in the erstwhile *Sabianiste* world. I would like to thank him here again for having introduced me to the late Alban Géronimi and to Sabiani's daughter Agathe, whom I might otherwise never have had occasion to meet.

Agathe Sabiani never tired of my badgering requests for information and introductions, and I would like to thank her for her patience and her hospitality. She was at all times frank and forthcoming and if there are any errors about her father in my work they are my own.

I would like also to extend my thanks to Madame M.-F. Maraninchi-Attard for letting me see her valuable work on the Corsican immigrants in Marseille, and to the other people I interviewed in Marseille and in Corsica: M Antoine Leonetti, Mme Dora Leonetti née Sabiani, maître Jacques Luciani, Mme Antoine Morelli, M Antoine Franceschi, M Roger Py, Dr Lucien Fredenucci, M. Finocchietti and, of course, the late Alban Géronimi.

I am very grateful to the entire staff of the *Archives départementales des Bouches-du-Rhône* for its help and forbearance during my work there. I would like in particular to thank the former director Madame Madeleine Vilar for supporting my efforts to gain access to closed archives and the *conservateur*, M. Christian Oppetit, for his invaluable suggestions and guidance through the rich *marseillais* archives. I have profited immeasurably from his knowledge of the city's recent history and of the sources for it, and hope my work will repay his assistance.

I would also like to thank the staff of the *Archives communales* in Marseille, where I worked on the census and on electoral lists.

In Paris my thanks go to M. Cézard and his successor Madame Bonazzi of the *Section contemporaine* of the *Archives Nationales*. I would also like to thank M. Jean Favier, the *Directeur des Archives de France* and the *Préfet de Police* for permission to consult closed archives. Finally, I would like to thank M. Gilles de la Rocque for his time and his help.

I would like to add my special thanks to Professor Bernard Wasserstein (Brandeis University) and Dr David Wasserstein (University College, Dublin), both of whom read the book in manuscript form and made valuable suggestions. I am grateful to Zelfa Hourani of Quartet Books for having introduced me to Robert Baldock and Ann Grindrod of Yale, with whom it has been a great pleasure to work. My thanks, also, to Dr Alex Pelin of Florida International University for his early advice on using computers, to Mireille Chemin, to Marita L. Wagner, and to Sandra Gerand.

I am grateful to the British Universities North America Foundation for a generous grant.

In Oxford I would like to thank the Taylorian Institution for a travel grant, Mr J.M. Prest and Dr Colin Lucas for their advice and encouragement, Dr Hartmut Pogge von Strandmann for guiding me to the *Wilhelmstrasse* archives, Dr D.A.L. Levy for permission to read his important Ph.D. thesis on 'The Marseille Working Class Movement, 1936–1938' (Oxford, 1982) and Dr Paul Griffiths of the Oxford University Computing Service for his extensive help and forbearance in working with me on the statistical and computing aspects of this book. I would also like to thank Dr D.B. Goldey, who began supervising my doctoral thesis and who continued thereafter to share his time and knowledge with me generously.

And last but not least, I thank my friend, former tutor and supervisor Richard Cobb for all. He made working on this thesis a pleasure when it might have been a penance, and for his company, his interest and his historical intuition I will always be grateful.

ABBREVIATIONS

AD   Archives départementales des Bouches-du-Rhône (Marseille)
AN   Archives Nationales (Paris)
APP   Archives de la Préfecture de Police (Paris)
CC   Commissaire Central (de police)
CD   Commissaire Divisionnaire (de police)
CJ   Cour de Justice (Aix-Marseille)
CS   Commissaire Spécial (de police)
EN   *l'Emancipation Nationale*
Int   Minister of Interior
LPM   *Le Petit Marseillais*
LPP   *Le Petit Provençal*
LVF   Legion des Volontaires Français contre le Bolchevisme
ML   *Marseille Libre* (later *Midi-Libre*)
MM   *Marseille Matin*
OPA   Office de Placement Allemand
PPF   Parti Populaire Français
PSF   Parti Social Français
Pref   Préfet des Bouches-du-Rhône
SFIC   Section Française de l'Internationale Communiste
SFIO   Section Française de l'Internationale Ouvrière (Socialist party)
SOL   Service d'Ordre Légionnaire
T   Microfilm series, (German Foreign Ministry) U.S. National
        Archives (Washington).

3   The Quai des Belges, c 1930

CHAPTER 1

The Confluence: Popular Politics in Pre-war Marseille

In 1970 two daughters of a once famous Marseille politician, Simon Sabiani, sued *Paris Match* for libel. The magazine had published an article calling their late father a 'bandit notoire', an epithet which, the court agreed, was defamatory. But it ruled that the plaintiffs could not themselves bring suit on their father's behalf.[1]

Most *Match* readers had undoubtedly never heard of the man, but the few who had could not have been surprised by what they read. They would have seen it before — seen Sabiani described two years earlier, for example, as venal and immoral — and they would see it again. A few years later he reappeared in a book on the drug traffic as an operator in the Corsican criminal *milieu*, a few years after that in a Marseille daily newspaper as an unscrupulous and ambitious influence-peddler, a lord of the underworld. If people remember the man at all, it is for the villainy of his cronies: *Sabiani, c'était le milieu, non?*[1]

This is surprising. Sabiani did have friends in the criminal *milieu*, but so did most local politicians, and Sabiani was much more besides: a hero of the first world war, a founder of the Communist party in Marseille, mayor of the city in all but name for four years, regional head of a major collaborationist organisation during the German occupation, and above all the leader of several thousand devoted friends and supporters, some of whom went into exile with him and some of whom paid for their loyalty with their lives. Even more than he, they have fallen into oblivion.

They are the losers whom history erases — temporary players whose sensational appearance closes to general obloquy, prelude to an obscurity they prudently do little to lift. They have no antecedents and no descendants. Devoid of apparent historical significance, they even come to resemble interlopers in their own day, espousing hair-raising causes — like that of the Nazi occupier — and stubbornly dis-

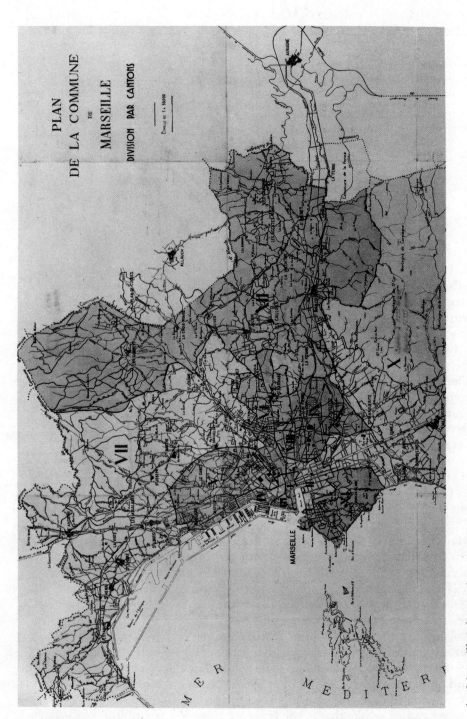

i   Marseille: the twelve cantons, 1931

regarding the most widespread sentiments of their compatriots. Then they disappear.

But the *Sabianistes* invite more than a study in the spectacle of transience. They successively stamped with their presence the wild politics of *Marseille-Chicago*, the 'fascism' of the Parti Populaire Français, and the increasingly sordid business of collaboration with the enemy: a singular itinerary illuminating controversial historical episodes and gradually revealing a logic of its own. Unruly and unattached, the *Sabianistes* started out clamouring for attention and ended up hiding wherever they could: who were they, and how did they come to grief?

The fourth canton was shaped like a riding boot: it began briefly along the high ground overlooking the *Vieux Port*, then turned north for a longer and wider stretch along the docks. Eleven other equally bizarre shapes overlay the city — electoral fictions conceived in 1884; some were peripheral, others central, and some, like the fourth canton, were neither.[2] It was a transitional canton, linking the dense nucleus of the old city, clustered around the port, to the sparse reaches of the new. Here the face of the city began to change; here the crowded streets of the *vieux quartiers* began to give way to the bleak stretches of factory and *terrain vague* announcing Le Canet, Les Crottes, and the endless industrial suburbs of the north. And here Sabiani established his base.

It was a small canton, dwarfed by the tenth in the south, which stretched over open country and even took in a coastal hamlet, or by the seventh in the north, with its industrial port of L'Estaque and its population scattered in clusters over the plateaux. The fourth covered less than one per cent of Marseille's huge surface area — twice that of Paris, five times that of Lyon — and was only a half-hour's walk from one end to the other.[3] But population compensated for size. There were perhaps 700,000 people in Marseille in 1936, after allowing for the inventiveness of the quinquennial census takers that year, and 50,000 of them were crowded into the fourth canton alone: it included some of the most densely populated streets in the city.[4]

They ran like furrows along the canton's southern heights, where the *vieux quartiers* ended their ascent from the water's edge — houses and walls clambering up the Butte des Carmes and the Butte des Moulins, through the first and third cantons and into the fourth. At their heart the *vieux quartiers* looked Italian or *niçois*: old stone houses two or three windows wide faced each other across narrow streets running with rivulets. The misnamed Grand'rue was only three meters wide.[5] Even more than its streets and houses the old city's Italian sailors, fishermen, dockers, vegetable merchants and artisans

ii Marseille: the fourth canton, 1924

of all kinds inspired the name by which other Marseillais knew it: *le petit Naples.*[6]

A third of all Marseille's residents had come, like the Italians of the *vieux quartiers*, from somewhere beyond metropolitan France. Since the late nineteenth century they had poured in from all over the Mediterranean and beyond, so that by the late 1930s there were 125,000 Italians, 20,000 Spaniards, 10,000 Arabs, 5,000 Greeks; and 60,000 Corsicans, French citizens but immigrants nonetheless; and 15,000 Armenians and 5,000 Russians, including a colony of Cossacks and their hetman, housed in wooden huts — Marseille, in Sabiani's day, was the most cosmopolitan city in France.[7] And the *vieux quartiers* included its most cosmopolitan canton, the first, striking to its many visitors:

> Women and their households sit in the doorways...Italians, half-slavs, native orientals, gypsy half-breeds...Neapolitan and Genoan women selling fried fish, onions and lemons; Bachins, natives of Genoa, Sardinia, or Sicily...[8]

They did not need the census to know that even excluding Corsicans, 40 per cent of the canton's population was foreign.[9]

At their summit in the fourth canton the *vieux quartiers* looked much the same but fanned out, between the edge of a famous red light district and a sixteenth century church — between the *quartier réservé* of Pierre MacOrlan's novel, 'twenty-five streets and alleys given over to the dark pleasures of the flesh' and the Eglise des Carmes on its hill above the port.[10] Some 25,000 people, half the population of the canton, crowded together here, sometimes at more than 1000 to the acre.[11] Densest of all was the quartier des Présentines, named for its prison but known for its Arabs. 'Here we are right in the middle of Arabia and Kabylie': the rue des Chapeliers was lined with cobblers' shopfronts, nameless Arab bars, and boarding houses where north African day labourers lived in furnished rooms. In fact, Arabs added up to only four per cent of the men in the fourth canton's *vieux quartiers*.[12] But like the Italians with their six per cent and the Armenians with their ten, they stood out. Compatriots tended to live in the same streets and cluster in the same professions: there were Armenian cobblers, tailors and seamstresses in the rue des Dominicaines, Algerian workmen in the rue Bernard du Bois, Italian masons in the rue Audimar. Together they contributed disproportionately to the wide base of the area's social pyramid: 25 per cent of the adult males were skilled or unskilled workers, 12 per cent were artisans, six per cent were domestic servants.[13] It was a 'quartier populaire'.

Towards the Boulevard des Dames the crowding began to ease, the workers to decrease, the officeworkers to increase — all signs that the *vieux quartiers* were ending, and the quartier de la Joliette was beginning.[14]

La Joliette was the closest the fourth canton came to having a *quartier bourgeois*. Some of the buildings here resembled those in the most opulent part of the city, around the Bourse in the second canton or the Chartreux in the sixth — massive façades, five or six windows abreast, the vestiges of a nineteenth century *haussmanisation* more austere than in Paris or Nice. They overlooked the docks and the liners unloading in the Bassin du Lazaret, and they housed, among others, employees of the great shipping companies and shopkeepers living off the commerce of the port. These were a distinctive feature of the *quartier*; many were Corsicans who had made good — immigrants of recent vintage who had prospered and left crowded tenements in the *vieux quartiers* for the more spacious flats of the Société Immobiliére.[15] Here they could enjoy Corsicans' company without enduring immigrants' privations; and one of them was Simon Sabiani.

But la Joliette had its humbler dwellings. Opposite Sabiani's flat in the rue de Forbin was a hostel for homeless men, and along from his subsequent home in the nearby rue Fauchier was a decrepit old house occupied by a bric-à-brac dealer. And it had its humbler residents: if factory workers, with about 12 per cent of the men of the *quartier*, carried only half the weight which they did in the *vieux quartiers*, then sailors, and in particular Corsican sailors, were two or three times as numerous. In Sabiani's voting ward sailors accounted for 12 per cent of the men, and more than a third of them were Corsican. There was even a home for Scandinavian sailors in the Boulevard de Paris.[16] Marginal itinerants peopled waterfront and dockside, notably the rue Mazenod:

> Birds of passage, employed in the boiler-rooms of the big liners...
> There they are in motley groups, dressed in blue overalls and droll coats. A mix of peoples: Ethiopians, Malagasys, Martiniquais, Senegalese...[17]

Indeed la Joliette, and the fourth canton itself, ended on one side in squalor, in the shanty town of the Lazaret: Spanish, Italian, Greek immigrants in huts of wood, or tin, or tar and pasteboard, and gypsies in tents and wooden trailers, and fetid alleys they had named, with black humour, after the city's richest streets — the rue St.-Ferreol, the rue Paradis, the rue de Rome. There was no running water, disease was endemic, plague broke out. The police hated the place. And beyond it in the fifth canton was more of the same: la Villette, huddled below the entrance to a sooty railroad tunnel. These were the dark spots of Marseille.[18]

On the other side la Joliette ended in factories — its residents complained about the fumes, to no avail — and in the industrial *quartier* of

Arenc. Long rows of greying warehouses linked to the docks by rail extensions rose above 'open lots, bars, uneven rooves, pink or ochre plaster, stained, grimy, faded....'[19] Factory workers rose again to almost a third of the adult male population; the canton ended here, in the middle of Arenc, but Marseille's industrial suburbs had already begun. The city was thinning out. Population densities, already falling in la Joliette, now dropped to below 200 people per acre, and out in the fifth canton, out past the dry-docks and the gasworks, they dropped to below 80. There were some dense working class concentrations — in la Madrague almost half the men were unskilled workers — but around were open lots and open land, presages of the Provençal country beyond.[20]

On the Boulevard de Paris, not far from the Scandinavian sailors' home, stood the Bar Raffé, one room on the ground floor of an apartment building, announced by a narrow doorway. It was a Sabianist bar. Across the Boulevard was the Bar Populaire, which was Socialist, at its Lazaret end the Bar Allegre, which was Communist. Nearby in the Avenue Camille Pelletan the bar at number 167 was called the Coullomb in 1928, when it was Communist, the Celona in 1934, when it was Socialist, and the Di Gugliemo in 1937, when it was Sabianist. The Bar de le Veranda in the rue des Enfants Abandonnés, near the Eglise des Carmes, was Communist, the Bar Casanova in Sabiani's rue de Forbin Sabianist — bars like these were the primary theatres of politics in the fourth as in every other canton.[21]

In them candidates inspired their supporters with words and regaled them with drinks. The practice delighted pundits and punsters. 'Monsieur le député Régis revitalises his voters so that they can revitalize his term of office' ('rafraîchit ses électeurs afin qu'en retour ceux-ci rafraîchissent son mandat') remarked one of them, and another dubbed a slate of candidates 'la liste du pastis', after its leader, the Socialist mayoral candidate Henri Tasso, connived at the suspension of the absinthe laws during the electoral period. Candidates drank too — another local Socialist, Toussaint Ambrosini, warned Léon Blum that to be elected in Marseille he would have to drink forty pastis a day.[22] Suitably fortified, candidates and supporters alike could open the proceedings: speakers, sometimes standing on table tops, reviewed their records in office, acknowledged the thanks of their friends and the ratification of their candidacies; new members signed on, old ones brought in contributions and made proposals for meetings and benefits and fund-raising rallies. Almost anything could be discussed.[23]

During election campaigns the meetings were frequent and widespread — on any one night there could be as many as 100 taking place around the city.[24] Attendance varied greatly, from 30 or less to four or five hundred; the largest bar meetings spilled out onto the pavement, where the audience could sometimes listen to a harangue relayed from within by a loudspeaker, and where curious onlookers — boys with bicycles — could sometimes join in.[25] Larger meetings called for more space. Salon and cinema owners let their premises to political parties for major rallies, sometimes quite ecumenically: the Olympia cinema in the eighth canton was host to 800 Royalists in April 1935 and to 1,000 Communists seven months later. The largest meetings of all took place in the open, in the public theatres provided by the city's squares. It took about 10,000 people to fill the Place Marceau, in the heart of the fourth canton, for a Sabianist rally in 1936. But these were exceptional. Mostly the meetings took place in bars, on weekday evenings or weekend mornings.[26]

Sometimes the participants formed cortèges afterwards and proceeded to their candidates' homes, where they would finally disperse, or to rival meetings in rival bars, where they would demonstrate. After a victory at the polls exultant supporters turned the streets themselves into the arena of politics. Tasso's re-election in the third canton in 1935 brought garlands of flowers to the bar-room doors and fireworks and pistol shots and revelry in the streets. Much the same took place a week later in the fourth canton, where Sabiani was also re-elected. The festivities could even turn to masquerade, mocking the loser and exhilarating the public: in 1928 Sabiani's supporters 'buried' his opponent Canavelli in a funeral complete with priest, choir boys, wooden coffin and burial — and with a few death notices in the bars of the fourth canton. They did the same to his opponent Duverger in 1924; victory without triumph was rare in these cantons.[27]

Any gathering, whether in the closed setting of the bar or the open air of the streets, could turn violent. Rival meetings often took place simultaneously and within sight of one another,[28] hecklers and saboteurs could choose their targets from the press, which usually published details of forthcoming meetings; at réunions contradictoires — semi-institutionalised free-for-alls — opponents were even invited to come and argue. These were recipes for violence.

It was not always clear how it started: all the police knew, on 9 October 1931, was that followers of Sabiani and followers of his Socialist opponent Ferri-Pisani had started shooting at each other in the Bar Auzers the night before. But mostly there was no mystery. Hotheads briefly disrupted meetings with flying raids — fired shots from car windows at Sabianists in their Bar Raffé in 1934, or Sabianists themselves shouted down socialists in the Bar Populaire opposite the Raffé in 1928. More determined saboteurs closed down meetings altogether. Any means were good — Socialists silenced a schismatic speaker with car horns and revolver shots in the third canton in 1937,

Sabianists drove Communists out of the Bar Allegre with trumpets, whistles, and loudspeakers in 1936, rivals within the right attacked each other's meetings with smoke bombs, stink bombs, and rancid missiles of *amadou poivré* in 1928. Communists in the Belle-de-Mai in 1930 adopted the simplest tactic of all: they moved in and took over a Socialist meeting. So did the Sabianists in 1924, wrecking a fourth canton bar in the process. In confrontations like these the aggressors normally encountered resistance, setting off a predictable spiral of violence: chairs were thrown, blows exchanged, shots fired; there were injuries and occasionally deaths.[29]

Out in the streets violence could erupt almost accidentally, as cortèges collided — in October 1937 the police wanted cortèges prohibited, after a collision between Communists and Sabianists in the fourth canton — and as rival newspaper sellers skirmished on common pavements. A fight in the Place Jules Guesde — again in the fourth canton, again in October 1937 — left two of them with bullet wounds. Most explosive of all were encounters between billposters, especially if they happened to be covering each other's posters with their own. An encounter of the kind in the tenth canton in 1934, between Socialist and right-wing billposters, left two dead and two wounded. During a single night in 1935, five men found lacerating rivals' posters were arrested and a sixth was shot during a pitched battle between billposters in Arenc. Violence of this sort was spontaneous.[30]

Then there was repeated violence — not always physical — to the electoral process itself, and by extension to the universal male suffrage on which the Third Republic rested.

The savaging began even before the campaign — to disfranchise unfriendly voters the men controlling the town hall had only to remove them from the electoral lists, using fanciful pretexts for multiple deletions; in 1928 over 500 Sabianist supporters in la Joliette were victims of the practice. Or they could add imaginary voters to the list: in 1922 87 of 114 voters said to be living in a nursing home were unknown there. Mere aspirants to office had to steal or destroy the electoral lists; the onset of a campaign was often heralded by break-ins at the Office of Electoral Lists. During the campaign the proliferation of bogus registration cards complemented the prior obliteration of *bona fide* voters, and the bar replaced the town hall as the distribution centre. *Le Petit Marseillais* found

> . . .a bar in the fourth canton where last Friday the owner had a supply of about 300 [voter registration] cards, in full view and in the full knowledge of the entire neighbourhood, and where some voters sought and *obtained* their card[s], which they had not been able [to do] at the town hall. . .

Candide quoted a bar owner's concluding argument in promoting the sale of his establishment: '. . . we have, finally, 146 voter registration cards which we will hand over with the sale'. With so many cards in circulation it was not surprising that some should turn up during the campaign in unlikely places: under a bench in a school playground, on a judge's desk — sent there by a repentant *fraudeur*.[31] By election eve the tricksters could attain new heights of ingenuity, pasting up counterfeit posters bearing spurious declarations of rivals' stepping down in favour of their own man — or even dying. But the climax came the next day.

On election Sunday, the architects of electoral victory turned their attention to the ballot and the ballot-box. With imaginary voters in-scribed on the lists, imaginary votes could be cast — votes by the absent, the deceased, the disappeared, votes by 'individuals brought in in a gang', votes by residents of other cantons. Ballot-box stuf-fing, generally known as *le toboggan*, further inflated the count, and long afterwards Sabiani's chauffeur Alban Géronimi remembered with pride his skill at ironing ballots together before introducing them as one into the box.[32] Such sleight-of-hand usually required the complicity of the *président* in the polling station — indignant voters repeatedly brought complaints against their partiality, which could be quite unequivocal: they were known to threaten voters with revolvers, empty the polling station without apparent motive, hold sudden conspiratorial meetings outside. Incumbents appointed them with care — *Marseille-Matin* reported that of 114 polling station *pré-sidents* in the 1937 cantonal elections, 82 were municipal employees and the rest worked under contract to the state or the city. Some of them at least could be relied on to turn a blind eye to even the crudest abuses — to ballots left uncounted, to a ballot box full even before the bureau had opened, or to the ultimate fraud, resorted to when all else had failed: the theft of the ballot box, *les urnes en promenade*.[33]

Electoral fraud could decide the outcome of an election without greatly distorting a party's overall share of the vote. It was a matter of tipping the balance, and Alban Géronimi recalled a wild scene during a first ballot count at a polling station in the fourth canton in 1937 — revolvers and confusion over 50 'votes' which would elect Sabiani or force him to a second round. Fraud was obvious if not overwhelming: 410 votes in a tenth canton bureau with 374 registered voters is only a discrete increment, but enough to sway an election. In 1924 the *Ligue pour la sincérité du vote* found 13,500 votes 'dubious', and in 1937 *Marseille-Matin* estimated that 16,000 were fraudulent: each figure, if accurate, would represent 11 or 12 per cent of all votes in those elections, and would consist of marginal fictions, favouring different sides, from polling stations all around the city.[34]

The agents of violence were sometimes professionals, the men of the *milieu*, like a 'well-known gangster (*nervi*)... and brothel-owner'[35] arrested after an attack by Socialist supporters on the office of electoral lists in 1937. The police recognised that no one had a monopoly over them: 'it is important to note, unfortunately, that [we] cannot single out M. Sabiani's teams alone'.[36] Sometimes they were petty criminals, like the four saboteurs, all with prior records, arrested at a meeting of the right in the ninth canton in 1929. Sometimes they were drifters, described by a lawyer defending them in 1939:

'You recruit naive or docile paupers, lead them into bars, you give them drinks, you excite them and when they've just about lost [any] sense the responsibilities they're about to incur, you take them to the polling station to commit the felonious act'.[37]

But the mainstream participants did not always find professionals or outsiders reliable — 'when there were set-tos the men from the milieu were always the last ones to arrive on the scene', Géronimi recalled with a trace of contempt; they would fight their own battles and assure their own defence. For the instruments of violence were at hand. Some regulars at meetings brought revolvers with them, some bar owners kept them under the counter, and if most were fired euphorically into the air, some were fired in anger. The owners of more primitive weapons — socialist and communist campaign workers with coshes (*nerfs de boeuf*), a voter with an ice-cutter — could have only one use for them. The habitués of violence were not necessarily its professionals.[38]

The authorities were almost powerless to prevent it. In 1929 Marseille had about 1,400 police, Paris 15,000; the police clamoured for reinforcement and pointed to political violence as an index of their impotence. They kept a small reserve at central headquarters to intervene when possible, and once on the scene they could erect barrages between rival meetings or marches, but, by their own admission, any preventive 'system' was chimerical.[39] Prefects were driven to outright bans, stopping short of suppressing the campaign itself: in 1937 they considered a ban on all public meetings and marches during the campaign, before banning loudspeakers alone. But bans were difficult to enforce. Posters proliferated anarchically, indifferent to the restrictions; meetings prohibited from taking place in public simply moved into private premises — like bars; the loudspeakers forbidden in 1937 kept reappearing, on cars, on trees, on houses.[40] Fraud, once done, could almost never be undone, unless there was an avalanche of evidence. The Conseil d'Etat or the Conseil de Préfecture would accept arguments but refuse to overturn the election, ruling that the complaint was too late, the margin too small, the evidence too slender; *fraudeurs* went to prison, their fraud went free.[41]

Sometimes leaders tried to restrain their followers: in 1937 Sabiani was able to tame a cortège of 700 supporters when it ran into Socialist opponents, and in 1935 he successfully forbade his people from using revolvers during a victory celebration. Sometimes they tried to forestall violence with appeals to the police, like that of the Socialist candidate Duverger in the fourth canton in 1925: 'an atmosphere of murder is settling on the Lazaret'. But mostly they themselves were to blame. In the mayoral elections of 1929 Sabiani, already a deputy, led his friends in a scuffle with Tasso's billposters at three in the morning, and Rouvier, a socialist candidate, invaded a right wing meeting at the head of forty followers. Like Sabiani they could not afford to lose face: 'If they draw their revolvers we'll draw our own!'[42]

Nor could they forgo the illicit perquisites of incumbency. Losers' complaints are recitals of outrages inflicted on them by incumbents during the campaign and on election day.[43] In or out of office, politicians had to employ professionals of the *milieu* as electoral agents. 'At the time we thought of it as banal,' a Sabianist supporter recalled fifty years later.[44] Tasso had the Guerinis, Rouvier had the Renuccis, Sabiani had Carbone and Spirito, all gangsters launched on the road to fame and prosperity by one political family or another. In return for their specialised services politicians provided protection, often at considerable cost to their public image: Rouvier's interventions on behalf of the Renuccis and Sabiani's proclamation of friendship for Carbone and Spirito provoked storms of criticism.[45] Political leaders had to protect anyone who rendered electoral services to them — bar owners in particular:

"You know?...I'll tell Sabiani...or Tasso"...Oh! Those two fateful names! You can't walk down the pavements of those ill-famed streets...without hearing them mentioned at every turning. The truth is that each bar-owner has his protector just as the serfs of old France had their lords.[46]

Tasso and his fellow-Socialist Corbani consorted with the felonious owners of neighbouring bars on the Quai du Port, and Sabiani provoked his first major political scandal when he came to the rescue of a friendly bar-owner implicated in armed robbery.[47] In relying on a bar-owner to provide an outlet for voters' cards or a false address for voters from out of town, a political leader might not know what else he was promoting, for the bar could be the home of less sophisticated crime — of stolen goods or a white slavery ring or a black market in false identity papers.[48] Politics was one venture among many.

But politics in this form shares with other bar-room crime its iconoclasm and its indifference to social convention. For a Géronimi there is nothing inviolable about another's ballot, and he is proud of his artistry in undermining democracy's most sacred ritual, the election. From a practical joke to physical murder, the gamut of political violence is a celebration of the power struggle. It is the will to prevail by any means necessary. It has an element of fun and stops well short of systematic terror, but its trademarks are force and intimidation; it is the pistol pointed at the taxi driver: 'Shout *vive Tasso* or I'll waste you!'.[49]

During an exchange in the city council Sabiani's Socialist opponent once declared that with Sabiani in office none of his protégés had a chance of a job:

Ferri–Pisani: If I pass on. . . a request for a job. . . I'm [only] doing what others do, but with this difference, that I'm convinced beforehand that my candidate will not be hired.
Sabiani: Eh! We'd certainly be wrong–headed to hire him. These are rules of the game ('c'est de bonne guerre, cela'). . .[50]

They both knew that behind all the brawling and the chicanery and the desecration of democratic institutions lay the pursuit of gain: the politics of services rendered and loyalty returned: the politics of clientelism.

So did the press, which reacted with sanctimonious disapproval to Sabiani's 'devoted creatures' in the fourth canton or Bouisson's ability to 'amass gratitude', or with vacant resignation to the entrenched system: 'The elected officials have built their clientèles. . . they are [now] reaping the fruits from individual favours performed for their voters'.[51]

A job was the ultimate favour, and successive municipalities in inter-war years distributed them extravagantly. They hired needlessly — in five years the street-cleaning force doubled, the rubbish remained. They laid off reluctantly — 400 temporary sanitation men hired during a strike in 1936 were still on the books three years later, long after the strike had ended. They spent prodigiously — ten million francs for the firemen in 1939, only 400,000 francs for their equipment. They were wastrels on the loose.[52]

Professional qualifications were irrelevant: only 123 employees, out of more than 2,000 hired during the 1930s, took the supposedly mandatory entrance test. Some of the city's tax collectors were illiterate. Worse, in 1938 at least 77 municipal employees, and probably more, had criminal records; one of them was a murderer. Hiring peaked in 1932, when Sabiani's town hall took on 815 new employees, but a scandalised national commission declined in 1939 to point its finger at any one municipality: the practice, it concluded, was endemic.[53]

Employment was the richest gift in a politician's hands, but whenever his electors ran afoul of faceless bureaucrats he had a fresh chance to ingratiate himself. He was a broker between the state and its citizens. The elected officials, deputies in particular, prevailed on judges to reduce fines, lift expulsion orders, delete prostitutes from the registers of *filles soumises*, reprieve criminals, grant naturalisations — between June and September 1939 Tasso intervened 70 times on behalf of protégés, 31 times to request their naturalisation. They arranged for identity papers, commercial permits, 'medical' exemptions from military service. No favour was beneath their dignity — a licence for a fishmonger to sell in neighbouring departments or for a bar to stay open late, a stay of eviction for an unemployed tenant:[54] the favour was the currency of clientelism.

And when its recipient voted for its donor he married honour to self-interest. When Sabiani's opponent Canavelli intervened in 1928 to prevent an unwanted transfer to Paris for a customs inspector, the grateful protégé repaid his debt with his ballot, openly proclaiming his choice. Nearly sixty years later he recalled an encounter with the victorious Sabiani on that election night:

'I was playing poker [in a café] on the Canebière when people on the terrace starting singing l'Ajacienne...they were acclaiming Sabiani. He saw me and said, "I won! In spite of you!" I explained to him that Canavelli had done me a favour and that I would [therefore] vote for him, always. And Sabiani approved. He understood honour, Simon did'.[55]

Simon understood honour: in another debate in the city council with Ferri-Pisani Sabiani declared that the workers he had hired 'most certainly and naturally are bound to think their support should go to me rather than you!'. Conversely the voter expected honourable behaviour from his elected representative and complained if he felt slighted. More than reproach is implied in a letter to Sabiani from a municipal employee in 1935:

'...You know...that to defend your administration I wasn't afraid to fall out with everyone...Well all that was a complete waste. I'm not even put forth for promotion...I place my trust in you. I *demand* to be your candidate'.[56]

It was a two-way street.

Private and vaguely illicit, the individual favour had a public and thoroughly conventional extension: the collective subsidy. To the tram workers the town hall was a source of richer pensions, longer vacations, larger sick pay; to the gas workers, of free gas and electricity; to its own employees, of job security granted *en masse*, sometimes, as in 1935, on the eve of elections — this was institutionalised largesse, and it repeatedly raised the eyebrows of Paris auditors.[57]

Candidates for re-election were careful to remind the municipal and franchised employees of their bounty in office. But of necessity they courted other collectivities, especially those strongly represented in their own constituencies — it was natural that Cana-velli and his successor Sabiani should fight for the pensions of customs inspectors, Tasso and Corsetti for those of sailors: the former abounded in St. Lazare, the latter in Petit Naples. It was no coincidence that Sabiani defended the rights of Algerian immigrants, so numerous in the Présentines, or that another fourth canton candi-date proclaimed his services to Corsicans, so numerous in Arenc and la Joliette.[58] They were trawling for support.

More impersonal, but just as conventional, were services to entire neighborhoods. Like individual favours they answered concrete re-quests: a misspelled letter to Tasso from some residents of the *vieux quartiers* asking that 'your and our neighbourhood' be cleared of pro-stitutes, a neighborhood association presenting its demands for im-provements at the *mairie*. Like individual favours they were rarely refused, if occasionally hedged with financial caveats. And like in-dividual favours they were received with praise and gratitude — the neighbourhood association in la Madrague referred to Sabiani as 'our likeable [sympathique] first deputy mayor, to whom our requests are never made in vain', and in their communiqués other associa-tions enumerated their acquisitions — lighting, paving, *vespasiennes*, dustbins — and thanked their municipal suppliers.[59] Such willing compliance by the town hall was grist to the critic's mill, and le Petit Marseillais condemned the Sabiani municipality for it: 'They have lived from day to day, ceaselessly hounded by neighbourhood asso-ciations, resurfacing here, lighting there...' But others made their support contingent on it, like the president of a neighbourhood asso-ciation, as he recalled after the war:

> I knew Sabiani in [1931–1932]...After he accepted the demands I made in the neighbourhood association of St.André, I joined his party. I campaigned for [him] during elections and we became great friends...

It was thanks to Sabiani, he said, that St. André had electricity in-stalled, streets repaved, pipes refitted, a tramline put in. Like the customs inspector who voted for Canavelli, he had good reason to honour his obligation.[60]

Financial control might have arrested the flow of favours, but with administrative power dissipated among the elected grandees them-selves, financial or any other control was not to be. It required a selflessness to which they did not even pretend. Nineteen city coun-cillors, attended by loyal but incompetent subalterns, ran 43 munici-pal services as personal fiefdoms, hiring almost at will, spending as though there were no budget and then presenting the municipal treasury with a *fait accompli*, giving free rein to contractors and not even reviewing their work, keeping poor records; the national authorities were beside themselves.[61]

Inevitably some of the councillors enriched themselves in office, like the butcher-turned-councillor who supplied the city's hospitals with meat, or the councillor in charge solely of the slaughterhouses found ordering carpets and linoleum, or the deputy who quietly transformed the city's printing press into a private concern — 'altogether singular vagaries' to the *cour des comptes*, but surely not to a Castel-Bénac, the venal official of Pagnol's Topaze: 'But, in God's name, who is city councillor? You? or me?'[62]

Efforts at reform came to nothing. When Flaissières and later Tasso tried instituting regular controls on expenditures they only provoked a vigorous defence on the part of indignant councillors, who balked at the assault on their independence and stayed the onset of accountability. Sabiani declared in 1930 that there were 1,000 superfluous employees in the Hotel de Ville, but he hired 315 the following year and 815 the year after that. He tried various reforms but bequeathed a 400 million franc debt to his successor, Tasso, whose successive premier adjoints resigned in despair over the futility of their own efforts at reform. By 1939 the debt had doubled, in spite of declining services, and only a 76 per cent increase in revenue would balance the municipal budget.[63] Marseille was bankrupt.

Dark, airless, dilapidated, the Hotel de Ville and its annexes — theatre of the financial and administrative anarchy — inspired less than awe.

> 'Alcoholism reigns in the town hall. All you meet on the stairs are deputies sleeping off electoral drinking (*cuvant des vins d'honneur*) and councillors dead drunk from champagne.'[64]

And Daladier's bewildered cry as he watched the *Nouvelles Galeries* burn out of control — a disaster which finally provoked the suspension of the *conseil municipal* and its replacement by an administrator from Paris — is a closing comment on the sorry inter-war chapter in the city's long history: 'But who is in charge here?'.[65] With private problems seeking public remedies and public services provided as private kindnesses, and with the frontiers of politics thus impossibly blurred, it was difficult to say, but 'la clientèle' would have been as good an answer as any.

Clientelism is so elastic a concept that its disciples have applied it to eighteenth century England, nineteenth century America, and twentieth century India. But it has a traditional association with Mediterranean societies, and Marseille was one of their meeting grounds — a meeting ground, in particular, of Italians and Corsicans.[66]

The Italians were more numerous, but unless they were naturalised — and about a quarter of them were[67] — they did not vote and could not hold public office. Possibly they compensated for their political marginality by participating in ethnic associations like *Il Progresso* or *La Fratellanza Italiana*, or in trade unions, or even in religious ceremonies like the *fête de la latinité*. Some of them attended political meetings, and some took part in the meetings of Italian socialists in exile, but even among the naturalised only Henri Tasso made a career out of politics.[68] It was not a natural route of ascent.

Corsicans, by contrast, pervaded the political landscape. They were already French, they already voted; they had lived in the Republic for as long as anyone else. They crowded into public office, administrative and elective. Corsicans accounted for ten per cent of the fourth canton's adult men, but twenty per cent of its male civil servants — more in la Joliette and in the streets off the Place Jules Guesde.[69] One contemporary urbanist saw them as a sort of administrative island in the *marseillais* sea, attributing their passionate interest in local politics to self-interest as well as to instinct.[70] And indeed their demographic weight in the city — about eight per cent — belied their elected numbers. Twenty-one out of 68 city councillors before and after the elections of 1935 were Corsican. All five candidates for deputy in the fourth canton in 1928 were Corsican. 'Marseille, first city of Corsica,' Flaissières had said in 1920, and the doctor-mayor's *mot* honoured the Corsicans in office as well as those in the streets.[71]

For the politics they practised were more than echoes of the politics they had left behind. In the Corsica of Sabiani's and Canavelli's childhood a *capi partitu* traded land for votes:

'I give my life and I could even say our fortune to our clients, and our clients give us their votes; that is our secret . . . yesterday they would have followed us to war, today they follow us to the ballot.'[72]

In Sabiani's native Niolu, where such private domains were rare, and where three-quarters of the land was collectively owned, mayoral *capriccio* made access to the commons easy for supporters and difficult for opponents; in a pastoral economy this was tantamount to distributing jobs. In 1886 in Casamaccioli, Sabiani's village, 34 supporters of the mayor paid 87 francs for the use of the communal lands, 37 opponents paid 1002 francs; 41 opponents paid almost four times the property tax of 56 supporters.[73] *C'est de bonne guerre, cela* . . . Then there were the municipal jobs themselves.

Paid jobs fall like manna on the clan in power. Cleaning the foun-
tains, watching over the peace of the dead, correcting the clocks,
collecting paltry local dues, guarding empty pounds...

A state service was an electoral weapon, and by the turn of the
century mayors were withholding birth or indigence certificates,
inflating medical relief payments, publicising the names of opponents
receiving charity: clinging to office as expected: *a mayor should die in
his sash.*[74]

Thus the ritual question on election day about the identity of the
victor — *for whom are those flags fluttering on the masts?* — reflected
material anxiety: 'his personal security and fortune are what the voter
risks on his ballot': politics, for the Corsican villager, was more than
a duty.[75] And it was to politics that he turned when he stepped
ashore in Marseille. From the emigrant's first stop, often among
family or friends in the *vieux quartiers*, the feelers would go out to
powerful acquaintances, ideally to co-villagers who had made good.
'A cousin has just landed on me, *I have him on my hand [je l'ai sur les
bras]*...if there were some way of getting him in somewhere...'.
With that central and recurring phrase, a semaphoric request for
help, the Calenzanais turned to the eminent émigrés from their
village:[76] to Jean-François Leca, the socialist *conseiller d'arrondissement*
in the third canton — 'I said to myself: with Leca in Marseille, he can
always find something for me somewhere', recalled one of his people
— and to Jean-François Guérini at the social assistance office and
even to the great Landry, the minister who created the Assurances
Sociales and helped staff its offices with protégés from Calenzana.[77]
Every year Sabiani found jobs for three or four arrivals from Casamaccioli alone, and when he was elected deputy in 1928 the entire
village rejoiced.[78] It was *le village en République.*

In Corsica the road to power and its blessings ran through the clan,
in Marseille through the party.[79] In the 1930s Casamaccioli still had
its two clans, more or less divided by the north and south sides of the
road running through the village and loosely including four or five
chiefs each; Sabiani had grown up with them. In Marseille they dissolved. Sabiani took no part in their distant warfare and back in the
village they even celebrated his distant electoral victories together.[80]
In Marseille the Corsican *amicales* transcended the clan — it was a
condition of their success that they do so.[81] But with so much still at
stake, the new party member of the city fought for office as bitterly
as the old clansman of the village, taking up some of the same weapons. Neither Corsica nor Corsicans, during Sabiani's childhood,
had a monopoly on electoral fraud and violence in the Third Republic.
But it had the highest incidence of elections overturned — one out of
every six communes had election results invalidated in 1886, almost

one in four in 1884. If Marseille had *les urnes [the ballot box] en promenade*, Corsica had *les urnes à la mer*; Sabiani's chauffeur Géronimi
had learned the tricks of the trade in his native Cassano, and the electoral 'enforcers' from the *milieu* were often Corsican immigrants: the
Tramonis before the first world war, the Guerinis, the Renuccis, and
Paul Buonaventure Carbone after. In Marseille, they said, 'the party
member. . .only lives for his party'; in Corsica, they replied, 'what is
right is what is good for the clan'.[82]

The Third Republic was hospitable territory; its statesmen and its
commentators knew and understood the politics of the clientèle.
Barthou saw the city councillor as 'the auxiliary, the intermediary,
the agent of the voter in the administration' and Tardieu thought of
the intervention on behalf of a constituent as the very essence of the
deputy's profession. Barthou, along with authors like Etienne Fournol and Jacques Fourcade, also knew that when professional men,
notably doctors and lawyers, entered local politics their clients became indistinguishable from their voters. Dr. Siméon Flaissières,
mayor of Marseille before and after the first world war, was a classic
example. The weight of the bar or café in any election was taken for
granted — 'the Café de Commerce is *also* a café', wrote Fourcade —
and the physionomy of the campaign, marked by the abuses of incumbency and the excesses of militancy, had already ceased to sur-
prise before 1914. Fourcade knew of a mayor in the Midi who
proclaimed his fraud in his speeches, and another author, Pierre de
Pressac, thought that the Corsican 'politics of the clientèle' were
simply a distilled version of the politics prevailing in the Midi generally.[83]

But certain cities were showcases for this sort of politics. Marseille
was one of them, and within Marseille the fourth canton, with its
immigrants, its poverty, its Corsicans, and its gangsters doubling as
electoral agents — it housed Carbone, his felonious brother, and the
Guerinis[84] — took pride of place. The press stigmatised it: *Le Petit
Marseillais* wrote of 'this electoral period, so agitated in the fourth
canton, which, alas, is really no honour to Marseille'. The Prefects
worried about it: 'Please have the polling places of the fourth canton watched *particularly closely*'. The police wearied of it: all is normal
in Marseille this year except the 'tumultuous meetings' of the fourth
canton.[85] And with good reason, for an election there rarely went
without *pastis*, processions, *les urnes en promenade*, a pistol fired
wildly into the air, and a basket of flowers for the victor.[86]

But where was the line between the clientèle and the electorate at
large? Between the politics of private interest and the politics of
public opinion?

A 'client', unlike a disinterested voter, had a debt to pay, but if the debt was weak his politics might stray. Sabiani's young upstairs neighbour theoretically owed his job in the *Ponts-et-Chaussées* to Tasso — his uncle, a socialist, had asked Tasso for help: 'I've a little nephew, [he's just] a guttersnipe' — but his vote and his loyalty went to the compelling presence downstairs.[87] The tailor in the rue Bernard-du-Bois may have thanked the Guerinis for their custom by introducing prostitutes to them, but there is no indication that he felt obliged to vote for their political employers.[88] Conversely simple electors had fitful attitudes to the wilder members of the clientèle. Sometimes they complained — on election Sundays indignant citizens denounced fraud by day and revelry by night. But sometimes they liked what they saw; they laughed and applauded.[89] The two political mentalities — that of citizenry and that of dependency — are not always distinct: there is a floating frontier between them.

But each has a typical collective expression: one has the raucous street cortège behind the candidate-hero, the other has the mass public meeting around the mobilizing issue. Each leaves a measure of its presence in local politics.

About 2,000 people took part in Sabiani's street celebration after his electoral victory in the cantonal elections of 1925; 2362 had voted for him. Even allowing for the presence of non-voters — notably children and foreigners — in street processions, the congruence between those who voted and those who went on parade for Sabiani was striking. It remained so until the war. In the cantonal elections of 1937 about 3,000 of Sabiani's supporters celebrated his victory; 3,471 had voted for him. Even in municipal elections, where the candidate's constituency took in another canton, the participants in the cortège coincided with the voters in his own canton. In 1935 about 4,000 people celebrated Tasso's re-election in the third canton, where 3,556 had voted for him, but he also owed his victory to 9,806 voters in the other cantons — the first and the eleventh — of his municipal constituency. In the same elections about 3,500 people took to the streets of the fourth canton to celebrate Sabiani's re-election; 3,217 of its residents had voted for him. His other voters that year — 2,391 in the sixth canton — appear to have stayed home on Sunday night. So it was in the municipal by-election of 1939: the size of Sabiani's cortège — about 2,800 people — corresponds to that of his vote in the fourth canton, but not to his total vote.[90] The numbers in all their monotony indicate a solid but unchanging core of personal supporters in the candidate's own canton: a clientèle.

By contrast the mass public meeting, organized around a national party or issue, surged onto the scene almost unannounced. During the mid-1930s it began to dominate the political landscape, dwarfing the more intimate encounters of the bar and the more personal cortèges of the streets. In the first six months of 1926 — six months of the Guerre du Rif and the mounting crisis of the Cartel — there had been only five open political gatherings of 1,000 people or more, one of them a royalist Mass attracting mostly curious onlookers.[91] In 1933 there were five again,[92] one of them a personal rally uniting a local faction with its leader — as it happened, Simon Sabiani. But in the first six months of 1934 there were 15. Only one was a personal rally, again organized by Simon Sabiani; most of the others drew partisan throngs to itinerant national figures — 4,000 socialists to Léon Blum, 4,000 Croix-de-feu to La Rocque — or mobilized multiple trade unions.[93] More people now marched to a public tune — to syndical sentiment, which mobilized 2,000 on Mayday 1933 and 35,000 four years later; to anger over a foreign war, especially the Spanish Civil war, which was drawing crowds of 10,000 in 1937 while the Rif war, in which French soldiers were dying, had brought out no more than 800 at once in 1926; to conservative patriotism, which mobilized at most 3,000 for the *fête de Jeanne d'Arc* in 1933 and 10,000 in 1937.[94] Attendance figures like these warrant more conjecture than conviction, but beside them the raucous enthusiasts of the *apéritif d'honneur* and of the candidate's cortège begin to look very small.

A stronger indication that the frontiers of the clientèle were receding comes from the simultaneous rise of new parties with little or no hold over the riches of office. At the beginning of 1934 police attributed the weakness of the Communist party to its parsimony; in Marseille, they said, members of a party expected some sort of recompense for their adherence. Two years later the party had 3,500 members and still only two *conseillers d'arrondissement*. Its success was that of the Popular Front and of a broad working class movement,[95] but on the right an equally unworldly novelty appeared in the shape of the Parti Social Français, heir to the avowedly anti-electoral Croix-de-feu: by 1937 the PSF had 15,000 members and not a single city councillor.[96] With the new parties came a new sort of leader. Neither François Billoux of the PC nor Jacques Arnoult of the PSF generated the popular affections enjoyed by Tasso or Sabiani; they had no garlanded photos in bar-room windows or cheering crowds below their balconies. Billoux had not even come to Marseille until 1934,[97] Arnoult never stood in an election. The focus of their supporters' affections was more distant: *le parti* itself, or a national symbol like La Rocque. It was a different kind of politics.

Its novelty never precluded a resort to conventionally violent tactics. The PSF had its armed felons and the PCF its murderous *hommes de main*.[98] The Communists valued the treasures of incumbency, demanding control over the rich social assistance office after their electoral success in 1936.[99] But members were displaying more abstract preoccupations. In 1929 SFIO had lost a quarter of its members after losing municipal power. In 1937, upset by events in the Soviet Union and Spain, and by the government's financial policy, communists began to leave the party — at a time when it was still riding a crest of electoral success. If some joined the PSF under pressure from their employers, others left because of its refusal to join the *Front de la Liberté*. If 5,000 shipyard workers followed a hearse through the streets in January 1937, it was to mark the demise of the 48-hour week, not of some hapless local politician.[100] New opinion mingled with old antics.

Taken together, such symptoms may translate no more than the encounter of demographic with financial reality. While the city's electorate was growing, its resources were dwindling. There were 70,000 registered voters in the six cantons of the 1931 elections, 77,000 in the same six in 1937. And certainly, if municipal hiring is a criterion, the local politicians were increasingly hard pressed to reward their proliferating voters. During the extravagant years of the 1920s municipal employees increased on average by about 40 per cent a year, a rate sustained until 1935 when the spectre of bankruptcy began to haunt the Hôtel de Ville. By the end of 1937 its tenants had to freeze hiring altogether.[101] And still the electorate kept growing.

But in another sense these are so many convergent indications that the compelling issues of the middle and late 1930s were severely testing conventional politics. Clients now confronted issues which clientelism could not resolve: it could provide jobs for a while, but it could not dispel the slump; it could arrange for exemptions from military service, but it could not dispel the growing threat of war. Nor could it assuage popular anger at the decrepitude of a régime to which it so visibly belonged. Into its own politics — pragmatic, local, and intensely personal — came the tide of mass politics: ideological, national, and anonymous. Its politicians had to struggle to stay afloat, to ride the confluence; and none had to struggle more than Simon Sabiani.

For his hybrid fourth canton had room for the new politics as well as the old, and the story of their encounter is the story of his career. Mass politics appeared in the form of the Communist party, spreading in from the northern suburbs into the industrial working class of Arenc, finally besieging Sabiani in his own stronghold, and *Sabianisme*, struggle to adapt and survive, embarked on an ill-conceived venture which eventually went grotesquely awry.

CHAPTER 2

The Rise of Simon Sabiani,
1919–1931

Simon Sabiani was born in 1887 in Casamaccioli, a pastoral village high in west central Corsica. His father had sold the family land and taken up accountancy in Bastia to support the family; his mother was a teacher in the local girls' school. He grew up, with four brothers and two sisters, in a modest house — candlelight, well-water, and a roof of wooden planks — wedged into a village descending in staggers down the sides of a mountain valley.

Both of his parents were politically active. Jean-Pierre Sabiani was a minor chief in one of the village's two clans, a rivalry in which his wife took a spirited part, even prevailing during the 1930s on her visiting granddaugher — Simon's daughter Agathe — to shun members of the opposing clan. Simon was a mediocre pupil but an energetic leader of village pranksters at home in Casamaccioli and of socialist *lycéens* at school in Bastia. He displayed his mother's factious if not her academic inclinations; politics ran in his blood.

In 1907 Simon left for Marseille, following in the steps of his older brother. Unsettled years followed, spent in abortive notarial studies, in shipping and haberdashery, in military service cut short by illness. Eventually he joined the entourage of Roch Olivier Colombo, a local Corsican politician of the moderate right who had found him a job at the *Compagnie des Docks*. By 1914 Sabiani was taking part in his patron's re-election campaign — a client, an apprentice, but as yet still a drifter.

In the end the war launched him on his career. He tore up his medical exemption papers, left for the front, lost an eye at Douaumont and returned with four citations including the *Croix de Guerre*; he survived. Three of his brothers did not, and the experience of the war turned the volunteer of 1914 into an ardent pacifist. He returned to civilian life and opened a small shipping company by the docks in

4 Young upstart and old Mayor: Sabiani and Flaissières (from *Le Bavard*, 30 March 1929)

la Joliette, but he soon lost interest in the business. His real interests lay elsewhere — with the pacifists and the internationalists on the far left of the Socialist party. The war had given him a cause — revolutionary pacifism — and a vocation to be an electoral politician.[1]

The emerging public personality was anything but pacific. Contemporaries, then and later, saw a violent temperament which was perhaps the dark side of physical courage but certainly an indispensable asset for an ambitious politician setting forth in the rough streets of the fourth canton. Sabiani did not shrink from bar-room confrontations — he even challenged a journalist to a duel in 1930 — but his violence was more verbal than physical, released in vituperative epithets. One opponent was the speculators' guardian, another a punctured windbag, a third a pale puppet with pretty hair and an empty head. He was a 'born militant, truculent orator and a remarkable leader of men', a firebrand who made up in mettle for what he lacked in physical attractiveness. He was a short man with a glass eye. But he fascinated his visitors:

> A stubborn face with the fixed glass eye introduces a strange note and accentuates the energetic mask, thin and excitable, coldly violent, no surprise that he should have become in our great Mediterranean port a gang leader with his own fanatics and his own legend.

His opponents saw demagoguery, his supporters sincerity — and both were right.[2]

The public mask hid few secrets other than an engaging *bonhomie*; the largesse which won clients for the patron also won friends for the man. To this day his neighbours and protégés remember him with affection: 'he had a rasping voice, he was small, not handsome, but he had charm'; 'warm, sincerely close to the poor, tender towards the aged and children, always available...'. But his moralistic speeches, resounding with civic injunctions and professions of personal honesty, reflected a certain sternness towards his three children and a private asceticism precluding alcohol or gambling or any extended leisure. His public contempt for the rich and the bourgeois matched a private indifference to money which often left him penniless and dependent on his wife — a Bastiaise of some means who had arrived in Marseille carrying a sack of gold — and even occasionally on his chauffeur. He was not venal: he gave money away. He saw it as a means to acquiring influence rather than the reverse. The politician was the person, the passenger captured in his chauffeur's memorable lament: 'Outside of politics he was nothing. He couldn't even drive'.[3]

'He appears to be seeking electoral office. . .': within three weeks of
the armistice Sabiani the militant Socialist was thinking of the following year's elections. As the first treasurer of the Socialist party's
newly created *comité de vigilance* he helped organize the party's campaign and took part in its meetings, where he denounced the war
and the rich and called for 'les soviets partout'. He also began
building his base in the fourth canton; by 1919 he was president of
the neighbourhood association of the wretched Lazaret and a notable
of the canton. But he was not strong enough to stand on his own,
and when he was elected city councillor in November 1919 he had
Flaissières and the *scrutin de liste* [voting by party list] to thank: he
came in on the old mayor's coat-tails, the thirty-fourth of thirty-six
on a list herding Socialists, Radicals and *Républicains de gauche*
together in a coalition called 'collectiviste'. 'Collectivism meant
nothing, we didn't believe in it', recalled one of Sabiani's friends, but
lip-service to Flaissières and his creation was a small price to pay for
an office in the Hôtel de Ville.[4]

Sabiani and his Socialist *co-listiers* had entered the election as the
candidates of a deeply divided party, for the creation of the Third
International in March 1919 had opened a rift among Socialists locally
as well as nationally. In Marseille supporters of affiliation — the
future Communists — had appeared almost at once, launching a
movement which by 1920 had absorbed or eclipsed the visionary
cliques proliferating on the far left of the party, such as the erratic
groupe communiste or the hybrid *groupe d'études sociales*, mostly inde-
pendents and anarchists, or the *groupe clarté* or the *jeunesses socialistes*.
From such footholds the missionaries of the Third International
moved on, carrying motions at successive departmental congresses
in 1920, and the vote of the Bouches-du-Rhône delegation at Tours
in December, already foreshadowed by its vote at Strasbourg in
February, completed their conquest of the local party.[5]

The subsequent schism in the Bouches-du-Rhône party left SFIC
with the troops but SFIO with the officers: most of the socialist *élus*
defied the members' vote at Tours and stood by the old party. The
few who did join the exodus, the few who could countenance the
Third International's famous twenty-one conditions, did so for different reasons: because Amsterdam's International had given way to
Moscow's, because the Socialist party had disgraced itself in the
union sacrée, because revolution was the order of the day; and among
them was Simon Sabiani.[6]

Since 1919 Sabiani had championed the Third Internaitonal, sometimes in the vaguest of terms:

  . . .It's necessary for us to go to Moscow. It will be the best way to
  eliminate those who are preventing the socialist party from fol-

lowing its ideal...the day the party is rid of those people, we would [sic] be able to envisage a general movement which will allow the installation of a collectivist régime while awaiting the communist régime.

But he spoke the language of revolution fluently. He decried the evils of militarism and urged resistance to an imminent mobilization; he denounced the *bourgeoisie* and called for the overthrow of capitalism. And he practised what he preached: he engaged his shipping company in the cause, sending clothing and 10,000 sacks of rice to his 'Camarade, Commissaire du Gouvernement des Soviets' in Odessa and offering half the proceeds of other trade with Odessa to the Bouches-du-Rhône Communist party. 'M. Sabiani,' declared the prefect, 'is one of the most ardent Communists in Marseille.'[7]

For two years revolutionary militant dovetailed with practical politician — Sabiani had both clients and comrades in the fourth canton. He still presided at the Lazaret association but he now had a seat on the social assistance office as well, a *carte blanche* to funnel municipal alms to his beggarly constituents. Later he candidly declared his priorities:

'Do you not know that, in the social assistance office, one does nothing but play politics?...You do not know the conditions under which the social assistance office's relief is given?...I stayed five and a half years in the social assistance office...I did what everyone else did...when I could please some friends I did so'.[8]

He denounced the coalition in power at the *mairie*, accused it of corruption and incompetence, and wooed voters with promises of integrity and generosity. A second-round election as *conseiller d'arrondissement* in 1922 crowned his efforts, making him the city's first elected Communist: a happy union between Communist ideologue and clientelist careerist.[9]

But the marriage could not last. Sabiani, like many of the early converts, had paid little attention to the Third International's twenty-one conditions and had never envisaged the purges which would turn a *potpourri* of apostate Socialists into a bolshevised party subservient to Moscow. If the party soon modified its millenarian conviction that the world was on the brink of a radical transformation, that 'Communism is at our door' as a leading *Marseillais* had put it just before Tours,[10] it retained an equally millenarian preoccupation with the purity of its members — a determination to resist the contaminations of the non-Communist world. The pre-Tours Comité de la Troisième Internationale had taken the first step by establishing an oversight committee to investigate the lives and the livelihood and even the hidden convictions of new members, 'so that only real

Communists are accepted', and the post–Tours inquisition came to anathematise any heretical affiliation. Freemasons, in a twenty-second conditon added by the Comintern in 1922, were to leave the order, sailors were to avoid the International Club and its non–Communist members; even the League of the Rights of Man was suspect for its Socialists.[11] In June 1922 alone the eighth canton section stigmatized its members for provoking too much discussion, for owing a job to the Socialist Tasso, for withholding subscription dues, for political dealings with the Socialists. One of them declared that he had never seen such a zoo [*pétaudière*] and that it was no wonder that members were 'getting the hell out' [*foutaient le camp*] of the party, now rank with mistrust. There had been 2,600 Communists in the Bouches-du-Rhône at the end of 1920, there were 900 at the beginning of 1923 — the shell left by defections and expulsions and by a diaspora of political refugees, some of whom found homes again in the ancestral SFIO and some of whom, like Sabiani, lived on in rootless exile.[12]

Sabiani's initial enthusiasms had eventually given way to deep misgivings over the party's cloistral rigidities. Revolutionary *élan* was one matter, political suicide another. He disliked the International's attempt to impose electoral tactics on the French Communists, the creation of a committee to control publications, the strictures on freemasons, the proposals to harness the unions to the party; he argued for pluralism. At the Gardanne congress in January 1923 the rift hardened. The International's faithful, grouped around the *Jeunesses communistes*, came to blows with Sabiani and his refractory friends, who defied a hostile *Comité directeur* two months later and boycotted a contrived congress. It was the final break. The 'résistants', like Frossard in the Central Committee, had excluded themselves from a Russified Communist party.[13]

There were about two hundred of them in Marseille, clustered around Sabiani's fourth canton delegation, which had followed him *en masse*.[14] With them he founded the *Fédération communiste autonome* and struck out anew, now free of the sectarian shackles of a party which seemed to reject the world.

But he retained its language. For the rest of the decade he railed at capitalists and warmongers, at Italian Fascists and French Socialists, at the Rif war and the occupation of the Ruhr; he defended Sacco and Vanzetti and the mutineers of the Black Sea. From time to time he shared platforms with his former comrades and even talked of reconciliation — idly, for nothing had changed. He and his friends still shrank from slavish conformity, still refused to be blind agents of Moscow, as one of them put it, and the party, more obdurate than ever, imposed humiliating conditions for readmission. One of its local leaders even proposed that politicians — 'like Sabiani' — who returned to the fold renounce all electoral campaigns for four years. Sabiani declined the invitation.[15]

The city's 'communistes résistants' or 'communistes autonomes' sang the International and presented themselves in their short-lived paper *La Vérité Communiste* as the standard-bearers of proletarian revolution: they had avoided the twin traps of Muscovite sectarianism and socialist class collaboration. They soon joined like-minded former Communists from elsewhere in France, first in an ephemeral electoral association early in 1924 and later in the hybrid *Parti Socialiste-Communiste*, founded in Boulogne in April 1923 and throwing together outcasts from SFIO and SFIC alike. For eleven years this eccentric party played host to Sabiani and his followers, who kept it alive in Marseille long after it had died in France.[16]

They were not the only left-wing nonconformists of the mid-nineteen-twenties trying to commandeer the cause. Louis Badina, a Black Sea mutineer and former Communist, had founded a 'Parti Fasciste Ouvrier Français' and was campaigning among disaffected Communists and trades unionists. He travelled to Italy, had ample means, and attracted the keen attention of the Italian Consulate; he was probably an early product of Mussolini's predilection for making trouble. Posters for Georges Valois' *Faisceau* began to appear in July 1926, appealing to Communists to desert their party: 'You are not Communist. . .'. But neither succeeded — both Badina's party and the *Faisceau de Marseille* had disappeared by 1927.[17] Sabiani fared differently.

For he had what none of them had: a popular base. He had the gypsies of the Lazaret and the Corsican friends who had followed him out of the Communist party: Lucien Mangiavacca, his partner in the shipping company and a former secretary of the Communist party's fourth canton section; Joseph Mussa, foreman in a canning factory and editor of *La Vérité Communiste*; Sylvestre Cermolacce, a customs inspector and a city councillor; and his old friend from the *Lycée de Bastia*, Gustave Chipponi, with whom he had put out a socialist paper and to whom he now gave most of his city councillor's salary.[18] He was also developing a base among the sailors of La Joliette. As a Communist he had led the violent *ripostes* by the *minoritaire* sailors to the bully-boys in the Socialist sailors' gang *le marteau*, and now he set about organising a new union among them. Corsican sailors were fixtures of his following — he took on their union leader Pierre Ferri-Pisani as his secretary, the sailor and bar owner Géronimi as his chauffeur, and later the gangster Carbone as his electoral enforcer: Carbone had begun his career as a cabin boy sailing to the middle east — and returning with opium — before moving on to more lucrative pursuits in the fourth canton.[19] They

were all ingredients in a potent brew of Corsican clientelism and revolutionary slogan, a mix of folklore and ideology perfectly portrayed
in Sabiani's victory procession after the cantonal elections of 1925: a
red flag bearing *vive Sabiani*, a white flag bearing a black cross for his
opponent Duverger, a cardboard coffin bearing an effigy of Duverger
himself and, to cap it all, a band alternating funeral marches with the
familiar air of the International.[20]

Sabiani's following in the fourth canton was strong enough to send
him to the *conseil d'arrondissement* in 1922 and the *conseil général* in
1925. But it was not strong enough for victory in the multi-canton
municipal or legislative elections. He had won his seat in the *mairie* in
1919 by joining Flaissières' list; he lost it in 1925 by standing alone at
the head of a *socialiste-communiste* list of his own. He fared no better
in the legislative elections of 1924, when his list won 28 per cent of
the vote in the fourth canton but only 12 per cent of the city at
large.[21] Clearly, if he was to expand his horizons beyond his cantonal
fiefdom, he needed electoral allies.

There was the Communist party, which sometimes co-operated
for obscure tactical reasons of its own. In 1925 it helped by standing
down in Sabiani's canton, and in the legislative elections of 1928 its
doctrine of 'class against class' played into Sabiani's hands by obstructing the Socialists. Sometimes it stood against him, probably
depriving him of votes, as in 1924. But it was not strong enough to
decide the outcome — throughout the decade it never swayed more
than six per cent of the fourth canton's or twelve per cent of the city's
voters.[22] By 1929 the party's leaders had withdrawn so far into their
sectarian shell that they proclaimed indifference to the municipal
elections that year.[23] Sabiani would have to turn elsewhere.

There was the *Parti Républician-Socialiste*, a small party of the moderate left torn by indiscipline and internecine squabbling. It could
count on some votes in the fifth canton, where its candidate Louis
Schurrer won as *conseiller d'arrondissement* in 1928 — only to be imprisoned for embezzlement three years later. But Sabiani's electoral
alliance with Schurrer and his party in 1924 brought him no closer to
victory than the Communist abstention did the following year: the
Parti Républician-Socialiste was too small.[24]

There was SFIO, which was too large. It had won 48 per cent of
the vote and four out of seven seats in the legislative elections of
1924; it could consent rather than submit to electoral alliances, could
afford to ignore its suitor's conditions and dictate its own, and when
Sabiani sat down with Tasso in 1929 the negotiations predictably
broke down.[25]

That left the clerico-reactionaries themselves, the men of the moderate right. After the Socialists they were Sabiani's favourite target; he and his colleagues sometimes assimilated the two, seeing in the Bloc National a mirror-image of the *Cartel des Gauches* and in the socialists and *modérés* of the *mairie* a sinister fraternity of business operators.[26] The *modérés* on the hustings were indeed nothing like Sabiani and his friends: of their elected officials in the 1920s only one was a Corsican immigrant and their six deputies between 1919 and 1928 were all men of industry, commerce or the liberal professions. So were 15 of their 23 candidates in cantonal elections between 1925 and 1931.[27] Their routine electoral victories in the second canton, which included the *Bourse* and the commercial heart of the city, returned deputies who took its interests to heart: the shipbuilder and deputy Hubert Giraud believed that its voters had elected him just as they had elected his fellow-*modéré* Adrien Artaud '[to] choose men capable of defending the interests of the commerce of Marseille' and once in the Chamber of Deputies he joined the *Entente Républicaine* 'not because it was the largest but because it assembled a number of Presidents of Chambers of Commerce'.[28] To Sabiani this was foreign ground.

They were on the whole men of measured if somewhat defensive views. They defended the Republic against its enemies on the far left and the far right, the 'policy of order' against parliamentary and syndical incoherence, the franc against fiscal extravagance, the Catholic schools against the laic and levelling left, the Treaty of Versailles against Germanophil critics; and they rallied around Poincaré when he returned to power in the summer of 1926.[29]

As a political organisation they were less a party than a web of like-minded men meeting in like-named associations, reading like anagrams from the limited lexicon of the Republican right: the *Comité Républicain*, the *Comité d'Union Républicaine*, the *Comité d'Union Républicaine Démocratique*, the *Comité Républicain d'Union Nationale*, the *Comité d'Union Nationale Républicaine*.[30] They linked arms nationally in the *Fédération Républicaine* and the *Alliance Démocratique* and locally in the *Grand Cercle Républicain*, an extended club founded in 1902 with premises on the Canebière by the stock exchange and later a few streets away in the rue Grignan. The *Grand Cercle* offered its thousand members a seasoned mix of gravity and levity: a talk on the recovered provinces or 'the difficult birth of the Third Republic' but also a *soirée artistique* or a ball 'with the famous Jazz-Hawaiien'. For 'one does not only discuss politics at the Grand Cercle, one savours the most agreeable entertainments . . .' and for much of the year the festivities of its members eclipsed the campaigns of its candidates.[31]

But during electoral periods the *modérés* revealed a different face. In spite of chronic rivalries — separate lists in 1924, pitched battles between opposing partisans in 1928, divided candidacies in 1932 —

they could mobilise powerful electoral machines and play the rough game of popular politics as well as anyone. Their men disrupted meetings and defaced posters and fought in one of the worst electoral incidents of the interwar years, a murderous encounter between bill-posters in Les Goudes in 1934. They won a third of the city-wide vote in the legislative elections of 1924, more in the municipal elections of 1925; they took a quarter of the fourth canton's vote in 1924 and a third in 1925;[32] and these were the votes Sabiani needed.

When they stood in 1924, Sabiani lost with 21 per cent of the vote; when they stood down in 1925, he won with 56 per cent.[33] Their gesture that year hinted at a tacit accommodation between the men of the *Grand Cercle* and Simon's raffish companions: together they would keep the Socialists out of the fourth canton. And out of part of the fifth, for in 1928 the slums of la Villette and the working class settlements of la Madrague in the north were added to Sabiani's own canton to form the legislative constituency he coveted; between them they could deprive the Socialists of at least one seat in the Chamber of Deputies. This they did. The first round of the 1928 elections left Sabiani in second place behind the Socialist incumbent Canavelli — he had done well in his own bastion, in la Joliette and Arenc, but not well enough in the newly added voting districts of the fifth canton, and even after the Communists helpfully stood down the second round looked doubtful.[34] The *modérés*, true to their pre-electoral promise, tipped the balance and sent Sabiani to Paris by withdrawing their candidate and releasing their 2,300 voters — not because they loved him more, but because they loved Canavelli less.[35] It was the start of a revolving dance, a *chassé-croisé* with the right which would last throughout Sabiani's career.

Part of the right would still have nothing to do with him, and in the city's major daily, *Le Petit Marseillais*, it spelled out its fears. Sabiani, whatever his politics, was a menace: 'M. Sabiani is a Communist who calls himself a Socialist without being one or the other' but 'his speeches [are characterised by] a distinctive violence' and even if the 'repentant Communist' no longer marched to Moscow's orders he still shared the aspiration of his former comrades — 'disembowel the bourgeois'. The paper scolded the wayward groups of the right who had given the upstart his *entrée*:

> M. Sabiani...evidently owes his election to...parties where one does not practice violence, but in which one sometimes forgets the notion of political solidarity.[36]

Sabiani had divided as well as exploited the *modérés*.

He looked to them again in the municipal elections of 1929, and the first round seemed to promise a renewed act of quiet collusion. Sabiani's campaign was by now familiar, all defamation and self-promotion and libel suits from the aggrieved occupants of the *mairie*, but he contained himself: he attacked the Socialists in power but spared the *modérés* in opposition. They returned the favour. *Le Séma-phore*, which had supported a royalist fringe list in 1924, even defended him, approving in particular of his attacks on the integrity of the city councillors.[37] But deference vanished in the second round, when the right maintained its list, and Sabiani repeated his trick of 1919: he attached himself to the octogenarian Flaissières, who had jettisoned his Socialist allies and assembled another bizarre but winning coalition, this time with Sabiani enjoying pride of place. The mayor kept his office and added Sabiani as his first deputy, after an election which garbled party identities and bewildered the press — *Le Petit Marseillais* saw in Flaissières' election 'the coronation of general electoral confusion'[38] — but which at least lifted any lingering doubt: Sabiani would sup with the devil as long as the devil had the votes.

One night in July 1928, aboard the Paris-Marseille *rapide*, Sabiani met the journalist Philibert Géraud, and by their journey's end the new friends had hatched a plan for what Sabiani now needed more than anything: his own paper.[39]

That year the Marseille press, dominated by *Le Petit Marseillais*, had ignored Sabiani's candidacy in the legislative elections, and in the municipal elections the following year it renewed the conspiracy of silence, broken only by an occasional first-round compliment from the right. Sabiani riposted by launching his own broadsheet, appropriately called *Les Élections*, for the duration of the mayoral campaign.[40] Now, with Géraud and soon with others, he developed plans for *Marseille-Matin*, a major daily to rival *Le Petit Marseillais*. It would live on public shares; it would open its columns to Sabiani; it would mark the *entente* between him and the *modérés* who had helped him enter the Chamber of Deputies. A transitional weekly, to be called *Marseille-Libre*, would pave the way, defending the Flaissières-Sabiani municipality, building a readership for the new daily, and then humbly effacing itself.[41]

Marseille-Libre was duly launched in January 1930, with Géraud as managing editor. Sabiani continued to work with the founders of *Marseille-Matin*: with Jean Fraissinet, a local right-wing shipping magnate, Admiral Lacaze, *académicien* and former minister, Fernand Raux, Clemenceau's police prefect during the war — with men who did not care for his politics but who shared his determination to break the monopoly of *Le Petit Marseillais* and its owner, Gustave Bourrageas, over the city's press. The posters announcing *Marseille-Matin* continued to cast *Marseille-Libre* as a passing herald for the new daily.[42] But by the time *Marseille-Matin* finally appeared, in May 1931, *Marseille-Libre* had become Sabiani's own herald. Its first issue, half hagiography, half scandal-sheet, had already provoked criticism for rapt attention to Sabiani — 'one cannot deny' protested the second issue, 'that the deputy of the third district is a political man' — and the backers of *Marseille-Matin* did not argue in September 1930 when the incendiary weekly declared its independence from them.[43] Once in league they probably gave Sabiani some money, but would not bail his operation out when it ran into financial problems, and once in print they gave him their qualified support but would not allow his signature at the foot of a column; they would let the unpredictable creature into the garden but not into the house. With his *Marseille-Libre* he could do as he wished.[44]

With or without *Marseille-Matin* Sabiani now had a loudspeaker which would carry his voice beyond the confines of his canton. But he had no extended organisation, no local branch or a national party, to turn readers into partisans. His phantom Parti Socialiste-Communiste had only one other deputy in the Chamber, and an involvement in the Parti d'Unité Prolétarienne — yet another fraternity of exiles, mostly former Communists and Socialists — had ended in recriminations after a month.[45] A *sauvage* in Paris, a *parvenu* in Marseille, Sabiani discovered the limits of his newfound influence in October 1930 when his best efforts failed to keep another Socialist from winning a fifth canton legislative by-election. He reacted by floating a short-lived electoral organisation in the canton, the Phalanges Prolétariennes, and a wider association promised to a longer life and quaintly named les Vrais Amis du quatrième et du cinquième canton:[46] the nucleus of a personal party to add to the propaganda of a personal paper.

Within the *mairie* Sabiani stayed in the shadow of the venerable Flaissières. When the doctor-mayor died, in March 1931, he suddenly found himself in the limelight, for although he was not and could not be a candidate for Flaissières' seat in the city council his support could be critical. It went to Eugène Pierre, the wartime mayor and candidate of the right. Sabiani declared that Pierre was a good man, even if he did belong to a 'socially regressive party', and he sent in the Phalanges Prolétariennes and even the gangster Carbone to lend a hand in the campaign. For the first time the partners in the silent *pas de deux* acknowledge that they were stepping in concert; for the first time a candidate of the right won over fifty per cent of the vote in the fourth canton; for the first time the *modérés* found themselves in Sabiani's debt, for Pierre could not have won without him.[47]

They soon repaid him. Pierre's friends in the city council contrived with Sabiani's to deny the socialists the mayoralty and hand it to the nonentity Georges Ribot, like Flaissières a doctor but unlike

Flaissières a figurehead, dismissed in the press as the nominal mayor and 'le roi fainéant' [lazy-bones king]. Sabiani now became the power behind the throne, the man who would give the Ribot mayoralty his own name. Pierre had unknowingly inaugurated a municipal era: the bewhiskered *modéré* entered the *mairie* with the gangsters Carbone and Spirito at his side, cheered in the street by the arch-conservative Jeunesses Patriotes and the anything but conservative Phalanges pro-létariennes, French *tricolore* and Corsican *tête de Maure* fluttering in the wind, and there to greet the parade of improbable friends was *le sympathique député* Simon himself, there to consecrate what he was happy to have called and what soon came to be called and what could only be called *Sabianisme.*[48]

CHAPTER 3

Sabianisme, 1931–1935

'We'll keep on hiring and as long as I'm here we'll hire my friends and only my friends! Them first, and then the others, if there's any room left!' *Sabianisme* was, first and foremost, a system of favours. Sabiani and his friends now held the purse-strings of patronage in their hands: he himself took control of the fire brigade and tax collection, both rich in jobs — no accident, either, that the firemen had barracks within his legislative constituency; the pliant Ribot took general charge of municipal personnel; the faithful Chipponi, of Bastia days, ran the all-important office of electoral lists. For the wife of a Corsican sailor of la Joliette, looking back more than fifty years later, Sabiani's private favours were all that mattered:

> The number of Corsicans he got into the police! The number of Corsicans he got into the Customs! He did a lot of good, a lot of good...everything else is just politics.

It was the horn of plenty, and corruption to his critics was generosity to his friends.[1]

Sabiani was following the practices of his day; his pork barrel was no larger than Tasso's or Flaissières'. But *Sabianisme* also had the ring of scandal to it — the ring of 'Marseille-Chicago'. The Parisian press had begun using the epithet when the first major scandal of Sabiani's career broke, the 'affair of the bandits behind the Bourse'. At the time Sabiani was Flaissières' first deputy; his presence in December 1929 at the trial of five 'bandits' accused of waylaying some bank cashiers behind the Bourse provoked storms of criticism, for one of the accused — the owner of a bar in the *vieux quartiers* where most of the loot was discovered — was the brother of Sabiani's political protégé Alexandre Eyssautier and was mysteriously acquitted. Worse, rumours began to fly that an escaped 'bandit' was none other than

Sabiani's brother. In its first issue *Marseille-Libre* mounted a vigorous counter-attack on the 'bandits in front of the Bourse' and on the Paris papers for their disparaging coverage of 'Marseille-Chicago': Sabiani's weekly was born and lived out its days under the sign of scandal.[2]

But it was his friendship with Carbone and Spirito that did the lasting damage to his name. Sabiani had served with one of the Carbone brothers in the same unit during the war, and had even found a flat for their mother in 1925. But his professional association with the senior and foremost Carbone, Paul Buonaventure, and by extension with his Sicilian partner Lydio Spirito did not begin until his political career was well underway — until 1930 when he came to the defence of the younger Carbone, on trial for the murder of a Senegalese procurer, and turned the *Cour d'Assises* into a political circus once again. The following year Carbone made his services available in the Eugène Pierre election, and in 1934 Sabiani provoked another scandal, this time of national proportions, by plastering Marseille with posters proclaiming his loyalty to the *milieu*'s most famous couple: 'CARBONE AND SPIRITO ARE MY FRIENDS'. Perhaps his complicity with them was no stronger than Tasso's with the Guerrinis or Rouvier's and Bouisson's with the Renuccis. But it was more brazen, so brazen that *Sabianisme* could never erase its stain.[3]

There were scandals in which he had no hand, above all the assassination of King Alexander and Louis Barthou on the Canebière in October 1934. Sabiani could protest, justifiably, that the *Sûreté Nationale* was to blame, that his *mairie* and its services were innocent, but it was another blow to the reputation of the city and its controversial first deputy.[4]

To cap it all, Sabiani's reign at the *mairie* coincided almost exactly with the worst years of the slump. In Marseille, a port city vulnerable to the vicissitudes of the world economy, it was sharper than elsewhere in France — between late 1930 and the peak year of 1935 unemployment almost tripled. Sabiani launched new municipal projects, including a stadium and a prison, he even urged the recalcitrant municipal employees to accept early retirement and a ban on overtime work, but caught in a stagnant economy between the contending demands of job creation and fiscal responsibility he only reaped charges of callousness from the left and extravagance from the right. It was a no-win situation.[5]

Throughout Sabiani's troubled heyday his followers flocked to his rallies in raucous *camaraderie*. 'It was just to have a good time,' recalled his son-in-law, who had been a *Sabianiste* since the age of eleven when he had carried the *afficheurs*' brushes through the streets of the third and fourth cantons. They all cheered him after every scandal, after the Carbone and Spirito posters and the assassination of Alexander and Barthou; they even cheered sporting surrogates, like the 'Sabianiste' boxer Kid Francis, a 'local kid' and an idol, whose match against Al Brown at the Arènes in July 1932 ended in chaos with the referee assaulted, the ring invaded, the stadium destroyed — pandemonium, the lasting image of *Sabianisme*.[6]

The organisation, such as it was, had two entwined branches, Sabiani's party and Sabiani's friends — the *Parti Socialiste-Communiste* and the *Amis de Simon Sabiani*.

The party was an electoral organisation, numbering 1,700 members by 1934 with a section in every canton. Some, like the seventh with five subsections and the fifth with eight, were large enough for subdivision. It was a loose confederation; the sections squabbled over electoral tactics, held unauthorised meetings, even tried to annex one another; an erratic *Commission Exécutif Fédéral* held uneasy sway, for some of the sections criticised it for weak leadership and others ignored it altogether. The fourth and fifth cantons were the hub of the party's activity: here the sections and subsections met several times a month, except for August when they did not meet at all and for electoral periods when they might meet every night, and here the party had most of its members, 756 out of a city-wide total, in July 1933, of 1294. The industrial seventh canton, with 255, took half the rest: it was a party of the northern *milieux populaires*, with Sabiani's home and legislative constituency at its centre.[7]

The *Amis de Simon Sabiani*, unlike the *Phalanges Prolétariennes* which were dissolved after their brief and noisy existence in the fifth canton, and unlike the *Parti Socialiste-Communiste* which remained rooted in Sabiani's own fief, grew to flourish in far-flung *quartiers* of the city. They were the offspring of the original *Vrais Amis* and started out early in 1932 as the *Groupe Sabianiste de la Joliette*, meeting in the Bar Casanova next to Sabiani's flat. They spread quickly, as long as Sabiani was in office — their membership claims were wildly exaggerated, but there were probably about 2,000 of them in 1934, scattered in 32 groups, some as far afield as the twelfth canton. The *Amis* were neighbourhood associations, like the *comités d'intérêts des quartiers*, only brazenly partisan, pandering to Sabiani and so bringing home a streetlamp here or a schoolhouse there; they were not, they said, 'an organisation to acquire certain favours' but a philanthropic family — and in a sense they were: they conveyed favours one way and thanks the other: a philanthropy in which the donors were also the recipients.[8]

The *Parti* and the *Amis* thus each had about 2,000 members around the beginning of 1934. How many belonged to both is unknown; there were therefore between two and four thousand Sabianistes enthusiastic enough that year to join an organisation; earlier perhaps 1,000 had joined the Phalanges Prolétarienness.[9] Who were they? Membership lists, if they were ever kept, have disappeared, but 843 names, recovered from press communiqués and traced to the electoral lists, allow a partial reconstruction: a social and ethnic sketch of the *Sabianistes* based on about a fifth of their members.[10]

It shows a lower middle class (*fonctionnaires* [government employees], shopkeepers, office workers and artisans) predominating with 53 per cent; a lower class (skilled and unskilled workers, sailors, dockers, and domestic servants) next with 39 per cent, miscellaneous professions making up the rest and an upper middle class (merchants and industrialists, liberal professions, landowners) almost entirely absent.

The *fonctionnaires* are the most numerous. Sabiani had courted them since the beginning of his career, seeking funds for the *Association Philanthropique des Douaniers corses*, salary increases for the postmen, more men for the police; or had intervened with the prefect on behalf of the municipal employees in general; or had tried to conquer their unions. They were, above all, the followers whom he could win over with jobs and services — a clientèle. Many, almost half, were Corsican, and they filled the ranks of his supporters out of all proportion to their weight in the population: twenty per cent of the sample of *Sabianistes* against six per cent of the men in the fourth canton. They were sacrosanct: 'Try to govern with your brain, but govern also with your heart...Economies on what? On the municipal employees? I insist...on hands off'. They were the *Sabianiste* core.[11]

By contrast the presence of shopkeepers (10 per cent), office-workers (11 per cent) and artisans (12 per cent) is unremarkable; it is commensurate to their presence in the population. Shopkeepers probably had their own sound reasons for joining. Most of the *Sabianiste* butchers came from the seventh canton: no coincidence that the canton's city councillor, in charge of the municipal slaughterhouse and a valuable man to a butcher, was also a *Sabianiste*. The bar owners were probably filling their standard political role. Other shopkeepers may have been tempted by commercial arrangements with the *Amis*, including the promise of member-customers in exchange for a discount. And Sabiani courted the shopkeepers as he courted the *fonctionnaires* — he attended their demonstrations and supported their demands. He did the same for office-workers, proposing that they share in their companies' profits, and for artisans, giving them advice in *Marseille-Libre* on tax exemptions; he took up their collective cause, pleading for the small shareholder and the small property buyer and for all the 'middle classes...crushed by capitalism'. It was only normal — they were his constituents.[12]

The lower middle classes dominate the sample without over-whelming it. They never swamp the important lower-class minority but within it the skilled workers stand out — with eleven per cent of the *Sabianistes* they exceed their share of the working population of the fourth and fifth cantons — and thus shift the centre of gravity further towards the lower-middle class, for they straddle the social frontier: they are artisans as well as workers.[13]

Their humbler colleagues are weakly represented: unskilled workers and day-labourers account for only 13 per cent of the sample, and without the short-lived *Phalanges Prolétariennes* they would account for even less. Their absence may reflect Sabiani's failure to develop a lasting syndical base. With most unions already attached to the socialist CGT or the communist CGTU, or split between them, he was unable to drive his own wedge and claim his own members. A prior personal following helped. He had acquired some influence among the sailors' CGT union, and when their syndical leader Ferri-Pisani deserted him and returned to SFIO Sabiani retained enough supporters among them to create a splinter union, setting off a long and bitter feud. Sailors correspondingly appear in the *Sabianiste* sample, accounting for about six per cent of the total; almost half of them are Corsican. They may be the exception proving the rule, suggesting that where Sabiani could not find union members he would not find partisans.[14]

More probably, the sample understates the lower-class presence in Sabiani's organisations. Unskilled industrial workers were unsuited to the bureau positions from which the sample is largely drawn; they might have joined and paid their dues without becoming secretaries or treasurers or even committee members. Likewise it lists few dockers, who abounded in the Lazaret and in parts of the fifth canton and among whom Sabiani had a small but vocal following, and it lists few unemployed, to whom the *Amis* sometimes gave free mem-berships — the lower class *Sabianistes* were more numerous than the sample suggests.[15]

Even adjusted, the profile by itself is only a succession of almost inconsequent percentages, at best sketching a socially muddled group close in its broad traits — a strong lower middle-class, a weak indus-trial working-class — to Sabiani's electorate; closer, quite naturally, to his own fourth than to the neighbouring fifth canton.[16] It broadly resembles the socialist party, to judge from 1365 bureau members in 1936: 49 per cent came from the lower middle, 30 per cent from the lower class, including only 19 per cent from the industrial working class.[17] But aggregates like these camouflage the telling anomalies —

the *fonctionnaires* and the Corsicans in particular. Among the *Sabianistes* the former are thrice and the latter twice as numerous as in the fourth canton.[18] They are the deformities distinguishing the profile.

And that was how contemporaries saw them. When Sabiani declared at a rally in the Alcazar cinema, 'Rarely in my life have I found a heart as noble as that of Carbone', the prefect described his audience of 2,000 as

> ...almost entirely Corsican...composed of members of the 'Association des Amis de Simon Sabiani', of municipal employees and low level employees [petits employés] of Corsican origin. On the whole the audience belonged to the workers' class.[19]

And *Marseille-Matin*, reporting on the same meeting, sniffed at the enthusiasm if not the background of 'the fanatics of local Sabianisme':

> ...this passionate harangue...visibly met the expectations of the audience. The success the speaker had bears witness once again to the vehement loyalty of friends who display for him, outside of any party considerations, a devotion so characteristic of the electoral mores of our community.[20]

There was nothing sinister or mysterious about them.

Outside of any party considerations, the *Sabianistes* adored the man, not the party — there were no cries of 'vive le Parti Socialiste-Communiste' — and it was vital to Sabiani that he transcend party loyalties. For his political position, even at the height of his power, was precarious.

He lived on borrowed votes. In the cantonal elections of 1931 he and his candidates won only 22 per cent of the city-wide vote — 21 per cent in 1934;[21] SFIO was still dominant. Sabiani's position within the fourth canton was very strong, but he still needed votes from the right to win in 1931 and the right was not entirely reliable. In the 1932 legislative elections only the local friends of the Fédération Républicaine would co-operate, and even one of their candidates balked and sided with the local Alliance Démocratique, as resolutely anti-*Sabianiste* as ever.[22] Sabiani owed his re-election in 1932 to a number of SFIO votes, probably his recompense for having taken on some socialists at the *mairie* during the preceding year.[23] He needed votes from both sides; he could not afford a political identity.

Nor could he put too fine a point on his social identity. He won when the voting was unconfined, when it made light of social geography. In 1932 les Présentines with their industrial proletariat voted for him, Saint-Lazare and Strasbourg with theirs voted against him; la Joliette with its artisans voted for him, le Canet and les Crottes with theirs voted against him; the dockside streets with their office-workers voted for him, the *quartier Oddo* with its office-workers voted against him — both, also, were weak in artisans: there was no solid class basis to his electorate. It was a social as well as a political medley.[24]

Sabiani, in short, was performing for a mixed audience and his ideological repertoire had to include something for everyone.

He periodically wheeled out the old idols and dusted them off — the local Cadenat or the national Jaurès or the international Trotsky, all dutifully deified, even the class struggle still a doctrinal fetish — but mostly he prudently kept them stored away. Sabiani and the columnists in his paper now found revolution along the lines of 1789, 1848, 1871, or 1917 impossible and Marxism itself, 'in its integral version', ineffectual. He still posed and was still hailed as an 'elevator [levier] of the working class' but the addition of middle class ingredients diluted the proletarian brew and led to the proclaimed conviction that 'middle classes' and 'proletariat' formed a single class. He still attacked the right, voting in the Chamber against Tardieu as he had against Poincaré, but he saved his harshest words for SFIO — it was 'bourgeois', 'an outdated party', the 'mainstay of capitalism', a traitor to the working class — and as early as 1931 he rejected the labels of left and right alike. He still preached internationalism and anti-bellicism, but he now upheld the defence of the nation against Germany and even of its colonies against Soviet subversion. Marxist and non-Marxist, proletarian and *petit bourgeois*, opposed to the right and opposed to the left, 'national and at the same time international', as *Marseille-Libre* declared in 1930 and repeated in 1933 — it was all a tissue of ideological equivocations.[25]

Sabiani in his speeches and Philibert Géraud in *Marseille-Libre* tried to reconcile the contradictions by finding some third way between right and left, and for a while, during 1933, they thought they had found it in the *néo-socialisme* of Marcel Déat and Adrien Marquet. For them SFIO's latest schismatics would sidestep Marxism by seeing to it that 'religious rituals of integral Marxism' were 'temporarily suspended'; Déat would settle class by marrying the proletariat to the middle classes, political identity by repudiating the parliamentary parties, and the role of the nation by making the state the architect of the new social order. But they soon forgot about Déat's Parti Socialiste de France — it never amounted to much in Marseille, and it even became a political liability when Marquet joined the Doumergue government in 1934. Their jangling ideology kept its *Sabianiste* name.[26]

Around the city no one knew what to make of it. For the communists Sabiani was a 'social-flic', a traitorous socialist. For the socialists he was a capitalist, a reactionary, a man of the right. For the right he

was a man of the left — surrounded, to make matters worse, by a
most alarming entourage. Elsewhere on the right he was a 'fascist',
elsewhere again a good sort enslaved by his electorate. No one could
agree on his identity. 'We confess to having never heard a complete
exposé of the doctrine of M. Sabiani', complained the conservative
l'Eclair, naively, for the reason was simple: there was no doctrine.[27]

The *Sabianistes* had difficulty defining themselves, let alone their doctrine. Some had so weak a sense of political identity that they casually
joined other parties, seeing in multiple memberships nothing incompatible with *Sabianisme*. It was a vexed question at section meetings.
Sabiani's political dependents came and went and came again: Ferri-
Pisani went back to SFIO in a fit of pique, Mangiavacca and Eyssautier wandered off but eventually returned to the fold. Charlatans,
masquerading as the *Amis de Simon Sabiani* to make the most of his
hour in the sun and gather what favours they could, further diluted
the *Sabianiste* identity.[28] And what exactly was Sabianisme? Sabiani
had first tried defining it as 'the irresistible force driving the political
sharks far from the *mairie*...however powerful they may be'. Later
Marseille-Libre tried

> ...a barrier, a constant call to order, a rallying symbol for honest
> men, a reassurance for peaceful citizens; an encouragement for
> activists motivated by an ideal of justice, discipline, and purity

— vacuous words which Philibert Géraud could only echo when he
attempted a retrospective definition in 1939. But he could see the
problem. Sabianisme, he said, had been 'perhaps not a doctrine, but
an action, perhaps not a party, but an élan of partisans'.[29] If the
leaders could not define it, how could the members?

In fact Sabiani was the essence of *Sabianisme*. He was the *raison
d'être* of political candidates like Grisoli, who claimed to model himself on him, or Chipponi, who only stood for an honorific office to
demonstrate his friendship for him; he was the guiding light of bar-
room eulogists like Mangiavacca, the 'leader...who directs us, who
instructs and motivates us, it's he who enlightens our minds with his
intelligence, his knowledge and his foresight'; he was the honorary
president of minor societies like the *Club Universitaire* and the *Sports
Athlétiques de St. Antoine*, and the father of a foot-race and the name
on a cycling trophy. There was even a Sabiani song.[30] And he encouraged the hero-worship. He belittled doctrinal differences, even
declared that between himself and his socialist opponent they did not
exist, and invited voters to decide on the man, not the party line:
'what distinguishes the candidates is not so much the programme as
honesty and sincerity': he was honest, his opponents were corrupt.

He was the friend of the poor, they were the friends of the rich.[31] The person was the doctrine.

People believed in him. His day was choked with friends, favour-seekers and dependants. They were at his door at the rue de Forbin and later the rue Fauchier by eight in the morning; they joined him at breakfast; they were waiting for him at the *mairie* when he arrived at ten.

> On the great stairs leading to the man whom some Marseillais call "the dictator of the city"...women sit on the steps, men lean against the stone banister. A little higher...I come up against a veritable mob...someone whispers that they're mostly favour-seekers.[32]

Every day, Sabiani declared, he received three or four hundred people. When he went home for lunch they were queuing up again, knowing his hours and counting on his generosity; he would ask them in. There were sometimes ten, sometimes fifteen, sometimes twenty of them, a neighbour recalled, there to share a *soupe corse* and complicate the life of Mme Sabiani. 'His poor wife, she moaned, she bellyached' — and she had to contend with it every day. Sabiani's daughter could not recall a meal without guests. Most were off the street but some were friends: 'there was everyone,' recalled the neighbour, 'a docker, a great lawyer, even a film actress, a gangster's girlfriend'. Carbone and Spirito were there occasionally; it was at Sabiani's table that an upstairs neighbour, a sea captain, renewed his acquaintance with Carbone — he had first known him as a *mousse* on his ship, he now met him as a *caid* of the *milieu*. There would be more people at the *mairie* in the afternoon, and more people again in the evening at the Café Glacier on the Canebière, where *le tout Marseille* congregated; there might even be more people at home later on, for sometimes Sabiani's doors would be open till midnight. Otherwise he would work on correspondence and read and smoke Egyptian cigarettes until late in the night. He did not sleep much. And the next day it would all start again.[33]

But the floodwaters of the Popular Front soon began to rise around the rickety house that Sabiani had built — soon threatened, in fact, to sweep it away altogether.

CHAPTER 4

Sabiani at Bay, 1934–1936

The alarm bell, when it sounded, was almost inaudible: the election in October 1934 of Jean Cristofol, a customs officer, to the largely honorific post of *conseiller d'arrondissement*. But Cristofol was a Communist, dismissed from the *douanes* after organising the great demonstration of the twelfth of February,[1] and his victory came in the fifth canton — in the outer voting wards of Sabiani's own legislative constituency.

The Communists had not won an election in Marseille since 1922, when Sabiani himself had been elected *conseiller d'arrondissement*. Since then their wretched electoral performance had brought them six per cent of the city's vote in the legislative elections of 1924, four per cent in the municipal elections of 1925, eight per cent in the legislative elections of 1928, never any more. They professed indifference to the results; their candidates were *candidats de principe*, they said, there after 1928 to block the 'social fascists' of SFIO. It was Comintern policy.[2] Their membership stagnated along with their vote: there were 592 of them in Marseille in 1926, 600 in 1934. But for a few able agitators, said the police, the party would not have existed at all. By then many of its cells were meaningless abstractions, a sham of a single man or a fiction woven around a café where two members would occasionally meet for an *apéritif*. The local party was bankrupt, its members indifferent, their dues unpaid. It was happening all over France, but the Central Committee in its consternation upbraided the *marseillais* item by item — there were too few members, and those there were had no political education, too few leaders, too few cells, too few *cahiers du bolchévisme*; there would have to be changes.[3]

Changes there were, but not until early 1934 when the national party itself began emerging from its sectarian cocoon. The Central Committee sent down one of its members, François Billoux, a *roan-*

nais fresh from reorganising the party in Alsace, to galvanise the wilting *provençaux* into action; cells and *rayons*, blessed with new independence, now bent the party's dogmatic rigidities and so began to enlist new members; 'suppleness' became the order of the day. Above all, the party joined arms with the Socialist demons of the day before — briefly in a joint demonstration of the CGT and the CGTU on the Canebière on the twelfth of February,[4] lastingly after June in the electoral 'unité d'action' pact. The party was now interested in winning elections, and Cristofol's victory in the fifth canton was the first fruit of its new strategy.

The party was stronger here — in the working-class districts of the Belle-de-Mai, just beyond Sabiani's legislative constituency, and of la Cabucelle, well within it — than anywhere else in the city.[5] Its vote had been consistently high in the fifth canton: 15 per cent in the cantonal elections in 1928, 16 per cent in 1931. Now, in 1934, Cristofol won 29 per cent of the vote in the first round and, with SFIO obligingly standing down, was elected in the second. He did best in the Belle-de-Mai, with 40 per cent in the first round, but alarmingly well, on average 25 per cent, in Sabiani's own fifth canton constituencies[6] — and Sabiani would be up for re-election as deputy here in the spring of 1936.

Sabiani had seen the threat right away — he had reviled the 'masquerade' of 12 February that winter, the 'new monstrosity' and 'amoral amalgam' of the *Front Commun* that summer, its 'seductive name' and its 'marching orders from Moscow.'[7] But for the time being he was beating the air. The partners in the *Front Commun*, once past their successful electoral experiment in the October cantonals, lost interest in one another and even began bickering again. Billoux's attacks on Tasso's social views the following spring, on the eve of the municipal elections, can only have deepened the socialist mayoral candidate's time-honoured hostility to the Communists.[8] It was at best a shaky alliance; besides, since 6 February 1934 Sabiani had been staring in bewilderment at a matching apparition — this one on the right.

That night he had managed a *sortie* from the besieged Chamber of Deputies and wandered aimlessly through the riot; he had preferred the sedition of the street to the legality of the Chamber. Back in Marseille he gave his reaction to *le six février* in a speech of incomparable incoherence. The left was to blame, for it had provoked the riot, but the right had manipulated the left, and it remained the enemy, especially the *Camelots du Roi*, even though it was not all bad...The *ligueurs* had impressed Sabiani. They were 'the entire population of Paris, men and women, come to the Place de la Concorde'.[9] And by far their most important formation, in Marseille as in all France, was the *Association des Croix-de-Feu*.

For the early years of their existence in France the Croix-de-Feu, founded in 1927 by an eccentric Parisian journalist and author, were little more than veterans in arms marrying comradely nostalgia to social paternalism. They organised requiem masses and patriotic plays and soup kitchens for the indigent; they blustered on occasion, as at Joffre's funeral in 1931 when their aggressive display offended other veterans' groups, or on the Trocadéro the same year when they invaded a disarmament demonstration, but mostly they avoided political confrontations. They limited their ranks to decorated war veterans and so kept their numbers down, to about 15,000 in 1931 and 36,000 by the end of 1932.[10] Two years later they were a mass movement. With La Rocque in command they had opened their ranks during 1933 and created satellite organisations: an influx of new members, probably from the *petite bourgeoisie*, probably embittered by the slump, probably alarmed by the *Front Commun*, swelled their numbers to 60,000 by the middle of 1934 and perhaps 150,000 by the end of the year.[11] Now the Croix-de-Feu talked about politics. Now they presented themselves in their pamphlets as an alternative to the parliamentary parties; now their posters spoke for constitutional reform and against the *décrets-lois*; now, more loftily, La Rocque foresaw a 'rallying of healthy forces for the installation of a new order'. They still disdained electoral activity and spurned joint action with others, but their closed fraternity had become an open movement, conservative in its ideals of 'Travail, Famille, Patrie' yet worlds apart from the traditional right in its organisation — the echelons marshalled against the disorder they saw spreading around them.[12]

It was much the same in Marseille. The Croix-de-Feu had appeared there at the beginning of 1930, 25 of them, led by Jacques Arnoult, a local industrialist with a factory in Marseille and an estate in the country; they grew slowly but steadily, to about 700 in the Bouches-du-Rhône in 1932, staging commemorative veterans' processions and sending children for summer holidays to a Var chateau made available by its aristocratic owner — a priest accompanied them.[13] But the Croix-de-Feu soon opened up — La Rocque was in Marseille in 1933 urging veterans and non-veterans alike to join the appropriate branches — and by the end of 1934 there were three to four thousand members in the Department.[14] A small sample shows them divided almost equally between lower middle and upper middle class members, with the lower or working class almost absent: a *bourgeois* presence much stronger than that among socialists, communists, or sabianists, reflected also in the presence of shipbuilders like Fraissinet and in the Croix-de-Feu discourse, but perhaps exaggerated in the sample.[15] With new members came new rhetoric. Local speakers offered obscure recipes for regeneration: a 'regrouping of the French in moral order and work' or the hot-headed Arnoult's 'necessary revolution strictly following the orders of our leader'. They and their national leaders stayed out of elections but allowed members to stand individually; they condemned 'parliamentary anarchy' but disliked certain parties more than others — while the *Front Commun* was anathema they did not disdain the premises of the *Grand Cercle Républicain* and even admitted some *modéré* politicians into their ranks.[16] By 1934, in Marseille as in France, the Croix-de-Feu were a political force if not a political party.

The communists called them fascists; so did the Royalists, who saw them as a threat and La Rocque as 'a plagiarised Mussolini, an ersatz Hitler'; right-wing intellectuals like Brasillach saw them as *bourgeois*, 'the cup of tea'; the traditional right sometimes approved of them, sometimes ignored them, sometimes tried to use them — Tardieu, wrote Fabre-Luce, saw all the *ligues* as 'an instrument to serve his own ambition' and La Rocque as '...a disloyal domestic servant.'[17]

Sabiani did not know what to make of them. At first *Marseille-Libre* echoed the left in likening them to the German *stahlhelm*, to Hilter, to the fascists. Later, in his reaction to the *six février*, Sabiani had some good words for them, 'all disabled comrades who had given their blood for the country', and for La Rocque, 'full of energy, full of knowledge, full of audacity and courage' — but he was glad that they had not succeeded that night. A few months later *Marseille-Libre* reverted to a disparaging view, and at the end of the year Sabiani's party supported proposals for their dissolution. But by March 1935 a non-committal tone prevailed: Sabiani, who had no time for the Jeunesses Patriotes or for the Action Française — 'you bore with me your talk of Maurras', he told a young Royalist neighbour — was nonplussed by the only local *ligue* of any size, the Croix-de-Feu.[18]

Soon *Sabianisme* began roughhewing its ideological defences against the new forces stirring on the left and right. The Parti Socialiste-Communiste, fearing that it would be taken for a member of the *Front Commun*, changed its name to the Parti d'Action Socialiste. Marxism was jettisoned, the class struggle sacrificed to the simpler, primal ideals of order, authority, and the defence of the national community: 'The nation first, for there is the foreigner who lies in wait for the slightest weakening and who would not hesitate to introduce some order among us...to his own profit!' These were conservative themes, and Sabiani had voted with the right in the Chamber for two-year conscription. But he insisted that his nationalism was different from theirs. He was a socialist, capitalism had failed and would disappear, his nation would be built on class cooperation within a strong and centralised state: 'I have bound myself,' he declared on the eve of the 1935 municipal elections, 'to the culture of a socialism of society within the framework of the nation'. It was a slapdash formula, and most of his ideas came from Déat to whom he occasionally attributed them, but when he harped on the theme and spoke of 'the altar of the fatherland' and of his pressing need to return to 'the ancestral shell' there was a hint of a siege mentality, of a defence hastily improvised against penumbral aliens threatening him and his kind.[19]

The first round results of the 1935 municipal elections confirmed Sabiani's worst fears. The Communist party was now as strong as the *Sabianistes* in Marseille — each had about 14 per cent of the vote — and, ominously, stronger in the fifth canton, where its inroads into the working class districts of the Belle-de-Mai and the Boulevard Durbec gave it 32 per cent of the vote to Sabiani's nineteen.[20] Cristofol's victory there the previous October was no fluke: Sabiani was facing a class-based communist conquest of his legislative constituencies.

Fortunately the fifth canton was not, this year, part of his constituency, for the municipal districts had been redrawn, amid furious allegations of partiality, and Sabiani's seat now combined the sixth instead of the fifth canton with his own fourth. For the time being he was safe. He had some help from the right: he declared after the first round that he would link arms 'even with the devil' to stop the *Front Commun* and so he did, entering the second round with support for and support from selected *modérés* — for some of them would still have nothing to do with him. One wing of the right withdrew its candidate in his sector, another stood fast and cost him the sixth canton, with its *quartiers bourgeois* around Longchamps and Les Chartreux, but his loyal supporters in the fourth canton saw him through.[21] He kept his seat on the city council.

But he lost the mayoralty. *The Front Commun* had held; everywhere the Communists had stood down between rounds in favour of the Socialists and deferred to them, releasing their supporters of the first round to vote for SFIO in the second. The upshot of it all was a city council with 24 socialists, six *modérés* and six *Sabianistes*. Tasso became mayor, the socialists took over the key municipal offices — including the office of electoral lists — and Sabiani was out in the cold once again.[22]

It was not long before he felt the consequences. The *Amis de Simon Sabiani* languished, subscriptions lapsed, members left: 'I joined the *Groupe des Amis de Simon Sabiani* in 1934 because I was employed in the Mairie, I had nothing to do with [the Groupe] after 1935...'.[23] An effort to revive the flagging organisation in September came to nothing, and the next month it merged with the Parti d'Action

Socialiste. At the end of the year the combined organisation could still only claim 1830 members, and they spent much of the annual congress exchanging recriminations over the electoral results of the spring. Worst of all, the *Front Commun*, soon known as the *Front Populaire*, showed no signs of failing. As always Tasso was unenthusiastic, and there were some tensions over the dock strike in the winter of 1935–1936, but Socialists and Communists continued to share public platforms, to denounce fascism and the *décrets-lois* — and they were faring menacingly well in the Belle-de-Mai and la Madrague — in the fifth canton.[24] Prospects seemed bleak for Sabiani.

From now on he castigated the *Front Populaire* almost daily. He blamed it — correctly — for his eviction from the Hôtel de Ville; he called it a threat to the Republic and to domestic peace and a municipal disaster. Events abroad, soon dominating the news, petrified the rift separating him from the left. Where the Socialists and Communists denounced the Italian invasion of Abyssinia, *Marseille-Libre* made little of it, or pointed to 'the savage Abyssinia of the Negus', or warned against driving Italy into the arms of Germany. Where they railed at the German occupation of the Rhineland, *Marseille-Libre* tempered its earlier treatment of Hitler and called for negotiations, seeing Germany as provoked by the Franco-Soviet pact or by sanctions against Italy; Géraud even ranted about 'an unjust war...against a Germany determined to resist the capitalo-communist menace'. War became the great polarising issue. Sabiani and his friends saw bellicose anti-fascist mobilisation as a boon for the left and a bane for the country, and they lost no time in saying so: the *Front Populaire* was the party of war.[25]

In all of this the government was almost forgotten, a noncombatant in the ideological hostilities. A climate of civil war was setting in — the more so as the Croix-de-Feu were growing as fast as the *Front Populaire*.

There were 250,000 of them in France by the middle of 1935, and 450 to 600,000 by the middle of 1936; in Marseille there were about 12,000 at the end of 1935 and between 15,000 and 20,000 by the spring of 1936.[26] It was a phenomenal growth rate — the fruit, probably, of an intense propaganda campaign and of a determined effort to extend their social roots downwards: between January and April 1936 two-thirds of their recruits in Marseille came from the working class, and if there were strike-breakers among the Croix-de-Feu there were also strikers.[27] Their confidence grew with their numbers. A local leader in Rouen declared that 250,000 Croix-de-Feu were ready 'at the propitious moment to fight the Popular Front and even if necessary to take power'; another in Paris said that if the *ligues* were dissolved 'the leaders of the Croix-de-Feu movement would not go along' and that they might have to take over 'the direction of the country's affairs if the situation required it'; Arnoult in Marseille spoke of an 'H Hour' and told his audience, 'you will receive the order the day you need to arm yourselves'. They all outshone La Rocque, who never spoke of a *coup d'état* and who on at least one occasion had to explain away Arnoult's reckless declarations. But he continued to build the political character of his *ligue*, issuing orders to support this or that candidate in the 1936 legislative elections. Arnoult, in transmitting them, announced that such decisions would never be needed again, as everyone in France would soon be a member of the Croix-de-Feu: he was riding a tidal wave.[28]

Sabiani reacted erratically. One day La Rocque was a great leader, and his *ligue* unquestionably preferable to the *Front Commun*; the next, following the views of some mutinous Croix-de-Feu subalterns, he was a source of national disunity, and the *ligue* too *bourgeois*; one day the *ligues* should be dissolved, the next they should live on; one day the Croix-de-Feu were on the right side, the next they were pro-capitalist and, anyway, ineffective. Géraud thought La Rocque too conciliatory, too appeasing.[29] The *Sabianistes* were confused.

And they were agitated. All these newcomers threatened to evict *Sabianisme* from the house of politics. Sabiani and Géraud and the unbridled columnists of *Marseille-Libre* continued to rail at the right as at the left, deriding the 'sterile conservatives' and the 'Marseillais de salon'. But now they kept up a running fire on the whole system itself: they joined the most radical elements of the Croix-de-Feu in promising to bring down the existing order. They looked at the bloody riots in Brest and Toulon in August 1935 and declared that 'never has the need for a new order been felt as much as this week...'. They declared that '...now, outside of the parties, above the aged doctrines...we will sweep away the régime that has to go', that there must be a 'vast auto da fé' and a complete transformation of the Republic. They even outdid the Croix-de-Feu radicals and attacked universal suffrage. In its place they vaguely proposed an authoritarian and *dirigiste* state, along the lines of Déat and *planisme*, but their discourse was more invective than corrective. They sought an explanation for the perversity of the times: Géraud, but never Sabiani, suddenly took to anti-Masonic and anti-semitic outbursts. The Freemasons, he said, would sacrifice France to their 'satanic Utopias', and Germany and Italy owed their regeneration to the overthrow of 'les artisans of disorder — the Freemasons and the GREAT Jews...'. Then he dropped the theme. These were the fulminations of marginality, of the excluded, of the imminently obsolescent. These were the signs that they were taking leave of political reality, and when Sabiani told his followers, 'I ask you to follow me at all costs. The hour is not far off when I will prove to you that the leader you've given yourselves is worthy of your sacrifice', it was

partly play of fancy and partly presage of some radical departure —
finally forced by the legislative elections in the spring of 1936.[30]

The campaign was rough in Sabiani's constituency, a dead heat with
at least one murder a side by the Socialists and Communists and one
attempted murder by the *Sabianistes*. The Communists were deeply
committed now in the fourth as well as in the fifth canton; they had
prepared their campaign well, issuing circulars to the *comités de rayons*
and creating *comités de bureaux de vote* and telling their people to pursue
the abstentionists who Sabiani thought were *modérés*; they denied
being a 'parti électoral' but what was true in 1932 was no longer true
in 1936. They called Sabiani a renegade from the proletariat, a Croix-
de-Feu, a fascist — 'the man who has eaten at everyone's table and
who, like Doriot, has ended up in complete fascism'. He fought back
with his customary pugnacity, accusing the socialists of fraud and the
communists — 'Parisians sent from Moscow' — of subversion.[31] It
all came to a climax in the Place Marceau, the large square at the end
of Sabiani's own rue Fauchier, on the evening of 21 April. He was
there, so was Billoux, perhaps 10,000 of their followers packed the
place, the *Sabianistes* in serried circles around the podium, the Communists around them. Sabiani spoke prodigiously, riding the heck-
ling, monopolising the meeting, knowing that at half-past nine buses
would come for the Communists; he proclaimed himself worthy and
them unworthy of the working class, but he never finished, for
around nine o'clock fighting broke out, revolvers were seen though
not heard, and the mass around him dissolved into eddies of frenzied
partisans. Billoux never did speak, but he had silenced Sabiani in his
stronghold, a violent ending to a violent campaign and a foretaste of
electoral upheaval.[32]
    Five days later the Communists swept the fifth canton and made
deep inroads into the fourth. In the Belle-de-Mai and beyond, into
the seventh canton industrial suburbs of St Antoine, St André and
l'Estaque, Cristofol led the Socialist of the sector;[33] in Sabiani's fifth
canton *bureaux* Billoux widened the Communist margins of the year
before, doing best in la Madrague, the most proletarian of all
Sabiani's *bureaux*.[34] The pattern recurred elsewhere: on the other side
of the city in St Pierre and Montredon, the Communist vote surged
in working class neighbourhoods.[35] And now *le parti* undermined
Sabiani's base in his own fourth canton. Billoux won about a fifth of
the vote there, but, more importantly, he did best where Sabiani
for the first time in his career did worst — among the slum dwellers
of the Lazaret and the workers of Arenc. Sabiani partly compensated
for his decline there by a strong showing in the less proletarian
neighbourhoods of la Joliette and the Boulevard des Dames, but in

5 Sabiani and his paper on the eve of electoral defeat, May 1936

the second round the discipline of the *Front Populaire* undid him. The Socialist candidate — his former friend and secretary, Ferri-Pisani — withdrew in favour of Billoux, and his margin in the fourth canton was too narrow to compensate for his losses in the fifth. Billoux was elected — as was Cristofol next door — and Sabiani was no longer a deputy.[36]

From now on the communist party was the enemy. It was 'bolshevism invading', 'Muscovite enslavement', an occult power working on the Socialists, Léon Blum, and all France. Above all it was foreign. 'Remember that today, above political parties, the problem...is simple: French or foreign?': the danger was not the worker on strike nor even the ideology of Marxism but the cosmopolitan mercenaries in the pay of 'the Russia of the Comintern'. Plots and conspiracies entered the language of *Sabianisme* — now a raid planned by the Communists, now 45 subversive Greek workers infiltrated into Marseille. June and July were wild, with demonstrations and street fights and Carbone and Spirito in the news again. A *Sabianiste* lorry driver was murdered. Communism became an obsession.[37]

On the right the Croix-de-Feu continued their ascent; they too did well by the elections. There were now 58 deputies favourable to the

Croix-de-Feu in the Chamber, including two from Marseille; meanwhile the June strikes swelled the *ligue's* ranks with alarmed new members. And the *ligue* became a party. The new government's dissolution of the *ligues* was a blessing in disguise, for it allowed La Rocque to declare that 'the time has come for us to go over to political action' and to assume the leadership of a *ligue* reincarnated as the Parti Social Français, rid of many of its old radical or intemperate elements — traitors to the Croix-de-Feu, he had called them — yet just as contemptuous of the placidities of the traditional right, of the 'conservatives or...moderates who think only of words and reject deeds...'. They would be different: 'We will organise ourselves along the lines of the Socialist party...'.[38] In Marseille there was some talk of absorbing the *modérés*, but it came to nothing and the PSF was launched on its own in a huge rally in July, 20,000 people filling the Arènes du Prado,[39] a juggernaut with the ideas of the right and the organisation of the left: a mass conservative party.

Like the rest of the right the PSF was eclipsed in the demonology of *Sabianisme* by the *Front Populaire*, and like the rest of the right it had the virtue of anti-communism. Sabiani had even been willing to meet in public with the assembled right in the call to arms following the elections. But the PSF threatened to engulf him, and Sabiani and Géraud finally decided to try to stem the tide. La Rocque became the apostle of 'home...family...and tranquility,' a faint-heart who asked his followers only to 'practice politics henceforth, just as in a good old traditional grouping, in the "Parti Social Français"' — he was bourgeois.[40] They would applaud his views but deflate his pretensions, and so began a new suite in Sabiani's wary dance with the right.

But for now, in July 1936, the situation was simple: *Sabianisme* was facing extinction. For all the charged climate and the talk of civil war, the twin extremes, yesterday disdaining electoral politics, today actively practising them, had entered the spacious premises of the Third Republic — the Communists as partners in the *Front Populaire*, the Croix-de-Feu as the Parti Social Français: they were now part of the system. Not so everyone in France: not so *Sabianisme*. It seemed to belong nowhere, a clan among parties, its Corsican chieftain anachronistic as well as *dépaysé*. It would have to adapt to survive: it, too, would have to transform itself.

Sabiani set about doing so. He looked for a way to transform his personal following into a wider party of the disaffected and the maladjusted, with an ideology to express their anger and an organisation to mobilise their strength; he looked for a way to dignify his incongruity, and in the Parti Populaire Français of Jacques Doriot he thought he had found it.

CHAPTER 5

'Fascism', 1936–1939

In July 1936 two friends of Sabiani, Joseph Carrega and Gustave Chipponi of Bastia days, hailed Antoine Franceschi from the terrace of the Café Glacier on the Canebière. They had heard that Sabiani was about to join Doriot's PPF; would Franceschi stay and help dissuade him? Ten minutes later Sabiani himself turned up and announced that yes, he was taking the 10 pm *rapide* to Paris, where he intended to sign up with Doriot, and that no, he would not reconsider: 'Shut up! You don't understand anything about politics! Yes, I'm starting a party, but you three won't be in it!' His mind was made up.[1]

Sabiani and Doriot had met in the Chamber of Deputies and by 1931 the two were friends. They made an odd pair: Doriot the physical colossus beside the unimposing Sabiani, his voracious appetites the antithesis of Sabiani's asceticism, a national figure next to a provincial unknown. But there was much to unite them. Both were heroes of the first world war, disaffected Communists, compelling speakers; both were obsessed by politics and the pursuit of power, and both were foiled by the developments of 1934–1936, left only with their personal fiefdoms in *milieux populaires* — Doriot with St Denis, Sabiani with the fourth canton. Over the years Doriot's affection for Sabiani, together with the kind of hypnotic fascination that he held for him, would survive their frequent and stormy quarrels.[2]

They began to converge after Doriot's expulsion from the Communist party in 1934 — ostensibly for heresy, for advocating *unité d'action* with the Socialists, for being right before the party was, but fundamentally for his visceral unsuitability to the discipline of the mass sect. His biographers have invoked opportunism and ambition to explain his rebellion, but probably, like Sabiani, he also nurtured deep-seated doubts about a Soviet presence in French politics.[3] In the months before the elections of the spring of 1936 *Marseille-Libre* applauded his anticommunism, seeing in him the antidote to a foreign hold over the French working class, a 'remarkable' speaker in the Chamber, an unheeded prophet.[4] He was a favourite before he was a *chef* — before the summer of 1936 when he founded the PPF.

The project had been brewing in Doriot's mind for some time, possibly since 1934. He had seen the failure of the Third International, the success of the fascists in Italy and of the Nazis in Germany, the miscarriage of the *néo-socialistes* and the normalisation of the Croix-de-Feu. He had concluded that there was room in France for a new sort of party, his party. It would assemble dissidents of all sorts, the sorts present at the *rendez-vous de Saint-Denis* and at the PPF's first congress in November 1936: the workers of St Denis who had followed him out of the old party, other dissident communists who now made up the *bureau politique* of the new party, hallucinating intellectuals like Drieu la Rochelle, schismatic Croix-de-Feu and disillusioned *modérés* like Alfred Fabre-Luce:

> Before, the modérés had always seemed to me a little ashamed of their own ideas: they held meetings by invitation only and feared big confrontations. It was reassuring to see that on the right too there was a populace...The irruption of the masses into politics seemed to call forth men of this type[Doriot]...The Communists had undertaken a primitive struggle in which their adversaries risked losing if they did not fight on the same terrain with the same weapons.

For Fabre-Luce as for others Doriot personified the vision of a stronger kind of politics and a stronger kind of state, and his appeal was strong enough to attract perhaps 100,000 members at the party's pre-war peak.[5]

For Sabiani and his diehards the creation of the PPF could not have come at a more propitious moment. Doriot's new party delivered them from oblivion: it promised to breath new life into a moribund organisation, to give it national and ideological identity and so recruit all sorts of new members, set against Communism and conservatism alike.

The inaugural rally took place in the *Arènes du Prado* on 26 July, the day after La Rocque's rally there launching the PSF — the culmination of a hectic month-long scramble for the starting line by the two new parties. Doriot arrived with Sabiani, climbed onto a tribune crowded with *Sabianiste* municipal employees, regional PPF officials, and friendly observers from the traditional right, and acknowledged the ovation of 15,000 people, enthusiasts among them saluting with raised arm as he saluted back. In shirtsleeves and braces he attacked Stalin, called for peace, trivialised the distinction between right and left, spoke of a mystical faith in nationhood; he pledged himself to fight the Communists with their own weapons and Sabiani, taking the standard of the section from him, pledged in turn the fealty of his followers: 'I take the oath of loyalty...We will follow you all the way in your struggle': a reckless and ultimately disastrous commitment.[6]

From the outset the ideologues of the PPF, in Marseille as in Paris, had an audience in mind: the doubting Thomases — and among them, the disaffected Communists of the working class and the disaffected conservatives of the middle class.

In working class neighbourhoods, like Arenc and St Lazare close to Sabiani's home or Montolivet and Mazargues further away, their posters and their stump orators blamed neighbourhood unemployment on the communists, urged the workers to recognize the advent of 'Thermidor' and of tyranny in the USSR, called on them to rally to the PPF.[7] They serenaded the susceptible — Arab immigrants, to whom they recalled the Koran's dire warnings about marching with the infidels, *alias* the Communists, and to whom they promised jobs; disillusioned Communist *miliciens* returning from Spain, whom they plied with gifts in money and kind; and disgruntled trades unionists, whom they sought to hive off into dissident unions and whose own CGT they briefly sought to infiltrate and undermine.[8] Their goal was as clear as Sabiani's *mot d'ordre* — 'the PPF wants to take root among the working masses' — and their strategy as simple as the headline in *l'Emancipation Nationale*: 'WORKER, YOU HAVE BEEN BETRAYED'.[9]

For the fence-sitters of the *petite bourgeoisie* they changed their tune. They challenged them to join the fray, appealed to their dormant fears. Mimeographed broadsheets were issued in Endoume and the Roucas Blanc:

> And you the fearful...you who have a 'position', a 'business', an 'industry', will you finally understand that supporting the Soviet agents in France with your neutrality is not a way to underwrite your life insurance?

Doubters within the PSF, at least, heard the PPF's call to action: '...a fairly large number from the parti social [français],' noted the city police, 'have decided to leave it for the parti populaire [français] which is more audacious and above all more combative'.[10] The PPF became the party of the 'small employers, small industrialists, small farmers' harried by taxes, impoverished by inflation, and despoiled by the 'anonymous trusts'; it would deliver the 'sacrificed' middle class as well as the 'betrayed' working class.[11]

What if their interests collided? Then the PPF would support the workers' demands but oppose their strikes and sit-ins, especially if they threatened the welfare of 'small shareholders' and 'small savers'. They would argue for and then against the 40-hour weeks; or they would deny any conflict, affirming that they were all part of the same class anyway.[12] It was the discord of *Sabianisme* all over again, only now in the PPF the makeshift *motifs* harmonised into a time-honoured theme: the theme of conspiracy.

For the Communists and their foreign masters had hatched a diabolical plot for the destruction of the middle class and the enslavement of the working class. They would drive the workers into suicidal strikes, 'bolshevise' or 'russify' where possible the middle classes, wreck the French economy, ignite civil war and destroy the country from within, and so leave it at their mercy.[13]

Worse, they would destroy the country from without by driving it into war. 'The French want peace, the parties of Moscow want war': they wanted to deflect Germany's aggressive designs away from the Soviet Union, but also to promote social chaos at home. The Spanish crisis broke just as the PPF was getting underway, and at once the party's leaders denounced the Communist call for intervention as 'Moscow's war'. Subversion in Spain and war in France had the same communist face and by January 1937 Sabiani, in an exemplary display of conspiracy fantasy, imagined that the Comintern, in the event of a setback in Spain, would unleash a revolution in France, in order to provoke Hitler's intervention, and a subsequent Franco-German war, true to Soviet design.[14] Less tortuously he and his new colleagues declared that the Communists were trying to push the country into a war with Germany for which it was unprepared. Because of the Communists and their Socialist accomplices France was diminished and had to reach some sort of understanding with a renascent Germany, whatever Germany was. Except for a few words of envy for its accomplishments and of disapproval for its excesses neither *Marseille-Libre* nor *l'Emancipation Nationale* had much to say about Nazism: all that mattered was to avoid a war that France would lose. The larger loomed the threat of war, the shriller grew the cries: after the Munich scare the PPF called for the dissolution of the Communist party and the incarceration of its leaders.[15] What went for Germany also went for Italy. The Communists, by advocating intervention in the Spanish civil war, were trying to push France into a war against a 'latin sister' with whom she had no quarrel. To Sabiani Hitler was a 'swine' ['salopard'] and Mussolini a 'trapeze artist', but *le parti* and its Soviet masters were the real warmongers — 'we will offer our hand to Germany if she gives guarantees of peace but we will always fight our only enemy,

Communism' — and he and Doriot greeted the Nazi-Soviet pact and the war which followed as the confirmation of their direst predictions.[16]

National regeneration thus depended on peace, and Communism was the foe of both. It was the anti-France, at work poisoning the nation, its defeated *miliciens* from Spain preparing a 'revolutionary putsch' in Marseille, its fifth columnists in the army laying plans for the siege of the city, its agents fomenting insurrection in France's north African colonies.[17] 'They are like parasites incrusted in human flesh' — with the stock-in-trade animal imagery of the conspiracy artist Doriot painted the communist portrait. And with the stock-in-trade appeal to some 'infantile fear of strangeness', the appeal of precursors exposing masonic, jesuitical, or semitic plots, he and his fellow ideologues endowed the conspirators with sinister foreign faces. Most obviously the Communists were Russian. But they also worked obscurely with an occult force called 'international capital', specially entrusted with the destruction of the French middle classes, and less obscurely with their benighted socialist minion, the Jew-foreigner at the head of the government. 'Léon Blum does not love France and cannot love it because he is not French', Sabiani once declared and, after the *Anschluss l'Emancipation Nationale* ran a cartoon showing Blum and Marx Dormoy in conclave: '...Peuh!...We've annexed France!' Jews are all right if they became French but those of the Front Populaire did not do so; those in the government even opened the floodgates to the foreign emigrants pouring into the country — and who only tried to wreck the French economy with strikes once they arrived. The communist phobia thus degenerated into fitful bouts of antisemitism and xenophobia, depending on temperament: febrile authors like Drieu la Rochelle in Paris and Géraud in Marseille ran to anti-semitism, Sabiani almost never. Sometimes it all came together in a chain of execration, like that put together by Sabiani's friend and protégé Mangiavacca: 'international Jewish and Anglo-Saxon capitalism'.[18] These were the faces of the Communist *Etranger*, the hydra-headed monster threatening the French national community.

But, providentially, the PPF was there. It would be the counter-commuist order, like the anti-masonic *Chevaliers de la Foi* under the First Empire or the anti-Jesuitical association in Eugène Sue's *Juif Errant*.[19] It would foil the 'outsiders of the inside, fomenters of civil war', as Sabiani called them, turn decadence into rebirth, and usher in some sort of new order, variously described as a victory of French civilisation, a 'directed economy', a 'new state', a 'French socialism for the French', not Russian, not totalitarian, but with 'authority above' and 'discipline below'. It would transcend right and left, especially the sterile parliamentary parties like the *bourgeois* PSF, and rally the new classless Frenchman, his arm raised in ritual salute to Jacques Doriot, *le chef*.[20]

All this the PPF wanted but failed to be. For beneath the surface glare of speeches and ideology, and in the half-light of motives and mentalities, a different PPF emerges, one that Sabiani did not and could not acknowledge.

At first all seemed to go well. At a *pro forma* session held four days after the inaugural *Arènes* meeting the Parti d'Action Socialiste voted to scuttle itself and follow Sabiani *en masse* into the PPF. Mangiavacca had to answer various questions — notably about whether the PPF upheld the 'proletarian ideal' — but there were no defections[21] and throughout August the cantonal sections were rechristened the PPF one by one, with a recitation of the party's statutes and a rousing speech from Sabiani. At least nine of the twelve sections retained their secretaries, a sign of continuity and personal loyalty, an act of self-immolation described in *Marseille-Libre* as a 'considerable mark of affection and trust'[22] — and for once the incendiary weekly was understating its case.

The core of loyalists was soon fringed with converts, the recruits of the late summer and autumn of 1936. By December the local party was claiming 7,000 members, by the new year 8,000. A credulous police commissioner parroted the figures, which were implausible, for at the time the eleventh canton — an important section — was only claiming 375 members, the third canton 300, and *Marseille-Libre* 5,000 subscribers, and by then it was the PPF paper for all of Provence. And how, within six months of its birth, could the PPF overtake the PCF with its 7,000 members and come abreast of SFIO with its 8,000? The same commissioner thought the PPF had 9,000 members in the Bouches-du-Rhône in 1938, and 7,200 in Marseille in the middle of 1939, but by then he recognised that half were not paying their dues — the party's membership in Marseille between 1936 and 1939 probably fluctuated between 4,000 and 7,000 at the most.[23]

Who were they, and why did they join? 408 can be identified and traced, 173 of them from post-Liberation trials or investigations, and 95 of these in turn give some motives for their membership: a partial sample, but a sample nonetheless.[24]

Seventy-eight per cent were workers, claimed Sabiani in the spring of 1937: this was sheer fantasy. Only 28 of the 426 members of the sample are workers, skilled or unskilled — a steep drop from the level of the earlier *Sabianiste* organisations, from 24 per cent to seven per cent, probably disguising an even steeper one, for the PPF sample draws on more of the rank-and-file than the *bureaux*-based

Sabianiste sample.[25] None of them joined to expurgate and rejuvenate the France of PPF rhetoric. At least four joined looking for work: an occasional rag collector, 32 years old and unemployed — 'I did it because I had been promised work' — who eventually left the party after finding work independently as a dishwasher; a mechanic, also 32, on the strength of a friend's word that he might find work through the party; a 28-year-old illiterate Algerian day-labourer, who had somehow met Sabiani and through him found a job at the *Raffineries de Sucre Saint-Louis*. A 25-year-old Algerian tinworker joined to show his gratitude: 'In 1938 I joined the PPF party in order to please Maitre Franchi [a prominent PPF member] who had represented me in a case involving a bicycle'. A worker from Vaucluse in a chemical plant in l'Estaque joined a PPF group on the factory floor 'for purely professional reasons'. And the political 'ideas' of a 25-year old jack-of-all-trades, sometime plumber and stonemason, were not ideas at all:

> I joined the PPF in 1936. Before, I had belonged to the Communist party, but I had changed [my] ideas because I found myself at one point without work and the CGT took no interest in my situation. I [therefore] joined the PPF...[26]

They are the only skilled or unskilled workers to reveal their motives, and conviction is not one of them.

The other members of the 'lower class' — domestic and service personnel, who drop from eight to four per cent, and sailors and dockers, who increase slightly, from about seven to nine per cent[27] — tell the same story. Some joined out of syndical ambition, like a Senegalese sailor who while frequenting a communist bar in the *vieux quartiers* joined SFIO, then the PSF, and finally the PPF: 'I joined the PPF in 1938...in order to get Sabiani's support for my sailors and compatriots whom I represented at the time...I never paid any dues...'. Some joined out of loyalty, like the 42-year-old taxi-driver from Bastia whose taxi Sabiani took in preference to others, or the Corsican sailor, barely literate, who had met Sabiani in the army in Aix in 1908 and later joined his following, or the 38-year-old docker with the guileless politics: 'I was always in Simon Sabiani's party, I voted socialiste-communiste when he was [socialiste-communiste] and I joined the PPF at is foundation'. Some joined out of personal gratitude, like the 50-year-old Corsican sailor of the Boulevard de Paris — 'I paid all [my] dues in order to please Sabiani who had rendered numerous services to my family'. Some joined in the hope of finding a job, like the unemployed seamstress, a *Bastiaise*, who left in disappointment 18 months later; some for multiple private motives, like the illiterate Corsican sailor of the *vieux quartiers* who had always followed Sabiani but who also, in 1936, hoped for a job in municipal tax collection. A PPF *concierge* at the *Cableries Phocéennes* in the fifth canton was anti-communist to the point of arguing with fellow-employees, and a docker found the PPF a 'suitable political party':[28] two instances of doubtful public conviction, in the lower class, against sixteen of credible private interest.[29]

Sabiani, in short, had lost many of his lower class supporters and those that remained, or those that joined, had little interest in the ideals of the PPF. They were clients as before.

Artisans, shopkeepers and office-workers could not give the party ideologues much hope either. Artisans — the most 'proletarian' element in the lower middle class — fall, in the PPF sample, to seven per cent of the total from an earlier level of twelve per cent: one of them, a mason, joined 'because Simon Sabiani lived in my neigh-bourhood'. Shopkeepers with nine per cent and office-workers with eleven remain about the same,[30] but so does their mentality. A bank employee signed up out of enthusiasm for the party's 'social policy', but the shopkeepers were pragmatism itself: a drysalter in Saint-Louis out in the seventh canton, tempted by the incentives offered by a commercial traveller and PPF recruiter; another drysalter, a Corsican in Sabiani's *quartier*, persuaded that a shipping company in la Joliette would buy his insecticide on contract if he joined the party; a grocer, also Corsican, also a neighbour, 'bound by friendship forever to Simon Sabiani', who had once found him a job in Cus-toms; a Corsican restaurant owner, another old friend of Sabiani's; yet another neighbour, the owner of a bar up in l'Estaque, who joined like so many others '[because] I had lived in Sabiani's neighbourhood for a long time and because I knew him. I joined the party to please him'; and his brother, who alone injected a dash of polemic into the mix: '[I joined] because the social programme pleased me and because having lived for twenty years in the Place d'Aix I knew Sabiani'[31] — these were dyed-in-the-wool *Sabianistes*, at best titular converts to the new mass party.

Fonctionnaires account for one-fifth of the PPF sample, unchanged from their earlier level, a stable and strong presence, stronger by far than among Sabiani's electorate in the fourth and fifth cantons. About one-sixth of all municipal employees in Marseille — 1,280 out of 7,603 — belonged to the PPF in 1938. It was no accident that their patrons and employers, the *Sabianistes* in the *mairie*, also accounted for one-sixth of the city councillors — six out of 36: to each faction its share of the municipal spoils.[32]

And here, among the PPF *fonctionnaires*, was the old *Sabianiste* clientèle in all its practicality and simplicity. Most were already employed at the *mairie* or, in a few cases, in a state branch like the post office, already owned their livelihood to Sabiani, and joined out of prudence, gratitude, or deference, like a fireman from la Joliette:

I joined the PPF in 1937 out of gratitude for its leader Simon Sabiani who had found a job for me as a fireman in the city of Marseille'

and a tax-collector from the Lazaret:

Sabiani had got me in as a tax-collector in 1928, and in gratitude I followed his politics...I was simply enrolled in the party...

and a dustman from la Madrague:

I was taken on at the Mairie in 1934 and to be agreeable to Sabiani I joined the PPF

and a painter from Arenc:

I joined the PPF because it was almost obligatory for municipal employees to join the party which Sabiani led

and an office-helper from la Barrasse — a native of Casamaccioli — and a blacksmith-turned-fireman from the Boulevard de Paris. Some were more forward, like the naturalised Italian municipal employee who joined expecting security of tenure and who was not disappointed, or the Corsican who joined expecting promotion and who was disappointed — and who resigned from the party. Some joined in recognition and some in hope of favours to their families, of a flat for a mother or a job for a brother or a sanatorium room for a sick daughter. Some had multiple services to repay, like the guard at the Saint-Pierre cemetery, a *Bastiais*, who owed his job to Sabiani in 1932 but who joined the PPF in 1936 'out of gratitude for the services which Simon Sabiani rendered to my family' — Sabiani might not control the *mairie* any longer, but still he had riches to dispense and still his dependents clung to him as to a lifeline.[33]

Sometimes they gilded necessity with idealism. A Corsican sailor-turned-city tax collector who probably owed his job to Sabiani was half-retainer, half-patriot: 'I had joined this party because I knew Simon Sabiani, I believed that it was for the good of France'. An official at the *Société des Eaux*, there since 1934 thanks to his former schoolmate at the *lycée de Bastia*, Simon Sabiani, an ardent syndical activist among the municipal employees as well as a party propagandist, laced affection for a patron with partiality for a programme:

Living in the same neighbourhood as Sabiani, I had frequent contacts with him, on a purely private and friendly basis...[I joined the PPF in 1936] out of gratitude to Sabiani and because the programme of the party had convinced me at the time.

Sometimes they believed in the PPF. A receiver at the city gas monopoly joined because the party's programme pleased him and his fiancée, a tramway employee 'out of political idea', another tramway employee seemingly to fill the void of celibacy with political conviction, for as a colleague said later, 'Before his marriage he spoke well of the PPF...but, since his marriage, he preferred to devote himself to the happiness of his young wife'.[34] But such conviction was rare. Thirty-seven of the *fonctionnaires* in the PPF sample give motives for their membership and only five cite conviction alone: all the others give some sort of private motive, occasionally straying onto the treacherous terrain of political opinion but never wandering far from the no-man's-land of *Sabianisme*. One-third were born in Corsica — compared to less than one-fifth of all the others in the PPF sample[35] — and as before they are the city's version of the *parenti, amici e aderenti* of the island's clan; as before they are the *Sabianiste* core.

How was the PPF to breathe ideological fervour into these people, turn clients into zealots? The neighbourhood activists joined for the wrong reasons too, to advance the cause of the *quartier* rather than that of the party or the nation, like Sabiani's old friend of the *comité d'intérêts du quartier* of Saint-Antoine or the Corsican from la Timone:

> In 1936, as treasurer of the neighbourhood association, to improve the neighbourhood, I had to appeal to Monsieur Simon Sabiani who replied, 'I only take care of men who join the PPF.' So, to satisfy my demands, I joined the party.

The party's enforcers, now on the *quais* hunting for imaginary communist arms smugglers, now on the docks waylaying a convoy they thought destined for Spain, were the same old drifters and criminals at loose ends and thugs from the milieu, no more interested in Spain than in any other official PPF obsession. And still the bar was the hub of political activity, still the Bar Raffé on the Boulevard de Paris the Sabianiste *siège* of the fourth canton, except that now it was called the PPF *siège*; still the barkeepers played their pivotal role, symbols of the tenacity with which the old politics resisted the new.[36]

But the new politics did break in, borne by intruders almost absent from the earlier *Sabianiste* organisations: the *bourgeois*. Merchants, managers, industrialists, journalists and lawyers and doctors and other members of the liberal professions rise from less than six per cent of the early *Sabianiste* sample to nearly twenty-five per cent of the PPF sample, offsetting the decline in skilled and unskilled workers and so raising the social centre of gravity. They came from the other side of the city: those in the sample are concentrated in the second and sixth cantons, their lower and lower middle class colleagues in the fourth and the seventh: the second, with the *Bourse* and the commercial district, was the *bourgeois* canton *par excellence*, the sixth less so, but it was still the canton of stately Longchamps-Chartreux-

Madeleine. They had different ethnic origins: only five per cent in the sample are Corsican, compared to twenty-eight per cent of the others, and more — thirty-three per cent compared to fourteen per cent — are from outside Provence. They were slightly older: only twenty-four per cent in the sample, compared to fifty per cent for the lower and seventy-six per cent for the lower-middle class, are under thirty-five.[37] They were different.

And they joined the PPF for a different motive: they joined out of conviction. For a securities broker '[the PPF] seemed to represent the party of order', and employers were undoubtedly impressed by the party's anti-communism, like the technical director of a factory — 'I joined the PPF in 1937 because of its social doctrine' — or the 52-year old manager of another factory — 'I saw social accomplishment in the PPF' — or the barely coherent director of a chemical company: '[I joined the PPF] not for its political ideas but for its social programme. I shared the ideas of Doriot but not those of Sabiani'. Or they were political animals. A sales director, treasurer of the Endoume section, 'got all worked up over an idea', said a colleague, was enthusiastic about the ideals of the PPF, but also, concluded a psychologist after the war, found in party politics a role 'which [merely] inflated his vanity without provoking the appearance of real ideas [delusions] of grandeur or personality disturbances'. And an accountant's rigorous profession did not preclude an uninterrupted flight of political fantasy, from SFIO in 1928 to Sabiani's Parti Socialiste-Communiste in 1931 to the Croix-de-Feu in 1934 to the PPF in 1936:

> I am a fervent collectivist. . .who then became the enemy of communism as the PPF depicted it for us. . .My dream would have been to see realised a truly French revolutionary unity. . .I have conducted no propaganda, other than [in support of] my ideas of co-operation which are applicable to all parties.

Others were intrigued by the novelty of the PPF, like the corporate administrator who joined 'a little out of curiosity, for information's sake', or the journalist at *Le Petit Marseillais* who went to the inaugural St. Denis meeting: 'I met Guitard and [Bertrand] de Jouvenel who [told] me that this party seemed to have a new spirit and on my arrival in Marseille I signed up'. Two joined out of friendship for Sabiani, including an engineer at the water monopoly who had served in his unit during the war, and only one, an Italian grateful to Sabiani for his naturalisation, signed up in recognition of services rendered — and as a masonry *entrepreneur* his upper-middle class credentials are doubtful. The remaining fourteen with motives to reveal joined because they liked what they heard; the ideologues' exertions were not all idle.[38]

They were rewarded with a two-tiered party: a new, ideological, largely *bourgeois* layer grafted onto an older, clientelistic, largely popular base.[39]

But the graft did not take. The police noticed first the contrast between 'members really sharing the views [sentiments] of the party' and 'purely Sabianiste members who have no Faith, no Party, no Conviction...'. Then they noticed the signs of disintegration: by 1939, with the Popular Front receding in time and the social climate settling down, apathy and desertions left little more than a core of about 3,000 paid-up *Sabianistes* '[who] have always blindly followed their leader, M. Sabiani, for motives more personal than political'. Some of the members saluted and sang the PPF song and went along with the ritual but it was only the homage that clan paid to party and anyway lent a vaguely ridiculous aspect to the proceedings. The eighth canton section celebrated the second anniversary of the PPF with a minute of silence for the party's dead, victims of political violence, followed by the oath to Doriot — 'I swear it' intoned with right arm raised — followed by free entertainment from a magician member, a lottery drawing and finally the singing of *France libère-toi*. Sabiani consistently upstaged Doriot. He could not help it. 'When Doriot spoke,' recalled Sabiani's young neighbour, 'there was polite applause; when Sabiani spoke there was uproar. He electrified'. The PPF came to celebrate *Sabianisme*, instead of the reverse — the Bar Raffé had both Doriot and Sabiani on the walls but the meetings were all Simon. The *Petits Pionniers Jacques Doriot* sang *France Libère-toi* in a circle around him, the eleventh canton section welcomed him with an 'Ode à Simon Sabiani': 'Honour to you, Simon, honour to your valour...With you and by you, the PPF will win'. It was a failed transformation, a failure finally captured in another recollection of the young neighbour: 'We were there because of Simon. We couldn't give a damn about the PPF'. ('On était là à cause de Simon. Le PPF, on s'en foutait').[40]

Claiming to be what it could not be, overtly indulging its fantasies and covertly surrendering its principles, the PPF blustered its way into French politics.

It boasted that it was French-financed and decried the foreign funding of the *partis de l'Etranger* even while surreptitiously pocketing Italian money, for certainly the Italian embassy in Paris and probably the *Casa d'Italia* in Marseille were quietly sponsoring its activities. Its secret foreign fund was one of the reasons Pierre Pucheu gave for resigning from the *bureau politique* in 1938, and the *tu quoque* with which the Communists parried charges of their own financial dependence on the Comintern.[41]

It upheld the middle classes against the 'capitalist trusts' even while raking in large sums from corporate contributors, including banks in Paris and shipbuilders in Marseille. Sabiani's chauffeur Géronimi went along to Fraissinet and Altieri to collect their contributions, and Sabiani himself was not above asking the local representatives of the *Compagnie Française des Métaux* for funds on two occasions between 1938 and 1940 — he was gratified with 500 francs each time.[42] How much the bankers and the businessmen helped is open to doubt. In Marseille, even with the party's other revenue from subscriptions, dues, and private donations, their contributions did not solve chronic financial problems — in April 1937 the eleventh canton section could not finance its monthly bulletin and in October Sabiani's own fourth canton section was 650 francs in debt.[43] But the party's penury only increased its dependence on its patrons: it could not afford the luxury of its rhetoric.

It derided the conservatives, new and old, even while trying to inveigle them into electoral pacts. The PSF, with about 13,000 members in Marseille in 1938, was much larger than the PPF and the smaller party had to play aspirant as well as accuser. Its members heckled PSF speakers, who in turn called the PPF a 'revolutionary party', but Sabiani sought and obtained the co-operation of the PSF in the fourth canton in the cantonal elections of October 1937 — only to deny angrily the following year that he owed his re-election to their support. In Marseille as in France the PPF tried to entice the PSF into the *front de la liberté* and when the PSF demurred, seeing a stratagem from which the PFF could only win and it could only lose, Sabiani like Doriot could accuse them of breaking ranks and of abetting the Popular Front with their 'harassment' and their 'ill will'.[44] They were false-hearted, trying to discredit and live off the PSF at the same time.

It claimed to rally voters from all sides but its only asset was Sabiani and even he needed pacts with the right to stay in office. The *Sabianiste* base in the fourth canton alone held firm, and Sabiani was re-elected *conseiller général* there in 1937, but he needed the withdrawal of the right to win and even so could not reconquer the ground lost to the Communists in the legislative elections the year before — he was still weakest in the working class wards of Arenc and the Lazaret, still strongest around the less proletarian Boulevard des Dames.[45] Elsewhere that year the PPF was on the decline, its candidates around the city drawing only 14 per cent of the first round vote compared to 21 per cent for the *Sabianistes* in the same cantonal elections six years earlier.[46] And Sabiani was the only member of the PPF in the city council — his five allies followed him but kept their own party labels: *Radical-socialiste/Union Républicaine Démocratique/ Républicain-socialiste* or ex-SFIO. In Marseille, whatever its claims, the PPF had no identity and no electorate beyond that of Simon Sabiani.

For most of the voters of the right and centre were deaf to its appeals. In the summer of 1936 it could exploit real fears in Marseille, the fears reported by police as late as March 1937: 'political anxiety, notably among the middle classes and the right wing parties...they say in these milieux that our country is moving with big strides towards bloody revolution'. But by 1938 and 1939 most voters probably thought that the PPF was tilting at windmills. The decline in the communist vote in the cantonal elections, the formation of the Daladier government in April 1938 and its final break with the Popular Front later that year, the failure of the general strike of November 1938, the drop in May Day attendance, from 25,000 in 1937 to 13,000 in 1938 to 4,000 in 1939 — the threat of upheaval, real or imagined, lost its hold. Late in the day the PPF could still strike some popular chords, such as the rancour, at the time of Munich, against the Communists and against foreigners who drew unemployment benefits while enjoying exemption from military service, and the support, outside of the Communists, for the recognition of Franco at the end of the Spanish war. But it had no monopoly over the themes — Daladier vigorously attacked the Communist party after Munich, even attributed strikes to foreigners, and sent Pétain to Spain as ambassador, and Daladier, in Marseille as in France, was popular. Both Doriot and Sabiani claimed, with some bitterness, that he had adopted their own policies. In the end the deepening gloom over the approach of war probably smothered whatever electoral appeal the PPF might have had. The party's speakers applauded Munich after prevaricating throughout September — Doriot had declared absurdly that France should give in on the Sudetenland but not allow Germany to take it by force — and along with almost everyone else accepted war as inevitable after the German entry into Prague: it seemed to have nothing to offer, other than conspiracy and ritual and revolutionary pretence.[47]

But it went on like a mechanical piano up to the outbreak of war. When the Nouvelles Galeries went up in smoke in October 1938 Sabiani and Géraud blamed Marxism and the Popular Front for the inadequate water supply; when the city council met its inglorious end in March 1939, dissolved by the national government and replaced by a special administration, they blamed the Popular Front for the city's disgrace. The voters went their own way: in February 1939 a municipal by-election confirmed the decline of the communist party and the stagnation of the PPF. It was a pointless affair, provoked by the six Sabianistes in the city council when they resigned in the unfulfilled hope of forcing a general resignation and a general election.

They won a routine re-election after a routine campaign, amid much indifference beyond their captive constituents: it gave the *Sabianistes* a chance to celebrate. In Marseille it was the last voting Sunday of the Third Republic. When war was declared Sabiani and Doriot were still railing at the communist conspiracy, and they continued to rail after the communist party was dissolved,[48] but by then their followers were at the front and no one else was listening.

Was this a fascist movement? Neither Sabiani nor Doriot called themselves fascists and neither sang the praise of fascist régimes abroad — not yet. But it would have been political suicide to do so. Sabiani parried accusations of fascism with countercharges of the abuses of antifascism;[49] it was an open question then and it is an open question now.

Sabiani's 'socialism within the framework of the nation', his indifference to parliamentary democracy and contempt for its parties, his flamboyant temperament and demagogic excess make him a kind of *marseillais* Mussolini even if his virtues, including some courage and loyalty, do not. But neither he nor his following carry the conviction of the early *squadristi* or *fasci*: the movement is fascist in appearance but not in reality: counterfeit fascism.

There was nothing fascist about the old *Sabianiste* core. Sabiani gave his faithful the bread of city jobs and the circuses of political meetings and the fun of his person and kept it going as long as he could. His 'I will hire my friends!' is no different from the self-serving generosity of the Neapolitan city councillor after him:

> . . . During my political activity, I try to get close to the people, interesting myself first, in what they need, a buiding license, papers for mains water, emigration, etc. . . and they remain obliged to me and it is easier to convince them to vote DC [Christian Democrat] . . .

or of the Bostonian ward politician before him:

> Is somebody out of a job? We do our best to place him and not necessarily on the public payroll. . . We do what we can, and since, as the world is run, such things must be done, we keep old friends and make new ones.[50]

Three port cities, three proclamations of 'clientelism' — and indeed clientelistic politics can be inimical to fascist penetration: they rely on the established order, fascist movements seek to overthrow it; their violence is limited and practical, fascist violence is terroristic and becomes an end in itself; they are ethnically inclusive, fascism, in some of its varieties, is racially exclusive; above all they are ideologically neutral, fascism ideologically charged. *Sabianisme*, whatever its critics said, was clientelism, and clientelism is not fascism.

The attempt to imbue it with a fascist or semi-fascist ideology was the result of an adjustment crisis. It was the modern costume donned by an archaism facing extinction. Already indifferent to the principles of democratic politics, *Sabianisme* reacted defensively to the swift rise of mass politics. Its discourse became a catalogue of the evils of modernism,[51] a denunciation of capitalism, internationalism, *bourgeois* parties, foreigners, Jews, Communism, finally culminating in the conspiracy theory of the PPF: the ideological equivalent of a persecution mania.[52] Indeed *Sabianisme* requires its communist menace as a psychotic requires his delusion, conjuring up a threat loudly contradicted by reality: communist intervention in Spain even when the war was about to end, communist bellicism even when itself more or less resigned to a war with Germany, communist influence even when the party had been dissolved.[53] It hoped to exploit the charged climate of the slump and the Popular Front and rally all who were frightened by the times.

But it failed. Neither the voters nor the old-time *Sabianistes* were interested, and the PPF stands as a political grotesquerie wrenched out of the process of change and a testimony to a controversial truth: that without enthusiastic popular support there is no fascism.

Outside Marseille the PPF fared no better. Historians have attributed its failure, like that of other 'fascist' movements, to the comparative weakness of the slump, the strength of the right and of the PSF, the association of the PPF with threatening foreign régimes, the hope offered by the Popular Front to groups who might otherwise have been tempted by more extreme remedies.[54] Outside Marseille, too, the success of the party among Jean Medecin's personal following in Nice, among the *pieds noirs* in Algeria, and among nonconformist intellectuals in Paris hints at adjustment crises of the marginal or the eccentric. Only further research will tell.

But in Marseille the PPF was no more than a phase in the history of *Sabianisme*: in 1924 the *Sabianistes* sang *l'Ajaccienne* and the International, in 1935 *l'Ajaccienne* and the *Marseillaise*, in 1939 *l'Ajaccienne*, the *Marseillaise*, and the PPF anthem. Only the Corsican element, and all that it implied, was constant. As war approached it seemed that the PPF might also be the last phase of *Sabianisme*; elections in 1940 might well have sounded its electoral death knell. But by then the Germans were in Paris, the Third Republic had ceased to exist, and *Sabianisme* found itself with an utterly unexpected stay of execution.

CHAPTER 6

Vichy's Rivals, June 1940 — November 1942

A crowd of several thousand had gathered on the *Place de la Bourse* at midday on 17 June when Pétain's voice came crackling through the loudspeakers. Most listened silently. Later, as defeat, armistice, and historical rupture sank in, emotions rose. Throughout the summer Vichy's agents listened to the telephone conversations and read the mail, and discovered hatred of the Germans, contempt for the Italians, support for the British and rancour at the politicians of the past — the artisans of defeat. For Pétain there was almost unanimous support.[1]

The city had come through the war almost unscathed. The Italian raid of 21 June, eleven days after Mussolini's entry into the war and the 'stab in the back', lightly damaged the Cathédral de la Major, the Vieux Port and l'Estaque,[2] but was trifling next to the destruction that lay ahead — the German dynamiting of the *vieux quartiers*, the American bombing of 1943 and 1944, the street fighting at the Liberation.

But the deprivations began almost at once. Housing, already in short supply before the war, was now in full crisis, for the city was flooded with refugees from all over France and beyond:

> A good part of France has withdrawn onto the Phoenician Vieux-Port, along with groups of all origins, in all conditions: Czechs, Poles, Belgians, Dutch and, among them, many Jews fearing Nazi persecution. Not one spot in a hotel, not one room to let, the stations overcrowded, people sleeping by night in the squares, clutching their bags...[3]

In September food supplies were rationed. Already during the phoney war some *marseillais* had complained about rising prices, denounced hoarders and heard rumours of bread and sugar rationing. They now accepted food tickets with gloomy resignation but resented the shortages and the truckloads of victuals sent north by the German representatives on the Armistice Commission to their colleagues in the occupied zone. By the end of summer black markets in food and petrol had taken root; by November cattle-raisers were withholding livestock in the expectation of price increases and some shopkeepers were speculatively hoarding their goods. These were harbingers: for the next four years food shortages in a city totally dependent on imports from the rest of France and overseas would go from bad to worse.[4]

The city's intellectual life was suddenly enriched by uprooted artists and authors — Paul Valéry, André Gide, Roland Dorgelès, André Breton, even Henri de Montherlant sitting on the Canebière reflecting on the triumph of paganism over Christianity.[5] But what the city gained in intellectual it lost in political diversity, for now the fissile politics of the Third Republic gave way to the bleak uniformity of Vichy, its arcane symbols and proclamations conveying some recondite sense of ancient unity.

The Quai du Port became the Quai du Maréchal Pétain, the Place Jean Jaurès the Place St-Michel, and unruly Hôtel de Ville a deserted dependency of Vichy's massive Préfecture off the Place de Rome; the city council, suspended, resurrected, then abolished altogether in September 1940, dissolved into a memory of the thirties. Now a regional prefect moved in, drawing in his wake two *secrétaires généraux*, one of whom later became *préfet délégué à l'administration de la ville de Marseille*. It was a recipe for administrative anarchy. Between the decree of March 1939 foreseeing a tenure of six years for the first *administrateur extraordinaire* and August 1942 five prefects came and went, of whom four were also *administrateurs extraordinaires* and three regional prefects. 'One cannot say,' one of them finally admitted, 'that the first test of this system has worked', and when the German troops arrived in November 1942 Vichy's civil servants were still wrestling with the intractable administrative problems of *la grande cité phocéenne*.[6]

The administrators in the Préfecture had supporting players in the local leaders of Vichy's mass veterans' organisation, the Légion Française des Combattants. They were military heroes with large families and sound politics: of 156 Légion leaders in the Bouches-du-Rhone, 82 had been *modérés* before the war; most of the rest had been in Action Française or the PSF or the parties of the parliamentary centre.[7] They posed as the conscience of the *Révolution Nationale*, sending the prefect earnest reports about public opinion, about a freemason still on the Tribunal de Commerce, about communist slogans on the walls of a *lycée*. The Légion, insisting that it was apolitical, devoted itself mostly to social paternalism, patriotic propaganda, and the welfare of its own members — 27,000 strong in the Bouches-du-Rhône by March 1941. It distributed food to the poor, organised sporting events and *Pétainiste* rallies and visits to the families of prisoners-of-war; it pressed the Préfecture with its members' demands for pensions and family allowances.[8] In fact it strongly resembled the early Croix-de-Feu, and was the closest Vichy had to an official party.

The old parties disappeared from view. In the autumn of 1940 Félix Gouin set about resurrecting SFIO in the Bouches-du-Rhône and by the following March he and Gaston Defferre, a minor Socialist from Marseille, had laid the groundwork for the new clandestine party. But most of the city's socialist politicians withdrew into private obscurity: Henri Tasso retired to La Ciotat, where he died in 1944; Dr Franchi confined himself to his medical practice; near Aix Léon Bon refrained from political activity even if he did not hide his Gaullist sympathies.[9] The Parti Social Français survived informally as the Progrès Social Français, with regional headquarters in Pau, some of its members keeping in touch and meeting occasionally but observing the ban on political activity — as La Rocque had instructed them. Late in 1940 Vichy's agents thought of the PSF people in Marseille as attached to Pétain — 'he's doing what he can, he has no choice', they heard one of them telling another over the phone — but suspicious of his entourage; otherwise they too stayed out of politics.[10] The parties of the traditional right disintegrated. A few of their pre-war leaders accepted appointive office — Ponsard in the Counseil National, Ripert in the Délégation Spéciale administering the city, Régis in the Chamber of Commerce. The others withdrew like almost everyone else: the *modérés* no longer existed, above or below ground.[11]

The Communists were in complete disarray. After the Nazi-Soviet pact and the outbreak of war the local party, dissolved and despised, struggled to maintain the morale of its members. During the *drôle de guerre* it illegally disseminated *L'Humanité*, sent down from Paris once a week, and issued clandestine pamphlets:

> Who is responsible for the war? Those in France who, like Laroque [sic], Doriot, Sabiani, learning the Hitler salute, give Hitler the assurance of their support in the event of war.

But members were scared, propaganda volunteers rare, bar-owners skittish about providing premises.[12] In January 1940 Joseph Pastor, a member in Marseille since 1930, tried to put together an underground party; later that year he put out a May Day leaflet and worked on a clandestine regional issue of *L'Humanité*. The police soon put a stop to his activities: they arrested him in September, 63 other Communist suspects in October, and dismantled the organisation, such as it was, in the Bouches-du-Rhône. Pastor escaped, only to be excommunicated from the party for demonstrating too much independence of spirit. During the winter of 1940–1941 another pre-war Marseille member,

Jacques Meker, resumed disseminating *L'Humanité* and occasionally
Rouge-Midi — decidedly more anti-Vichy than anti-German in these
days of the Nazi-Soviet pact — but by his own admission the local
Communists survived on titbits from Paris:

> If, at that time, there was a Marseille region of the party in place, it
> was inactive [ne se manifestait pas], and material sent from Paris
> was received enthusiastically.[13]

Political parties were illegal but the Communist party was more
illegal than most.

Party politics, in short, were dead, along with the *ancien régime* in
which they had flourished.

This delighted Sabiani. He hailed a 'cleansing wind' which would
blow everywhere on the rotting remnants of the old order. In fact he
had been anticipating the demise of the Third Republic even before it
scuttled itself, and his first bitter reaction to the news of the German
breakthrough had been to attack the régime and foresee its overthrow: 'The UNIQUE authority which, following normal probabil-
ities, will not be long in imposing itself in all domains will do well to
watch for profiteers...'[14]

He had been in Marseille at the time, improbably commanding
an anti-aircraft unit. After the outbreak of war he had eventually
succeeded, in spite of his age and infirmity, in enlisting and had even
spent some time on the Italian front. In March he had returned with
his unit to Marseille; in June and early July he had quickly abandoned
whatever thoughts he might have had of carrying on in North Africa
— Pétain, Doriot, and the British attack at Mers-el-Kébir all contri-
buting. In early July, too, he and Carbone had driven frantically to
Port-Vendres on the Spanish border to retrieve his son François, a
volunteer in the *chars d'assaut*, and then about to leave for London.
Sabiani had arrived just in time — a day later he would have had a
son with the Free French for the duration of the war.[15]

And now, a month after the armistice, he was baying for the blood
of the *ancien régime*. *Marseille-Libre*, after appearing as a shortened bi-
weekly during the phoney war and the *débâcle*, now resumed weekly
publication. Then Sabiani had continued to warn of the Communist
menace in articles signed 'Matricule X'; now he dropped the pseu-
donym and along with his friends attacked republican democracy
instead:

> The worst enemy of France was the electoral régime

and

...the mass of the citizenry is scarcely capable, on its own, of discerning its true interests...

and

14 Juillet 1789 — 14 Juillet 1940. One hundred and fifty years of demagogy will have sufficed to annihilate the work of ten centuries of continuous labour.

They demanded the dissolution of the city council in Marseille and ideological 'detoxification' in France: the defeat had released all their latent hatred of modern republican politics.[16]

With vengeance they attacked the hateful symbols — Jews, foreigners, freemasons, Communists. Especially Jews: protected before the war by tacit taboos and the loi Marchandeau, they now became fair game. Anti-semitic items began to appear regularly in Marseille-Libre, some of them borrowed from L'Emancipation Nationale which had set up shop in Marseille: cartoons, innuendoes, references to hoarders and smugglers, attacks on Jewish deputies now abroad. For the first time Sabiani joined in, denouncing 'the Jews...responsible for our misfortunes', echoing Doriot — 'it will have to come to a stop [il faut en finir] with the Jews', Doriot had said, and called for the creation of a Jewish state somewhere beyond Europe, finally running up against even Vichy's censors.[17] As before the Jew was also the faceless foreigner, who now wore an English as well as a Russian mask. England was Mers-el-Kébir, Dunkirk, Dakar, Libreville; its victory would be the victory of capitalism, its supporters in France, who somehow included the PSF, were threats to the new order. It was, in Sabiani's conspiracy-fantasy, 'Anglo-Saxon capitalism, underpinned by the dark power of freemasonry and of international Jewry of finance and business'. The Communists, arch-villains before the war, were still the Russian party and yesterday's warmongers, but censors and circumstances — the Nazi-Soviet pact — discouraged too concentrated an attack and they made way in the rogues' gallery for the Jews, their functional equivalent in the demonology of the PPF.[18]

In fact, like the other parties, the PPF officially no longer existed. But like the PSF it had resurrected itself with a name change — it became the 'Mouvement Populaire Français' — and it now kept itself alive in the unoccupied zone with publications, ceremonies honouring its dead, youth activities, and thinly disguised references to its prewar identity: 'Notre combat pour le Pays, la Patrie, la France'. Subsidiary organisations, like the Amis de l'Emancipation Nationale, could still recruit members: in December the 'Mouvement' could assemble 344 delegates from North Africa and the unoccupied zone at a national meeting. It was better preserved than any of the other prewar parties, and it intended to play its role.[19]

For the PPF still proposed to save the country, to transform 'the resolutions of Vichy into living reality', to keep the Révolution Nationale on course, safe from unrepentant democrats, Action Française reactionaries and PSF *conservateurs*. It issued reminders to Vichy that the decrees of the autumn were only a beginning, that 'the entire superstructure of our new State remains to be built', and to galvanise popular sentiment it set about creating revolutionary committees in offices and workplaces — by December, it claimed, there were 27 of them. Sabiani had revolutionary words for the revolutionary cause: 'Give me five or six hundred heads and I promise you that afterwards the country will be happy and tranquil': the early months of Vichy were to be the dawn of the new state, and the PPF would marshal its 'best soldiers'.[20]

It did not work out that way: Vichy quickly disappointed Sabiani and the ultras of the PPF. From the outset Doriot and his lieutenants had had their doubts about Vichy's 'revolution'. 'We don't believe in it', Barthélémy had said, and Doriot had gone further:

> The revolution of Vichy might have impressed the Peruvians or the Brazilians. The Germans and the Italians know what a real national and popular revolution is.[21]

But they had suppressed their scepticism while their own role at Vichy hung in the balance, while the protracted intrigues of the late summer and autumn of 1940 pitted them against rivals like Déat. Then, in the winter, the rift opened again. Sabiani kept silent about the men around the *Maréchal* but in December he began to attack 'those who only conserve' and 'those who want to downplay the importance of the ideas of Jacques Doriot'; in February Géraud declared that the *Révolution Nationale* was in trouble. Vichy reciprocated their suspicion. Sabiani later accused its civil servants of systematic obstruction during the autumn and winter of 1940–1941, and the editor of *L'Emancipation Nationale* claimed that censors then had suppressed 203 articles in the paper and edited over 400.[22] When the prefect named Sabiani to the Commission administrative of the Bouches-du-Rhône Vichy's inspectorate was aghast:

> ...It was he who was the first to unfurl the red flag in Marseille... Was supported by men who are outcasts of society...It is a provocation to the motto of the Maréchal to put him forth today.

And in June Sabiani enraged the local director of the Centre de Propagande de la Révolution Nationale when he tried to have their rally cancelled so that Doriot could speak instead. He eventually had his way, but Vichy forbade an open air meeting. The pattern had set in: Sabiani did not like Vichy, and Vichy did not like him.[23]

'Collaboration', as a theme in the minds of the ultras, was initially an ideological by-product of such tension. For the ultras of the PPF it was an index of earnestness, a promotional slogan proclaiming their superior sincerity, and they only adopted it in the winter of 1940–1941, when their rift with Vichy hardened. Even after the armistice, in late June and early July, *Marseille-Libre* had declared that the war would go on. It quickly dropped the theme, taking shelter behind Pétain, but in September Sabiani still tempered his attacks on the Jewish bankers of the City of London with a now pathetic jingoism: 'I could not kneel without shame before our present victors'. There were signs of a forward flight into collaborationism that autumn when Sabiani voiced his dread at the prospect of an English victory over Germany, seeing a struggle between capitalism and 'the real socialism', and again after Pétain's encounter with Hitler at Montoire, when spectral visions suffused Géraud's gibberish:

> The Pétain-Hitler meeting. . . is the evident meeting of subjective elements, of cosmic perspectives fixed on the unchanging face of eternity. . . [it is] the expression of a will which surpasses our intelligence.[24]

But it was still a matter of following Pétain. Not until that winter did collaborationism become a matter of outdoing the faint-hearts in the Hôtel du Parc — the more so as Doriot himself now adopted an ultra-collaborationist line once and for all.

Doriot's early pronouncements on collaboration were like a weather-vane, changing according to his hopes for Vichy. In August, sceptical of Vichy, he was enthusiastically for it, seeing Germany as the architect of the new European order and France as one of its builders. Then he equivocated, while manoeuvering to assert himself at Vichy. He called vaguely for 'collaboration' between France, Italy, Germany and Spain, but in December, in an oblique reference to Déat, he declared that he was 'one of the most prudent men in Paris in relations with them [the Germans]'. Finally, from February on, he called collaboration a historical necessity, claimed that he had always been for it and demanded that obstacles in its path be swept away. Just as there would be revolution instead of reform, there would be collaboration instead of *attentisme*; the creation of 'a modern and strong state, of a sort close to that of other European states' required it.[25]

Sabiani followed. For him as for Doriot collaboration became the emblem of the social vision which Vichy was betraying. They, the revolutionary collaborators, were pitted against the 'sad little men' of the old order angling for an English victory. He demanded vengeance on them, expecting none himself should Germany lose. He did not go as far as either Doriot or his colleague Géraud — both were in Paris and prone to eulogising the *occupants* — but in the spring of

1941 he attributed to Hitler the 'formal intention of bringing about peace in Europe by an understanding among all peoples': he had finally crossed the frontier from *Pétainisme* into ultra-collaboration-ism.[26]

Collaboration became the issue in itself, rather than the reflection of frustration, after the German attack on the Soviet Union and the creation of the Légion des Volontaires Français contre le Bolchévisme — the most extreme form of collaboration possible. The ultras in Paris were soon falling over one another in the rush to monopolise the French volunteer unit,[27] and Doriot finally stole the show and broke out of his political impasse by leaving with the first LVF contingent in September.

But in Marseille there was no competition — the PPF ran the LVF from the start. The PPF transformed its offices into recruiting stations and orchestrated an intensive propaganda campaign, spending whole weeks doing nothing else; articles in *Marseille-Libre* and *L'Emancipation Nationale* reassured potential légionnaires — misleadingly — that they would wear French uniforms, posters glorified Doriot outside Moscow, parties for the children of volunteers honoured the absent fathers.[28] Much of this was Sabiani's doing. Like Doriot he had greeted the German invasion of the Soviet Union as a deliverance, and he now threw himself heart and soul into the cause of military collaboration. He signed on recruits himself in the first floor offices of *Marseille-Libre* on the rue Pavillon, he wrote articles, organised a promotional committee, raised funds; he presided at departures of the *légionnaires*, seeing them off at the Gare St Charles. He even put in an appearance at the LVF barracks in Versailles when a contingent left for the East in December 1941, for amongst its ranks was his son François, and this time he let him go.[29]

Military collaborationism intensified the domestic discourse of the PPF in Marseille as in Paris. The choice was between 'the new European order and the Soviets everywhere', and the LVF was the measure of the PPF's commitment to the new order. It was at grips at home and abroad with the same old villainous duo: the *conservateurs*, now identified as the Gaullists, the PSF, and the Anglo-American plutocracy — 'La Rocque + Les Juifs + Les FrancsMaçons [sic] + Les Anglais = Mers el Kébir. Vive Pétain et Doriot', read the PPF slogans on the walls — and the communists, whom Sabiani like the others now reinstated as the senior villain: 'Stalin is still enemy number one and Roosevelt and Churchill are his odious associates'.[30]

The PPF leaders needed the LVF more than the Germans did — the *Militärbefehlshaber* deliberately kept the numbers down by rejecting recruits as unfit for service. And they needed it more than Vichy did: Pétain's government were for the most part cool to the LVF. In the southern zone *its* legion, the Légion Française des Combattants, even disseminated leaflets discrediting *their* legion, the *Légion anti-bolchévique*, as it came to be known. Vichy's censors forbade publication of photos of Doriot at the front and would not let Géraud even suggest that Pétain had any interest in the LVF.[1] To Vichy the LVF was the creature of the Paris ultras, out of hand and out of control, and in the summer of 1942 Laval, now back in power, tried to reclaim it and turn it into a Vichy-run Légion Tricolore. He failed. But he did succeed in keeping the *doriotistes* from monopolising it[2] — and so further chilled the already glacial relations between Vichy and the PPF.

In Marseille, the more Sabiani devoted himself to the LVF, the more he scorned Vichy. In March 1941 he had resigned as a commissioner in the Légion Française des Combattants. In September of that year he demanded that it be purged of freemasons and false Communist converts. In April 1942 it was 'We'll have to drop the Légion, we can't count on it any more', as told to a friend over the telephone — and to Vichy's listening agents.[3] Meanwhile Vichy was telling Géraud how little they liked his anti-*bourgeois* diatribes and withholding funds as well as paper supplies from PPF publications. For in spite of the presence of the PPF sympathiser Paul Marion at the Secrétariat à l'Information, subsidies were hopelessly inadequate and Lebrun at L'Emancipation Nationale lost no time in telephoning the Secrétariat to say so: 'If, in spite of your kind financial help, I do not find the modest million I need, we've had it...as far as the printing press goes, they're telling me to go take a walk'. Laval's return raised but then quickly shattered their hopes for new influence at Vichy — in the summer of 1942 his government even forbade the wearing of the PPF blue shirts.[34] Even though Vichy was a political hodgepodge Sabiani's attitude to it, after the false start in 1940, came to resemble his attitude before the war toward the traditional right, now so visible in Vichy during these first two years: they were people with whom he had to deal but with whom he had nothing in common. He disliked and distrusted them.

The violent incidents of 14 July 1942 only heightened animosity. That day members of the PPF fired from the windows of the *siège* in the rue Pavillon onto a crowd of hostile demonstrators. They were shouting 'Sabiani the assassin!' and 'death to Doriot!', and earlier the Canebière had resounded with their discordant cries, the confused sounds of protest and resistance: 'Down with Laval!' 'Long live Pétain!' 'Long live de Gaulle!' 'Long live Laval!' 'Down with de Gaulle!' 'Bread without ration tickets!'. Two women were killed; Vichy arrested and interned five members of the party, including Sabiani's old friend Mangiavacca, and Sabiani was beside himself. He flaunted his disgust with Vichy over the telephone in September:

This very moment a record in the surveillance room must be turning and recording everything we say . . . That poor Maréchal is surrounded by ignoble and cowardly people . . . His only real friends are us . . . Meanwhile poor Mangiavacca is interned. . . .

And that month, after the English attack on Madagascar, Sabiani's colleague Peter, at *L'Emancipation Nationale*, thought the government's passivity a 'scandal'. They had given up on Vichy.[35]

But they were more isolated than ever before. Sabiani's PPF had failed once again. In the spring of 1942 Sabiani could still pin his hopes on the LVF as a way out of the impasse and could even plan to replace Doriot on the Russian front — 'at bottom the life one leads here,' he told a friend over the phone, 'is not interesting and when we return we'll at least be able to impose our will'.[36] But nothing came of it. And by then it was already obvious that the LVF was not living up to the expectations of its founders. The authorities noted the low level of recruitment: the propaganda had fallen on deaf ears. It was the same for every other cause the PPF promoted. The prefects' reports on public opinion in Marseille are a window onto the party's desolation: it preached collaboration, the *marseillais* were sceptical or hostile from the Montoire handshake on; it reviled the English and the Americans, they were anglophilic; it recruited for the Russian front, they cheered the news of Russian successes; it had hopes for Laval, they never liked him; it promoted his *relève*, calling for volunteers for work in Germany, they scorned it.[37] Rarely can the hagiography of the missionaries have corresponded so neatly to the demonology of the natives. Few listened; few joined.

But some did — about 1500 or so, to judge from police estimates in 1940, 1941 and again in 1942.[38] The party had shrunk, but it still had its followers. After the Liberation the *Cour de Justice* of Marseille tried or investigated 167 of them:[39] who were they this time?

They appeared to be the same as before: their occupations and birthplaces suggest that the social and ethnic composition of the party had hardly changed. There was still a lower class element, again weak in industrial workers, stronger in sailors and dockers, of about twenty per cent; there was still an upper middle class, strong in businessmen, also of about 20 per cent; there was still a predominant middle class of about 50 per cent in between, half of it *fonctionnaires*, the perennial *Sabianiste* core. Corsicans still accounted for about twenty per cent, more among the *fonctionnaires*.[40] The PPF still made its home in the fourth and fifth cantons — almost forty per cent of its members lived there. Another fifteen per cent came from the more *bourgeois* second and sixth cantons.[41] Statistically speaking it was the same party.

This is not surprising: two thirds of its members had joined before the war and never resigned. They probably stayed in for the same reasons they had signed on.[42] They still hoped for favours, like the fireman who had entered the brigade in 1929 through Sabiani's good offices and who stayed in after the armistice in gratitude for other favours, or the vegetable wholesaler, *Sabianiste* since 1930, who asked Sabiani in 1942 to intervene at his forthcoming trial for illegal price increases — and who incidentally contributed 20,000 francs to the PPF. Or they needed work, like the fireman who found himself on the streets after the dissolution of the fire brigade in 1941, or the unemployed security guard: 'As a PPF[member] I asked my leader Sabiani to find me a job'. Or they stayed on out of life-long habit, like the municipal employee who had known Sabiani as a schoolboy at the *lycée de Bastia* and who had followed him in and out of bar-rooms and political parties ever since — these were the clients with constancy, *Sabianistes* through thick and thin.[43]

The newcomers, the remaining third who joined after 1940, reveal a similar medley of motives, if they reveal motives at all.[44] A bar owner wanted a license to reopen, a sailor wanted a flat in the Groupe Clovis Hugues, a taxi driver took the gangster Carbone to Peron's restaurant on the Corniche five or six times and when his raffish passenger handed him a membership card in December 1940 — 'I'm giving you a nice Christmas gift' — he wisely accepted it. Some needed to find a job, like the employee at the electrical works to whom Sabiani promised a job in the police if he would join the PPF, or the secretary who left 800 francs a month in an insurance company for 1,600 at *L'Emancipation Nationale*. Some were trying to keep one, like the municipal driver who signed up for protection, fearing that as the son of an Italian immigrant he would soon be unemployed. Others, especially if they were young, joined under pressure from family or friends, like the eighteen-year-old electrician, son of a fervent member, or the seventeen-year-old baker, unschooled and illiterate, who joined at his father's urging.[45] Others, better off, knew that an invitation to a PPF congress in Paris would get them across the normally impassable demarcation line — knew that they could sign in at the rue Pavillon just before a congress, hand over two photos and some money, sometimes 1,200, sometimes 2,000 francs, and walk away with the prospect of seeing friends, relatives or colleagues in Paris. It worked for all sorts: during the third party congress in May 1941 for an electrician, a salesman and a vegetable merchant, during the fourth in November 1942 for an office worker, a cashier, a cosmetics dealer, a medical student, a businessman, and a grocer enjoying his first visit to the capital. Some of them never attended the congress at all, even though they needed their cards stamped to avoid embarrassing questions at the demarcation line on the way back: they were the most casual of members.[46]

Newcomers and veterans alike must have heard Sabiani call for a German victory over the Soviet Union, heard him praise 'the delicate sentiments which...Chancellor Hitler and the German high Command have demonstrated'.[47] Some at least must have liked what they heard, must have believed in Franco-German collaboration. But they were hardly likely to broadcast such views at the Liberation, and there is predictably little talk of conviction from the wartime members investigated by the courts. A retired dockworker claimed only to affect conviction when he asked Sabiani to prevail on the Compagnie Générale Transatlantique to increase his pension:

> If in some of these letters I express ideas which conform to the ideas and directives of the PPF it was only to interest Sabiani in my lot...

And a barrister came close to a confession:

> [I joined] in part because quite a few of my friends, Corsicans like myself, were in the party and in part because this party invoked the political ideas of the Maréchal [and had] a vigorous social policy.[48]

This is not much to go by, and even avowals as rapid as his are rare.

But low levels of activity suggest low levels of enthusiasm, and the PPF, in these early years of the war, was a party of laggards. Some — about ten per cent — cared enough to sell the party's papers and distribute its leaflets. But forty per cent of the members of pre-war vintage were so lethargic that post-Liberation investigators could find no trace of their activity, and another thirty per cent only attended a few meetings or paid one or two visits to the rue Pavillon.[49] By October 1942, a month before the Germans rolled in, a pre-war member from the fifth canton had all but given up, as he wrote to Sabiani:

> [I know that] you are not at all satisfied with the running of the organisation...I am not in the least surprised...among the *cama-rades*, covered with various more or less justified excuses, prevails a state of mind devoid of enthusiasm, dominated by indifference, indolence and [by] a negligence to which we are alas accustomed.

And when at most 1,000 turned out to hear Doriot in June 1941 Sabiani and the other PPF leaders were in despair. Even these probably included stage extras, for the day before someone had called

Sabiani's flat: '[do we need] to send people tomorrow?' 'Yes,' Dora Sabiani had answered in her father's absence, 'a lot, even'.[50]

More distressing than indifference was desertion. The veterans were leaving. A *Sabianiste* loyalist, around at least since the days of the Parti Socialiste-Communiste, finally left after hearing Doriot at the fourth party congress early in November 1942; Doriot, he declared in his letter of resignation, was no longer a servant of France. Even Géraud resigned in July 1941. And the converts of the heady days of 1936 and 1937 were probably dropping out — of the 22 who joined out of conviction in the pre-war sample, 13 had left by the end of the war.[51] As early as July 1941, with Germany seemingly invincible, the police were intercepting letters from doubting Thomases among the party's rank-and-file, and in October that year, with the news of the first German reverses, one of them spelled out the fears:

> Quite a few of the boys are beginning to get discouraged and fear what will happen to us after the war...The outcome of the war is certain...[Instead of] articles constantly talking of victories and the new order [we need articles] showing that we will have nothing to fear later on...We have already been noted...We thought we could take shelter behind the Maréchal, but he seems to be pretty compromised himself.[52]

Of the 167 members in the sample, 42 had left by November 1942, and 24 of these had joined before 1940; eight of them left that month, after the Germans occupied the city.

Conviction could not hold them, but Sabiani still could. He had seen better days; he was stripped of much of the patronage he had commanded ten years earlier; the vegetable wholesaler was condemned for his illegal prices, the security guard found work on his own, the bar-owner never did get his licence. Sabiani's promises were often empty: 'he bluffed a lot', his chauffeur recalled.[53] But he still had some influence in the Préfecture, still had friends in the private sector, still rendered services when he could. He was a generous man. When his dentist wanted to visit Paris Sabiani handed him and his wife an invitation to the fourth party congress — 'M. Sabiani knew very well that I wasn't going to attend the congress'; he and M. Sabiani even threw in an invitation for another of the dentist's patients. He still had his followers, whatever their political persuasions — a Corsican sailor, a follower at least since 1936, proclaimed Gaullist views but *Sabianiste* affections, an apolitical attachment reflected again in the post-Liberation comment from a witness about a neighbour under investigation: 'I knew that he was Sabianniste [sic] but I don't know if he belonged to the PPF'.[54] When word got around that Sabiani and Doriot had quarrelled at the fourth party congress — though it was shortlived — the entire *marseillais* delegation marched out singing *l'Ajaccienne: Sabianistes* one and all.[55]

But it was slowly rotting away. 'I had noticed great confusion within the party,' recalled a member who left in October 1942. 'Many members no longer showed themselves while new ones came in to join'.[56] With many of its old members gone and its leader running out of trump cards, his movement isolated and his rhetoric ignored, *Sabianisme* began to attract the opportunists of the occupation, some of them criminal — it began to show the first signs of its ultimate degeneration.

The first indication is statistical. The PPF during the first two years of the war broadly resembles the PPF before the war, but the surface similarities obscure a contrast within the wartime party: there are more unemployed among the newcomers than among the old members — twenty per cent compared to three per cent.[57] There are too few to allow any conclusions, and those that there are show no particular penchant for criminal activity, but they mark the beginning of a descent into marginality soon to go out of control.

Random criminal elements, present in the murky depths, began freely floating to the surface. PPF rowdies, defended by Sabiani as crusaders against the black market, smashed Jewish shop windows on the Canebière in August 1940 and again in March 1941.[58] Most were mere vandals. But some were murderers as well. In April 1941 four of them, arrested after daubing anti-semitic slogans on the pavement, resolved in their resentment first to blow up a synagogue and later to assassinate Marx Dormoy, the Jewish minister of the interior who had tried unsuccessfully to suspend Doriot before the war. They quickly carried out their first project and waited until May for the second: a time bomb killed Dormoy in his hotel room in Montélimar while the original conspirators attended the PPF congress in Lyon. One of them later boasted of the crime:

> I was in favour of swift punishment of the men responsible for the defeat. . .I thought that to create a truly revolutionary spirit, it was necessary to strike and supplement Justice. . .I cannot remember which one of us had the idea first to do away with the former minister. . .

They had tried out Action Française before the war, Vichy's paramilitary *groupes de protection* after the armistice, the PPF after that. Their ringleader had probably been a Franquist agent in Spain during the civil war. They were miscreants at large, 'eternal malcontents', the Vichy police called them,

eternally impatient, they do not appear to have followed the discipline of parties and, after joining for a few months, they always assumed the role of dissidents. . .

Vichy imprisoned them in 1941, the Germans released them in 1943 and employed them as agents and informers: treason to cap vandalism and assassination. Three were later mysteriously murdered in Nice.[59] But by then the PPF had others like them.

These were the hard elements. Meanwhile the members of the soft majority, most of them holdovers from the thirties, idled or shirked or left. The party was drifting towards a new identity.

Other collaborationist organisations were already finding their identities.

In Marseille, unlike Paris, the PPF was the only ultra party — the only party preaching fascist revolution — of any consequence. Marcel Déat's Rassemblement National Populaire did not open a branch in Marseille until 1943, and then never exceeded 60 members; Eugène Deloncle's Mouvement Social Révolutionnaire never opened a branch at all. Marcel Bucard's avowedly fascist Francistes had existed in Marseille since 1936, when an unemployed and thrice-convicted criminal opened a one-room branch, but they had never exceeded a few hundred and were now insignificant: in November 1942 only twenty members attended a meeting.[60] But collaborationism, in its protean diversity, was developing other varieties, and in one of them the PPF finally found its calling.

There was a Pétainist variety, that of the officials and administrators carrying out Vichy's collaborationist initiatives, notably its antisemitic measures. It was the greyest and most ambiguous of all varieties, for it included an essential Vichy paradox: the anti-German collaborationist.

It was epitomised in Marseille by Rodellec du Porzic, the naval officier and police chief. He was an ardent Pétainist — an Action Française supporter and an old fashioned nationalist, a *lieutenant de vaisseau* who had managed to get his ship to Casablanca in June 1940 before Darlan sent him to his unlikey new post in Marseille in the autumn. He despised the Germans. He knew of the secret mobilization system in the Gardes Mobiles Républicaines, of arms *caches*, of escape routes and forged documents used by the early naval *résistants*, and he turned a blind eye. He had no time for the ultras and he tried to have Sabiani interned after the Bastille day *fusillade* of 1942. But when Vichy began using foreign Jews as bargaining chips in its negotiations with the Germans and the internments and the deportations began, he carried out his orders efficiently and, according to some, zealously. Between August and September four convoys carrying

1,600 foreign Jews left Marseille for the camp des Milles, near Aix. Du Porzic remarked darkly to a colleague:

> I know well that the measures we are taking are very painful, but if you knew what I know you would think that it might perhaps be better to let these foreigners leave rather than soon see French people leave.

Later he resigned, and at the Liberation charges against him were dropped — as they were for eleven of seventeen other Vichy officials, burdened like him with unenviable responsibilities.[61]

But some other Vichy officials did worse and fared worse. The one-time police inspector at the camp des Milles later blackmailed Jews while in du Porzic's service, and a few — not all — of the *administrateurs provisoires de biens juifs* enriched themselves even while reviling their despoiled Jews: a retired colonial *fonctionnaire* previously living on 1,000 francs a month inflated his income as well as his rhetoric when he took over a Jewish hatter's shop.[62] These were the first predatory beneficiaries of any kind of collaboration, in this case *collaboration d'état*.

Collaboration of the Pétainist variety in official grass roots organisations was largely lip service to Vichy. The Légion Française des Combattants was hardly collaborationist at all, and its members, unless they had belonged to proscribed wartime groups as well, were left alone at the Liberation. Its local leader supported collaboration only 'in the economic sense' and his colleagues saw the Paris ultras — the PPF in Marseille — as 'in foreign pay'. Its members, all veterans, joined, they said, 'to do as everyone else did', 'to show trust in the Maréchal', 'because it took care of the prisoners' — the Légion, at the time, was the only relief organisation for the prisoners in the stalags.[63] But it had its hotheads and extremists too, pulling down Marianne in official buildings, expressing dissatisfaction with the pace of Vichy's reforms, exasperating the Prefects. There was nothing intrinsically collaborationist about such excesses. But when a *légionnaire*, an archivist for the railways, denounced colleagues for Gaullist sympathies and boasted of doing so he came close to the limit. And when a retired colonial official — 'a drunkard, more stupid than nasty' — complained of Communists in the sports club and held his fist on his head with his thumb in the air in imitation of the German helmets of the First World War (that was what the French needed, he said) he exceeded the limit. These were the first runaway Pétainists.

They were marginal — the Légion was vast, amorphous and inhospitable to free-wheeling zealots. There were more of them in the Légion's shock troops, the *service d'ordre* launched in January 1942 with the former *cagoulard* Joseph Darnand at its head.

The Service d'Ordre Légionnaire was more than its name implied.

In Marseille its members put on social and charitable functions, including parties for the children of prisoners, but they also swore an oath of allegiance, attended monthly meetings, distributed propaganda, and paraded in uniform — khaki shirt, dark trousers, *beret basque* and triangular emblem. Some of them began gratuitously policing the city, reprimanding bar-owners for staying open late, and a few took on more sinister political roles by breaking up illicit meetings: in August 1942 they smashed the bottles and threatened the owner of a bar on the Boulevard Banon where carousers had sung parodies of the Petainist anthem, *Maréchal nous violà*. A few attended special courses in street fighting, supposedly in preparation for a Communist insurrection. Their officers were armed. And unlike the members of the Légion they fell foul of the courts at the Liberation, for in February 1942 Darnand swore them to an anti-Gaullist, anti-communist, anti-masonic and anti-semitic crusade and in July he urged them to volunteer for the Russian front.[65]

Many of them, like so many in the PPF at the time, found themselves members of an organisation which later adopted collaborationist rhetoric. Almost half of the members before the German occupation in November were transplants, sometimes forced, from the Légion.[66] *Commissaires* in the Légion found themselves members whether they liked it for not — one of them was told that it was merely a change of title. Rank-and-file members were not always given the chance to refuse: 'one day, we were called together to fill out the entry forms for the SOL'; 'I was enrolled in the SOL without being asked for much of an opinion'. But there was a larger contingent of enthusiasts than in the PPF. One-fifth joined out of conviction of one kind or another — because they were ardent Pétainists or because they thought it was their duty. Among them were the lingering optimists who later left the SOL or helped the resistance and who could still believe, before November 1942, that 'le Maréchal was playing a double game', that they were joining a 'camouflaged army', a 'disguised army' and that collaboration was 'temporary and designed to attenuate for the moment France's misfortunes'.[67] There were not many like them in the PPF.

And unlike the PPF the SOL had few unemployed — only about five per cent.[68] Few joined it in the hope of finding work, although some bowed to professional pressures, like the gardener in the semi-rural tenth canton who obediently gave his employer two photos and let him take care of the rest.[69] Conversely it had a stronger upper middle class component — twenty-five per cent to the PPF's sixteen. They filled no special role — the SOL officialdom was roughly evenly divided between *fonctionnaires*, lower middle class members and upper middle class members — but they formed its distinctive element from the start.[70] The SOL did not have a strong popular base.

The sorting out began in the summer of 1942, with Darnand's radicalisation of the SOL. Sixteen of those known to have resigned did so in the late summer and early autumn, apprehensive or disillusioned or even disgusted. Some wrote letters of resignation, others used excuses — a factory director and *chef de trentaine* left in feigned protest over a ban on beards. There would be more sorting out in November and December, when the Germans arrived and at least another 14 left, and more in the next two months, when at least 34 left as the inexorable process culminated in Petainist paramilitary collaboration — when the SOL became the *Milice*, the PPF's chief rival.[71]

The PPF was already threatened by the SOL and made a few attempts to seduce its members, chiefly with propaganda.[72] In November 1941 it gained another rival when another variety of collaborationism, the *salon* variety, appeared in the shape of the Groupe Collaboration.

That month the extended social and cultural club of Alphonse de Chauteaubriant, Georges Claude and Professor Grimm opened its offices on the Rue St. Ferreol in the heart of the commercial district. It began filling its shop front with various anti-masonic and collaborationist pamphlets and organising lectures on the new order in Europe — in 1942 Grimm gave three and Georges Claude one: flanked by the German, Japanese, Spanish and Finnish consuls he asked his listeners whether they wished to be proud members of the new Europe or not. But it was discussion group collaborationism, mere words: it promoted the LVF without signing in recruits and spread the word without taking any action. It was, as the Foreign Office in London noted, a soft-sounding PPF: 'The group derives its appeal from the fact that it says the same things as the PPF but that it says them far more politely'.[73]

Its members, who numbered at most 1000 in the Bouches-du-Rhône,[74] were probably more polite as well. Almost forty per cent of those investigated at the Liberation were from the upper middle class — mostly lawyers and teachers.[75] Many joined out of cultural curiosity, intrigued by the pamphlets at 25 or 50 francs in the rue St Ferréol window — an English teacher by those on German life, a banker and a shopkeeper by those on Franco-German trade, a history teacher, who soon began giving talks on Goethe and Schiller, by those on German architecture. For them and for others the activities of the *groupe* probably provided a welcome escape from the humdrum life of 1942. A postman, 'a tinkerer in his spare time', thought it might subsidise his tinkering and his inventions — he had always wanted a laboratory of his own. And the *groupe* began offering German lessons at 50 francs a month, a bargain that a translator at the post office could not pass up. Possibly they thought Franco-German collaboration a good thing; one or two even said so later: 'I was in favour of collaboration'.[76] But next to the PPF the Groupe Collaboration was almost frivolous, and it inspired deep mistrust among the more plebeian *doriotistes*, including Lebrun at *L'Emancipation Nationale*:

> [They're with us] as long as we're serving them but the day they no longer need us they'll drop us.[77]

It was the party of the *salon*, the PPF the party of the street.

Decorous as it was it harboured some hard or zealous members. In Sénas, just outside Marseille, an active member organised 'groupes de protection' and began denouncing 'gaullo-communistes' in the community. Some members in the *groupe*'s youth organisation, the Jeunesses de l'Europe Nouvelle, began practising the Nazi salute[78] — later the *Groupe* disowned its youth, destined to a noisy role when the Germans arrived, too noisy for the sedate parental organisation.

Even before they arrived active collaboration was possible. If the Germans would not come to the *marseillais*, the *marseillais* could go to the Germans — and some did.

Some went to work for them. Between May 1942, when a *bureau de la main d'oeuvre pour l'Allemagne* opened in the rue Beauvau, and early July 1531 volunteers from the Marseille region signed up for work in the Reich. At the end of the summer Laval's *relève* briefly revived the flagging volunteers: the first to leave was a 26-year-old Italian woman, unemployed and illegally resident in France since before the war: she was given a heroine's send-off, with flowers and good wishes and officials on the *quai* at the Gare St Charles.[79]

She was typical. A third of all who signed up before November were looking for work.[80] They were unemployed or, like a young circus trapeze artist stuck in Vichy's dreary *chantiers de la jeunesse*, unemployable. Or they had jobs but could not resist the prospect of higher salaries: a furnace-maker with five children left his hourly ten-franc pittance for 6,000 francs a month; a baker volunteered after a row with his employer over his wages. Simple escape — typified again by the outward-bound Italian — was also a powerful motive: 'I left on a sudden impulse [coup de tête], because I was living on bad terms with my wife, from whom I'm now separated'. A young prostitute left for Germany in September after quarrelling with her parents, she was imprisoned there after being found with a French prisoner of war, and returned pregnant to Marseille — where her quarrels with her parents probably resumed.[81] Like the rarely fulfilled hope of releasing a relative in a stalag, escape was a classless motive. But work and wages were not: three-quarters of Marseille's volunteers before November 1942 were either unemployed or from the working class.[82]

Mixed in were some doubtful elements, petty criminals at loose ends — an unemployed sailor and known black marketeer, an ex-salt miner convicted five times, a sometime white slaver convicted six times, a gunsmith and police informer fearing his victims' vengeance. Also mixed in were the ubiquitous hard collaborators, those who turned on their compatriots. An industrial designer denounced his co-workers for anti-German sentiments, an engineer escaped from his lowly German factory assignment by taking radio and espionage training in Wiesbaden — he later went to work as a German agent in Perpignan.[83] He was the ultimate in opportunism, unbridled and uninhibited.

But, apart from such exceptional cases, voluntary work in Germany was a harmless form of collaboration, looked on lightly by the courts at the Liberation.[84] They took quite a different view of the most extreme form possible, military collaboration — the LVF. Yet many of the LVF volunteers were similar men with similar motives.

Almost half the LVF recruits from Marseille before November 1942 were unemployed — a ship's cook without a ship, a soldier without an army, a photographer without any film — and a further fifth were employed in working class professions.[85] Unlike their civilian counterparts in the *relève* they were all men of military age, but like them they wanted escape, most often from oppressive or hostile relatives, or work, or money, as Lebrun at *L'Emancipation Nationale* told Sabiani over the phone:

> **Lebrun**: In this Légion, there are people who are sincerely taking part in the anti-Bolshevik struggle, like us, and there are crooks [margoulins] who are after money.
> **Sabiani**: Who are only after that [money]![86]

Some of the *marseillais* in the LVF, like some of those in the *relève*, were retarded or mentally ill, like the paranoid schizophrenic, probably delirious and hallucinating, who somehow joined the LVF after a dispute with his father in August 1941. A few — like Sabiani's son — joined the LVF believing in the anti-communist crusade, just as a few had signed up for the *relève* believing in Franco-German co-operation.[87] The LVF had more unemployed.[88] It probably had more criminals and more derelicts — 'quite a few fruitcakes [pas mal de gens un peu à la cloche]' had initially signed up, as a PPF organiser recognised over the phone two months after recruitment had begun; some of them disappeared before they ever reached the LVF barracks at Versailles and some of them were refused once they got there, as Roger at *L'Emancipation Nationale* shouted over the phone:

> . . .I don't want any more of this comedy of giving 800 francs for a return trip to jolly little men [bonhommes] who are refused. . .and I can tell you there are a lot of them![89]

At least forty per cent had criminal records when they signed up.[90] But collectively the men of the LVF and the men of the *relève*, in the early days, broadly resembled one another.

They fared completely differently. The *relève* volunteers worked as stonemasons in Saxony or sawmill employees in Vienna or bakers in Mehringen.[91] The LVF recruits travelled from Versailles to a camp near Deba in occupied Poland and thence, many of them, to Kruzhina and the front. Around Smolensk and Moscow, in the winter of 1941 to 1942, the adventure turned into a nightmare: combat units sustained casualties; returning recruits spoke of a forced march between Smolensk and Viazmak in which stragglers and invalids were shot. In Smolensk, one of them claimed, 'human meat is hung in butcher shop windows'. Some were killed, some deserted. Some returned frozen to the bone: an accountant from the Belle-de-Mai, a barber from the *vieux quartiers* and a sailor from the tenth canton were all evacuated from the front early in 1942 with frozen hands or feet, never to return — the barber returned to collaboration but not to combat, more prudently signing up for the *relève* at the end of the summer.[92] After 1942 the men of the LVF — those in the field did not exceed 2,500 or so at any one time from all over France — were assigned to anti-partisan action, if they saw action at all.[93] Of the *marseillais* some, like the barber, found their way back and some stayed on until the very end.

The volunteers for the *relève* and the LVF were the first active collaborators in the southern zone and in Marseille. They were not the Pétainists of the Service d'Ordre Légionnaire or the *bourgeois* of the Groupe Collaboration. They were unhappy or unemployed or at loose ends, people to whom collaboration offered tempting opportunities and even the chance to change their lives. They naturally had the lion's share of the hard collaborators — the criminals, adventurers and profiteers willing to turn on their compatriots or take up German arms. Until November 1942 they had to travel to make good, but that month the *occupant* came to them, and in Marseille a broker soon emerged to marry the opportunists to the opportunities: the PPF. Sabiani, stalemated, marking time, the frustrated leader of a fading party, now became the patron of the active collaborators and they his last clients.

In June 1942 François Sabiani was killed in action outside Smolensk. He became an instant PPF hero, this time a legitimate hero, for he had died courageously, in battle under fire, carrying a French standard in a German uniform. Doriot exploited his death shamelessly, angering Sabiani and his family, who resented the sale of cards bearing François' photograph and remembered his letters complaining of

Doriot's *fainéantise* at the front. At the flat in the rue Fauchier police noted 'complete collapse', and a neighbour found Madame Sabiani 'very affected...[she] told me that her husband would have done better not to be involved in politics'. But Sabiani was more committed than ever: from now on the war against Russia became a veritable vendetta.[94]

And from now on his only allies were the Germans. The German foreign ministry had already singled out Sabiani as a key man in the southern zone — they even exaggerated his influence, thinking it extended as far as Lyon[95] — and in the summer of 1942 the local PPF, in its isolation, drew closer to the German consulate. 'I have the proof of a close entente locally between the PPF milieux and the German General Consulate', the prefect announced to Vichy, probably referring to the reports of his eavesdroppers. They revealed a personal link between Sabiani and the German consul, Count von Thun, Sabiani thanking the Count for his condolences on François' death, the Count thanking him for sending over a *bouillabaisse*. The Count was troubled by the incidents of 14 July and questioned Sabiani endlessly over the phone — how could the demonstrators have reached the PPF *siège*? How many of them were there? Who fired first? Was Sabiani having troubles with the police? And what about his old friend Chipponi? Possibly he was only gathering information for a routine report to his ministry, but later in the summer he telephoned Sabiani's home to find out where he was, *L'Emancipation Nationale* to set up a meeting 'for a tour d'horizon of your organisation', and the PPF *siège* to protest about the musical chairs in the party — 'why these constant changes?' In August he gave Guillet of *L'Emancipation Nationale* 20,000 francs and promised him more: whatever games their colleagues were playing in Paris, the German diplomats in Marseille were fostering Sabiani and his PPF.[96]

Rejected by the city, abetted by the occupant, waiting for its role, the PPF was ready to practise what it preached when the German troops rolled in: a collaborationist party became the party of the collaborators: and so *Sabianisme* embarked upon its final transformation.

CHAPTER 7

The Dregs of Society,
November 1942 — August 1944

The morning papers on the twelfth carrying the prefect's appeal for calm were barely off the presses when the first German units arrived, like tourists, at the Gare St Charles. Soon mobile kitchens and armoured carriers and camouflaged lorries came clanking and grinding down the Boulevard d'Athènes, turned into the Canebière, spread around the Quai des Belges and the Vieux-Port and the centre of the city. The men moved into the *lycées*, their strange vehicles into the city's squares, and by nightfall Marseille, for the first time since 1815, was an occupied city.[1]

The German commander, General von Fischer, set up staff headquarters — the *Platzkommandantur* — in the Hotel Splendid, across the street from station. Later a *Feldkommandantur* responsible for the Bouches-du-Rhône beyond Marseille set up shop in the Hôtel de Bordeaux down the boulevard and a regional *Oberfeldkommandantur* took over a large villa in the Boulevard Périer, on the other side of the Vieux-Port.[2] Beyond it, at the very end of the rue Paradis — number 425 — another villa, set in a pleasant garden, housed the occupier's police and security services, the *Sicherheitspolizei* and *Sicherheitsdienst*, known technically as the *Reichssicherheitshauptamt* but popularly, if somewhat incorrectly, as 'la gestapo'.[3]

A glimpse of the members of the armistice commission entering or leaving the Hôtel Louvre et Paix, a parade in a newsreel, perhaps a stalag guard — until 12 November 1942 most *marseillais* had never seen a German uniform.[4] That day they watched in consternation if not in panic, like Lucie in André Ducasse's *Quand ma ville ne riait plus*:

In the morning on the 12th, people lined up on the Canebière to watch the tanks which had been all over Europe go by...Lucie... atop the tram...went unendingly past the grey trucks, the machine guns pointed skywards, all those dusty, troubled, brutal men...[5]

That day the prefect imposed an eight pm curfew and a night-time blackout. Von Fischer added a ban on fishing and later on sailing. Food shortages worsened almost at once, as traffic in the port came to a complete halt and three million tons of goods stood useless on the docks. But the population remained calm. Quite a few even went out strolling the following Sunday, 'as in the days', reported the prefect drily, 'when the free zone deserved the adjective without any qualifications'. There were no disturbances. Von Fischer even persuaded the prefect to shorten the curfew on the twenty first, and later he himself lifted the ban on fishing. The Luftwaffe's orchestra began giving public concerts on the quai des Belges, the Wehrmacht's on the Canebière.[6] The Germans settled in.

Gun turrets appeared on the Corniche, the beginnings of submarine base on the Cap Janet, a concrete wall on the high ground between *Bonneveine* and the Roucas-Blanc — incidentally sealing off the popular beach at the Prado. Officers requisitioned villas overlooking the sea. Basso's restaurant on the Vieux-Port became something called a 'Kameradwirtschafthaus', the Brasserie du Chapitre on the Boulevard d'Athènes a 'Soldatenheim' — a 'monkey-house' to the *quartier's* more senior habitués. The cinemas of the Canebière — the Rex, the Majestic, the Trois Salles — were turned into 'Soldatenkinos', their uniformed spectators enjoying the right of way behind cordons and police as their *séances* spilled out onto the crowded street: the most trivial and the most rankling of precedence.[7]

Staggered shocks, punctuating the daily resentment, began shortly after the Germans arrived. First came the fears sparked off by the scuttling of the fleet and by the fatuity of Vichy, which broadcast lively concert music even as Marseille itself resounded with the explosions from Toulon harbour. There was now, reported the prefect, a sense of total defencelessness. Wild rumours began to fly: France was about to enter the war on Germany's side, the crews of the martyred ships were locked up in hotels in Aix-en-Provence, the Germans had seized all of the city's remaining food supplies.[8] Time dissipated the rumours, but in the new year came the evacuation and destruction of the *vieux quartiers*, decided upon by the Germans for obscure reasons but carried out with preliminary help from the *marseillais* police and Service d'Ordre Légionnaire.[9] There was incredulity — the *Marseillais* must be terrifying, people said, if 10,000 troops and police were needed to evacuate 22,000 of them. There was also anger — the evacuees were not compensated, the ruins were not cleared. Above all there was anxiety — what was in store for the city next? A year later, in February 1944, the German evacuation of the Mediterranean coastal zones and consequently of several thousand residents of the city's dockside streets revived apprehensions: it looked like the *vieux quartiers* scenario all over again.[10] Destruction did come, but this time from the air and from the Americans, who bombed the city that May in an apparent — and unsuccessful — attempt to hit the station, killing 2,000 people in ten minutes and demolishing whole neighbourhoods, including parts of the Belle-de-Mai. 'See how the Americans come to liberate us', said a carpenter there at the time; 'what have you, that's war,' said another.[11] The battle at the liberation in August 1944, when Monsabert's troops had to fight their way up to Notre Dame de la Garde and the Germans blew up the famous bridge across the *Vieux Port*, marked the violent finale to an occupation more devastating than it ever was in Paris or Lyon.

Meanwhile deportations of various kinds multiplied.

By the autumn and winter of 1942 the *relève* had fallen so far short of German expectations, in spite of Vichy's promotional efforts and the proliferation of recruitment bureaux between the Opera and the Canebière, that *inspecteurs du travail* had to designate the volunteers, in particular bachelors and childless married men. The introduction of the *Service du Travail Obligatoire* in February 1943 institutionalised forced labour, and as exemptions steadily disappeared departures steadily rose: 2,200 conscripts left from Marseille in July 1943 alone — compared to 597 volunteers in June the previous year — bringing the total for the year to about 12,000.[12] By June 1944, when the Germans suspended the STO, at least 16,000 had left for the Reich from the dreaded building in the rue Honnorat, next to the station and fittingly facing the *Platzkommandantur* in the Hôtel Splendid on the other side. Two thousand of them never returned.[13]

Deportations of foreign Jews had already begun before the Germans arrived. Refugees had transformed the city's essentially *bourgeois* pre-war Jewish population of 25,000 into an inchoate mass of 40,000, many destitute and homeless, and into a human reservoir for Vichy's antisemitic collaborationist initiatives.[14] There was some resistance in the local administration to Vichy's measures, but not enough to prevent the deportations of August 1942, and the following February the Germans deported many of the foreign Jews evacuated from the *vieux quartiers*. At least 4,000 Jews, French and foreign, were deported from Marseille during the war, and probably more, even allowing for voluntary departures, for in 1944 only 15,000 were left.[15]

Fewer *résistants* were deported: there were fewer of them to deport. Within three weeks of the German arrival the inevitable happened and someone took a potshot at the *occupant*. The harmless attack — a few *pétards* set off among some German vehicles on the Boulevard Garibaldi — nettled the *Kommandantur* into demanding a list of Communist leaders to be taken hostage: the prefect, Joseph Rivalland, refused. But in January an attack on the Hôtel Splendid provoked 18 arrests, and so began a familiar monthly spiral of sabotage and retaliation: three more 'terrorist' actions that month, eight in February, 21 in April, 19 in November, nine in June 1944, 21 again in July, alternating with some Geman *coups*, like that of April 1943 in which 75 *résistants* were deported.[16] There were never very many combatants, men prepared to take up arms against the occupant — perhaps 1,000 in Marseille and another 1,000 elsewhere in the Bouches-du-Rhône by the insurrection of August 1944. But numbers like these leave out the non-violent *résistants*, like Rivalland, or one of his successors, Emile Maljean, who exasperated the *Feldkommandantur*, resisting its demands for the arrests of striking workers in the spring of 1944, or the strikers themselves, or the President of the Chamber of Commerce, who met the Germans only to thwart their designs, only to keep a crane in the port or some cable equipment out of their hands — these were *résistants* as well, and their numbers are unknowable.[17] The SD at the end of the rue Paradis may have killed several hundred *résistants* and deported some 2,200 others from Marseille and the surrounding region, of whom half never returned. But some of the deported Jews, *résistants* or not, are included: the numbers are imprecise, but conscripted workers led the deportees, followed by Jews and then by *résistants*, and among them the Jews fared the worst.[18]

The acts of sabotage and assassination alarmed people. The *marseillais* had demonstrated hostility to the Germans as early as March 1941, when they laid flowers at the site of King Alexander's assassination to mark their support for his successor's stand in Yugoslavia, and Bastille Day 1942, when 20,000 demonstrators took to the streets. Now the prefects reported helplessly that they were indifferent to Vichy and its pronouncements, that they preferred the British and American broadcasts and that they continued to demonstrate their views during cinema newsreels with laughter and conspiratorial coughing. They were sympathetic to the young men on the run from the STO — the *réfractaires* — and to the Jews once the deportations had started: 'the most fanciful rumours have spread about the fate of those concerned', the prefect noted after the *rafles* of August 1942, adding elsewhere that the *marseillais* were beginning to see the Jews as martyrs. Hunger concentrated their hatred of *occupants* seen to be intent on starving the *occupés*.[19] Yet they had little enthusiasm for the bomb-throwers. Amidst the deprivations, destruction and deportations they represented yet another threat, first of reprisals and later of civil war:[20] a French threat to add to the German.

But threats to the many were opportunities to the few — to the few active collaborators who came forth daily to profit from the German presence. For the Germans needed workers to build the wall behind the Prado and the emplacements on the Corniche, telephone operators and messengers and porters to run the Hotel Splendid, gardeners to maintain the grounds at the SD villa, cooks and waiters to run the *Kameradwirtschafthausen* and the officers' mess. And they found them. They found the 'soft' collaborators, men and women who voluntarily entered the service of the *occupant* without harming their compatriots. But the Germans also needed agents to root out STO *réfractaires*, bounty-hunters to bring in Jews for deportation, informers to betray *résistants*. They found them too, in much smaller numbers — the 'hard' collaborators, whose service on behalf of the *occupant* always threatened and sometimes doomed their own countrymen, and who eventually gave *Sabianisme* its lasting and ignominious *niche* in local history.

Sabiani, with the Germans in town, suddenly regained his old role, severely tested during the recent barren years, and emerged once again as a broker between private followers and public authorities. He was the most important collaborationist leader in the city, he said all the right things, he was on friendly terms with the Consul, who attended the unveiling of the commemorative plaque for François in July 1943 along with a major representing the *Wehrmacht*; he was a useful man to an occupant not always satisfied with the prefects' cooperation: well worth occasional gratification.[21]

Sometimes Sabiani had only to prevail on some French civil servant to help matters along, to help a mechanic open his shop or a claimant obtain payment from the *sécurité sociale*. But now he could intercede with the Germans as well, a power prized by job-seekers and job-holders alike — by a *lorrain* police employee, desperate for more remunerative work, who asked him to approach to SD, and by an employee in a factory working for the *Kriegsmarine*, whom Sabiani promised security of tenure if he joined the PPF. Old members could always approach him for favours, but newcomers sometimes travelled a winding access road before gaining a hearing: a social worker seeking the release of a friend from German hands asked her PPF hairdresser, who asked a local party official, who asked Sabiani. Sometimes they travelled the road in vain: sometimes Sabiani bluffed. A welder who joined the party on Sabiani's word that he would help revoke a fine for cigarette contraband gave up after fifteen days: 'seeing that Sabiani wasn't doing anything I went home'. But usually Sabiani did his best for old and new members alike. He did not give up when the Germans rejected the *lorrain* police employee, who had only turned up in the rue Fauchier after meeting with intermediaries, including Sabiani's chauffeur Géronimi — he found him a job as a translator in a construction company working for the Germans. For an unemployed accountant whom he had known since the early thirties Sabiani first tried the *assurances sociales*, where the salary was too low, then the *Kriegsmarine*, where the job was too demanding, and finally Vichy's Gardes Mobiles Républicaines, where the protégé settled down as a secretary. Shortly after the Liberation, with his old patron gone, useless, an overnight liability, he prudently joined the Communist party.[22] Sabiani would probably not have been surprised.

If there had been enough jobs and favours to go around this would have been the heyday of *Sabianisme* all over again, with the Liberation a rerun of the mayoral defeat of 1935. Some of the diehards were still in, no more ideological in *Marseille allemande* than in *Marseille-Chicago*. After the Liberation only an allusion datemarked the continuing loyalty of a Corsican municipal employee:

> He spoke of Sabiani a lot [said a witness]. I've the impression that Sabiani had great influence over him and if Sabiani had been Gaullist, G…in my opinion would have been [too].

A hospital worker said much the same: 'If Sabiani became Communist, I would be Communist too'; so did a psychologist about a somewhat slow, probably retarded sailor who had followed Sabiani until the end:

> When pushed, the accused reveals himself to be incapable of developing any kind of political opinion, and he also comes back to his first statement, that he had simply 'followed Sabiani'…Pushed [again], he reveals himself to be incapable of providing accurate information on the European situation and even on the real sense of the various parties.

And so did an examining magistrate to an equally loyal grocer from la Joliette:

> You followed him without demonstrating in this respect the discernment one might have wished for.

Sabiani still had his devotees.[23]

With the *occupant* on his side *le sympathique Simon* could both threaten the free-loaders and reward the faithful: he could threaten to have them sent to Germany. Sabiani, in the second half of the war, was a leader mixing indulgence with asperity as his friendships vied with his convictions. Ever since François' death he had castigated the laggards for profiting from the party while ignoring the cause. By the spring of 1944 he had drawn up a list of 'bad activists', members who did nothing for the PPF and who he thought ought to go and work in Germany. He expelled a young furnace-maker from the party: '. . . Sabiani took my membership card away on the grounds that I didn't attend meetings'; he threatened a young industrial designer who had not attended a single meeting with the STO; he told an ideologically indifferent tram-worker not to expect any help from the party. All three had joined hoping to avoid the STO. He wanted his men to cross the Rubicon and told one of them: 'you'll be involved [mouillé] like the others!'[24] But Sabiani the friend offset Sabiani the enforcer. When the Germans arrested the son of an old friend for resistance activities he immediately intervened to have the boy released. When they arrested his former friend and former foe, the socialist Ferri-Pisani, he did the same, this time with no luck: Ferri-Pisani went to Buchenwald. When Vichy's Commissariat-Général aux Questions Juives began pursuing his young Jewish neighbour he took him under his wing, and later covered his flight from the STO to Toulon: '. . . he never said anything to me about it, he knew me as a child and took care of me'. When another friend, this one an illiterate Corsican sailor whom he had known since childhood, asked him to save his son-in-law from the STO, he obliged. And whenever yet another old friend, a retired civil servant, asked him to intervene on behalf of friends, Sabiani ignored his known hostility to collaboration and collaborators.[25] Sometimes he asked the friends in need to join the PPF or to step up their activity if they were already in. But he knew what sort of members they were: and so the Jekyll and Hyde act went on.

It was the same old clash between ideologue and patron, the pre-war dualism now a wartime paradox. The ideologue, launched on a course from which there was no longer any turning back, travelled to Paris regularly to meet with Doriot and the other PPF leaders and the LVF committee; he gave speeches all over the south exalting the new order in Europe and lamenting the incomprehension of his benighted compatriots. In April 1943 he spoke in Perpignan, later that month in Toulouse, in May back in Marseille at a regional party congress, in June in the Gers, in July in Clermont-Ferrand.[26] In between the patron attended to his clients, whoever they were, redressed their grievances when he could, at least once refunded a membership fee when he could not, mediated disputes and avenged bar-room affronts — 'one of my men has been hurt [touché]', he told the owner of a bar in Le Merlan where a violent argument had broken out over a poker game, 'the guilty must be found and brought here'. The two Sabianis wrestled, the outcome uncertain, however trifling the stakes. When his old friend Lucien Mangiavacca sought his help in exempting his son from the STO he was at first unyielding:

I'm not crawling into my shell [je ne me cache pas derrière mon doigt]. I want German victory at all costs. My son went and got himself killed in Russia, I don't see why yours can't go work in Germany.

Later he relented and asked only that Mangiavacca's son join the PPF in return. Still later he expelled him, seeing him only as an STO-dodger and wayward sort with two previous convictions. He had decided that the young Mangiavacca was an undesirable member: he had changed his mind: one Simon had prevailed over the other.[27]

In the end he turned in the performances in war that he had in peace: the spellbinder, 'trembling with emotion and running with perspiration' as he left the platform; the battle-axe, declaring after a fatal incident outside the PPF offices that 'they should have killed not one but a hundred'; the tireless patron, whose secretary later recalled typing nothing but '[answers to] various requests, answers to job requests, requests for recommendations. . .'; the devil-may-care veteran seated alone without a bodyguard on his suitcase in the corridor of the Marseille-Lyon train, knowing full well that he was a marked man; Sabiani, essentially, had not changed.[28]

Sabiani had not changed but by the Liberation the PPF had. During the twenty-one months of the German occupation, the last twenty-one months of its existence, an influx of new members transformed the party. At least a quarter were unemployed, compared to one-tenth before November 1942; one-third were from the working class, compared to one-fifth before; only six per cent were *fonctionnaires*, compared to twenty-five per cent before, and only seven per cent, against seventeen before November 1942, were from the upper middle class. Few of the new entrants were Corsicans — seven per cent compared to twenty-one before November 1942. They came from all over the city — the fourth and fifth cantons were losing their privileged place, claiming only 20 per cent of the new members against 40 per cent before. They were younger — 55 per cent were under the age of 28 against only 15 per cent before. The Corsicans going, the *fonctionnaires* almost gone, plebeian, even marginal, ethnically patternless, the fiefdom around la Joliette forgotten — this was *Sabianisme* mutilated almost beyond recognition. What were all these newcomers doing in the party? And why had they come there to do it?[29]

Many of them were not doing anything. At least a third of the party's new members attended a few meetings only or, more often, managed to stay away altogether.[30] Sometimes they were browbeaten into attending a rally, a major party congress or even an occasional roll-call, the summons implicitly acknowledging their perversity:

> I hope you'll be among those who answer the call. Those who do not turn up will be regarded by the Leader as members uninterested in the Party and punitive measures will be taken.[31]

Coercion like this could round up perhaps one to two thousand — the probable extent of the party's membership — for a major event, like a regional congress, where members knew what to expect: flags, photos of Doriot, Sabiani in party uniform (which irritated him) haranguing the crowd and denouncing Communists, Freemasons, Jews, *bourgeois* and *affameurs*. Threats could also bring them to party headquarters, now on the Canebière, where they would find an equally ritualistic routine, with sentries and raised-arm salutes and a nightly taking down of the colours. Sometimes they were made to wear the party's blue shirt and black tie.[32] Few can have done so enthusiastically.

Some were probably afraid. *Résistants* killed their first PPF member in Marseille in September 1943; they killed two more in the first six months of 1944, and threatened many others; they detonated bombs in the party offices in June and July 1944. When the killing began some members left in fright.[33] Others stayed in, but they had good reason to practise political discretion: the public hated the PPF. It was the party of the *occupant*. Anyone seen in the building on the Canebière was asking for trouble: passers-by skirmished with the arrogantly saluting sentries, angry women demonstrated about the price of bread, bombs went off and even a neighbourhood prostitute declared to an acquaintance that one bomb was not enough.[34] The PPF was a focus of resentment, and it made sense to stay away.

But mostly they stayed away because they had never been very interested in the party to begin with.

At least half of them — half of the layabouts, the new members who did little or nothing — had joined to avoid the STO.[35] Membership in the PPF or in another collaborationist organisation normally provided protection against the dreaded trip to a German factory, so that Sauckel's STO swelled the ranks of collaborators and *résistants* alike. Exemption was informal: the PPF promoted the STO in public and could only court the fugitives in private, so that they joined expediently, furtively, accidentally. If they or a relative were lucky enough to know Sabiani, a tacit understanding — membership in the party in return for freedom from deportation — could suddenly save the day, as it did for the young Mangiavacca and for the student whose father at the last minute got him out of the *rue Honnorat* the antechamber to deportation, with an appeal to Sabiani. Later the student, ostracized for his inadequate militancy, had to hide

from the PPF as well as from the STO. Often the worried potential
conscripts hit on the idea by accident, at the suggestion of a friend or
a client. The barman at *la Potinière* on the Vieux-Port, threatened by
a summons from the *Office de Placement Allemand*, signed up after a
crisis consultation with his customers across the *zinc*. He once
marched in uniform in a PPF parade when Doriot came to town,
under threat of expulsion; otherwise he took little part. He even hid
other fugitives from the STO. Three other barmen, all working at
the bustling *Colibri* on the Place de la Bourse, joined in July 1943 in
exactly the same way — one of them counselled by a neighbourhood
bookseller and PPF member who happened to take his *apéritifs* there.
One helped avoid the six-day compulsory work stint, which the
Germans had introduced in March 1943 along with the STO to man
their projects and guard the rail-lines, for favoured *Colibri* clients.
Another sheltered some Jews. A third joined the FFI: these were poor
militants indeed. Escaped conscripts, men who had jumped the
convoys carrying them to the Reich, also came to the PPF, hoping to
avoid a new journey or to acquire valid legal papers. They had no
other interest in the party. Fugitives like these came to the party, but
sometimes the party came to them — sometimes recruiters enticed
probable conscripts with the promise of freedom. They found them
in bars — an illiterate and unemployed docker in the *bar Figaro*,
conveniently close to the party headquarters — and in dance-halls: a
nineteen year-old, taken and then released with an exemption when
he joined the party's youth organisation; and above all in the halls of
the rue Honnorat itself: a twenty-two-year old shopkeeper, his deportation papers for the salt mines in Upper Silesia torn up before
his eyes when he joined the party. The recruiters were sometimes
honest and sometimes venal: the docker paid the normal 100 francs
to join, the Silesian-bound shopkeeper 5,000. The STO inspectors
themselves took bribes: why should not the party's recruiters? The
opportunities were legion.[36]

The PPF had other laggards: the other half of the inactive members
who had joined for some other reason and then shunned the party as
best they could. They feared the Germans in some other way — a
roadworker because his wife was Jewish, a plumber's apprentice because he had argued with a German engineer, a shopkeeper because
his son had joined and then deserted the SS, a taxi-driver because
they were requisitioning cars. They thought they could use the party
without the party using them. Or they feared Vichy, like the harried
freemason or the mutinous 20-year old on the run from the *chantiers
de la jeunesse* or the Opera director sacked for trying to put on operas
by the Jews Offenbach and Strauss. Or they sought protection from
the law, or they wanted to get to Paris — a plethora of motives, each
commanding only casual allegiance to the party.[37]

Collectively the inactive members changed the social composition of the party. Almost a quarter of those who had joined in flight from the STO were unemployed, another third from the lower class — about half of them skilled or unskilled factory workers, a social group particularly vulnerable to the STO. By contrast *fonctionnaires*, the old *Sabianiste* core, were officially exempt from the STO, a privilege accounting for their absence from the STO-dodgers in the PPF and by extension for their dwindling presence in the party at large.[38] Among the motley crew of otherwise motivated idlers no social group prevailed, but the marginal element, the men on the run, also helped depress the party's social centre of gravity. If the typical *Sabianiste* before the war — even until November 1942 — was the Corsican municipal employee, the typical member now was an unemployed fugitive, a man who had fallen foul of the German or of the French authorities or of both, a twenty-six year old stonemason and petty thief who joined in flight from the STO and from the police:

> It is clear indeed that it is difficult to speak of honour, of dignity, of energetic resistance, to a subject like this, who besides. . .seems to have tried to take the easy way out. . .he worked as the chances came. . .he was to be found frequenting the "dancing" establishments of the rue Thubaneau where the clients are used to living by their wits. . . .[39]

He is the story behind the statistics: new conditions, new clients.

All of the party's inactive members were 'soft' collaborators; their collaboration stopped at membership in a collaborationist organisation: it was harmless to their compatriots. But some of the party's active members, who took on duties once they joined, were as innocuous as their idle colleagues.

A few — probably not more than five per cent of all the new members after November 1942 — found manual or clerical work in the party.[40] Some found jobs as secretaries or *concierges* at the party's headquarters, some as clerical employees in the subscription or editorial offices of *L'Emancipation National*, a few even as cooks; some, the recipients of Sabiani's gifts, found jobs through but not in the party — a porter at the *service municipal de ravitaillement*, an electrician at the *Kriegsmarine* works in the Parc Chanot, a driver at the police headquarters. But they were a handful compared to the crowd of STO-evaders and other fugitives huddled idly under the party's umbrella.[41]

Some of the party's young showed some enthusiasm for the cause. Some became proselytes in the party's 350-member Jeunesses Populaires Françaises, dragooned into disseminating propaganda, putting up posters, occasionally parading in the streets; they provoked the prefects and ruffled Vichy, which saw the JPF as a political rather than a youth organisation and so withheld legal recognition. Some of the members attended twice weekly meetings at the party headquarters where they listened to their regional leader on 'Russia and England' or Sabiani on their duty to save France from Communism; some helped assure security at large party meetings.[42] This was an active form of party membership but another harmless form of collaboration, and only some, perhaps a third, of the members of the JPF went that far. A further quarter managed to do little or nothing, losing themselves in the crowd of their like-minded elders. Most of these 'soft' collaborators of the JPF had joined to avoid the STO — the young, at loose ends, job-hunting and just out of the *chantiers de la jeunesse*, were the *Office de Placement Allemand*'s favourites.[43] They, more than anyone else, needed a way out; they, more than anyone else, were susceptible to the blandishments of the party's recruiters.

Many of the party's new office employees, or the members it managed to place elsewhere, and the more active members of the JPF were probably unemployed when they joined.[44] They and their inactive colleagues, collectively the soft or harmless collaborators, account for much of the party's overall social composition — about half were unemployed or from the working class. Their heterogeneous origins diluted the party's ethnic character — less than a tenth were Corsican — and their youth depressed its age level: over half were under the age of twenty-eight, young job-seekers or fugitives from the STO.[45]

What did such collaborators believe? Few, naturally, proclaimed a collaborationist credo after the Liberation, but few explicitly denied one. Expediency is not incompatible with conviction; possibly every belief rests on a bedrock of self-interest; the marchers photographed in the PPF *défilés* do not look cynical or sceptical or insincere. Some undoubtedly agreed with Sabiani, as others had before the war, that France was menaced by 'bolshevisation' and that Stalin, not Hitler, was the real danger. But how convinced could they be when so many combined resistance of one sort or another with membership in the PPF? Half of the passive PPF members, the reluctant militants, were able to prove after the Liberation that like the barmen of the *Colibri* they had helped *réfractaires* or Jews or *résistants*, or even joined the FFI before the Liberation.[46] A few gave resistance networks inside information on members and meetings; a few sabotaged party offices; many, less dangerously, turned a blind eye to *résistants* in their workplaces and used their friends in the party to exempt *réfractaires* from the STO. The post-Liberation court had little against the owner of a bar in what was left of the *vieux quartiers* — he had joined the party in May 1943 after receiving an STO summons, had torn up others in his bar in front of customers, had protected résistants including the head of the Communist cell of the Place de Lenche; he had attended two PPF meetings and had finally been thrown out of the party by Sabiani in May 1944, a year after he joined.[47] Men like him were able to prove that their membership in the party was practical rather than principled: that they were victims rather than villains: that they were totally opposite to their other colleagues, the 'hard' collaborators, the men who made the newspapers and later the history books.

One line of their work was chasing *résistants*.

'I'm no angel but it was no party time either [Je ne suis pas un ange mais ce n'était pas le temps des bonbons]': in his last and unsuccessful appeal for clemency Ernst Dunker *alias* Delage, *Scharführer* in the counter-espionage section of the Marseille bureau of the Reich security services, adopted a war criminal's only possible defence, that he was a victim of circumstance and that in a gentler time he would have been a gentler man.[48]

Perhaps: he had ended up arresting and torturing the *résistants* of Marseille and Provence largely by accident. Born in Halle in 1912, imprisoned for theft in 1931, a hotel receptionist for most of the thirties but a bartender in Berlin at the outbreak of the war, he took part in the French campaign as a corporal and was finally seconded to a staff unit near Dunkirk. Gifted in languages — he soon came to speak excellent French — Dunker was spotted, trained as an interpreter, and assigned first to a unit in St German-en-Laye and later to the security police (*geheim Feldpolizei*) in the prison camps. He must have done well: in August 1942, still an interpreter but now an *SS-Scharführer*, or sergeant, he bagged a job at SD headquarters in Paris in the rue des Saussaies. There he proceeded to burn the candle at both ends and so by the end of the year landed in prison again, this time for black marketeering and desertion. Early in 1943, released from prison but also from his idyllic Paris posting, he went south in disgrace to take up yet another interpreter's job in yet another SD *Abwehrstelle*, this time in Marseille, in the villa at the end of the rue Paradis.[49]

The combined services of the SIPO and of the SD had penetrated the southern zone well before its occupation in November 1942. Their agents had operated under cover of the Red Cross, the Consulate, the Armistice Commission, probably also of German industry, so that when the Germans arrived in force they had only to lift the pretence and transform the six existing SD *Einsatzkommandos* in the south — those in Limoges, Lyon, Montpellier, Toulouse, Vichy and Marseille — into official Kommandos. The rue Paradis became a regional bureau, with dependent branches — *Aussendienststellen* — in Nimes, Avignon, Nice, Digne and Gap.[50] For most of the occupation *SS-Stürmbahnführer* Rolf Mühler, who had been a member of the German police delegation in Vichy and head of the SD in Rouen, presided over five sections of the Marseille bureau, the most important of which, section IV, carried out arrests, interrogations, and general security operations including the pursuit of Jews, Communists and deserters. And it was in Section IV that the lowly *Scharführer* Dunker went to work when he arrived in February 1943.[51]

Next to the mostly professional German agents in section IV Dunker was something of an oddity. Possibly he felt he had something to prove; probably he wanted to regain the confidence of his superiors in Paris. Whatever his motives, he quickly made himself indispensable, thanks to a command of French stronger than that of his colleagues, and began taking part in arrests and interrogations, writing some reports and translating others, providing his services indiscriminately in subsection IVA (Communists and *résistants*) and IVE (counter-espionage): administrative fictions which, he later said, it was impossible to respect. Soon he began to arrest and torture his first *résistants*, the first of at least several hundred he would have deported during his eighteen-month career; and he also began to hire local French agents.[52]

The fifty or sixty German officials of the Marseille bureau could not operate without the several hundred local agents — Dunker put their number at 200, other estimates are higher — whom they soon took on.[53] Most were informers, telling the men at the rue Paradis what they knew about *résistants* or hidden arms supplies or black market stocks. They boasted semi-official status, complete with letters of protection which kept the local police at bay while the Germans were in town but which fascinated the courts after they had left, for anyone enjoying such protection, whether an informer or not, also enjoyed a personal card in an SD index file which survived the occupation almost intact.[54] Smaller in number but greater in notoriety were the active agents, the full-time collaborators who took part in operations of the SD, including arrests and interrogations, and most of whom Dunker — he put their number at 17 — hired himself. A time-honoured practice, he later declared in his defence:

> The SD in Marseille didn't do anything different from what the English, American, French and Russian [security] services are doubtless doing this moment [1948] in their respective zones of occupation in Germany.[55]

It was a superficially convincing but ultimately irrelevant argument:

he was not charged with hiring French agents and informers but with torturing and murdering their compatriots.

Dunker's active agents were a motley crew. One was Spanish, a former Barcelona policeman. At least seven were former *résistants*, six of them arrested and turned under varying degrees of torture. One, twenty-four year old Blanche di Meglio, gave away many of her former colleagues at *Franc-Tireur* before Dunker — who by then was operating under the *nom de guerre* of Delage — took her on as secretary and mistress. Another, Jean Multon *alias* Lunel, was a prize catch: at the time of his arrest and conversion he was regional second in command of Combat, and promptly led Dunker-Delage to Maurice Chevance, his Combat commander of the eve. Chevance slipped through the hands of his captors, but Lunel proved his worth again while on loan in Lyon, where he helped deliver the MUR agents René Hardy and Jean Moulin to his new masters — including Klaus Barbie. They sent him back to Marseille with an appreciative letter of recommendation: if he was not needed in Marseille could they have him back in Lyon? One *résistant* came forth voluntarily. Aptly code-named Catilina for his treachery, he led Dunker-Delage and his colleagues, in return for money, to 39 FFI agents in the south-east, including some radio operators who were all doubled in turn: betrayal, voluntary or not, was the stock-in-trade of the war against the resistance.[56]

From the other side, balancing the seven turned agents, came six less guileful men, psychopathic or criminal or merely marginal: six members of the PPF.

Two were notorious. One was Antoine Tortora, a member of the party since 1937, once a sailor and a prize-fighter, known as 'Antoine the boxer' and now as 'the torturer' for the grisly skills he practised in Dunker-Delage's own office. The other was Gaston Daveau, a thrice-convicted mechanic who had joined the party in 1936 and the LVF in 1941 and whose brutality during arrests and interrogations was such that even Delage tried to restrain him. There was also Daveau's Italian mistress, Marguerite Magno, 'la belle rousse', divorced and unemployed, whom he had initially inveigled into trailing one 'Thérèse the seamstress' through the streets of the city and who now worked full-time for him. They lived together in Tortora's seedy hotel in the rue du Musée, behind the Canebière. All three when they met Delage were already working for an SD official and hotel guest who had come down from Paris to investigate an organisation repatriating grounded English airmen. The visitor from the rue des Saussaies more or less forced them onto Delage, Daveau later said. But Delage put the raffish trio to good use. With occasional help — one 'Marcel l'Ukrainien' lent a hand now and then

— they carried out repeated arrests, including the *rafles* of April 1943 and the bungled attempt to seize Chevance; with occasional help Tortora tortured the prisoners at the rue Paradis while Delage's Blanche passed round drinks and refreshments. Then complications arose. First 'la belle rousse' took to jewelry theft as well as to a German sergeant and was reassigned to a more quiet spot in the SD; then Daveau shot at her in a fit of jealousy, became quite unmanageable, and was finally deported to Sachsenhausen; then Blanche di Meglio plotted clumsily with two disaffected agents to murder Delage and was deported to Ravensbruck; finally Antoine *le boxeur* met his end in a resistance ambush in Aix-en-Provence, plausibly concluding an implausible story, one which even the most credulous cinema audience would greet with scepticism.[57]

Daveau and Tortora were Delage's closest associates, but at least four other members of the PPF joined his team of French auxiliaries, probably finding their way to him through party contacts. One, an occasional factory worker, had frequented Sabiani's chauffeur's bar in the 1930s and another was Tortora's own cousin, once a sailor like him.[58] They carried out the same sort of work, including arrests. They probably carried no official party recommendation, but the party did nothing to hold them back and through them it established itself within the SD, a privileged interloper untroubled by patriotic scruples: it had become a pool of talent from which Dunker-Delage could draw.

Dunker-Delage and others: the SD had a rival in Marseille as in all Europe: the Abwehr. It had its own Dunker-Delage, the nameless 'Albert'. In his early forties, possibly of Belgian origin, speaking correct French, dark, athletically built, always well-dressed, always wearing his grey hat with the borders turned down, and often seen with a blonde woman who may have been English and who claimed to be his wife — 'Albert', as he was still calling himself when he escaped at the Liberation, was anonymous but not incognito. He lived with his *soi-disant* English wife in a requisitioned flat in the rue Llandier, off the Prado, had an office at the *Kriegsmarine* in the Hôtel Louvre et Paix on the Canebière, and kept a room in the Hôtel de Rome just off the Quai du Rive Neuve where he received black marketeers and their wares; he ate in the restaurants and drank in the bars around the Opera and the Vieux-Port; and there he recruited his agents.[59]

'Albert' and a colleague — there was at least one other Abwehr agent in Marseille, one 'Rolf', or Wolfgang Sandhage, a 'type alcoolique' — especially liked interviewing candidates in the bar of the Hôtel de Noailles on the Canebière. There they recruited a chemical worker, first to sell dyes for a German company at 10,000 frances a month and then to help find radio-operators for eventual use behind

Allied lines after the invasion. There they persuaded a lowly Préfecture errand-boy, who was soon spending 15,000 francs a month on his girlfriend, to report on his superiors; they even ensnared the barman with 5,000 francs a month and insignificant proving missions before sending him to Germany for radio training.[60] They, more than Dunker-Delage, wanted to build a network.

In this they had some co-operation from the PPF. In 1942 Doriot, encouraged by Colonel Reile of the Abwehr in Paris, had decided to develop a secret PPF intelligence network, unknown even to members of the *bureau politique*. It would ferret out resistance arms depots and radio communication lines, collect political and diplomatic secrets from embassies and consulates, undertake various specialised missions including the penetration of North Africa and, at Reile's request, counter-espionage operations; it eventually had about 60 agents, including some North African delegates who had been trapped at the party congress in November 1942 when the allies invaded their homeland, and four regional centres in the south — including one in Marseille.[61] An official nominally employed at *l'Emancipation Nationale* — 'René Page' — began putting agents to work in Marseille for an Abwehr officer based in Aix-en-Provence, Albert's superior, Major Werner and before long he began showing results. Soon three PPF agents, tempted by salaries of six and ten thousand francs a month, began setting up transmitting and receiving stations in villas in an eastern suburb, les Trois-Lucs. And soon a Corsican OSS agent, arrested in Carcassonne and doubled after days of torture, and three of the North African PPF agents were falsely communicating with Algiers and so setting up traps from their pseudo-*résistants'* flat in another eastern suburb, Saint-Jérôme. For all its failures — the four men parachuted into Algeria and shot as soon as they landed, the agent sent to Switzerland to uncover communist propaganda centres and caught almost at once by the vigilant Swiss, the collapse of the Spanish radio-operators' network — Doriot's secret network had its successes, and the flat in Saint-Jérôme was one of them.[62]

Gradually the SD took over the network, riding roughshod over Doriot and the Abwehr alike. Doriot even tried to have the North African ring dismantled, angry that Nosek of the SD should be running it at will. In Lyon Klaus Barbie was constantly asking the PPF agents to work for him. In Toulouse the main PPF agent went to work independently for the Germans. And in Marseille Dunker-Delage began himself to arrest the agents set up by the false *résistants* of Saint-Jérôme; 'Albert' and 'Rolf' left the *Kriegsmarine* and the Canebière and moved into the SD and the rue Paradis, minor actors in the larger drama unfolding in Berlin.[63]

But whether in the Louvre et Paix or in the SD villa, 'Albert' seems to have hired most of his PPF agents just as Dunker-Delage did, on his own and at his pleasure, whatever Doriot and Reile and 'René Page' of *l'Emancipation Nationale* were concocting. A hotel *chasseur*, prison guard and garage attendant who had joined the PPF to avoid the STO met him through a tailor already working for him. He went along to a bar on the Canebière, probably the Noailles, agreed to undertake various missions in return for 3,000 frances a month, and was soon checking up on a suspicious railway employee in Toulon, a suspicious radio operator in Marignane, the suspicious clients of a bar in la Milière. He made a fool of 'Albert'. Sometimes his mistress, a dancer in the 'El Rancho' nightclub and a former prostitute, accompanied him on his espionage missions; sometimes he fabricated his revelations, once limiting his investigation to a quick drink at the bar. He did not take his duties very seriously, unlike a former Préfecture employee and party member who met 'Albert' from time to time in Bar Titin on the Place de l'Opéra and who may have sent Antoine Zattara, the police chief and resistance leader, to his death in Germany.[64] Neither came to 'Albert' on behalf of the PPF, unlike the agents in the party's secret network, but neither was atypical: if Dunker-Delage could find his men among the party's ranks, so could 'Albert'.

With Doriot's secret network, with the Abwehr and the SD doubling one another, with Vichy's agents to boot, the Midi became a rats' nest — it was almost impossible, a PPF official declared to the *renseignements généraux* after the war, to employ anyone not already working for someone else. One former *cagoulard* seemingly worked for Vichy, the Germans, and the PPF all at once.[65] And even this did not exhaust the options open to the *marseillais* PPF members willing to act against the resistance, for in 1943 the *Waffen-SS* entered the act and set up its own French anti-resistance unit: the Légion Brandenbourg.

In German uniform and under the command of German officers, the *marseillais* recruits in the Légion Brandenbourg were trained near Pont St Esprit in the Gard to protect military objectives or fight the *maquis* or spy on gaullists and communists. Eight out of twelve *marseillais* members tried by the civil courts after the Liberation came from the PPF. Most probably never saw action against the *maquis*; some ended up in the LVF or the *Waffen-SS* itself, some others went to Germany, one joined the FFI. Some may have gone in unawares: a witness declared that the camp in Pont St Esprit was full of dupes who had signed up for a school and found themselves in a military formation. But once again the PPF furnished the lion's share, this time deliberately: five of the eight joined at the urging of party officials and one was an official himself, the secretary of the eighth canton section.[66] Perhaps the PPF in Marseille was trying to take over the new unit, just as Doriot in Paris was trying to take over the new French *Waffen-SS* brigade;[67] perhaps it was trying to impress the Consulate or the occupants of the Hôtel Splendid; whatever its motive, the PPF found the men to send.

It found them often, but not always, among the unemployed, the poor, the drifters: the classic source — but men like Tortora and Daveau do not lend themselves easily to classification. Seven out of twelve of the men it sent to guard prisoners — mostly *résistants* — in the Baumettes, were unemployed; at least four of the eight in the Légion Brandenbourg were drifting or on the run when they signed up. Twenty-seven out of 50 Abwehr or SD agents convicted after the Liberation were unemployed or from the working class; not all were from the PPF — some had come on their own — but the PPF was the privileged broker: it had become an employment agency for spies, informers, and turncoats.[68]

Another line of work was chasing *réfractaires*, the fugitives from the STO.

The Hôtel Californie was a narrow three-storey building on the Cours Belsunce, number 60, rising above some Arab bars and overlooking the gaping lot behind the Bourse and the Vieux Port beyond. It was one of the city's least known hotels until the early months of 1944, when it suddenly became one of the best known — it became the headquarters for perhaps two hundred French inspectors scouring the city in search of conscripts and *réfractaires* to send to Germany. They were working for Dr Lucke of Section III of the SD — political and economic matters, black marketeering, banks, voluntary or involuntary workers for the Reich — and his Alsatian deputy and interpreter; they were feared and hated; and their largest brigade, claiming the whole of the hotel's second floor, consisted of members of the PPF.[69]

Misnamed the *Schutzkorps* or *Comité pour la Paix Sociale*, also known as the *brigade Battesti* after its energetic leader, the PPF contingent at the Hôtel Californie had perhaps 100 men, each of whom arrived every morning at half-past seven. One of them lived in Les Pennes-Mirabeau and took the bus in every morning, alighting at the Cours Belsunce — a daily commuter's routine journey. There was a roll-call, and Battesti would then hand each one ten slips bearing the names and addresses of men wanted for the STO. They went out in pairs looking for the hapless conscript-to-be; if they found him they would take him to the rue Honnorat for pre-departure formalities; if they did not they would sometimes take a relative hostage or seize the family's ration cards until he materialized. They did all this for money. In addition to a monthly salary ranging from three to six thousand francs they received 100 francs for each man they brought in.'[70] They were bounty hunters.

The most active and the most successful went on a ten to fifteen day course at the Caserne Mortier in Paris, where Geman officers trained them in the use of firearms — nothing more sophisticated than old model revolvers and rifles — and in some rudiments of soldiering. They returned to Marseille with contracts, a first monthly salary, and a German authorisation to carry arms — in May 1944 alone the academy in the Caserne Mortier launched thirty *marseillais* members of the PPF, out of a total that month of 92 trainees from the city, on their new careers.[71] Some made multiple arrests, even farming out their services beyond the confines of the city, as in May 1944 when a covey of Battesti's men descended on Perpignan, reaped its crop of conscripts and rewards and returned, raiding Montpellier on the way back. Nevertheless, catching the *réfractaires* was hard work — for every 100 they hunted about 80 got away. Some of the men in the brigade merely watched, lurking around cafés and restaurants and public places and drawing up lists of suitable candidates. Some of their colleagues merely drove lorries or carried out menial tasks back at the Hôtel Californie. Some merely had clerical functions at the Office de Placement Allemand in the rue Beauvau, maintaining files or keeping track of *requis* and *réfractaires* alike.[72] But the manhunt was the most common as well as the most lucrative line of work for the PPF in the field: of 197 tried after the Liberation for working for the Hôtel Californie or the OPA, at least 113 pursued, arrested or guarded their compatriots bound for the workplaces of the Reich.[73]

'My activities in the PPF had one purpose only: to earn money', a member of Battesti's brigade declared after the Liberation: he was typical. A former sailor joined '. . . because I could earn fairly substantial sums fairly easily', a former customs inspector 'because I had three children to bring up'; a rural policeman found his salary of 1,700 frances a month inadequate; the commuter from Les Pennes-Mirabeau, a drifter, occasionally employed in cinemas or as a handyman, suddenly began dressing well. Some had themselves joined the party to avoid the STO and later succumbed to the lure of the Hôtel Californie, like the printer at *Le Petit Marseillais* who joined the party to avoid the STO but left his job six months later and accompanied a squad of inspectors to Montpellier and Sète. It could be a gradual descent: an STO conscript joined the PPF in Germany, came back, joined the OPA in the rue Beauvau to avoid being sent back, became an orderly there and later an inspector at the Hôtel Californie. But few claimed to have been coerced.[74] Few cared about Germany: of 141 tried after the Liberation, 34 had occasionally helped protect *réfractaires* and 28 had helped the resistance in some way, a reality grudgingly acknowledged by an examining magistrate:

> Certainly like all your friends in the Hôtel Californie you rendered a few services but this in no way attenuates the deeds you're accused of.[75]

Greed was their overriding motive.

Even more than their colleagues chasing *résistants*, the PPF members chasing *réfractaires* were poor or unemployed: over fifty per cent. About a third were under the age of twenty-eight, but their age profile is otherwise unremarkable, as is their ethnic background: only five per cent were Corsican. Forty per cent had been born in Marseille. It is the predictable statistical portrait of a group assembled only by extraordinary circumstances and united only by ordinary greed.[76]

Another line of work was chasing Jews.

Charles Palmieri was born in Marseille in 1911, the eighth of nine children of a quayside Corsican bar-owner. He left school at twelve and went to sea, first in the merchant marine and then in the navy; back in Marseille later he tried house-painting and in 1933, thanks to Sabiani, the *mairie*. Three years later he joined the PPF along with two similarly grateful brothers, the hunchbacked dwarf Victor — a tailor's apprentice, a chimney-sweep, a welder, finally an employee in Sabiani's *mairie* — and the idle and alcoholic Alfred, who stood and lost as the PPF candidate in the impregnable socialist first canton in 1937. Charles lived by 'expédients', including car theft, and he continued to do so after 1940, trying his hand first at black marketeering, then at spying, and finally at the most lucrative 'expédient' of all, Jew-hunting.[77]

Palmieri began black marketeering as a retailer. He smuggled fruit and vegetables across the demarcation line from Marseille to Paris, where his wife Jacqueline or 'Jacky' ran their bar, Le Mirliton, a PPF haunt in the rue Thérèse frequented by Sabiani and Doriot when they were in town. Later he sold it and bought l'Oasis in the rue du Pont-Neuf, which Jacqueline, Victor and Alfred managed while he moved into wholesale black marketeering, buying tires and Cognac and anything he could find in Marseille to resell in Paris. Through some Parisian cronies he began dealing with willing Germans, once landing in prison for trying to sell them the very goods he had stolen from them, and by 1943 he had already met several of their agents, probably including 'Albert', in the Hôtel de Noailles in Marseille. Thereafter his career moved swiftly. First, Keller of the *Contrôle Economique Allemande* began paying him 10,000 francs a month and three per cent of the value of whatever blackmarket stockpiles he could uncover — as it happened, soap, food, trucks, and dyes. Then, in October 1943, Kompe of Section IVE of the SD — counterespionage, Delage's section — hired him to organise an intelligence network disguised as a German purchasing organisation with offices at the other end of the rue Paradis. Then, early in 1944, Bauer of Section IVB — Jews — hired him to find, arrest, and bring in Jews living in Marseille and throughout Provence.[78]

Palmieri kept the same cover. The *bureau d'achat*, known as the *bureau Merle* after his own code name, continued buying, selling and trafficking from the foot of the *rue Paradis*, sandwiched into an *entresol* between a ground-floor bookshop and his own flat on the floor above. But he and his brother Alfred, who now joined the operation, devoted most of their energies to *la chasse aux juifs*. They hired agents and paid them 5,000 francs a month: informers to find Jews and mark their towns and villages in red pencil on *cartes Michelins, hommes de main* to arrest them and bring them back in the truck Bauer had provided, and volunteers to stand by, often in the *Amical Bar* around the corner, and lend a hand if the operation was large enough. They went all over Provence, east into the Basses-Alpes and north into the Drome, to Cavaillon and to Vaison-la-Romaine, at least ten times to Avignon. Their expeditions ranged from several hours to several days, their catch on each from one to fifty; and for each arrest Charles received 1,000 francs.[79]

He was quite normal, a psychologist found after the Liberation, 'with an alert and intelligent expression'. He liked nightclubs and expensive suits from *chez Severin* next door on the rue Paradis and above all money: 'everyone likes dough [pognon]' he repeated, 'but you have to know how to get it cleverly'. He said he hated Jews. 'Round- and baby-faced, choleric and brutal at times', he drove around town in a grey Citroën *traction-avant*, armed with a revolver and sometimes a machine gun. He was 'the quintessential criminal [le truand à l'état pur]'. Alfred was cut in the same cloth — 'Smaller, an alcoholic face, drinks and smokes heavily. Always armed...hatred of the Jews even more pronounced than Charles'. Victor, 'le bossu', who was running l'Oasis in Paris and had married a prostitute there, was in and out of the *bureau Merle*, at least once joining in an expedition to Avignon; so was Palmieri's wife 'Jacky', who now lived in the Grand Hôtel and moved back and forth between Paris and Marseille. Late in June 1944 Bauer ordered them to Cannes, where they took up with the local PPF, moved into the Villa Conchita and started all over again, there and next door in Monte Carlo.[80]

How many hunted Jews for the *bureau Merle*? The *bureau d'achat* was more than a cover: it bought and sold, so that the *entresol* at the foot of the rue Paradis pullulated with dubious hucksters and black marketeers, with a Turkish gold dealer whom the Germans distrusted, an ex-LVF 'brute' from Avignon known simply as 'Toto', an unemployed mechanic from Peugeot — their participation in the *bureau's* ventures may have stopped at the contraband they peddled. A salesman from North Africa, marooned by the Allied landings there in November 1942, claimed he did no more than sell wine, liqueurs, and chocolates to the *Kriegsmarine* through the good offices of the 'Merle' brothers and their 'bureau'.[81] Nineteen people were tried after the Liberation for full-time association with the *bureau*: convincing evidence of their work was available for ten: only six without doubt participated in *la chasse aux juifs*, the remaining four in theft or black marketeering. But suspects and witnesses spoke of teams of auxiliaries, many of whom had disappeared by then, voluntarily or involuntarily — their real number is as elusive as the comings and goings in the *bureau* itself. Whatever their number, the background of the *bureau's* associates brought to trial resembles that of their fellow-collaborators hunting *résistants* or *réfractaires*. Of sixteen whose professions were known, six were unemployed, the others scattered through the social spectrum. Even if they had a nominal profession they could be drifters, candidates for the *bureau's* special work. 'If you're at loose ends some day, come see me, I'll take you on', Palmieri told an old friend of his in the *Bar Amical*, a 'hair-dresser' who had been in the LVF and then in Germany as a volunteer worker. It was the same sort of work, and they were the same sort of people: only the victims were different.[82]

They were mostly poor or unemployed: collectively the PPF men chasing *résistants*, *réfractaires* or Jews resembled the PPF men working as cooks or sweeping the halls or avoiding the party altogether. But they had one interest, the others many; they were driven by shared greed, the others by individual fears; they were the team-mates, the others the unwilling onlookers. They were birds of a feather.

Their skills were convertible: they could do each other's work. The retired PPF rural guard who arrested *réfractaires* in Montpellier also arrested at least one Jew in Marseille — he took over her apartment — and said, 'I'm off to arrest Jews. I only arrest Jews. I can sense them at 100 metres'. A fellow-habitué of the Hôtel Californie, also aboard on the Montpellier expedition, later accompanied two of Delage's PPF auxiliaries to arrest some *résistants* in Aix. Another may have arrested as many Jews as *réfractaires* — he lived in a furnished room in the rue Curiol, appended 'German police' to his name on the door, and told a woman from whom he was trying to buy names and addresses of local Jews, 'after the war I'll change sides [après la guerre je retournerais ma veste]'. Charles Palmieri's brother Victor spent

more time at the Hôtel Californie on the Cours Belsunce than at the
bureau Merle on the rue Paradis, for he brought in at least nine and
possibly fifty *réfractaires*.[83] They were all stalking a defenceless quarry,
and they all shared the same mentality: the criminal mentality.

Few contented themselves with their stipends and commissions.
Battesti's and Palmieri's men blackmailed their own victims as well
as each other's, they robbed the relatives and pillaged the homes; on
their expeditions Delage's men took jewels and money as well as *résistants*. Palmieri's interpreter — who had met him through the pro-
miscuous 'Jacky' and begun moving up and down the rue Paradis,
carrying messages between the SD at one end and the *bureau Merle* at
the other — blackmailed the Jewish owners of a shoe store in Salon
for 35,000 francs and looted their store before sparing them from
deportation. Five of Battesti's men took 38,000 francs from a Jewish
woman and had her deported anyway. Another took a bedridden
invalid to the rue Honnorat when his wife failed to pay up.[84] Some
already enjoyed discretionary income from unrelated crime, from
contraband or prostitution or petty theft — at least one third of
Battesti's men already had criminal records when they joined the
Hôtel Californie.[85] And anyone connected with the SD, even
indirectly like Palmieri's men, could carry an SD card with which he
could try to threaten, blackmail, or arrest passers-by, like the
unfortunate Dr. Combarnous in the novel of André Ducasse:

> You know: one of the pimps who stop you in town: "Police alle-
> man-de!" and ask for your papers in a Vieux-Port accent

— the phony police theft [*vol au faux policier*], in which the SD card
brought its bearer a reward just for staying away, was the simplest of
all extortions. Occasionally the Germans tried to control it;
occasionally they deported headhunters more interested in booty
than bounty.[86] But they were powerless to suppress it, powerless to
prevent them crossing and re-crossing the invisible frontier separating political from common crime.

It was a continuum. At one end were criminals like Sabiani's old
friends Carbone and Spirito, who were more interested in smuggling
than in anything else. Nosek of the SD, seemingly bypassing Doriot,
tried unsuccessfully to recruit them in the North African intelligence
network and soon gave up; he used them as

> ...black marketeers and suppliers of rare goods...Our two
> gangsters...were simply occasional auxiliaries of the SD...[they
> were] eager to seize any opportunity to promote their illicit
> traffickings (tobacco, white slaving, black market, brothels,
> etc...).

But Spirito's bar on the Vieux-Port was a notorious haunt for SD agents, and Carbone's younger brother arrested *résistants* with one of Delage's men — he also tried blackmailing a stockbroker in the company of Rolf Mühler's barber. Another brother did some recruiting for the *Légion Brandenbourg*. The famous couple were no more innocent politically than morally.[87] At the other end was Battesti, a fanatic who harangued the members of the PPF on the Canebière and spurred on the inspectors of the Hôtel Californie, but who doubtless winked at the licence and greed of his recruits. In between was the tangled web of everyone else, including some *résistants*. The *milieu* criminals working for the resistance continued to run their bars, cabarets and brothels, thriving with their *collabo* confederates in a jungle of Byzantine plots and obscure rivalries. Joseph 'Jo-Jo' Renucci, the pre-war socialist *homme de main* and resistance spy in the *milieu*, cultivated his old partner in crime Charles Palmieri not to inform on the *bureau Merle* but to wage a gang-land feud with the Bony-Laffont gang of SD auxiliaries in the rue Lauriston in Paris. He was rumoured to be working with the SD in Nice, and to frequent the headquarters of the local *milieu* there in the Hôtel Excelsior and the Hôtel Hermitage, but after the war no one, the courts included, doubted the value of his contribution to the resistance. Loyalties could be contrived — Jean Grimaldi, another pre-war gangster, was killed after his *milieu* rivals cunningly deceived the SD into believing that he was a leading *résistant*. Loyalties could be ignored — a thrice-convicted thief, a baker when he was not in prison, frequented the bar of a famous *milieu* collaborator, François Carbone, with a false identity card from the bar of the equally famous *milieu résistant* Antoine Guerrini. And loyalties could be changed — one black marketeer joined the *maquis* to escape the police and then the SD to escape German punishment. But once in the *milieu* always in the *milieu*: however fractious its members, it was a binding family.[88]

Their world was small, confined to the few short streets running between the Vieux-Port and the Place de l'Opéra. Spirito's Bar Amical on the rue Pavillon was a favourite PPF hangout, packed with Palmieri's men when they were not at the *bureau Merle* just around one corner or at Chez Kiki or the Cintra in the rue Beauvau just around the other. Sometimes they went a few steps up the Canebière to the bar of the Hôtel Noailles, where Palmieri's wife 'Jacky' enjoyed her new wealth and where 'Albert' interviewed his candidates. Jeannot Carbone, the great Carbone's younger brother, had Le Studio on the Quai du Rive Neuve, a semi-private establishment up a flight of stairs, and the Mistral in the rue Molière just off the Opera — both were run by a *réfractaire*-hunter, the brother of his mistress 'Lily', and both were *rendez-vous* points for PPF members and SD agents. It was in the Studio that one of Dunker-Delage's agents boasted of the plot to kill him, a rashness costing him his life

and Delage's Blanche di Meglio her freedom. Next to the Mistral —
with its nineteen-year-old cashier and its seventeen-year-old wait-
ress, one a black marketeer, the other an SD informer, both members of the PPF *Jeunesses Françaises Féminines* — was La Poularde, a
restaurant catering to German soldiers and some PPF SD auxiliaries,
and at the end of the street, on the corner of the rue de la Darse, was
Le Gaulois, also run by one of Carbone's friends and also a stop on
Albert's rounds. Two streets down, in the rue Glandèves, was another German restaurant, la Mère Michel, next to the Kid Kat and
its busy owner 'Madame Daisy', the mistress of 'Georges Boyer',
who was Avignon's answer to Charles Palmieri and who had begun
his *collabo* career in the bars of this very *quartier de l'Opéra* — the *quar-*
tier de l'Opéra was a *quartier chaud*. 'Ruled', as the police noted after
the Liberation, 'by the law of silence', crawling with '. . .numer-
ous individuals in somewhat special professions' and 'bar owners of
the same mentality', it was the spinning hub of the Franco-German
mafia.[89]

And it was now the hub of the PPF — no accident that the *tenan-*
cier of the old Bar Raffé on the Boulevard de Paris, the pre-war *Sa-*
bianiste and PPF seat in the fourth canton, now left the party in
disgust: 'our party has degenerated into a bunch of gangsters'.[90]
After the Liberation the members of the PPF found to have chased
résistants, *réfractaires* or Jews, to have blackmailed, stolen or murdered, were only a fraction of all PPF members tried.[91] But they were
the party's hard core, the most active and determined elements —
they *were* the PPF. The rest of the party, reluctant or passive, still existed; many of the pre-war section leaders were still nominally *en*
poste.[92] But their sections no longer met and their members no longer paid. The national party was heavily in debt and Paris had little
money for Marseille. The Germans gave 10,000 francs a month to
help with propaganda expenses and there were probably some private donations.[93] But the money was being made elsewhere, and it
was being made for private purposes. The party officials were
irrelevant and so, increasingly, was Sabiani.

Sabiani was losing control of *Sabianisme*. His convictions pulled him
one way, his better instincts the other, and meanwhile his followers
were running riot.

In the *résistants* he saw Stalin's agents and the 'terrorists' who were
bombing his offices and assassinating his colleagues, including his
old friend Dominique Tomasini, who had joined and left the Communist party with him. But even as he clamoured for revenge he
shrank from civil war. If he dwelt on vengeance — 'blood, unfortunately, calls for blood' — he endorsed restraint, declaring that

6 German
soldiers on the
Calanques

'passion must cede to reason' and 'here we don't commit murder'.[94]
If he sent several men off to the Légion Brandenbourg counter-
resistance camp near Nîmes and once, in July 1944, accompanied an
expedition against the *maquis* near Simiane he also intervened on
behalf of arrested *résistants*, incurring Delage's suspicions — the
untiring *Scharführer* of Section IV may even have searched his
apartment.[95] If he sent men to detain a saboteur suspected of
bombing the PPF headquarters, he was also disgusted with them for
killing him in a bungled arrest operation. If once he interrogated and
threatened a suspected stockpiler of resistance arms, once he also
intervened to rescue a *toulonnais* police officer from the brutalities of
his PPF captors, repay him the money they had stolen, and send him
on his way with a warning to keep quiet. As always, his bark was
worse than his bite, his violence more verbal than physical. *He bluffed
a lot...* And he harboured no illusions about the calibre of his latest
acolytes, themselves real men of violence: they were 'cowards' and
'murderers', the *toulonnais* police officer said as Sabiani saw him out,
and his improbable saviour could only agree: 'battle is joined, I [have
to] take whatever I [can] find'.[96]

Likewise he could only watch as criminals corrupted his crusade for the STO. The Battesti brigade at first operated from the PPF headquarters, under Sabiani's nose, and he later told people going to work for the Hôtel Californie that 'in joining the social justice corps [Schutzkorps], the young are working for the resurrection of France and the grandeur of the country'. He even sent a few people to work there, including Palmieri's brother Victor, le bossu. But when he learned that some of the 'inspectors' were running a false identity card business he tried to break it up, and when an old friend asked him for work he suggested he enter the Hôtel Californie to watch the trouble-makers there, 'the PPF elements... whose conduct was plaguing him', but nothing ever came of it. He could sooner disband than reform the Battesti brigade.[97]

Over Palmieri and the bureau Merle he had no control at all. He and Palmieri had quarrelled at the party congress in November 1942, over a year before Palmieri became Monsieur Merle, and thereafter they had nothing to do with one another. Palmieri had attended PPF meetings during his Paris days, the days of Le Mirliton and l'Oasis, but once in Marseille he stayed away from the siège on the Canebière. He worked independently for Kompe and Bauer of the SD; Sabiani was out of the picture, doing nothing to match his deeds to the anti-semitic words he had been uttering since 1940. Once, early in 1944, he brought a Jewish shopkeeper to a party meeting to identify the four PPF thieves who had robbed him of 150,000 francs — the man was later arrested by Palmieri's men anyway.[98] Sabiani did not matter.

By the spring of 1944 he was so hard up that Philibert Géraud had to take him on as a consultant to his paper Actu at 15,000 francs a month. And converts, like funds, were hard to come by — he had given up, he said, trying to convince people that the Comité d'Algers was a communist cell and that Stalin was turning Poland into a Soviet outpost. Beggared and frustrated as well as dethroned, he could only look on at the half-world of the PPF around him, the débris of his twenty-five year old political family, a kingdom of outcasts in which the king had ceased to rule. Sabianisme had gone haywire.[99]

CHAPTER 8

The PPF and Others, November 1942 – August 1944

'Stupid blindness', Sabiani called it; moral flabbiness, said the PPF
Abwehr agent Roger Peter *alias* René Page:

> ...The French people make me think of streetwalkers who cry
> every time they go upstairs with a client, knowing they lead a bad
> life, but who start all over again as soon as they're through.[1]

The shortsighted French had failed them. Sabiani and 'Page' and the
last of the party's fanatics wrung their hands and bemoaned their
isolation even as their pack of pariahs ran loose into the hostile
world.

But they had some company. There were other men and women
who for one reason or another, in one way or another, at one time or
another lent a hand to the city's uninvited guests. They were thinly
scattered throughout the city, some in rival French organisations,
some acting on their own, and their random resort to the practice of
collaboration united them into a diffuse family, one in which the
ne'er do-wells of the PPF stood out all on their own.

Pétanist collaboration, among Vichy's local officials, remained
as mixed and ambiguous as before the German occupation of the
southern zone. As before, the Commissariat Général aux Questions
Juives took on corrupt employees trying to despoil the expropriated
Jews as well as blameless ones trying to protect them. At the trial of
the deputy-director of the *Commissariat* no less than 32 Jews came
forth to testify on his behalf, to thank him for services rendered,
property saved, Germans fended off. More questionable were the
practices of an *administrateur provisoire* who protected the French but
probably defrauded the foreign Jews and the investigations of an *inspecteur* who verified religious identities, at least once in the company
of a German officer. The mix ran through the echelons of Vichy's

civil service, from the aggressive propagandist in the Délégation régionale à l'Information to the *chef de liaison* resisting and obstructing the Germans at every turn to the *directeur adjoint* at the STO working for the resistance: a scratch below the bleak surface of 'l'Etat français' reveals a mosaic of loyalties and convictions, a mockery of official uniformity and of 'la collaboration d'état'.[2]

Below its administration Vichy's organised support was crumbling fast. By 1943 the Légion des Combattants was a shadow of its former self. By November that year sixty per cent of its members in the Bouches-du-Rhône had left; the following month its main departmental office closed. It carried on mainly as a charitable organisation, a reminder of the growing irrelevance of the early mythology of Vichy.[3] By contrast its illegitimate child, the Service d'Ordre Légionnaire, began to go its own way. After the German occupation in November 1942 its recruitment began to change — probably more were now leaving than joining, but among the new entrants workers and the unemployed began to rise and new motives began to dominate: forced transfers from the old Légion no longer swelled the ranks, but escape from the impending STO, by the beginning of 1943, probably did. Along with new members the SOL began to take on new functions, unthinkable in the hands of its parent Légion. On the night of 11 November members living in the country beyond Marseille obeyed their instructions and guarded intersections for some German motorised units already coming through, and at the end of January others helped evacuate the residents of the Vieux-Port. They were lending a hand, helping the evacuees carry what belongings they could, but that week they were the occupant's auxiliaries, ripe for their transformation at the end of the following month into a new Vichy creation, the product of the radicalisation in progress there: the Milice.[4]

Swiftly, before the end of May, the Milice and its local *chef* Max Knipping — a war hero and former *cagoulard* just like the national *chef* Joseph Darnand — set out to turn the SOL into a fascist militia. Marcel Bonte, the former SOL leader and *résistant*, helped launch the Marseille Milice but quickly abandoned his illusions and resigned. The discourse was now at times authentically fascist: martial, xenophobic, anti-semitic, anti-democratic and occasionally pro-Nazi. Before the end of May, too, the Milice was preparing for civil war. In addition to its headquarters in the Lycée Thiers — behind the grey STO building in the rue Honnorat — and its *service social* in the rue Chiappe it set up fortified barracks in Château Gombert where it began training and drilling several hundred recruits from Marseille and the surrounding region, the first of the soldiers of the Milice, the Francs-Gardes. And before the end of May the resistance had the

Milice in its sights, for it had assassinated two of its local leaders and was vowing to bring down more.[5]

It was a provocative presence. From the outset, the prefects reported, the public at large hated it, seeing a toady of the occupant and a 'tool of the worst of the German police'. The prefects themselves disliked it, for it repeatedly slighted their authority, issuing secret contingency plans for an Allied invasion, freely requisitioning supplies, refusing — 'if necessary by force', Knipping said — to let the Préfecture have one of its cars.[6] It was a law unto itself.

It said the same as the PPF; it probably had about as many members, between 500 and 1,000; and it had very roughly the same social composition. About 25 per cent of its members were from the working class, about a third from the lower middle, including more *fonctionnaires* than the PPF now had; about an eighth of its members came from the upper middle class. In one important respect it was different from the PPF: it had fewer unemployed, eleven per cent to the PPF's 25.[7] But, statistically speaking, it resembled the PPF much more than did the SOL.

Perhaps one fifth of its members had come from the SOL or the Propagande du Maréchal. Most of the members of the SOL had dropped out along the way or managed to refuse induction into the Milice when the time came — of 460 tried or investigated after the war, only 101 had ever ended up in the Milice.[8] They were the left-over Pétainists, the last vestiges of an earlier, ambiguous variety of collaboration consistently scorned by the PPF.

But as in the PPF, the largest contingent consisted of fugitives from the STO. Between a quarter and a third of all *miliciens*, almost as many as in the PPF, had signed up to escape the STO, some as an insurance against ever receiving a summons, some the very day they received the summons, some at the last moment, under pressure at the rue Honnorat itself. It was very tempting —

> So I joined the Milice to avoid going to Germany, because it was simpler for me, because it allowed me to be close to my [family] and my work. I didn't have all the uncertainty [that would arise from] leaving for an unknown *maquis* with possible reprisals against my family

— and could be entered into quite casually, as an STO-ridden butcher discovered when he slaughtered a pig for a friend and later received a Milice card in thanks. Whether Sauckel's victims joined the Milice or the PPF was a matter of indifference and accident. 'In two months it'll be all over', a butcher's boy was told by a friend in May 1944, 'hide out in the Milice or the PPF [in the meantime]'.[9]

The other *miliciens* had joined for all sorts of reasons, mostly but not always apolitical. An illiterate carter —

> ...simple, hard working, very fond of his children, but incapable of understanding the meaning of his actions, notably when it came to politics

— joined only for the sake of his family; a customs inspector, PSF before the war, only for the sake of his beliefs:

> ...I've always had right-wing political ideas. So I wanted to join the Milice, which in my eyes was an *organisation nationale.*

Perhaps five per cent joined out of conviction, like the career military officer who felt it was his duty; another ten to take advantage of jobs or privileges at the Milice; another five under pressure from family or friends; others for multiple reasons — the mix of motives was no different in the Lycée Thiers from that in the PPF on the Canebière.[10]

But once inside, the new *milicien* found a totally different organisation. The Milice was organised along paramilitary lines into four *centaines*: one formed of recruits from outside Marseille, another of *marseillais*, another of the Francs-Gardes and about 30 north Africans, and the fourth, the smallest *centaine*, of clerks and secretaries, the *service administrative.* The *centaines* and their constituent *trentaines* and *dizaines* were units of indoctrination as well as regimentation, for their leaders gave regular talks on Jews, freemasons, communists, and collaboration.[11] They were trying to create a political army.

There was much more to do than at the PPF. Like its remote ancestor, the Légion Française des Combattants, the Milice wanted to play a social and humanitarian role, to provide as well as to punish. It rooted out black market stocks and distributed the goods to the poor in the Belle-de-Mai and Endoume, organised food convoys, watched over food tickets, looked into the administration of hospitals. It also policed the city, carrying out random identity checks in the Gare St Charles. All this required manpower and a fleet of vehicles — paying jobs for the recruits; in short, many more than the PPF could possibly create. The Milice needed cooks at the Lycée Thiers and at Château Gombert, drivers for its cars and trucks, guards for its garage, relief workers for its social agency, and it was willing to pay them between three and six thousand francs a month. About a quarter of all *miliciens* took up such menial civilian tasks, harmless to their compatriots, the activities of 'soft' collaboration.[12] The Milice, much more than the PPF, was a source of normal jobs and normal livelihoods.

And much more than the PPF, the Milice was an organised counter-insurgency force. By January 1944 Darnand had declared war on all who helped the resistance:

We are dealing with two types of people...on the one hand, the bands in the *maquis* who are not very numerous; on the other, the mass of people guilty of complicity by supplying them, informing them, sheltering them. I will strike the latter as hard as the former...

In Marseille the *deuxième service* of the Milice began to arrest and torture *résistants*. It even had a formal 'Service des arrestations, section urbaine' whose employees arrested suspects and took them for interrogations, sometimes very active interrogations, to the villa at 425 rue Paradis or to the Lycée Thiers. Often the ubiquitous 'Albert' of the Abwehr was present at the torture sessions in the *lycée*, there to take charge of the victim once the *miliciens* had extracted a confession. But the Marseille Milice made its name and its enemies in operations beyond the city. From the opening weeks of 1944 until the Liberation in August it sent armed squads, sometimes 100- or 150-strong, on ever-deepening anti-*maquis* forays into Provence and even beyond — into the Vaucluse and even the Massif Central to the north and west, into the *provençal* Alps and even Savoie to the north and east. Some of the expeditions amounted to little more than verifying the identities of villagers or searching for reported arms caches. But in June in Aups, in the Var, where *résistants* had killed some German soldiers, they took suspects and executed them, as they did later that month in Lourmarin in the Vaucluse, and in July in Gap and Vals, and in August in Boulbon and Vallabrègues. Sometimes there were ambushes and chaotic night-time exchanges of small arms fire, sudden engagements seemingly marked on both sides by confusion and ineptitude but also by the open enmity of outright civil war.[13]

As many as one fifth of all *miliciens* tried in Marseille after the war had gone along on such expeditions. Many never fired a shot. They were cooks or stretcher-bearers or sentries detailed to guard equipment, suddenly summoned from idleness like the carpenter's assistant who had joined the Milice to escape the STO:

You have been designated to leave on a mission. The moment has come for the Milice to act and to support our Leader Joseph Darnand's work of purification. I ask you to kindly come this evening at 6.30 to the Place Strasbourg. Measures will be taken against those who refuse and deportation to Germany is envisaged for those who disobey orders.

The others were Francs-Gardes, more prepared but not always more willing, for many of them were official conscripts. When the unit was formed in May 1943, Vichy instructed the Prefect to recruit 240 young men 'liable for the STO' from the military classes of 1940,

1941, and 1942. After that the Milice found its own foot-soldiers, and over the months a strong marginal element probably crept into the barracks at Château Gombert; none of the Prefect's inaugural recruits were unemployed, about one fifth of those tried at the Liberation were — more than in the Milice as a whole and almost as many as in the PPF. Not all of the Francs-Gardes were dragooned into raiding villages and firing at 'terroristes' — only half of those tried at the Liberation had done so — but in every operation they were the spearhead, the distinctive sign of the *Milice*, and they had no counterpart in the PPF.[14]

As in the PPF, many in the Milice tried to avoid doing anything at all once they had joined. They were the 'not very militant *miliciens*'. Between a quarter and a third managed to attend a few meetings only or stay away altogether. But the Milice was more hostile to indolence than the PPF, its leaders more sovereign, its members more tame. Even the laggards had more to do than their counterparts at the PPF — they sometimes had to guard railways buildings or goods and parcels at the station. After 27 May 1944 everyone had more to do, for everyone was called out to clear away the rubble and guard the ruins left by the American bombing raid that day, and after D-Day the last idlers lost all protection when Darnand mobilised the Milice and they had to move into the Lycée Thiers or run away.[15]

As in the PPF, there were criminals at work. There were looters in the raided villages, black marketeers in the Milice canteen, *faux policiers* in the streets. There were at least some *miliciens* in the Hôtel Californie, led by the alcoholic and brutal Charles Ringo. He shared a hotel with one of Delage's PPF agents and his mistress: here, in the *milieu*, Milice and PPF came together. Their bars were next to each other in the *quartier de l'Opéra* — Maxim's, the main Milice bar, stood in the middle of the rue Beauvau, surrounded by the haunts of Palmieri and Carbone and 'Albert'. *A chef de centaine* in the Milice owned it; his protégé and fellow-*milicien* earned one sobriquet — 'Jean the Barman' — inside it and another — 'Jean the Killer' — outside it. But criminals were incidental to the Milice, intrinsic to the PPF. When Ringo, a *chef de centaine*, went to work at the Hôtel Californie the Milice expelled him, and many of his hirelings there had no connection with the *Milice* at all. The Milice checked the criminal records of its recruits, a formality which would have decimated the ranks of the PPF, as Darnand's colleagues at the *Maintien de l'Ordre* in Vichy knew at the outset:

> We recognize. . . that in ignoring the recruit's past we risk making the same mistake committed by the PPF, which today consists of highly dubious activists, [and] in which the procurer rubs elbows with the thief, and the murderer with the swindler.[16]

If criminals still found their way into the Milice — and they did — many more found their way into the PPF; if members of the Milice, whatever their past, blackmailed, robbed or murdered, — and they did — many more did so in the PPF.[17] By the Liberation the typical *milicien* was still a soldier, willing or unwilling; the typical PPF member a bounty-hunter.

For the Milice, unlike the PPF, was a working organisation, the final perversion of Pétainist collaborationism; unlike the PPF, it had a semi-official mission; unlike the PPF, it deserved its name. It was an army, the PPF was a mob.

Salon collaboration, abstract, untested, and typified by the Groupe Collaboration, began to decline as soon as the Gemans arrived and the *Groupe* had a chance to practice what it preached. The Prefects stopped reporting about it; new members stopped joining it. It tried crude ploys to attract members — it persuaded one of them that it was 'a successor to the Légion', drew others with the promise of free German lessons and then made them pay 25 francs and join, signed members up without their knowledge, after they had bought a photo of Pétain in the rue St-Ferréol office or taken the *Groupe's bulletin*. Those who joined now seemed to come from all walks of life, although the *bourgeois* element was still strong and conviction perhaps still ran higher than elsewhere:

> [I joined] out of resentment at the Allies whom I held responsible for the death of my father during the Allied landings in Casablanca in November 1942.

But the scattered newcomers did not compensate for the departing old members.[18]

The *Groupe's* youth organisation, the Jeunesses de l'Europe Nouvelle, was also an essentially frivolous form of collaboration. The *Jeunesses* were more vocal and had broken away in 1942, reduced to some thirty tiresome enthusiasts, *lycéens* saluting and signing letters with a 'national-socialist handshake', uniformed girls cavorting with German soldiers, bored adolescents looking for fun and excursions. It was a noisy version of its ailing parent. A few received some military training at the hands of the Germans; they were the only ones to play out the precepts of the Groupe Collaboration. Otherwise they did not matter.[2] They resembled the Jeunesses Francistes, who broke shop windows and upstaged their diminutive parent organisation — the Prefect once confused it with the equally diminutive Rassemblement National Populaire — in playing at National Socialism. A few of them, too, went all the way, inveigled by a ringleader into working for a while for Ringo at the Hôtel Californie, but the rest were dilettantes, like the *philo* student who created a society to spy on his schoolmates, complete with a national-socialist oath, and who decorated his copy-book with uniforms, salutes, and insignias. 'Unfortunately or rather fortunately,' he later declared, 'the membership of this society never exceeded three.'[19]

As before, the PPF had little to do with the Groupe Collaboration or the Francistes or their wayward offspring. It had nothing in common with the *Groupe* and its type of collaboration, and if there were tensions with the Francistes they, like the RNP, were too small to threaten the only ultras of any weight in town, the PPF. It was in a position to monopolise the active collaborators and bind them over to German masters and employers, a task neither for the Milice nor for the Groupe Collaboration: but it soon found that such collaborators found it simplest to bypass it altogether.

As before there were volunteers for work in Germany; as before they were mostly unemployed or from the working class, looking for work, wages, or escape. 'I left France in order to get away from the degrading life I had to lead at home' — but their new life was rarely an improvement over their old. A pipe-fitter who left for Germany after quarrelling with his fiancée ended up in a detention camp in Poland after trying to escape; a 23-year-old day-labourer who left 'on the spur of the moment' spent 22 months in prison in Germany for listening to the BBC; a 45-year-old factory worker, unemployed when he volunteered early in 1943, wrote home complaining of his straw mattress and his blighted hopes: 'workers in France have nothing to envy [here]'.[20]

As before there were volunteers for the Russian front. As before they collectively resembled the volunteers working in Germany, with an even stronger contingent of unemployed. So did the recruits in the French *Waffen-SS Sturmbrigade*, created in July 1943 as German losses mounted in the East. The two were socially almost indistinguishable. They recruited next door to each other — the Waffen-SS on the Canebière, the LVF in the rue Paradis — and they signed up men with identical motives and identical backgrounds.[21] They signed up men who were in fear — the LVF a 17-year-old, afraid to go home after being sacked by his employer for stealing two packets of cigarettes, the Waffen-SS an 18-year-old, fearing family and police after escaping from a juvenile delinquents' home. They signed up men who were in despair — the Waffen-SS a 16-year-old ward of the state, homeless and adrift, who lied about his age, the LVF a 24-year-old occasional shipyard worker, living in squalour with mentally diseased relatives and no way out:

In joining the LVF with all of its promised perquisites he seems to have thought he would find a way of improving on a hitherto doubtlessly miserable life;

and they signed up men who were in parental disfavour: the Waffen-SS a 19-year-old drifter who had quarrelled with his father, the LVF an 18-year-old mason:

> ...After I'd gambled away my weekly pay my mother berated me and told me that if I didn't recover the money she would send me to my father [from whom she was separated]...unable to find the money, I signed up...in the LVF, in the rue Paradis.

Many had criminal records; many were retarded or mentally ill. The *légionnaires*, in these last 20 months of the occupation, went to Kruzhina and the front, where some of them fought Russian partisans; the *brigadiers* were sent to training camps in Alsace and even in Prague. If they did not regret their rashness then, they did later: 'It was', said one of them to a post-Liberation magistrate, 'the worst blunder of my life'.[22]

But for the active collaborators opportunities in Marseille were now much greater. They did not have to go to Germany or risk their lives at the distant front if they did not want to, for German employers were now in town, ready and willing to hire them.

In Marseille as in France, the largest was the *Organisation Todt*, which built coastal fortifications and bunkers and military installations all over France and employed, directly or indirectly, perhaps half a million French workers in the process. In Marseille it took over the Hôtel du Levant in Sabiani's rue Fauchier, and soon various candidates came forth asking about jobs.[23] Not surprisingly the volunteers at the Hôtel du Levant resembled those at the Office de Placement Allemand — almost as many were unemployed or from the working class, and almost as many were simply trying to improve their lot. For the German-speaking Polish immigrant, left penniless when her husband died and their *patisserie* closed, then employed successively as cook, governess, and dishwasher, the *Organisation Todt* was a deliverance: it gave her a job as a translator at 3,658 francs a month. For the *employé de commerce*, dissatisfied with his 1,800 francs a month, the *Organisation Todt* was a step up: it gave him a job running a canteen, probably at 4,500 Francs a month. A few, certainly fewer than those who went to Germany, joined hoping to escape, like the 17-year-old, 'thought to be rather simple-minded', who joined in the wake of an unhappy love affair'. Unlike their confrères in Germany some — perhaps 15 per cent — joined to escape the STO. A paying job in Marseille was preferable to slave labour in Germany. Whatever their motives, the recruits performed tasks more varied than in any other collaborationist organisation. They drove trucks in the transport corps, the *Légion Speer*, repaired telephone lines, loaded and unloaded freight trains, built walls and earthworks. The *Organisation Todt* also employed engineers, interpreters and accountants, whose presence helps to account for the middle class element, stronger than among the volunteers in Germany. Not everyone worked in Marseille: applicants at the Hôtel du Levant were told to expect a change of scenery and some, especially drivers, were sent as far away as Brest and St Malo. One or two strayed into the land of the 'hard' collaborators when their contacts began to multiply — a radio operator was offered six and then eight thousand francs a month by a German agent, possibly 'Albert', to begin developing a secret network of post-invasion operators: he did not refuse. But apart from them the employees of the *Organisation Todt* were harmless to their compatriots, collaborators of convenience whom the courts later viewed with indulgence.[24]

The *Kriegsmarine* hired the same sort of people, mostly workers to help build blockhouses and the submarine base at *Cap Janet*. The Wehrmacht in the Hôtel Splendide and its dependencies took or kept on an array of service personnel, some of them routine hotel professionals like the receptionist who had begun his career at the Crillon in Paris and had moved on to Marseille via hotels in Cannes and Aix-les-Bains. Others were more unusual, like the escaped Jewish prisoner of war whom they paid 5,000 francs for each car he could find to requisition. The SD in the rue Paradis needed service personnel too — gardeners for the grounds, servants for the 'bar', cleaning ladies for the offices:

> While I was working at Bauer's I heard the cries of Jews under torture. When I went in to clean the offices, I would find bloodstains on the floor.

All three, *Kriegsmarine*, *Wehrmacht*, *Sicherheitsdienst*, needed interpreters to communicate with suppliers, employees or even prisoners. German speakers were not difficult to find, especially among the Alsatians or Lorrainers living in the city. Half of all interpreters working for the Germans had been born in Alsace or Lorraine. Most were trying to elude the *Wehrmacht*, which was conscripting their countrymen. Some had been in Marseille since before the war, others had fled during the *débâcle* and now, with the Germans at their heels once again, had nowhere else to go. Others, from Alsace-Lorraine and all over France, simply fancied salaries of 5,000 Francs a month.[25] The occupation, temporarily, had shuffled the cards in their favour.

The rarer the *métier* the more coercive grew the Germans. They had to browbeat a few of the interpreters into service, mostly with threats of deportation, and many more industrialists and *entrepre-*

neurs. About half of all the contractors in Marseille began working for the Germans under duress, for they had their employees as well as themselves to worry about. They faced deportation of the work-force, or shutdown of the plant, or direct requisitioning with out-siders brought in if they refused to carry out the construction work or naval repairs or provide the raw materials which the Germans were demanding. Some contractors came forth voluntarily, like the two salvage experts who offered to recover material from the scuttled ships at the bottom of Toulon harbour, or the clerk who wrote to the *Kriegsmarine* offering to buy and sell scrap metal for them — and who never received a reply. Some slid into contracting work to the Germans — they were resuming pre-war trade, today selling locally what yesterday they had exported, or, more often, they were meeting German demands as mediated by the Préfecture or, more often still, they began dealing indirectly with the Germans through French trade associations and gradually cut out the middle-men. Recalcitrant or not, some contractors made handsome profits, for the Germans were willing to pay; but some saved the day for *réfractaires*, for they inflated their personel rolls with the names of employees who never set foot in the plant, thereby exempting them from the STO: they were better *résistants* in German service than out of it. The two salvage experts sold to the Germans while giving to the resistance, earning profits from the former and gratitude from the latter. Lurking around wherever there was active collaboration, a few hard or even villainous elements disfigured the comparatively peaceful practise of trading with the enemy. Dismissal of an emplo-yee for any reason now often meant the STO, revelation of his sus-pected communist sympathies worse. Sometimes, like the director of an armaments company requisitioned by the *Kriegsmarine*, the em-ployer was transmitting German threats rather than issuing his own; sometimes, like the outspokenly Pétainist employer who asked his employees to spend less time listening to the BBC and more time working, politics could masquerade as business. Economic colla-boration was as varied and ambiguous, the practice of patriots as well as profiteers, as official Pétainist collaboration: another answer, if one were needed, to the doctrinaires of class uniformity.[26]

With active collaborators on German payrolls, in German uni-forms, at German headquarters, the PPF became superfluous. Sabi-ani gave away what jobs he could; the party continued officially to monopolise the LVF. But Sabiani did not control many jobs and no one needed him or the party to join the LVF: the role of broker lost its usefulness. Besides, most people hated the PPF.[27] They avoided it like the plague. If a plumber had to work for the *Organisation Todt* or a factory owner for the *Kriegsmarine*, why incur the visibility and the ostracism of membership in the PPF unless it was absolutely necessary? The active collaborators went quietly to work; Sabiani went noisily to his meetings; and the PPF went steadily to ruin.

'It must be said that in Marseille as in the whole region one meets more and more French women accompanied by Germans...': the prefect Lemoine, in the summer of 1943, was only reporting the obvious. Amorous collaboration was on the increase. In the PPF and the Milice women were restricted to small subsidiary organisations — political and paramilitary formations were almost inaccessible to the women of the day; where there were jobs women could fill, at the *Splendide*, in the *Kriegsmarine*, among the volunteers in Germany, and where there were diversions they could enjoy, as at the Groupe Collaboration, their presence was stronger. But casual collaboration — independent, episodic, unorganised — was fully open to both sexes and its best known variety, *la collaboration horizontale*, was almost exclusively feminine.[28]

Its full extent is unknowable: the civil courts after the Liberation convicted 65 women in Marseille of *débauche*, of *relations suivies or amicales*, of *rapports intimes* with the Germans during the occupation, but such adventures were the least likely of all to come to formal trial. Their real number was undoubtedly much higher.

Most began at work. A professional *rapport* led to an amorous one: a secretary at a requisitioned company, a cook at the *Kriegsmarine* on the island of Frioul, a chambermaid in the requisitioned Hôtel de Madagascar, another chambermaid in the Fort St Nicholas — chambermaids alone made up about one fourth of the women involved. It could be a matter of necessity — 'I had relations with that man because I was hungry'; or of habit — a secretary, the *amie* of a Jew arrested in 1943, lost count of his German and French successors at the *Organisation Todt* in 1944. It could be a matter of trade: 'I did have relations with those soldiers...From the favours I bestowed on [them] I reaped food and small gifts'. Mostly it was a matter of affection, rarely as melodramatic as the woman who followed a *Wehrmacht* doctor all the way to Marseille after he had saved her from the ruins of bombedout Lorient, but it was sometimes strong enough to outlast the Liberation — strong enough for some to smuggle letters and parcels to their former German *amants* prisoners of war in the Fort St Nicholas. Sometimes ill-gotten gains — clothing taken during an arrest, even a requisitioned flat — found their way into the hands of the *collaboratrice*: then amorous collaboration became larcenous as well. Probably some of them obligingly adopted collaborationist rhetoric: Germanophilia was a prudent pose for women out to enjoy themselves with the men of the hour.[29]

Private and unofficial arrangements with the Germans could be practical as well as passionate — surreptitious services, privately rendered and privately rewarded. The Germans had official French buyers and *bureaux d'achat*, like the *Bureau Merle*; but they also bought informally themselves, rifling the black market for a stock of almonds, several hundred kilos of tomatoes, 262 sheep, 12,000 bottles of Armagnac, all the stuff of a twenty-month-long *festin*. They also solicited private and unofficial services — some *Wehrmacht* officers a laundress to take in washing, some *Kriegsmarine* officers a painter to lend them his piano.[30] For their French partners this was surely the most innocent collaboration, the point where the word lost its stigma if not its meaning.

The villains of casual private collaboration, unlike the Prefect's *femmes accompagnés d'allemands* or the occasional purveyors of goods and services, were the *corbeaux*, the denouncers. Malice was their only motive. First came zealots denouncing complete strangers, overheard uttering Gaullist, communist or anti-German views — there was often a reward for turning them in. Then came neighbours, landlords and tenants denouncing one another, then spouses and lovers, then employers and employees, finally business colleagues and associates. Ostensibly these turned each other in for listening to the BBC, for harbouring *réfractaires* or foreign Jews, for voicing Gaullist or communist views, for hiding arms, but nearly always a more prosaic grievance lay behind the loathing letter to the SD: a dispute over rent, a bad marriage, a rivalry at work, or simple jealousy:

> [The only reason] I was arrested was because my neighbours in the quartier had ill-feelings towards me because I had the nicest vegetable garden.

The letters did not always reach their destination — Vichy's *contrôle postal* intercepted them, or the senders, anonymous or not, withdrew them in a timely gesture of remorse — and even if they did their recipients did not always act on them. Sometimes the denunctiation was spurious — no arms were unearthed, no *réfractaires* were found. But sometimes it bore fruit. Once a 21-year-old barmaid turned her father's bar in the northern suburb of *la Valentine* into a brothel for German soldiers and then denounced him to the SD when he reproached her for doing so. He was deported and never returned.[31] It was an act as villainous as any performed by Palmieri's men: some of the *corbeaux* of the occupation could hold their own with the worst of the PPF.

And it was among them that the PPF made its inroads into the ranks of the casual and occasional collaborators. It had no hold over the anarchy of the Franco-German black market: it was not a trading association. It had no hold over *la collaboration horizontale*, either: it was not a social club. But it did have a hold over the *corbeaux*: it had

more of them in its own ranks than any other collaborationist organisation and it relied on them in the population at large. Even the
few women who joined to meet Germans were often the sort who
had made a clean break and might think nothing of denouncing rivals
or relations. The barmaid who sent her father to his doom was encouraged by an older and looser woman who had joined the PPF 'to
make good on the Germans':

> Your father wasn't nice [pas chic] to speak that way, we ought to
> go to the rue Paradis.

And an illiterate Algerian woman, a former prostitute, joined the
PPF and promptly threatened to denounce anyone in the neighbourhood who annoyed her. The practise went with the premises. Men
who turned in Jews or *réfractaires* for money also turned in neighbours for vengeance — no qualms of conscience ever troubled the
unemployed Algerian, a regular at the SD, the PPF, and the Hôtel
Californie, who had his brother-in-law deported after quarreling
with him. *Corbeaux* or not, the party's bounty-hunters lived off the
city's informers — Palmieri's men their disclosures about Jews,
Battesti's about *réfractaires*, Delage's about *résistants*. Palmieri relied
on his army of professional *indicateurs* but also banked on the unknown tipster, the hotel-keeper who brought four of Palmieri's men
to the scene when he suddenly denounced his neighbour for harbouring former Jewish guests of his. They also turned honourable men
into informers — they extracted the name of a Jewish employee from
a stubborn accountant only by taking him to the rue Paradis and by
applying pressure on his wife.[32] The PPF was a constant provocation
to turn on one's neighbour or compatriot, the informers' benefactor
and thus the patron of the worst elements of unorganised and organised collaboration alike.

Very few *marseillais* collaborated during the war — less than one per
cent of the total population.[33] Those who did made up a tiny *potpourri* of styles and mentalities, a microcosm of the wider world with
the social, sexual, and ethnic proportions shaken up or distorted.
There were more unemployed, more men, fewer Italians — but glo-
bal indices like these are misleading if not meaningless. The heavy
taxonomy of the census is no answer to the who or the why of collaboration — repeatedly, unmistakably, people from similar backgrounds became dissimilar collaborators. Different opportunities
awaited them and different accidents befell them, so that genres of
collaboration developed, each a different pastiche: none represented a
class, none monopolised a mentality. But each developed its distinctive blend, made of the language of its leaders, the circumstances

of its creation, and the motives and backgrounds of its adherents: and as the brief and unprecedented episode ended, each genre had produced its own travesty.

Pétainist collaboration, initially made of the mythology of Vichy, the demise of the Third Republic, and the good intentions of some adherents, produced the soldiers of the Milice; *salon* collaboration, initially the product of the theories of Franco-German understanding, the naïveté and frivolity of its members, and the smiles of the *occupant*, produced the strutting and window-smashing youth of the Jeunesses de l'Europe Nouvelle; and active collaboration, made of the material needs of the *occupant* and the opportunism of the *occupés*, produced the parasites of the PPF.

Each genre had threatened to go out of control from the start: each had harboured hard elements, criminals or mercenaries or zealots, the predators of the occupation. The inexorable logic of collaboration brought them to the fore, so that by 1944 they formed a kind of counter-society, with the parasites of the PPF a violent underclass.

Palmieri's and Battesti's and Delage's men were marginal to society but central to the party. They were the active minority giving the party its character: their prosperity was the city's misfortune. It was a national pattern, for elsewhere in France too the PPF had become the party of the parasite. By 1943 and 1944 *marginaux* and *déclassés* were providing the hard core of its membership in the Nord, the Alpes-Maritimes, the Gironde, probably Paris as well. Not everywhere: in Dijon the party was predominantly *bourgeois*. But the PPF was probably in general more marginal, younger, more violent and in every way less respectable than Déat's Reassemblement National Populaire.[34] Marginality is ancillary if not identical to parasitism, and marginality was what the police and the prefects noticed in the party's bounty-hunters, the Groupes d'Action de Justice Sociale. In Montluçon, the *procureur* complained, 'these would-be groups of social justice' were really groups of convicted criminals, armed and often drunk as they went about their searches. In the Eure their 30 members arrested at will, led by a convicted swindler. In the Indre-et-Loire, the Prefect said,

> Some of the agents... of the PPF have behaved like veritable gangsters and have not hesitated, under the pretence of maintaining order and policing the population, to carry out veritable gangster operations for their own profit.

— the party *permanence* was the scene of violent quarrels as its resident thieves fell out with one another. Even the party's unrepentant apologist later recognised it: the members of the *Groupes d'Action* were, he said, 'thieves, swindlers, maquisards, diverse deserters'.[35]

They and their party were as much an affront to Vichy as to the re-

sistance. In Paris they declared themselves 'absolutely anti-govern-
mental', in Brittany they were behind the 'Roc Breton' separatist
movement, in the Vosges they threatened the police and ignored the
Prefect. They were an affront to the other collaborators as well.
Darnand, as *Ministre du maintien de l'ordre*, decried their licence and
their arrogance. In the Indre-et-Loire the local Groupe Collaboration
was 'literally floored' by them. Above all they were an affront to
the public. Everywhere it saw them as informers and *mouchards*, in
Montluçon as 'a branch of the German police run by the French
against the French', in the Var as potential soldiers of the *Wehrmacht*
if the Allies landed.[36]

But soldiering was not in the nature of the PPF, whatever the
hallucinations of its ideologues. When the Allies did land in the Var
on 15 August, Sabiani and his remaining followers were hastily
piling into cars and lorries, and when Monsabert's troops reached
Marseille four days later their convoy was heading up the Rhône
valley in the general direction of the German border.

CHAPTER 9

To Sigmaringen and Back,
August 1944 – September 1956

During his last, fantasy-filled summer in Marseille Sabiani was still dreaming of victories. He was also warning of massacres. In July he told people that public order was collapsing and that the PPF, far from being a 'valet' of the Germans, was the only solution. At the end of the month he organised a meeting in spite of Vichy's interdictions — Vichy had long since ceased to matter — and told the 150 members who bothered to turn up that the Germans would soon turn the tide with new weapons, with the V1, V2, 'all the way to the V9'. He told them that the PPF would soon take power, that members who missed the next meeting would go to the salt mines instead. Two weeks later, on 14 August, he sent word that the resistance would shoot anyone unlucky enough to fall into its hands and that everyone should prepare to leave the next day.[1]

He may have been bluffing, trying to mobilise his remaining followers with his remaining weapons, first hope and then fear. But probably he was sincere. Doriot, for one, believed in the new weapons and no one, in the civil war then reaching its climax, could shrug off the spectre of a bloodbath. Sabiani, as he prepared to leave Marseille, thought he was withdrawing to regroup and return on the crest of events to come.

Few followed him — certainly no more than 100 members, possibly no more than 50, and their families.[2] They had believed him: they were afraid of reprisals, and they were the members who had the most to fear. Many had worked for the Hôtel Californie, for 'Albert' and the Abwehr or Delage and the SD; some, party officials or propagandists, had been too visible for post-Liberation comfort; and a few were Sabiani's last remaining *dependenti, parenti i amici*, an old uncle for whom he had found work, a young nephew for whom he had found shelter. The others, perhaps about 750, stayed behind.[3]

The Milice, as always better organised, set up the convoy; it provided the trucks and the drivers, separated the women and children from the men, and turned a *sauve-qui-peut* into an orderly *exode*. More of its members, perhaps as many as 200, went along, and like the members of the PPF they had no idea where they were going. They were told first that they were going to Avignon, which they did; then they went on to Lyon, with more difficulty: there was bombing and strafing from the allies in the air and attacks from the *maquis* on the ground. Families were separated. Finally, at the end of the month, the convoy came to a halt in Nancy.[4] There compromised collaborators from elsewhere in France rejoined their *provençal* colleagues, and there the Milice and the PPF parted company.

The PPF moved on to Neustadt, across the Rhine. Doriot had sent word that his old friend there, the *Gauleiter* Josef Bürckel, the force behind the greater 'Westmark' and the eviction of 70,000 French citizens from Lorraine, was offering accommodation. So it was that in September the party's 5,000 nomads moved into the hotels, villas and official buildings of Neustadt and the surrounding vineyards, and so it was that Sabiani, his wife, and his daughters Agathe and Dora moved into a house with Doriot, his wife, mother and two daughters. It was not the happiest *ménage*: Doriot disgusted Agathe. He drank and womanised, she felt, while they desperately tried to save the party.[5] The exiles began to bicker.

Sabiani, in any event, did not stay long in Neustadt. At the end of September Doriot rejected a German proposal to move the party to Sigmaringen — he wanted nothing to do with Vichy's government-in-exile — and instead dispatched Marcel Marschall and Sabiani there as his official representatives. The bulk of the party's administration moved to Mainau, on Lake Constance; Sabiani and Marschall moved to Mengen, outside Sigmaringen, setting up an office in a converted shop, and Sabiani, his family and his faithful chauffeur Géronimi moved into the Hotel Bayer, where they stayed until the very end.[6]

The *marseillais* who had followed them to Germany began to scatter. They found jobs, often with Sabiani's help, in factories and *centres d'accueil*; they misbehaved, said 'dirty kraut [sale boche]', fought with one another, and went to prison; they worked for the party, if they could, putting out propaganda in Mainau and looking for members everywhere else, among the French all over Germany. But the largest contingent, if the trials of survivors are any indication, went to the party's espionage and sabotage schools.[7]

Even before the party had crossed the Rhine, Doriot, with some support from the SD, was setting up a subversive network of agents and *saboteurs* to operate behind allied lines. By the middle of September fifteen of them may already have been at work and by the beginning of November another hundred were in training at the new technical school near Wiesbaden — 82 men and 27 women, all volunteers from the party or French recruits from work or prisoner-of-war camps. There, in a deserted chateau, they began learning about weapons, radio, sabotage, codes and covert work, the basics of subversion. Nearby in 'secondary schools' they began to specialize, in intelligence gathering at Wiesbaden, in sabotage at Reutlingen, in counter-espionage at Usingen — where the director was none other than Roger Peter *alias* René Page, the party official who had worked at *l'Emancipation Nationale* in Marseille, run the agents in St-Jérôme and Les Trois Lucs, and called the French a nation of prostitutes.[8]

Problems developed almost at once. A German unit took over most of the chateau at Wiesbaden for its own use, turning the agents into refugees until they eventually found new premises in Lindau; the SD raided the school at Reutlingen as it had the PPF network in France, hiving off trainees and provoking mass desertions; Doriot quarrelled furiously with Nosek of the SD throughout the winter. By March only 30 were at all suitable for clandestine work. The Abwehr transplanted 25 men from Reutlingen to Italy, planning to send them on to southern France, but the project went awry after quarrels with Barthélémy, the PPF delegate to Mussolini's rump republic of Salò, and some of them deserted and joined the Italian partisans. In the end no more than 15 graduates of the PPF academies in Germany were dropped into France, where they were promptly arrested. In late April, with the Russians in Berlin, the others were given money and new identities as employees of the *Organisation Todt* and told to return to France on their own.[9]

Sabiani probably had little to do with the schools. He may have had a hand in the Italian adventure, for a PPF-trained agent arrested in Italy in March claimed that he was en route to Provence to spread anti-communist propaganda there at Sabiani's behest. He may have sent one or two candidates to Wiesbaden or Reutlingen. But mostly he tried feverishly to breathe new life into the phantom party — he looked after old members and signed up new ones among the wandering French exiles, so that his life in Mengen became a sad mockery of his life in Marseille. Céline caught it in *D'un château l'autre*:

> One place that was picturesque was Sabiani's PPF headquarters... the PPF, the biggest of the 'parties of the future'... Sabiani ran this Party office... it had two showcases... both full of sick people in the worst possible shape... Sabiani himself stayed in the back room... he took applications, handed out membership cards, which he signed and stamped... Sabiani drew a big crowd... if

he'd dished out something to eat in addition...he'd have recruited the whole town, including the Boches...'

Even at the end, Barthélémy recalled, after Doriot's death late in February on the road from Mainau to Mengen, 'Sabiani was dreaming of combats'. He was running what was left of the party with a Marschall '[who] spoke with the voice of wisdom' and another member of the *bureau politique*, Christian Lesueur, but by the end of April, as the American units closed in, the 'combats' were over. Sabiani, his family, and Géronimi made their harrowing way south across the Austrian Alps along with other survivors, bombed and strafed all along the way; in Innsbruck some gave up and turned back to await their American captors, but others, including Sabiani and family, kept on until Milan. There the convoy dispersed. Some were arrested, some gave themselves up; Madame Sabiani and Agathe found friends and slowly began trying to make a living, Géronimi struck out on his own, and Sabiani went into hiding. His public life was over.[11]

From Nancy the Milice had also moved on, but it had turned south towards Ulm, where it set up the first of several camps. In all there were about 10,000 *miliciens*, including their families, in Germany and soon, like the members of the PPF, they began to go their separate ways. The *miliciens* from Marseille as from everywhere split up — about a fourth stayed in camps cooking, cleaning, collecting firewood or doing nothing at all. Another fourth found jobs in German factories or on German farms; others — perhaps a tenth — went to Sigmaringen to join Pétain's remaining retinue, to work as orderlies or members of his guard until it was dissolved in January 1945. In the spring they all fell into French or American hands — some were sent to Italy in March, where they were arrested in April, some surrendered in Germany, some wandered back on their own.[12]

They were luckier than their remaining *marseillais* colleagues, the remaining fifth or so who had gone east to Wildflecken to join the *Division Charlemagne*. Thrown together in the autumn of 1944 from about 2,000 *miliciens*, 2,500 surviving LVF and Waffen-SS volunteers, and 3,500 French civilians from the *Légion Speer* or the German merchant marine, the *Division Charlemagne* was the last chapter in military collaboration. The Germans created it, ending the story that the ultras had opened in the summer of 1941. It was a final tribute to the tangle of even one variety of collaboration, for billeted together at Wildflecken were the mutinous mercenaries of the LVF:

...They had fought the war in their own way, as adventurous, feuding Frenchmen. Their indiscipline was the butt of much banter [avait fait jaser] in the headquarters...

and their counterparts from the Stürmbrigade:

> ...the survivors of the Assault Brigade...had truly acquired the German mentality, used only German orders, German ranks, German formulas...

and the *miliciens* who arrived singing *Sambre et Meuse* and *la Madelon*:

> ...at a *chasseur*'s step — Darnand came from the *chasseurs* [alpins] — carrying arms and kit, beret over the ear, decorations spread over their kaki or navy blue uniforms. They were truly very anti-German in spirit, and were not afraid to show it.[13]

About a quarter of the *marseillais* in the *Division Charlemagne* came from the *Milice*, the rest from the LVF or the *sturmbrigade*. Only a few came from the workers in Germany. But many, wherever they came from, were tattoed with the sign of their blood group, made to swear an oath of allegiance to Hitler, and sent in late January, undermanned and underarmed, to the front in East Prussia.

There they were overwhelmed by the Soviet army. At the end of February they were driven back from Hammerstein and encircled at Kärlin and again at Neu Stettin on the Hel peninsula. Some broke out and made their way back along the Baltic coast, to be taken later by the Americans. Some had deserted earlier, exchanging their SS-uniforms for civilian clothing and passing themselves off to Russians or Americans as escaped STO-deportees — one *marseillais* erased his tatto with a hot iron to make good his new identity. The others were killed or taken prisoner. The lucky ones left behind at Wildflecken survived. They had fallen ill or failed the courses or gone to prison for indiscipline, and now they melted away — one *marseillais* rejoined the Milice and was later taken by the Americans, another went to Italy, a third returned to France with false papers. By the time the Russians reached Wildflecken there was no one left.[15]

While military collaboration was coming to an end in the Pomeranian snow, the French volunteer workers still in Germany began leaving bombed out workplaces or presenting themselves on the spot to the advancing allied armies. Some barely survived — a baker from St Rémy de Provence wandered in the streets of Bremen for a month after his bakery was destroyed in October 1944, then shipped out on the armed merchant vessel *Weserstein* carrying food supplies between Bremen and Dantzig until it too was destroyed in Pillau harbour in April 1945, then worked on the liner-turned-hospital ship *Europa* and was still on board baking bread when the Americans arrived in Bremen two months later. Some may have wanted to stay — a baker in Mehringen who had left in Laval's *relève* of September 1942 had met and married a German girl there. Like the others he was repatriated by Allied units who often took the French volunteers for unwilling conscripts.[16]

But at home there were witnesses, pay slips and enlistment froms at the *Office de Placement*, and when the volunteers returned they found themselves in court side by side with others facing far more charges.

Back in Marseille the FFI had begun fighting on 21 August, de Monsabert and units of his Third Algerian Infantry Division had bypassed Toulon and come down the Canebière on the 23rd, and, after some fighting, General-lieutenant Schaeffer and his 24th German infantry division had surrendered on the 28th.[17]

In Sabiani's fourth canton, where it had all started twenty-five years before, new foreign employers and new French politicians began courting the same old inhabitants. People had taken to the cellars during the fighting, cut off and without food as *miliciens* and some PPF joined the German resistance and fired indiscriminately from the rooftops of la Joliette. Then people returned home, held up for a while by some Moroccan soldiers inexplicably barring the way. In September an American manpower agency opened its doors in the rue de la République at one end of the canton, calling for 15,000 workers of all kinds, and in the mined and ruined docks and *bassins* at the other end American military engineers were offering 250 francs a day and free food to all willing hands. The locals were only too delighted — they emerged in droves. They were more suspicious of the politicians. For a time they refrained from politics and resisted the new waves of propagandists — they were hesitant to commit themselves, the police noted, 'before the government's position is clearly defined'. But some turned on recent symbols with a vengeance. At the rue Fauchier FFI ransacked Sabiani's flat and a crowd tore down François' commemorative plaque with paving stones, uttering cries of hatred.[18]

Along with François' plaque the last traces of the PPF vanished within days of the Liberation. Party officials had already destroyed most of the archives. Only a truncated membership list survived, thanks to the *résistant* gangster Barthélémy 'Mémé' Guerini and some of his friends, who went into the party's offices on the Canebière in the chaos of the night of the fourteenth and retrieved it. They turned it over to the police, but not before Guerini had made a copy for himself. On the first of September the *Jeune Garde Socialiste* moved into the building and put up a sign: 'New management. Enlistment here of FFI volunteers against the criminal Simon Sabiani'. A week later they put up a new sign: 'Premises disinfected'. FFI and FTP arrested known or suspected members, whatever their actions during the occupation, and killed some and brutalised others. A few PPF diehards were still exchanging fire with the FFI around the Boulevard Oddo in the middle of September, and in October gunmen in a passing car on the Boulevard National suddenly fired on passers-by. They were said to be 'PPF', but no one really knew, and no one ever found out, for the car sped away down the *boulevard* and disappeared into the fog of post-Liberation rumour and *on-dit*.[19]

People said that *Milice* and PPF *maquis* were gathering around Mont Ventoux, led by 'scarface' Jeannot Carbone [Jeannot le balafré], and they repeated other canards, but the victors now began to unnerve them as much as the losers. They took fright at the swift descent from liberation into anarchy, a sentiment tacitly shared by the police:

> Many people are saying that the phony police [*faux policiers*] are starting to operate again, this time with new titles, and that searches and arbitrary arrests go on for the most part under false pretexts.

Personal vengeance was running riot:

> ...anyone with personal enemies in the *comités d'épuration* feels threatened

and the FTP and the FFI were rapidly losing their liberators' halos:

> ...people are likening their procedures to those of the Milice or the PPF...threatening bearing...reckless way of handling their weapons; requisitions, arrests, searches...many people from all social levels believe that we are in a fully-fledged civil war.

Unidentified bodies were beginning to appear, in the Jarret, in St Julien, in the St Pierre cemetery, left there by groups of FFI. A police inspector was murdered by former prisoners in FFI uniforms. Fire mysteriously destroyed most of the police archives in the rue de l'Evêché. People wanted it stopped.[20]

So they were relieved when the special *Cours de Justice* were established. Some Communists disapproved — they would have preferred summary judgements, summarily carried out — but most others welcomed the opening trial as an end to lawlessness. It took place on 11 September: in the dock was an Armenian who had joined the PPF to keep his bar open and had then gone to work for the Hôtel Californie. He had arrested at least one *réfractaire*. He was sentenced to death and shot the next day.[21]

It was a harbinger of trials to come. Over the next two years the civil courts in Marseille let off two-thirds of the members of the PPF with *non-lieux* or acquittals or mere loss of their civic rights: they were the members of the party's passive majority. But when the courts were severe their target was often a member of the party's active and violent minority. They sentenced 166 to death, of whom 55 were members of the PPF; 67 to life imprisonment, with or without hard labour, of whom 16 were members of the PPF; and 115 to prolonged prison sentences of ten to 25 years, of whom 22 were members of the PPF. The others were likely to be *miliciens*. Between the two of them they absorbed the most punishment.[22]

Sabiani's oldest friends fared unevenly. If they had stayed away from the PPF they had little to fear. The courts investigated Gustave Chipponi, his schoolmate from the *lycée de Bastia* and protégé of the 1920s, and Georges Ribot, the *maire fainéant* of *Sabianisme* and Marseille-Chicago, and left them alone. Carbone had been killed in a train crash in 1943 and Spirito was in Spain or in North America. But the journalist Philibert Géraud, who had left the party in 1941, was arrested in Paris in November 1944, spent ten years in prison and died in misery. And Lucien Mangiavacca, his early partner in the *maison de transit* and long-standing protégé, had remained active in the PPF and, worse, had allowed Sabiani to find him a job writing summaries of the daily press in the SD villa at the end of the rue Paradis. He was sentenced to death: others who had done more at the rue Paradis got off far more lightly: he was clearly paying for his patron. He was executed on 30 November 1944, surrounded by a jeering mob.[23]

Palmieri and his brother Alfred joined the exodus to Germany and went through the Reutlingen sabotage school. They were among the few ever sent on a mission. Like the others it was a fiasco — they were to sabotage a pipeline and were dropped into Burgundy along with three SS agents, who promptly disappeared with the supplies, leaving them to be arrested rather ignominiously by local *gendarmes*. Alfred took poison; Charles promptly offered his services to French military security. They considered his offer but soon thought better of it and handed him over to the judicial authorities. He was executed in 1946 after telling all. Of the three Palmieri brothers only Victor, *le bossu*, survived: his death sentence was commuted to hard labour for life.[24]

'Albert' of the Abwehr was last seen heading out of town on 15 August, behind the wheel of a black Ford cabriolet with the fair 'English' woman at his side. At the rear was an oversized petrol tank: clearly he was planning a long drive. He was never seen again. The owner of the Hôtel de Rome in the Cours St Louis complained to DST agents that he had left without paying his bill.[25]

Dunker-Delage was the only German in the Marseille SD to face the firing squad. His superior, Rolf Mühler, was sent to Poland in

7   Shells landing near Notre Dame de la Garde, August 1944

May 1944 and was arrested later in Ratisbon by the Americans, who imprisoned him in Dachau. In 1954 he was extradited to Marseille for trial, sentenced to 20 years hard labour and soon sent back to Germany, where he ended his days as a drinks wholesaler in Mannheim. But Delage was arrested in Paris in May 1945, tried in Marseille by a military court in 1947, and sentenced to death. He cheated the executioners for three years with appeals and hints and staggered revelations, some of them fabricated, about his French colleagues, but he was finally executed in 1950 and died shouting in his fluent French 'Vive l'Allemagne! A mort la France!'[26]

Sabiani's wife and daughters returned courageously to Marseille in 1947 and began rebuilding their lives. The faithful Géronimi, after striking out in the *sauve-qui-peut* of northern Italy in the spring of 1945, was arrested by the Italians near lake Como, escaped, went south to Naples where he was arrested by the Americans, escaped again, stole bicycles and cars for a while, went to Rome and Civita Vecchia, stowed away on a ship for Sardinia and then again on a ship for Corsica, hid out in the Corsican hills for two years, went to Marseille hoping to catch a ship for Argentina, was noticed, denounced, arrested, tried — and acquitted for services rendered to the resistance. Géronimi was a loyal man: he helped his friends which ever side they were on. He died in Marseille in 1984.[27]

Sabiani was condemned to death *in absentia*. He was in Italy at the time. Within days of the Liberation Marseille was rife with rumours about him — he had been arrested at the Swiss border carrying 67 million Francs, he had met his remaining devotees secretly in Marseille, he had planted agents in the *comités d'épuration* to foil their investigations. He had been sighted, *France-Soir* reported: 'Doriot's former right-hand man strolls along the Ligurian coast [making plans] to take to the Corsican hinterland [maquis]". In fact Sabiani hid in Italy as long as he could, until the beginning of 1947 when searches forced him all the way to Buenos Aires. He stayed there for seven years. As before he was penniless and as before he gave himself up to the demon of politics. He sold watches on the quays and harangued French sailors there, particularly if they belonged to the CGT, about the communist menace. He joined Peronist demonstrations. He even sent a recorded speech to help his son-in-law rally the old *Sabianistes* in 1953 and reclaim the fourth canton from the Communists. The effort failed, predictably, but for a minute Sabiani held sway again, across the continents, and he must have enjoyed it.[25]

The following year he moved to Barcelona and tried running an import-export business, as he had nearly forty years before in Marseille. There was a small French colony there, including some *marseillais* and former collaborators — they knew one another and often gathered in the *Bar Maurice* and the *Bar Baleares* in the Chinese quarter. Carbone's younger brother Jeannot was there; so was Maurice-Yvan Sicard, who had put out *l'Emancipation Nationale* in Marseille during the war; and as always Sabiani made new friends. Above all Barcelona was close to Marseille, so that friends and relatives could take the bus down the coast at weekends to call on him. It was close to Corsica, too, so that he could pay a clandestine last visit in 1955 — he arrived too late — to see his dying mother.[29]

When he died in Barcelona the following year under the assumed name of Pedro Multedo the French Consulate was nervous about letting the family bring him back, but it soon relented after friends he had made in Barcelona intervened, and in the old fourth canton a small crowd appeared on the *quai*, there to see Simon off with flowers and good wishes as the ship taking him back to Casamaccioli pulled away from the docks of la Joliette. *Sabianisme* had survived.[30]

CONCLUSION

Virtue Gone Mad

At first glance the story of *Sabianisme* is straightforward. It is the story of a Corsican machine politician who made a mistake. Nothing in his background or personality pre-ordained his disastrous choice in 1940: his career could have followed any number of different paths but he simply took a wrong turning and kept going resolutely until the end. But the more perplexing questions remain: why? And what was the *Sabianisme* that went astray with him?

It was difficult enough to place in its own day. At best it was a kind of counterfeit fascism before the war, even anomalous within the national PPF, whose leaders called it 'the autonomous republic of Marseille'; a rootless party marking time at the beginning of the war, and hardly a party at all at the end. After the war a few *Sabianistes* appeared in some of the ephemeral extreme right-wing organisations — Jeune Nation and the Parti National Français.[1]

The electorate of the Front National today — 'popular, battered by the rigours of the recession, or conservative, driven towards the extreme right by a complete rejection of the left'[2] — may bear some superficial resemblance to the supporters of the PPF before the war, and its ideology, identifying now Marxism, now Islam, as the historical threat to Western civilisation, may bear an equally superficial resemblance to the free-floating conspiracy-mania of the PPF. But Sabiani was not hostile to immigrants, who were as numerous in Marseille in his day as they are today; and *Sabianisme*, whatever the ideology of the PPF, was as much the ancestor of *Defferrisme* as of the local Front National, for Defferre's patronage was Sabiani's patronage, less blatant, less crude, but more extensive.[3] Historically *Sabianisme* is a dark horse.

Throughout his political career Sabiani was an outsider. He belonged to the small, rough, inarticulate politics of the clientèle; he

La 'lumière' politique

8 The three faces of Simon Sabiani

never outgrew the camaraderie of the trenches; he was at home among small groups of men. Mass democratic politics never had any room for him, and he began and ended his career calling for their abolition: he began by preaching Soviet Communism and ended preaching German Nazism. In between, excluded from the new politics of the day, he demanded that the régime be swept away, then joined a semi-fascist fringe party funded partly from abroad. In 1940 he thought his chance had come again. Each chapter in his mercurial career is a study in maladjustment.

He was a political nomad who made many friends but never found a home. There was thus a compensatory and obsessive side to his patriotism, a night-and-day harping on the theme which convinced his daughter that *la patrie* came before her or the rest of the family.[4] Communism was the complementary obsession, the demon threatening him and the country alike. He began belabouring the theme while under threat in the mid-1930s and never stopped — he confounded his own fate with that of the country, and the more marginal grew his position the more alarmist became his patriotism, a chiliasm of the outsider.

He was only at home with his followers and dependents, whoever they were and wherever he found them. He was not very discriminating: he did not mind who they were as long as they were loyal to him. This was his nemesis. It helped him in the early 1930s but destroyed him in 1943 and 1944. He was loyal to a fault — his proclamation of friendship for Carbone and Spirito in 1934 did him no good and his acceptance, even troubled, of the criminals who took over the party in 1943 and 1944 destroyed his reputation for ever. From the first days of his careers to the last, he took whoever came his way — 'I take what I find' — and the patron of the poor was also the apologist of the Hôtel Californie.

During his career he tried repeatedly to turn his clients into militants. But they were outsiders too — increasingly so as the years went by. The apolitical clan of Marseille-Chicago became progressively more incongruous; the PPF came close to rejecting the whole Republican system both before and during the war and ended its days as a rabble of social outcasts. Along the way Sabiani tried mobilizing them with every theme in the ideological lexicon. At first, during the 1920s and still during the heyday of *Sabianisme* in the early 1930s, he rallied lower and lower middle class followers and spoke of class. Then, with the PPF, he rallied some *bourgeois* elements and spoke of nation; finally, a collaborator out of control, he swept up the human refuse of the city and spoke briefly of race. There is a rough convergence between each of the mobilising myths of twentieth century politics and each successive family of *Sabianistes*. But even more obvious is the repeated failure to make the convergence work, the unremitting quest for a coherent political family, the unending cycle of ambition and frustration. *Sabianisme* in its PPF garb finally failed as a modern party because it lacked the essential fit between core ideology and core membership which sustained the other parties of left and right. The only lasting core *Sabianisme* could boast was a personal one, and it lasted until his death, but friends never made a modern party. Through all the social transformations and ideological somersaults the pattern emerges: Sabiani the ambitious outsider trying to politicise apolitical dependents. He collected but never mastered his followers. The people flocking to the rue Fauchier in the 1930s were no more interested in politics than Palmieri's and Battesti's bounty-hunters ten years later. In their very different ways both were political marginals, and collaboration was the last expression of a *Sabianisme* which could find no political home.

That poorly integrated groups are unguided missiles, that society ignores them at its own risk and peril, that they will sooner or later find a leader and that under certain circumstances they can do a great deal of damage — the story of Sabiani's following is a study in the hazards of marginality. The story of Sabiani's person is a study in the hazards of conventional virtues. More than a reminder that virtuous men can preside over vicious doings, his life is a warning that traditional virtues like courage or loyalty or generosity — his virtues — can be positive menaces if harnessed to the wrong cause. They can go mad — and in Sabiani's case they did.

APPENDIX I

The Social and Ethnic Composition of the Fourth and Fifth Cantons

The tables on the following pages give the social and ethnic composition of the adult male population (ie the voting population) of Sabiani's legislative constituency — all of the fourth and part of the fifth canton. They are based on a person-by-person count of the *listes nominatives* in the 1936 census. The professional classifications, based generally on the *Code des Catégories socio-professionnelles* (6th edn., 1977) published by the *Institut National de al Statistique et des Etudes économiques*, are given below.

(LOWER OR WORKING CLASS)

1. Unskilled workers: Journaliers, manoeuvres, ouvriers, mineurs.

2. Skilled workers: Chaudronnier, ferblantier, soudeur, fondeur, mouleur, zingeur, décupeur, étameur, ajusteur, monteur, perforeur, forgeron, charron, machiniste-opérateur, métallurgiste, mécanicien, carrossier, charbonnier, ramoneur, peintre, imprimeur, typographe, camionneur, tuyauteur, grutier.

3. Domestic and service personnel: Domestique, concierge, ménagére, lingère, chauffeur, cuisinier, serveur, barman, jardinier, coursier, commis, vendeur, magasinier, chargeur, gardien, surveillant, charretier, caviste, livreur.

4. Dockers, sailors: Docker, marin, navigateur, pêcheur.

LOWER MIDDLE CLASS

5. Artisans: Electricien, menuisier, ébéniste, serrurier, charpentier, plombier, maçon, terrassier, tuilier, platrier, armurier, miroitier, étalagiste, chiffonier, cordonnier, tailleur, couturier, tapissier, matelassier, cimentier, tanneur, graveur, boiseur, modeleur, chapelier, chemisier.

6. Shopkeepers: Liquoriste, coiffeur, boucher, charcutier, épicier, boulanger, patissier, savonnier, brocanteur, restaurateur, tenacier de bar, hôtelier, limonadier, mercier, confiseur, laitier, poissonier, papetier.

7. Office workers: Employé, vendeur, téléphoniste, caissier, contrôleur.

8. Fonctionnaires: Sapeur pompier, gardien de la paix, employé municipal (octroi, voirie, canal, pompes funèbres, etc.); douanier, fonctionnaire d'état (PTT, Préfecture, and PLM/cheminot); employé des eaux, tramways, gaz ou électricité (monopoles).

UPPER MIDDLE CLASS

9. Liberal professions: Avocat, médecin, dentiste, journaliste, publiciste, enseignant, pharmacien, ingénieur, vétérinaire.

10. Commerce and industry: Gros commerçant, négociant, entrepreneur, transitaire, bijoutier, horloger.

11. Senior employees: Cadre, contremaître, chef d'équipe, comptable, représentant, assureur, courtier, interprète.

OTHER

12. Unemployed: includes retirees (the census rarely distinguishes).

13. Other: artiste, clergé, soldat, cultivateur, apprenti.

Fourth Canton

Bureau de vote N°28 (Rue d'Aix — Place Jules Guesde — Boulevard de la Paix — Boulevard Dugommier — rue des Convalescents; total population: 12616).

Class	Occupation	A*	B	C	D	E	F	G	H	I	Total
Lower	1. Unskilled workers	217	31	26	230	2	64	239	116	31	956
		22%†	3%	3%	24%	2%	7%	25%	12%	3%	(23%)
	2. Skilled workers	93	9	14	20	2	28	48	3	15	232
		40%	4%	6%	9%	1%	12%	21%	1%	6%	(6%)
	3. Service personnel	84	9	17	16	0	29	68	11	13	247
		34%	4%	7%	6%	0%	12%	27%	4%	5%	(6%)
	4. Dockers, sailors	42	34	7	11	2	5	43	10	26	180
		23%	19%	4%	6%	1%	3%	24%	5%	14%	(4%)
Subtotals		436	83	64	277	6	126	398	140	85	1615
		27%	5%	4%	17%	4%	8%	24%	9%	5%	(38%)
Lower middle	5. Artisans	176	8	29	218	5	30	105	6	30	607
		29%	1%	5%	36%	1%	5%	17%	1%	5%	(14%)
	6. Shopkeepers	121	21	28	97	14	37	88	11	19	436
		28%	5%	6%	22%	3%	8%	20%	3%	4%	(10%)
	7. Office workers	226	15	6	12	3	59	163	13	8	505
		44%	3%	1%	2%	1%	12%	32%	3%	2%	(12%)
	8. Fonctionnaires	29	9	1	0	0	14	52	0	1	106
		27%	8%	1%	0%	0%	13%	49%	0%	1%	(3%)
Subtotals		552	53	64	327	22	140	408	30	58	1654
		33%	3%	4%	20%	1%	8%	25%	2%	4%	(39%)
Upper middle	9. Liberal professions	14	1	1	4	0	4	17	1	5	47
		30%	2%	2%	9%	0%	9%	36%	2%	10%	(1%)
	10. Commerce and industry	27	0	2	4	0	7	15	1	0	56
		48%	0%	4%	7%	0%	12%	27%	12%	0%	(1%)
	11. Senior office workers	63	2	7	8	0	18	42	2	7	149
		42%	1%	5%	5%	0%	12%	28%	1%	5%	(4%)
Subtotals		104	3	10	16	0	29	74	4	12	252
		41%	1%	4%	6%	0	11%	29%	2%	5%	(6%)
	12. Unemployed	244	17	21	153	3	43	140	13	49	683
		36%	2%	4%	22%	4%	6%	20%	2%	7%	(16%)
	13. Other	10	2	3	5	0	5	10	2	1	38
		26%	5%	8%	13%	0%	13%	26%	5%	3%	(1%)
Totals		1346	158	162	778	31	343	1030	189	205	4242
		32%	4%	4%	18%	1%	8%	24%	4%	5%	(100%)

* A = born in Marseille, B = Corsica, C = Italy, D = Turkey = Armenian. E = Spain, F = Provence, G = elsewhere in France, H = Mahgreb, I = all other.
† The percentage in columns A thorugh I is the percentage of the given occupation born in the given place; that in the 'total' column, is the occupation's percentage of the total male population. (Total percentages occasionally come to 99 or 100 because of rounding off of constituent).

Fourth Canton

Bureau de vote N°26 (rue d'Aix — rue des Présentines — rue des Chapeliers — rue des Grands Carmes — rue Puvis de Chavannes; total population: 9001).

Class	Occupation	A*	B	C	D	E	F	G	H	I	Total
Lower	1. Unskilled workers	167	33	49	47	15	16	72	104	3	506
		33%†	6%	10%	10%	3%	3%	14%	21%	1%	(17%)
	2. Skilled workers	139	17	27	25	5	27	28	2	2	272
		51%	6%	10%	10%	2%	10%	10%	1%	1%	(9%)
	3. Service personnel	105	11	20	18	10	16	32	9	5	226
		46%	5%	9%	9%	4%	7%	14%	4%	2%	(8%)
	4. Dockers, sailors	46	19	12	15	6	15	22	29	15	179
		26%	11%	7%	8%	3%	8%	12%	16%	9%	(6%)
Subtotals		457	80	108	105	36	74	154	144	25	1183
		39%	7%	9%	9%	3%	6%	13%	12%	2%	(40%)
Lower middle	5. Artisans	138	13	60	75	15	26	33	12	0	372
		37%	3%	16%	20%	4%	7%	9%	3%	0%	(13%)
	6. Shopkeepers	109	18	55	52	13	43	46	16	6	358
		30%	5%	15%	14%	4%	12%	13%	5%	2%	(12%)
	7. Office workers	157	16	6	6	0	56	58	2	3	304
		52%	5%	2%	2%	0%	18%	18%	1%	1%	(10%)
	8. Fonctionnaires	35	12	0	2	0	23	24	0	0	96
		36%	13%	0%	2%	0%	24%	25%	0%	0%	(3%)
Subtotals		439	59	121	135	28	148	161	30	9	1130
		39%	5%	11%	12%	2%	13%	14%	3%	1%	(39%)
Upper middle	9. Lib. professions	14	2	0	1	0	5	5	0	0	27
		50%	7%	0%	4%	0%	18%	18%	0%	0%	(1%)
	10. Cce. and industry	20	8	5	3	1	8	13	1	4	63
		32%	13%	8%	5%	2%	13%	20%	2%	6%	(2%)
	11. Senior office wkrs.	54	4	3	5	2	13	15	0	4	100
		54%	4%	3%	5%	2%	13%	15%	0%	4%	(3%)
Subtotals		88	14	8	9	3	26	33	1	8	190
		46%	7%	4%	4%	2%	14%	17%	1%	4%	(6%)
	12. Unemployed	179	22	40	35	7	44	35	24	6	392
		46%	6%	10%	9%	2%	11%	9%	6%	1%	(14%)
	13. Other	15	1	3	4	1	3	2	1	0	30
		50%	3%	10%	13%	3%	10%	7%	3%	0%	(1%)
Totals		1178	176	280	288	75	295	385	200	48	2925
		40%	6%	10%	10%	3%	10%	13%	7%	1%	(100%)

Fourth Canton

Bureau de vote N°27 (rue Audimar — Boulevard des Dames — rue des Grands Carmes; total population 4174).

Class	Occupation	A*	B	C	D	E	F	G	H	I	Total
Lower	1. Unskilled workers	90	12	20	16	1	27	46	8	3	223
		40%†	5%	9%	7%	1%	12%	21%	4%	1%	(16%)
	2. Skilled workers	61	2	7	4	0	12	10	2	5	103
		59%	2%	7%	4%	0%	12%	10%	2%	5%	(7%)
	3. Service personnel	23	6	8	3	1	10	7	1	2	61
		38%	10%	13%	5%	2%	16%	11%	2%	3%	(4%)
	4. Dockers, sailors	23	31	7	2	1	15	12	4	3	98
		23%	32%	7%	2%	1%	15%	12%	4%	3%	(7%)
Subtotals		197	51	42	25	3	64	75	15	13	485
		41%	10%	9%	5%	1%	13%	16%	3%	3%	(34%)
Lower middle	5. Artisans	45	0	14	20	1	17	7	0	3	107
		42%	0%	13%	19%	1%	16%	6%	0%	3%	(7%)
	6. Shopkeepers	44	6	10	12	3	15	24	1	3	118
		37%	5%	8%	10%	3%	13%	20%	1%	3%	(8%)
	7. Office workers	118	14	6	4	0	39	31	2	1	215
		55%	6%	3%	2%	0%	18%	14%	1%	1%	(15%)
	8. Fonctionnaires	29	8	0	0	0	18	9	1	0	65
		45%	12%	0%	0%	0%	28%	14%	1%	0%	(4%)
Subtotals		246	28	30	36	4	89	71	4	7	505
		49%	5%	6%	7%	1%	18%	14%	1%	1%	(35%)
Upper middle	9. Lib. professions	7	3	0	0	2	6	5	0	0	23
		30%	13%	0%	0%	9%	26%	22%	0%	0%	(2%)
	10. Cce. and industry	12	0	0	1	0	4	9	1	1	28
		43%	0%	0%	4%	0%	14%	32%	4%	4%	(2%)
	11. Senior employees	36	5	4	1	0	16	30	3	1	96
		37%	5%	5%	1%	0%	17%	31%	3%	1%	(7%)
Subtotals		55	8	4	2	2	26	44	4	2	147
		37%	5%	3%	1%	1%	18%	30%	3%	1%	(10%)
	12. Unemployed	154	13	9	19	0	45	34	0	1	275
		56%	5%	3%	7%	0%	16%	13%	0%	1%	(19%)
	13. Other	5	0	0	0	0	2	2	0	0	9
		56%	0%	0%	0%	0%	22%	22%	0%	0%	(1%)
Totals		657	100	85	82	9	226	226	23	23	1431
		46%	7%	6%	6%	1%	16%	16%	1%	1%	(100%)

Fourth Canton

Bureau de vote N°25 (Ave. Camille Pelletan — rue Fauchier — rue de la Joliette — Boulevard des Dames; total population: 6276).

Class	Occupation	A*	B	C	D	E	F	G	H	I	Total
Lower	1. Unskilled workers	157	20	19	26	5	34	54	0	2	317
		49%†	6%	6%	8%	1%	11%	17%	0%	1%	(15%)
	2. Skilled workers	114	12	15	4	4	24	27	1	2	203
		56%	6%	7%	2%	2%	12%	13%	1%	1%	(10%)
	3. Service personnel	77	14	6	4	1	14	34	2	3	155
		45%	9%	4%	3%	1%	9%	22%	1%	2%	(7%)
	4. Dockers, sailors	39	56	7	5	2	22	39	4	5	179
		22%	31%	4%	3%	1%	12%	22%	2%	3%	(8%)
Subtotals		387	102	47	39	12	94	154	7	12	854
		45%	12%	5%	5%	1%	11%	18%	1%	1%	(40%)
Lower middle	5. Artisans	107	10	24	37	10	18	23	3	5	237
		45%	4%	10%	16%	4%	8%	10%	1%	2%	(11%)
	6. Shopkeepers	64	11	9	13	6	25	28	2	2	160
		40%	7%	6%	8%	4%	16%	17%	1%	1%	(7%)
	7. Office workers	185	14	7	1	2	43	46	5	4	307
		60%	5%	2%	1%	1%	14%	15%	2%	1%	(14%)
	8. Fonctionnaires	43	26	0	1	1	16	19	0	0	106
		41%	24%	0%	1%	1%	15%	18%	0%	0%	(5%)
Subtotals		399	61	40	52	19	102	116	10	11	810
		49%	8%	5%	6%	2%	13%	14%	1%	1%	(38%)
Upper middle	9. Lib. professions	6	1	0	0	0	8	5	0	0	20
		30%	5%	0%	0%	0%	40%	25%	0%	0%	(1%)
	10. Cce. and industry	13	2	5	1	0	4	6	0	0	31
		42%	6%	16%	3%	0%	13%	20%	0%	0%	(2%)
	11. Senior employees.	49	3	0	3	1	12	38	0	4	110
		44%	3%	0%	3%	1%	11%	34%	0%	4%	(5%)
Subtotals		68	6	5	4	1	24	49	0	4	161
		42%	4%	3%	2%	1%	15%	30%	0%	3%	(8%)
	12. Unemployed	122	32	9	24	6	31	43	2	2	271
		45%	12%	3%	9%	2%	11%	16%	1%	1%	(13%)
	13. Other	17	2	0	0	0	3	6	0	0	28
		61%	7%	0%	0%	0%	11%	21%	0%	0%	(1%)
Totals		993	203	101	119	38	254	368	19	29	2124
		47%	10%	5%	6%	2%	12%	17%	1%	1%	(100%)

Fourth Canton

Bureau de vote N°24 (rue Fauchier — rue de la République — rue de Forbin — Boulevard de Paris; total population: 5596).

Class	Occupation	A*	B	C	D	E	F	G	H	I	Total
Lower	1. Unskilled workers	118	18	7	5	5	23	58	0	5	239
		49%†	7%	3%	2%	2%	10%	24%	0%	2%	(13%)
	2. Skilled workers	94	13	7	2	3	13	17	3	4	156
		60%	8%	4%	1%	2%	8%	11%	2%	3%	(9%)
	3. Service personnel	60	20	3	0	0	23	23	1	5	135
		44%	15%	2%	0%	0%	17%	17%	1%	4%	(8%)
	4. Dockers, sailors	65	90	8	1	7	20	37	1	19	248
		26%	36%	3%	1%	3%	8%	15%	1%	8%	(14%)
Subtotals		337	141	25	8	15	79	135	5	33	778
		43%	18%	3%	1%	2%	10%	17%	1%	4%	(44%)
Lower middle	5. Artisans	107	10	18	5	3	14	14	3	5	179
		60%	6%	10%	3%	2%	8%	8%	2%	3%	(10%)
	6. Shopkeepers	55	14	6	3	2	15	18	1	6	120
		45%	12%	5%	2%	2%	12%	15%	1%	5%	(7%)
	7. Office workers	130	26	3	5	1	29	54	2	0	250
		52%	10%	1%	2%	1%	12%	22%	1%	0%	(14%)
	8. Fonctionnaires	71	37	3	2	0	18	20	0	0	151
		47%	24%	2%	1%	0%	12%	13%	0%	0%	(8%)
Subtotals		363	87	30	15	6	76	106	6	11	700
		52%	12%	4%	2%	1%	11%	15%	1%	2%	(39%)
Upper middle	9. Lib. professions	14	2	0	0	1	4	2	0	1	24
		58%	8%	0%	0%	4%	17%	8%	0%	4%	(1%)
	10. Cce. and industry	7	2	0	0	0	0	6	1	0	16
		44%	12%	0%	0%	0%	0%	37%	6%	0%	(1%)
	11. Senior employees.	31	7	0	0	0	12	10	0	2	62
		50%	11%	0%	0%	0%	19%	16%	0%	3%	(3%)
Subtotals		52	11	0	0	1	16	18	1	3	102
		51%	11%	0%	0%	1%	16%	18%	1%	3%	(6%)
	12. Unemployed	96	23	7	0	2	21	24	0	3	176
		54%	13%	4%	0%	1%	12%	14%	0%	2%	(10%)
	13. Other	9	1	2	0	0	3	3	0	1	19
		47%	5%	10%	0%	0%	16%	16%	0%	5%	(1%)
Totals		857	263	64	23	24	195	286	12	51	1775
		48%	15%	4%	1%	1%	11%	16%	1%	3%	(100%)

Fourth Canton

Bureau de vote N°115 (Boulevard de Paris — rue de Forbin — Boulevard Maritime; total population: 5620).

Class	Occupation	A*	B	C	D	E	F	G	H	I	Total
Lower	1. Unskilled workers	129	40	18	2	4	28	46	2	1	270
		48%†	15%	7%	1%	1%	10%	17%	1%	0%	(13%)
	2. Skilled workers	105	20	10	3	1	27	28	4	0	198
		53%	10%	5%	1%	0%	14%	14%	2%	0%	(10%)
	3. Service personnel	53	21	6	0	2	15	17	3	2	119
		44%	18%	5%	0%	2%	13%	14%	2%	2%	(6%)
	4. Dockers, sailors	72	129	18	2	0	14	21	0	0	256
		28%	50%	7%	1%	0%	5%	8%	0%	0%	(13%)
Subtotals		359	210	52	7	7	84	112	9	3	843
		43%	25%	6%	1%	1%	10%	13%	1%	0%	(42%)
Lower middle	5. Artisans	65	22	10	3	4	9	20	1	0	134
		48%	16%	7%	2%	3%	7%	15%	1%	0%	(75%)
	6. Shopkeepers	51	17	8	5	4	15	22	0	1	123
		41%	14%	6%	4%	3%	12%	18%	0%	1%	(6%)
	7. Office workers	163	39	9	1	3	36	59	0	1	311
		52%	12%	3%	0%	1%	12%	19%	0%	0%	(15%)
	8. Fonctionnaires	56	58	3	1	0	23	26	0	0	167
		33%	33%	2%	1%	0%	14%	16%	0%	0%	(8%)
Subtotals		335	136	30	10	11	83	127	1	2	735
		46%	18%	4%	1%	1%	11%	17%	0%	0%	(36%)
Upper middle	9. Lib. professions	6	0	0	0	0	2	4	0	0	12
		50%	0%	0%	0%	0%	16%	33%	0%	0%	(1%)
	10. Cce. and industry	5	3	1	0	0	2	5	0	0	16
		31%	19%	6%	0%	0%	12%	31%	0%	0%	(1%)
	11. Senior employees	36	4	1	0	0	20	13	0	3	77
		47%	5%	1%	0%	0%	26%	17%	0%	4%	(4%)
Subtotals		47	7	2	0	0	24	22	0	3	105
		45%	7%	2%	0%	0%	23%	21%	0%	3%	(5%)
	12. Unemployed	139	56	26	3	3	35	41	2	0	305
		46%	18%	8%	1%	1%	11%	13%	1%	0%	(15%)
	13. Other	13	4	0	0	0	3	2	0	1	23
		56%	17%	0%	0%	0%	13%	9%	0%	4%	(1%)
Totals		893	413	110	20	21	229	304	12	9	2011
		44%	20%	5%	1%	1%	11%	15%	1%	1%	(100%)

Fourth Canton

Bureau de vote N°23 (rue Peysonnel — le Lazaret — avenue d'arenc — Boulevard Mirabeau — Boulevard de Paris; total population: 9313).

Class	Occupation	A*	B	C	D	E	F	G	H	I	Total
Lower	1. Unskilled workers	245	23	81	6	71	43	93	14	0	576
		42%†	4%	14%	1%	12%	7%	16%	2%	0%	(19%)
	2. Skilled workers	145	21	20	0	17	30	54	0	4	291
		50%	7%	7%	0%	6%	10%	18%	0%	1%	(9%)
	3. Service personnel	97	19	30	1	15	35	48	5	5	255
		38%	7%	12%	0%	6%	14%	19%	2%	2%	(8%)
	4. Dockers, sailors	69	53	14	2	37	18	45	7	22	267
		26%	20%	5%	1%	14%	7%	17%	2%	9%	(9%)
Subtotals		556	116	145	9	140	126	240	26	31	1389
		40%	8%	10%	1%	10%	9%	17%	2%	2%	(45%)
Lower middle	5. Artisans	154	18	37	5	27	15	28	5	3	292
		53%	6%	13%	2%	9%	5%	10%	2%	1%	(9%)
	6. Shopkeepers	70	13	13	3	23	15	26	3	2	168
		42%	8%	8%	2%	14%	9%	15%	2%	1%	(5%)
	7. Office workers	211	25	5	0	3	37	88	2	1	372
		57%	7%	1%	0%	1%	10%	24%	0%	0%	(12%)
	8. Fonctionnaires	70	49	2	0	2	25	39	4	1	192
		36%	25%	1%	0%	1%	13%	20%	2%	0%	(6%)
Subtotals		505	105	57	8	55	92	181	14	7	1024
		49%	10%	5%	1%	5%	9%	18%	1%	1%	(34%)
Upper middle	9. Lib. professions	8	0	0	0	0	5	7	0	0	20
		40%	0%	0%	0%	0%	25%	35%	0%	0%	(1%)
	10. Cce. and industry	18	4	3	2	2	5	5	0	3	42
		43%	10%	7%	5%	5%	12%	12%	0%	7%	(1%)
	11. Senior employees.	28	7	2	1	0	6	19	2	0	65
		43%	11%	3%	1%	0%	9%	29%	3%	0%	(2%)
Subtotals		54	11	5	3	2	16	31	2	3	127
		42%	9%	4%	2%	2%	13%	24%	2%	2%	(4%)
	12. Unemployed	266	39	43	5	19	54	58	6	3	493
		54%	8%	9%	1%	4%	11%	12%	1%	1%	(16%)
	13. Other	15	3	6	0	3	4	2	1	0	34
		44%	9%	18%	0%	9%	12%	6%	3%	0%	(1%)
Totals		1396	274	256	25	219	292	512	49	44	3067
		45%	9%	8%	1%	7%	9%	17%	2%	1%	(100%)

Fifth Canton

Bureau de vote N°34 (ave. Camille Pelletan — rue St. Lazare — rue de Crimée — rue Honnorat; total population: 6361).

Class	Occupation	A*	B	C	D	E	F	G	H	I	Total
Lower	1. Unskilled workers	183 45%†	16 4%	26 6%	52 13%	5 1%	39 9%	68 17%	13 3%	8 2%	410 (21%)
	2. Skilled workers	86 60%	5 3%	6 4%	2 1%	1 1%	13 9%	23 16%	4 3%	4 3%	144 (7%)
	3. Service personnel	78 57%	4 3%	6 4%	4 3%	1 1%	8 6%	25 18%	4 3%	6 4%	136 (7%)
	4. Dockers, sailors	22 28%	14 18%	8 10%	0 0%	0 0%	8 10%	18 23%	4 5%	5 6%	79 (4%)
Subtotals		369 48%	39 5%	46 6%	58 7%	7 1%	68 9%	134 17%	25 3%	23 3%	769 (40%)
Lower middle	5. Artisans	146 58%	3 1%	16 6%	29 12%	1 0%	16 6%	31 12%	1 0%	8 3%	251 (13%)
	6. Shopkeepers	35 38%	2 2%	9 10%	3 3%	1 1%	13 14%	21 23%	2 2%	5 5%	91 (5%)
	7. Office workers	228 65%	8 2%	5 1%	1 0%	1 0%	27 8%	79 22%	2 1%	1 0%	352 (18%)
	8. Fonctionnaires	48 34%	8 6%	1 1%	0 0%	0 0%	29 21%	52 37%	1 1%	1 1%	140 (7%)
Subtotals		457 55%	21 2%	31 4%	33 4%	3 0%	85 10%	183 22%	6 1%	15 2%	834 (43%)
Upper middle	9. Lib. professions	12 54%	1 4%	0 0%	0 0%	0 0%	3 14%	6 27%	0 0%	0 0%	22 (1%)
	10. Cce. and industry	4 40%	0 0%	0 0%	0 0%	0 0%	3 33%	3 33%	0 0%	0 0%	10 (1%)
	11. Senior employees.	28 58%	1 2%	0 0%	1 2%	0 0%	7 15%	10 21%	1 2%	0 0%	48 (2%)
Subtotals		44 55%	2 2%	0 0%	1 1%	0 0%	13 16%	19 24%	1 1%	0 0%	80 (2%)
	12. Unemployed	122 48%	9 4%	13 5%	21 8%	2 1%	18 7%	46 18%	5 2%	16 6%	252 (13%)
	13. Other	5 62%	0 0%	0 0%	0 0%	0 0%	1 12%	2 25%	0 0%	0 0%	8 (0%)
Totals		997 51%	71 4%	90 5%	113 6%	12 1%	185 9%	384 20%	37 2%	54 3%	1943 (100%)

Fifth Canton

Bureau de vote N°35 (Boulevard de Strasbourg — Caserne des douanes — Boulevard National — rue de Turenne; total population 7672).

Class	Occupation	A*	B	C	D	E	F	G	H	I	Total
Lower	1. Unskilled workers	157	10	30	3	2	60	103	26	5	396
		40%†	2%	8%	1%	0%	15%	26%	7%	1%	(17%)
	2. Skilled workers	65	4	11	0	1	9	18	1	1	110
		59%	4%	10%	0%	1%	8%	16%	1%	1%	(5%)
	3. Service personnel	41	3	7	0	7	11	17	0	1	87
		47%	3%	8%	0%	8%	13%	19%	0%	1%	(4%)
	4. Dockers, sailors	26	15	1	3	0	4	12	3	2	66
		39%	23%	1%	4%	0%	6%	18%	4%	3%	(3%)
Subtotals		289	32	49	6	10	84	150	30	9	659
		44%	5%	7%	1%	1%	13%	23%	4%	1%	(28%)
Lower middle	5. Artisans	85	8	23	5	7	7	27	0	5	167
		51%	5%	14%	3%	4%	4%	16%	0%	3%	(7%)
	6. Shopkeepers	50	4	9	2	2	8	16	1	1	93
		54%	4%	10%	2%	2%	9%	17%	1%	1%	(4%)
	7. Office workers	169	12	2	2	1	59	122	3	3	373
		45%	3%	0%	0%	0%	16%	33%	1%	1%	(16%)
	8. Fonctionnaires	100	160	3	0	1	83	350	2	1	700
		14%	23%	0%	0%	0%	12%	50%	0%	1%	(29%)
Subtotals		404	184	37	9	11	157	515	6	10	1333
		30%	14%	3%	1%	1%	12%	39%	0%	1%	(56%)
Upper middle	9. Lib. professions	11	3	0	1	0	1	4	0	0	20
		55%	15%	0%	5%	0%	5%	20%	0%	0%	(1%)
	10. Cce. and industry	15	2	1	0	0	1	4	0	0	23
		65%	9%	4%	0%	0%	4%	17%	0%	0%	(1%)
	11. Senior employees.	21	1	1	2	0	10	10	1	0	46
		46%	2%	2%	4%	0%	22%	22%	2%	0%	(2%)
Subtotals		47	6	2	3	0	12	18	1	0	89
		53%	7%	2%	3%	0%	13%	20%	1%	0%	(4%)
	12. Unemployed	140	35	12	1	1	18	68	3	3	281
		50%	12%	4%	0%	0%	6%	24%	1%	1%	(12%)
	13. Other	11	3	3	0	0	2	6	0	0	25
		44%	12%	12%	0%	0%	8%	24%	0%	0%	(1%)
Totals		891	260	103	19	22	273	757	40	22	2387
		37%	11%	4%	1%	1%	11%	32%	2%	1%	(100%)

Fifth Canton

Bureau de vote N°36 (Avenue d'Arenc — la Villette — Boulveard National — Boulevard de Strasbourg; total population: 13682).

Class	Occupation	A*	B	C	D	E	F	G	H	I	Total
Lower	1. Unskilled workers	349	44	135	3	129	94	169	11	3	937
		37%†	5%	14%	0%	14%	10%	18%	1%	0%	(24%)
	2. Skilled workers	180	19	34	0	14	10	59	3	0	319
		56%	6%	11%	0%	4%	3%	18%	1%	0%	(8%)
	3. Service personnel	129	9	26	2	24	16	27	3	1	237
		54%	4%	11%	1%	10%	7%	11%	1%	0%	(6%)
	4. Dockers, sailors	116	42	100	0	54	24	25	4	1	366
		32%	11%	27%	0%	15%	7%	7%	1%	0%	(9%)
Subtotals		774	114	295	5	221	144	280	21	5	1859
		42%	6%	16%	0%	12%	8%	15%	1%	0%	(47%)
Lower middle	5. Artisans	184	11	65	1	40	21	37	4	1	364
		50%	3%	18%	0%	11%	6%	10%	1%	0%	(9%)
	6. Shopkeepers	106	3	44	0	21	21	37	5	6	243
		44%	1%	18%	0%	9%	9%	15%	2%	2%	(6%)
	7. Office workers	308	8	8	0	1	83	211	4	1	624
		49%	1%	1%	0%	0%	13%	34%	1%	0%	(16%)
	8. Fonctionnaires	96	17	12	0	1	38	74	2	1	241
		40%	7%	5%	0%	0%	16%	31%	1%	0%	(6%)
Subtotals		694	39	129	1	63	163	359	15	9	1472
		47%	3%	9%	0%	4%	11%	24%	1%	1%	(37%)
Upper middle	9. Lib. professions	7	2	0	0	0	1	7	0	0	17
		41%	12%	0%	0%	0%	6%	41%	0%	0%	(0%)
	10. Cce. and industry	13	1	4	0	1	5	7	1	0	32
		41%	3%	12%	0%	3%	16%	22%	3%	0%	(1%)
	11. Senior employees.	53	1	3	1	2	13	19	1	1	94
		56%	1%	3%	1%	2%	14%	20%	1%	1%	(2%)
Subtotals		73	4	7	1	3	19	33	2	1	143
		51%	3%	5%	1%	2%	13%	23%	1%	1%	(4%)
	12. Unemployed	229	21	40	2	31	39	68	1	0	431
		53%	5%	9%	0%	7%	9%	16%	0%	0%	(11%)
	13. Other	17	2	4	0	0	1	1	0	0	25
		68%	8%	16%	0%	0%	4%	4%	0%	0%	(1%)
Totals		1787	180	475	9	318	366	741	39	15	3930
		45%	5%	12%	0%	8%	9%	19%	1%	0%	(100%)

Fifth Canton

Bureau de vote N°111 (rue Kleber — boulevard National — boulevard de Strasbourg; total population: 0000).

Class	Occupation	A*	B	C	D	E	F	G	H	I	Total
Lower	1. Unskilled workers	94	15	23	6	4	59	93	3	0	297
		32%†	5%	8%	2%	1%	20%	31%	1%	0%	(22%)
	2. Skilled workers	46	3	7	1	1	14	11	2	0	85
		54%	3%	8%	1%	1%	16%	13%	2%	0%	(6%)
	3. Service personnel	27	3	3	1	4	10	11	1	0	60
		45%	5%	5%	2%	7%	17%	18%	2%	0%	(4%)
	4. Dockers, sailors	18	15	9	1	2	5	4	1	0	55
		33%	27%	16%	2%	4%	9%	7%	2%	0%	(4%)
Subtotals		185	36	42	9	11	88	119	7	0	497
		37%	7%	8%	2%	2%	18%	24%	1%	0%	(37%)
Lower middle	5. Artisans	46	5	20	0	4	6	12	1	0	94
		49%	5%	21%	0%	4%	6%	13%	1%	0%	(7%)
	6. Shopkeepers	34	2	6	0	3	11	18	0	0	74
		46%	3%	8%	0%	4%	15%	24%	0%	0%	(5%)
	7. Office workers	82	20	1	0	0	51	99	0	0	253
		32%	8%	0%	0%	0%	20%	39%	0%	0%	(19%)
	8. Fonctionnaires	52	31	4	0	0	48	37	1	0	173
		30%	18%	2%	0%	0%	28%	21%	1%	0%	(13%)
Subtotals		214	58	31	0	7	116	166	2	0	594
		36%	10%	5%	0%	1%	19%	28%	0%	0%	(44%)
Upper middle	9. Lib. professions	9	0	0	0	0	1	6	0	0	16
		56%	0%	0%	0%	0%	6%	38%	0%	0%	(1%)
	10. Cce. and industry	8	1	0	0	0	0	2	0	0	11
		73%	9%	0%	0%	0%	0%	18%	0%	0%	(1%)
	11. Senior employees.	15	5	3	0	0	5	7	2	0	37
		40%	13%	8%	0%	0%	13%	19%	5%	0%	(3%)
Subtotals		32	6	3	0	0	6	15	2	0	64
		50%	9%	5%	0%	0%	9%	23%	3%	0%	(5%)
	12. Unemployed	80	21	14	4	3	21	31	1	0	175
		46%	12%	8%	2%	2%	12%	18%	1%	0%	(13%)
	13. Other	6	0	0	1	0	2	2	0	0	11
		54%	0%	0%	9%	0%	18%	18%	0%	0%	(1%)
Totals		517	121	90	14	21	233	333	12	0	1341
		38%	9%	7%	1%	2%	17%	25%	1%	0%	(100%)

Fifth Canton

Bureau de vote N°37 (avenue d'Arenc — Gare d'Arenc — rue de Lyon — chemin des Aygalades; total population: 9001).

Class	Occupation	A*	B	C	D	E	F	G	H	I	Total
Lower	1. Unskilled workers	262 40%†	10 1%	48 7%	77 12%	12 2%	43 6%	176 27%	20 3%	12 2%	660 (29%)
	2. Skilled workers	154 58%	5 2%	18 7%	2 1%	6 2%	22 8%	48 18%	5 2%	6 2%	266 (11%)
	3. Service personnel	84 46%	7 4%	16 9%	3 2%	8 4%	14 7%	42 23%	5 3%	2 1%	181 (8%)
	4. Dockers, sailors	35 34%	6 6%	8 8%	12 11%	4 4%	6 6%	17 16%	8 8%	8 8%	104 (4%)
Subtotals		535 44%	28 2%	90 7%	94 8%	30 2%	85 7%	283 23%	38 3%	28 2%	1211 (52%)
Lower middle	5. Artisans	123 45%	8 3%	21 8%	8 3%	5 2%	24 9%	78 29%	1 0%	3 1%	271 (12%)
	6. Shopkeepers	68 43%	2 1%	13 8%	2 1%	8 5%	20 13%	40 25%	2 1%	4 2%	159 (7%)
	7. Office workers	15 22%	2 3%	0 0%	0 0%	0 0%	23 34%	27 40%	0 0%	0 0%	67 (3%)
	8. Fonctionnaires	48 34%	9 6%	1 1%	0 0%	3 2%	33 23%	45 32%	1 1%	1 1%	141 (6%)
Subtotals		254 40%	21 3%	35 5%	10 2%	16 2%	100 16%	190 30%	4 1%	8 1%	638 (28%)
Upper middle	9. Lib. professions	10 59%	0 0%	0 0%	0 0%	0 0%	2 12%	5 29%	0 0%	0 0%	17 (1%)
	10. Cce. and industry	13 37%	1 3%	0 0%	0 0%	1 3%	3 9%	16 46%	0 0%	1 3%	35 (1%)
	11. Senior employees.	8 35%	2 9%	2 9%	0 0%	0 0%	4 17%	7 3%	0 0%	0 0%	23 (1%)
Subtotals		31 41%	3 4%	2 3%	0 0%	1 1%	9 12%	28 37%	0 0%	1 1%	75 (3%)
	12. Unemployed	174 47%	16 4%	28 8%	14 4%	8 2%	31 8%	88 24%	3 1%	5 1%	367 (16%)
	13. Other	15 75%	0 0%	0 0%	1 5%	0 0%	2 10%	1 5%	0 0%	1 5%	20 (1%)
Totals		1009 44%	68 3%	155 7%	119 5%	55 2%	227 10%	590 25%	45 2%	43 2%	2311 (100%)

Fifth Canton

Bureau de vote N°39 (rue de Lyon — Place Oddo — Boulevard Oddo — Boulevard Demandols; total population: 6047).

Class	Occupation	A*	B	C	D	E	F	G	H	I	Total
Lower	1. Unskilled workers	238	19	69	9	16	29	130	1	9	520
		46%†	4%	13%	2%	3%	6%	25%	0%	2%	(29%)
	2. Skilled workers	90	9	9	1	1	10	17	0	4	141
		64%	6%	6%	1%	1%	7%	12%	0%	3%	(8%)
	3. Service personnel	35	0	4	2	1	4	16	1	1	64
		55%	0%	6%	3%	2%	6%	25%	2%	2%	(3%)
	4. Dockers, sailors	28	16	6	9	0	1	29	0	3	92
		30%	17%	6%	10%	0%	1%	31%	0%	3%	(5%)
Subtotals		391	44	88	21	18	44	192	2	17	817
		48%	5%	11%	3%	2%	5%	23%	0%	2%	(45%)
Lower middle	5. Artisans	65	5	17	0	3	2	14	3	2	111
		58%	4%	15%	0%	3%	2%	13%	3%	2%	(6%)
	6. Shopkeepers	49	4	9	2	0	7	12	0	1	84
		58%	5%	11%	2%	0%	8%	14%	0%	1%	(5%)
	7. Office workers	163	11	12	1	5	29	129	1	2	353
		46%	3%	3%	0%	1%	8%	36%	0%	1%	(20%)
	8. Fonctionnaires	14	3	0	0	0	7	27	1	0	52
		27%	6%	0%	0%	0%	13%	52%	2%	0%	(3%)
Subtotals		291	23	38	3	8	45	182	5	5	600
		48%	4%	6%	0%	1%	7%	30%	1%	1%	(33%)
Upper middle	9. Lib. professions	6	0	0	0	0	3	4	0	1	14
		43%	0%	0%	0%	0%	21%	28%	0%	7%	(1%)
	10. Cce. and industry	1	0	0	0	0	1	1	0	1	4
		25%	0%	0%	0%	0%	25%	25%	0%	25%	(0%)
	11. Senior employees.	18	4	1	0	0	9	7	0	0	39
		46%	10%	3%	0%	0%	23%	18%	0%	0%	(2%)
Subtotals		25	4	1	0	0	13	12	0	2	57
		44%	7%	2%	0%	0%	23%	21%	0%	3%	(3%)
	12. Unemployed	147	10	18	6	4	16	101	0	3	305
		48%	3%	6%	2%	1%	5%	33%	0%	1%	(17%)
	13. Other	13	0	1	1	0	1	4	0	0	20
		65%	0%	5%	5%	0%	5%	20%	0%	0%	(2%)
Totals		867	81	146	31	30	119	491	7	27	1799
		48%	4%	8%	2%	2%	7%	27%	0%	1%	(100%)

Fifth Canton

Bureau de vote N°119 (Boulevard Oddo — Traverse du Moulin à Vent — Boulevard de la Mediterranée; total population: 11551).

Class	Occupation	A*	B	C	D	E	F	G	H	I	Total
Lower	1. Unskilled workers	456	47	252	138	64	85	347	210	23	1622
		28%†	3%	15%	8%	4%	5%	21%	13%	1%	(45%)
	2. Skilled workers	117	8	38	4	6	8	23	1	0	205
		57%	4%	18%	2%	3%	4%	11%	1%	0%	(6%)
	3. Service personnel	77	9	22	3	5	3	19	3	1	142
		54%	6%	15%	2%	3%	2%	13%	2%	1%	(4%)
	4. Dockers, sailors	13	6	27	23	1	2	9	12	7	100
		13%	6%	27%	23%	1%	2%	9%	12%	7%	(3%)
Subtotals		663	70	339	168	76	98	398	226	31	2069
		32%	3%	16%	8%	4%	5%	19%	11%	1%	(58%)
Lower middle	5. Artisans	108	12	64	18	8	6	20	2	2	240
		45%	5%	27%	7%	3%	2%	8%	1%	1%	(7%)
	6. Shopkeepers	89	4	44	16	4	10	23	3	3	196
		45%	2%	22%	8%	2%	5%	12%	1%	1%	(5%)
	7. Office workers	219	18	15	2	4	54	323	2	0	637
		34%	3%	2%	0%	1%	8%	51%	0%	0%	(18%)
	8. Fonctionnaires	26	3	3	0	1	3	11	0	0	47
		55%	6%	6%	0%	2%	6%	23%	0%	0%	(1%)
Subtotals		442	37	126	36	17	73	377	7	5	1120
		39%	3%	11%	3%	1%	6%	34%	1%	0%	(31%)
Upper middle	9. Lib. professions	4	0	0	0	0	1	5	0	0	10
		40%	0%	0%	0%	0%	10%	50%	0%	0%	(0%)
	10. Cce. and industry	6	1	1	0	0	0	5	0	0	13
		46%	8%	8%	0%	0%	0%	38%	0%	0%	(0%)
	11. Senior employees.	14	0	2	1	0	3	1	0	0	21
		67%	0%	9%	5%	0%	14%	5%	0%	0%	(1%)
Subtotals		24	1	3	1	0	4	11	0	0	44
		54%	2%	7%	2%	0%	9%	25%	0%	0%	(1%)
	12. Unemployed	133	9	63	18	10	9	56	7	2	307
		43%	3%	20%	6%	3%	3%	18%	2%	1%	(9%)
	13. Other	14	0	3	2	0	0	1	0	0	20
		70%	0%	15%	10%	0%	0%	5%	0%	0%	(1%)
Totals		1276	117	534	225	103	184	843	240	38	3560
		36%	3%	15%	6%	3%	5%	24%	7%	1%	(100%)

Fifth Canton

Bureau de vote N°120 (Chemin de la Madrague ville — Chemin du Littoral — Camp des Abattor is — Chemin du Cap Janet; total population: 4341).

Class	Occupation	A*	B	C	D	E	F	G	H	I	Total
Lower	1. Unskilled workers	75	14	43	27	4	39	39	8	4	253
		30%†	5%	17%	11%	2%	15%	15%	3%	2%	(21%)
	2. Skilled workers	78	4	15	5	2	20	23	2	2	151
		52%	3%	10%	3%	1%	13%	15%	1%	1%	(12%)
	3. Service personnel	37	5	10	2	2	11	14	0	2	83
		45%	6%	12%	2%	2%	13%	17%	0%	2%	(7%)
	4. Dockers, sailors	42	24	9	12	2	20	30	0	3	142
		30%	17%	6%	8%	1%	14%	21%	0%	2%	(12%)
Subtotals		232	47	77	46	10	90	106	10	11	629
		37%	7%	12%	7%	2%	14%	17%	2%	2%	(52%)
Lower middle	5. Artisans	48	4	14	5	1	5	6	0	5	88
		54%	4%	16%	6%	1%	6%	7%	0%	6%	(7%)
	6. Shopkeepers	46	5	10	5	3	11	8	0	2	90
		51%	5%	11%	5%	3%	12%	9%	0%	2%	(7%)
	7. Office workers	41	9	1	2	0	40	48	1	3	145
		28%	6%	1%	1%	0%	28%	33%	1%	2%	(12%)
	8. Fonctionnaires	15	1	1	1	0	7	10	2	0	37
		40%	3%	3%	3%	0%	19%	27%	5%	0%	(3%)
Subtotals		150	19	26	13	4	63	72	3	10	360
		42%	5%	7%	4%	1%	17%	20%	1%	3%	(29%)
Upper middle	9. Lib. professions	5	1	0	0	1	2	4	0	0	13
		38%	8%	0%	0%	8%	15%	31%	0%	0%	(1%)
	10. Cce. and industry	2	0	0	0	0	1	1	0	0	4
		50%	0%	0%	0%	0%	25%	25%	0%	0%	(0%)
	11. Senior employees.	19	4	1	1	0	5	11	3	1	45
		42%	9%	2%	2%	0%	11%	24%	7%	2%	(4%)
Subtotals		26	5	1	1	1	8	16	3	1	62
		42%	8%	2%	2%	2%	13%	26%	5%	2%	(5%)
	12. Unemployed	72	13	5	3	0	26	31	4	4	158
		46%	8%	3%	2%	0%	16%	20%	2%	2%	(13%)
	13. Other	14	0	1	0	0	0	0	0	0	15
		93%	0%	7%	0%	0%	0%	0%	0%	0%	(1%)
Totals		494	84	110	63	15	187	225	20	26	1224
		40%	7%	9%	5%	1%	15%	18%	2%	2%	

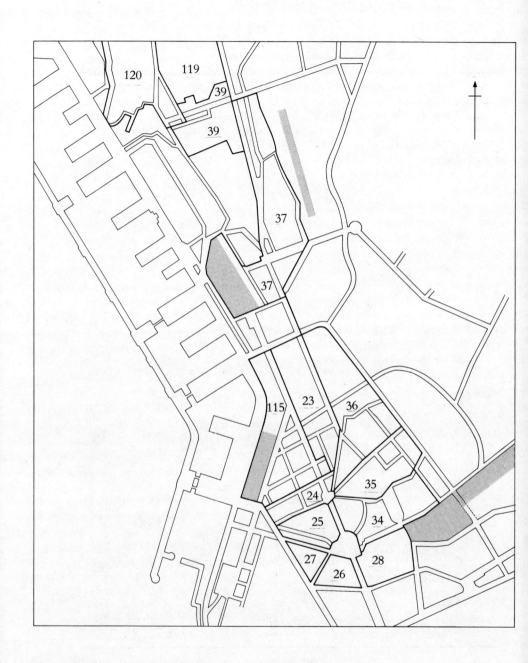

iii   Marseille: the twelve cantons

APPENDIX II

The Social Composition of the Sabianist Organisations

Professions

Class	Occupation[1]	1931–5[2]	PPF/1936–9[3]	PPF/1940–2[4]	PPF/1943–4[5]
Lower	1. Unskilled workers	118	13	4	14
		14%	3%	3%	6%
	2. Skilled workers	87	15	10	17
		10%	4%	7%	7%
	3. Service personnel	71	17	8	30
		8%	4%	5%	13%
	4. Dockers, sailors	53	36	9	15
		6%	9%	6%	6%
Subtotals		329	81	31	76
		39%	20%	21%	33%
Lower middle	5. Artisans	104	28	3	11
		12%	7%	2%	5%
	6. Shopkeepers	81	36	13	31
		10%	9%	9%	13%
	7. Office workers	92	50	16	13
		11%	12%	11%	6%
	8. Fonctionnaires	167	92	33	12
		20%	22%	23%	5%
Subtotals		444	206	65	67
		53%	50%	45%	29%
Upper middle	9. Lib. professions	10	28	4	0
		1%	7%	3%	0%
	10. Cce. and industry	12	23	10	5
		1%	6%	7%	2%
	11. Senior employees.	30	50	12	10
		4%	12%	8%	4%
Subtotals		52	101	26	15
		6%	25%	18%	6%
	12. Unemployed	10	17	19	58
		1%	4%	13%	26%
	13. Other	8	3	4	14
		1%	1%	3%	6%
Totals		843	408	145	230
		100%	100%	100%	100%

[1] Classifications as in appendix I, except that 'unemployed' do not include retirees but do include people with no steady job or 'sans profession bien défini'.

[2] Sources: 240 members of the Phalanges prolétariennes (1931–2), 380 members of the Amis de Simon Sabiani (1931–5), and 232 members of the Parti socialiste-communiste (1931–5), identified in published communiqués and traced to the electroal lists.

[3] Sources: 285 members as in note 1 above, 126 from postwar trials in AD500U series (see appendix III) and who therefore overlap with those in note 4 below.

[4] Source: 167 known to have been PPF members between June 1940 and November 1942 (information on professions for 145) from AD500U series.

[5] Source: idem, for 254 members known to have joined after Nov. 1942.

Ethnic Origin[1]

Birthplace	1931–5	PPF/1936–9	PPF/1940–2	PPF/1943–3
Marseille	387	154	67	150
	45%	41%	40%	59%
Corsica	179	92	35	18
	21%	25%	21%	7%
Provence	77	28	13	20
	9%	7%	8%	8%
Other France	110	75	34	36
	13%	20%	20%	14%
Italy	64	8	3	10
	7%	2%	2%	4%
Spain	11	0	0	1
	1%	0%	0%	0%
Mahgreb	15	0	10	10
	2%	0%	6%	4%
Turkey (Armenia)	1	10	0	1
	0%	3%	0%	0%
Other	6	6	5	7
	1%	2%	3%	3%
	850	373	167	253
		AGE[1]		
14–20	3	21	14	85
	0%	6%	8%	34%
21–35	249	139	57	115
	29%	37%	34%	45%
36–50	374	148	67	39
	44%	40%	40%	15%
51–65	180	59	22	12
	21%	16%	13%	5%
Over 65	43	9	7	2
	6%	1%	4%	1%
	849	376	167	253

[1] Sources as for professions overleaf.
[2] Discrepancies in totals for professions, age and ethnic origin result from availablility of only partial information in some cases.
[3] Includes 22 *Phalangistes* over the age of 60.

APPENDIX III

The 500U Series in the Archives Departementales Des Bouches-Du-Rhone

In October 1944 ninety *Cours de Justice*, established by a decree of the month before, began trying individuals all over France suspected of collaborating with the enemy during the occupation. Two months later *Chambres civiques* began trying individuals suspected of less serious actions, such as simple membership in a collaborationist party, according to a new offence known as 'indiginité nationale' and applied retroactively. In Marseille the *Cour de Justice* tried its first case on 11 October 1944 and its last on 31 July 1946, 1491 suspects in all; the *Chambre civique* tried its first case on 6 December 1944 and its last also on 31 July 1946, 869 cases in all; in addition the courts granted 1203 *non-lieux* (distinct from acquittals) to individuals who did not collaborate at all or who did so in a in a manner not punishable by law.[1] The dossiers of the 3563 cases, containing the detailed charges, the pre-trial depositions of witnesses for and against the defendant, and the judgement and sentence of the court though not the minutes of the trial, are assembled in 295 thick *liasses* or bundles, stored in the *Archives départementales des Bouches-du-Rhône* and making up, together with 110 other bundles mostly from the *Cour de Justice* of Arles, the 500U series. According to the provisions of the archival law of 1978, such documents are closed to researchers for 100 years, but the *Procureur de la République*, after some hesitation, granted permission to go through the series on the general condition that the names of the defendants were not to be mentioned.[2]

The courts themselves, set up to put a stop to six weeks of near anarchy and 'justice expeditive', became and have remained the subject of some controversy. There was controversy over the law itself. For the most part the procedures followed those of the *Cours d'assises* very closely and guaranteed the defendants' rights. But the *juge d'instruction* lost his power to decide after his investigation whether a suspect's case was actionable, ceding it to the *Commissaire du Gouvernement*: thus a fundamental principle of French penal law, according to which the decision to prosecute must be decided independantly of the prosecution itself, was overturned. More seriously,

[1] R. Aron, *Histoire de l'épuration*, ii, 218, 110–11; figures are my court from AD 500U series. There were in addition, 1233 cases tried by the *Tribunal militaire permanent* (theoretically responsible for judging paramilitary actions against the FFI or the French army although many such actions were also judged by the *Cour de justice*, and after December 1945, for judging foreigners. Their records were not accessible.

[2] I have felt free to mention names in the few cases in which the press or subsequent published material have already done so.

the retroactive nature of *l'indignité nationale* appeared to violate the principle, as old as the consitution of 1793, that the definition of a crime must precede its commisssion. But the most bitter controversy raged around the sentences of the courts: the members of the juries were themselves fromer *resistants*, unavoidably injecting politics into justice and giving rise to questionable sentences. Pierre Laval's chauffeur lost all civic rights for five years simply for being Pierre Laval's chauffeur. In Marseille a hotel keeper lost his civic rights for ten years just for subscribing to the *Pétiniste* paper *Libération*. Sentencing was often arbitrary and tended to be harshest while memories of the occupation were still fresh, growing more lenient as time passed. A defendant's lot could depend as much on luck and timing as on law: thus Christian de la Mazière's lawyer's primary tactic was to delay as long as possible.[1] It was a questionable sort of justice.

Critics of the courts, by contrast, did not often call into question the pre-trial *instruction*, assembling the evidence for and against the defendant. Indeed they implicitly applauded it when they argued that the evidence presented did not justify the sentence imposed. Christian de la Mazière saw his *juge d'instruction* some fifteen times before his trial for a total of about thirty hours, and although his lawyer could not always be present, de la Mazière did not complain of injustice during the *instruction* itself. The inclusion of extensive and numerous depositions from *temoins à dècharge* in the dossiers of the Marseille collaborators, and of psychological examinations where the *juge* thought appropriate, justifies a similar level of confidence in the pre-trial process once taken in hand by a professional *juge d'instruction*. What happened in court is another matter.

The material thus assembled, forming the bulk of the 500U series, nonetheless calls for circumspection when used as historical evidence. In addition to its value as a source on the systems of collaboration in place during the war, it provides three major sorts of information — about the social background, the activities, and the motives of the collaborators — but each is subject to certain problems of credibilty and interpretation.

Professional background

At his first interrogation the suspect provided basic information about himself, including his date and place of birth, his marital status, and his profession. It is not always clear, however, whether the profession given is that at the time of arrest, at moment of entry into collaborationst activities, or the pre-war profession: the three may well have differed. Very often the suspect's subsequent account of his life and wartime activities resolves the doubt: for the purposes of the statistical analyses in chapter 6–8 the profession used is that at the moment of entry into collaboration; where this is not clearly available the profession taken is the prewar profession; and where this is not available the profession taken is that given, with no further explanation, at the *interrogatoire de premiére comparution*. For the pre-war PPF — 173 of those investigated had joined the PPF before the war — the pre-war profession is the same as the profession upon joining the party and is normally specified; where it is not the profession used is that given during the first interrogation.

---

[1] R. Aron. *op. cit.*, ii, 92–6, 102–108; P. Novick, *The resistance versus Vichy. The Purge of Collaborators in Liberated France* (New York, 1968), pp. 157–184; H. Lottman, *The People's Anger. Justice and Revenge in Post-Liberation France* (London, 1986), p. 165; AD 500U35, A. Mag...8 March 1945; Christian de la Mazière, *Le rèveur casqué* (Paris, 1976), p. 226 (de la Mazière had served in the *Waffen-SS*).

[1] Christian de la Mazière, *op. cit.*, p. 236.

Collaborationist activity

The nature of the defendant's collaborationist activity emerges from his own state-ments, the statements of witnesses, including relatives, neighbours, or colleagues, and the conclusions of the *juge d'instruction*. Normally the three sorts of evidence are congruent, and a reliable picture emerges. But problems arise when the types of evidence conflict.

This happens, most commonly, when the defendant flatly denies the charges against him and the supporting evidence from witnesses. Often the denial is implau-sible and can be rejected by the historian as it was by the *juge d'instruction*: a suspect denies being in the *Waffen-SS* despite a partially erased blood-group tattoo (see p. 141); a *milicien* denies guarding prisoners at Avignon and La Tour d'Aigues but was seen by separate witnesses doing so; a suspected member of the PPF denies all, without any explanation, when different witnesses report seeing him selling papers outside the PPF *siège*, wearing a German uniform and carrying arms.[1] But some-times the denial, in spite of some evidence supporting the charge, is not inherently implausible: a member of the *Groupe collaboration* who declared on 11 November 1942, the day the Germans occupied the southern zone, that it was the happiest day of his life, explains that it also happened to be his wife's birthday; a suspected member of the PPF, thought to have guarded prisoners in the Baumettes, is unknown to all the other prison guards. Sometimes the declarations of the witnesses are unconvincing. When two 'camarades' come forth to denounce a local industrialist as 'cette personne PPF notoire, nazi de coeur, grand admirateur de l'hitlérisme, propagandiste et recruteur de la LFDC, SOL et Miliciens...' etc., scepticism is more than justified. Likewise witnesses who accused a worker at the *Entr'aide sociale* of repeated pro-Nazi declarations had earlier been accused by her of stealing. In such cases the conclusions of the *juge d'instruction* and of the court itself are the only basis for a historical conclusion (for purposes of statistical analyses). The member of the *Groupe Collaboration* was convicted; the suspected prison guard was acquitted; the industrialist was convicted on the basis of other evidence; the worker at the *Entr'aide sociale* was acquitted.[1] In such cases, therefore, the defendant has been taken to have performed the actions for which he was convicted. Only very rarely is the con-clusion reached by the *juge d'instruction* and the court (as distinct from its sentence) incomprehensible and at odds with the assembled evidence.

In most cases the *juge d'instruction* and the defendant together, often after confron-tations with witnesses, and in the presence of the defendant's lawyer, produce a plausible version of events.[2] When a member of the PPF declares that he rarely went to meetings and stayed away from the party he is speaking tendentiously, but when witnesses confirm his inactivity, or when no evidence of any other kind is found, and when the *juge d'instruction* and the court believe him, the historian is justified in believeing him as well.

Motive for collaboration

In many cases defendants give reasons for joining a collaborationist party or under-taking collaborationist action. Such assertions were more difficult to prove or dis-

[1] AD 500U series, *liasses*: 166, M. La...28 May 1946; 91, L. La...8 May 1946; 141, V. Mar...3 May 1945.

[1] There is no evidence at all of torture or brutality at this point, but some defendants initially arrested by members of the FFI retract confessions made at the time —

medical examinations sometimes confirm that they had then been tortoured — and such earlier confessions lose historical as well as legal validity.

[1] AD 500U: 38, P. Me...13 June 1945; 133, A. Fan...12 July 1946; 17, G. Du...8 March 1945; R. Gro...25 July 1945.

prove than assertions about activity, and the likelihood of fabrication is therefore stronger.

Often witnesses confirm the defendant's explanation of his actions — neighbours or colleagues confirm, for example, that defendants joined the PPF to avoid the STO. Often explanation is entirely plausible — when unemployed workers took up well-paying jobs in the *Organisation Todt* it is likely that they did so for the money. Patterns emerge — of volunteer workers in Germany or in the LVF signing up in the wake of some domestic dispute, for example — suggesting that the motives given are not fabricated: coincidence is too strong.[1]

But occasionally the motives are clearly fabricated. If a bank employee joined the *Groupe Collaboration* in December 1941 in order to secure the release of his brother from a prisoner-of-war camp, why did he not resign — he stayed in until August 1944 — when it became clear his brother was not coming back? How could a *milicien* have joined the *Milice* to escape the STO when he was working for a requisitioned company and thus already exempt from the STO?[2] In such cases the given motive has been rejected and none has been entered for the defendant in the statistical analyses. If some motives are invented, others are hidden: few defendants, in post-Liberation Marseille, are likely to admit conviction or pro-Nazi sentiments if they ever had them: the historian must look elsewhere for indications of the level of conviction among the collaborators, not reflected in the 500U series or in the conclusions drawn from it.[2] There is thus a margin of error in the collective analysis of motivations, making conclusions reliable only if the patterns and the numbers are suppricently loud and clear for confidence. Otherwise conclusions must be qualified.

Evidence about pre-war motives is less difficult to assess. It relates almost entirely to 173 members of the PPF who had joined before the war, 95 of whom give motives for doing so.[4] The practical motives given by so many, especially the municipal employees, are entirely plausible: if they are hiding their convictions why do others who joined admit their own so freely? Their confession of loyalty to Sabiani, furthermore, could be just as dangerous: if they are hiding motives then why not hide that one? Fears may have modified their versions of reality, especially if they remained in the party during the occupation, but again a credible pattern emerges, lending itself to qualified conclusions.

Caveats about credibility, therefore, can moderate but do not undermine the historical value of the 500U series. Provided that its revelations are not always taken at face value it remains an incomparable source for the study of wartime collaboration in almost all its forms.

---

[1] Cf. pp. 189, 191, 216, 275–276.

[2] AD 500U: 23, L. Gar...6 Dec. 1944; 63, J. Mel...6 Dec. 1944.

[3] Cf. p. 22[2]

[4] Cf. p.

The Social Composition of the Main Collaborationist Organisations[1]

Class	Occupation	PPF (1940–44)	SOL (1942–3)	Milice (1943–4)	Gr. Coll. (1941–4)	Hot. Cal. (1944)
Lower	1. Unskilled workers	21	20	51	3	8
		4%	5%	8%	2%	6%
	2. Skilled workers	27	32	47	4	8
		5%	7%	7%	3%	6%
	3. Service personnel	46	40	78	8	16
		9%	9%	12%	6%	11%
	4. Dockers, sailors	35	3	13	2	9
		7%	1%	2%	1%	6%
Subtotals		129	95	189	17	41
		26%	22%	28%	12%	29%
Lower middle	5. Artisans	20	28	46	6	6
		4%	6%	7%	4%	4%
	6. Shopkeepers	55	33	54	13	18
		11%	8%	8%	9%	13%
	7. Office workers	34	37	57	19	4
		7%	9%	9%	14%	3%
	8. Fonctionnaires	64	59	57	9	24[2]
		13%	13%	9%	6%	17%
Subtotals		173	157	214	47	52
		35%	36%	32%	34%	36%
Upper middle	9. Lib. professions	12	34	22	19	0
		2%	8%	3%	14%	0%
	10. Cce. and industry	20	17	17	11	1
		4%	4%	3%	8%	1%
	11. Senior employees	36	68	66	18	3
		7%	15%	10%	13%	2%
Subtotals		68	119	105	48	4
		14%	27%	16%	34%	3%
	12. Unemployed	90	26	82	19	36
		18%	6%	12%	14%	25%
	13. Other	32[3]	41[4]	76[5]	8	10
		7%	9%	11%	6%	7%
Totals		492	438	666	139	143
		100%	100%	100%	100%	100%
	Occupation unknown	28	22	45	7	10
Totals		530	460	711	146	153

[1] Source: 2541 dossiers in the AD 500U series (all individuals belonging to the main organisations). Occupational classifications as in Appendix II.
[2] Includes 15 school or university students.
[3] Includes 11 police.
[4] Includes 24 agricultural workers.
[5] Includes 32 agricultural workers.

Class	Occupation	Vol. Wkrs. (19: 41–4	LVF 41–4	Waffen- SS 43–4	Org. Todt. 43–4	Kriegs marine 43–4	Komman- dantur[1] 43–4)
Lower	1. Unskilled workers	21 15%	9 12%	5 16%	14 8%	3 12%	2 2%
	2. Skilled workers	16 12%	4 5%	1 3%	13 7%	2 8%	4 4%
	3. Service personnel	18 13%	8 10%	3 9%	32 18%	1 4%	25 26%
	4. Dockers, sailors	5 4%	3 4%	2 5%	9 5%	3 12%	4 4%
Subtotals		60 44%	24 31%	11 34%	68 39%	9 36%	35 36%
Lower middle	5. Artisans	4 3%	3 4%	0 0%	15 9%	0 0%	4 4%
	6. Shopkeepers	8 6%	3 4%	4 12%	7 4%	0 0%	9 9%
	7. Office workers	2 1%	2 1%	1 3%	11 6%	0 0%	3 3%
	8. Fonctionnaires	8 6%	6 8%	3 9%	2 1%	0 0%	8 8%
Subtotals		22 16%	14 18%	8 25%	35 20%	0 0%	24 25%
Upper middle	9. Lib. professions	1 1%	1 1%	1 3%	6 3%	1 4%	1 1%
	10. Cce. and industry	0 0%	1 1%	0 0%	5 3%	1 4%	3 3%
	11. Senior employees	4 3%	6 8%	1 3%	10 6%	5 20%	5 5%
Subtotals		5 4%	8 10%	2 6%	21 12%	7 28%	9 9%
	12. Unemployed	39 29%	31 40%	11 34%	41 24%	9 36%	23 24%
	13. Other	10 7%	0 0%	0 0%	9 5%	0 0%	6 6%
Totals		136 100%	77 100%	32 100%	174 100%	25 100%	97 100%
	Occupation unknown	10	12	10	12	5	15
Totals		146	89	42	186	30	112

[1] Includes 58 employees of the SD (many service personnel) as well as those of *Wehrmacht* staff headquarters.

NOTES

Preface and Acknowledgements

1. R. Brasillach, Notre avant-guerre (Paris, 1941), p. 282; P.-M. Dioudonnat, *Je Suis Partout, 1930–1944. Les Maurrassiens devant la tentation fasciste* (Paris, 1973), p. 373 (quote from P.-A. Cousteau in *Je Suis Partout*, 17 Sept. 1943); R. Soucy, 'The Nature of Fascism in France', *Journal of Contemporary History*, I, i (1966); E. Weber, 'Nationalism, Socialism and National Socialism in France', *French Historical Studies*, 2 (spring 1962); R. Girardet, 'Notes sur l'esprit d'un fascisme français, 1934–1939', *Revue française de science politique*, 5 (1955); J. Plumyène and R. Lasierra, *Les fascismes français, 1923–1963*, (Paris 1963), p .23.

2. Ernst Nolte, *Three Faces of Fascism* (2nd. end., New York, 1969, tr. from German edn., Munich, 1963), pp. 51–182; R. de Felice, *Fascism. An Informal Introduction to its Theory and Practice* (New Brunswick, 1976), p. 92; S. Grossman, 'L'Evolution de Marcel Déat', *Revue d'histoire de la deuxième guerre mondiale*, 97 (1975); A. Bergounioux, 'Le néo-socialisme. Marcel déat: réformisme traditionnel ou esprit des années trente', *Revue historique*, CCLX/2 (1978); J. Plumyène and R. Lasierra, *Les fascismes français, 1923–1963* (Paris, 1963),

pp. 86–88; Z. Sternhell, 'Anatomie d'un mouvement fasciste en France. Le Faisceau de Georges Valois'. *Revue française de science politique*, vol. 26 no. 1 (Feb. 1976); J. Levey, 'Georges Valois and the Faisceau: the making and breaking of a fascist', *French Historical Studies* 8 (1973); Yves Guchet, *Georges Valois* (Paris, 1975), pp. 242–246; R. Brasillach, *op.cit.*, p. 29.

3. Paris, 1983; Bertrand de Jouvenel sued; Raymond Aron testified in his support. Cf. also Z. Sternhell, 'Sur le fascisme et sa variante française', *Le Débat*, 32 (Nov. 1984); Z. Sternhell. 'Emmanuel Mounier et la contestation de la démocratie libérale dans la France des années trente', *Revue française de science politique*, 6 (Dec. 1984); Z. Sternhell, 'Socialisme nationale n'égale pas national socialisme', *Le Monde*, 11–12 March 1984.

4. Gilbert Comte in *Le Monde Diplomatique*, March 1985; J. Julliard, 'Sur un fascisme imaginaire — à propos d'un livre de Zeev Sternhell', *Annales ESC*, March 1985; M. Winock, 'Fascisme à la française ou fascisme introuvable?', *Le Débat*, 25 (May 1983); Shlomo Sand, 'L'Idéologie fasciste en France', *Esprit* Aug.-Sept. 1983; J.-M. Domenach in *Esprit*, *Aug.-Sept. 1983; Raymond Aron in*

L'Express, 4 Feb. 1983; J.-P. Entho-ven, 'Fascistes, si vous saviez', Le Nouvel Observateur, 18 Feb. 1983; P. Burrin, 'La France dans le champ magnétique du fascisme', Le Débat, 32 (Nov. 1984).

5. J. Plumyène and R. Lasierra, op.cit., pp. 116 ff.; R. Rémond, Les droites en France (2nd. edn., Paris, 1982), pp. 216–217; M. Winock in Histoire, 1980, p. 45; P. Milza, Les Fascismes (Paris 1985), p. 294.

6. A. Jacomet, 'Les chefs du francisme: M. Bucard et Paul Guiraud', Revue d'histoire de la deuxiéme guerre mon-diale, 97 (Jan. 1975); M. Winock in Histoire, 1980; R. Rémond, op.cit., pp. 211–216; P. Machefer, 'L'union des droites, Le PSF et le Front de la Liberté, 1936–1937', Revue d'histoire moderne et contemporaine, Jan.-March 1970; J. Plumyène and R. Lasierra, op.cit., pp. 28–31; M. Anderson, Conservative Politics in France (Lon-don, 1974), p. 54; R. Soucy, 'Cen-trist Fascism': the Jeunesses Patriotes', Journal of Contemporary History, 16/2 (April 1981).

Two recent books on 'French fas-cism' do not attempt, either, to an-swer such questions. R. Soucy, in French Fascism: The First Wave, 1924–1933 (New Haven and London, 1986) tries to suggest on the basis of a few leading members that the Fais-ceau was predominantly middle class (p. 101). Generally he characterises whole movements as fascist on the basis of criteria which are never very clear, referring to royalist fas-cists as well as republican fascists (p. 25), centrist fascists, etc. P. Burrin in La dérive fasciste, Doriot, Déat, Bergery, 1933–1945 (Paris, 1986), asks new questions about ideas, in particular about the process of 'fascisation' which led Doriot and Déat, in his view, to a kind of derivative, secondary, defensive fascism, but he has much less to say about their diffusion or appeal.

7. R. Rémond, op.cit., p. 217; P. Milza, op.cit., p. 299; R. Girardet, 'Notes sur l'esprit d'un fascisme

français, 1934–1939', Revue française de science politique, 5 (1955) re limi-tations on evidence; J.-P. Brunet, Jacques Doriot. Du communisme au fas-cisme (Paris, 1986), pp. 231–232 and St Denis la ville rouge (Paris, 1980), pp. 407–408 quotes the party's own statistics giving 49 per cent of the delegates at the Nov. 1936 congress and 37 per cent at the March 1938 congress as 'ouvriers', as did H. Coston, Partis, journaux, et hommes politiques d'hier et d'aujourd'hui (Paris, 1960), pp. 124, 129 and M.Y. Sicard, Histoire de la collaboration (Paris, 1964), pp. 16 ff. and likewise D. Wolf, op.cit., pp. 190–192, where he believes the percentage of 'ouvriers' to be 'manifestement exagéré', a view supported by the evidence for Marseille above.

8. Cf. P. Milza, op.cit., pp. 296, 297.

9. J.-A: Vaucoret, Un homme politique conteste: Simon Sabiani (thèse de doc-torat de troisième cycle, Université de Provenee, 1979).

Chapter 1

1. Paris Match, 17 Jan. 1970; E. Sac-comano, Bandits à Marseille (Paris, 1968), p. 75; A. Jaubert, Dossier D...comme drogue (Paris, 1974), pp. 38–39; Le Provençal, 8 June 1986; comment of Marseille taxi-driver, 17 Dec. 1983.

2. AN F²2234, Rapport de l'inspecteur général des services administratives to Int., 20 April 1933.

3. Ibid; Journal Officiel 29 Dec. 1938., Project de loi tendant à une nouvelle organisation administrative de la ville de Marseille. Marseille covered 23,000 hectares, Paris 10,000, Lyon 4,400, and the fourth canton 107.

4. No one knew, and no one knows, what the population of Marseille was in the 1930s. It was given as 803,000 in the 1931 census; G. Rambert, in Marseille. La formation d'une grande cité moderne (Marseille, 1934), pp. 445–450, thought that

643,000 would be a more realistic figure. The city's population was perhaps 700,000 ten years later, cf. J.-P. Beauquier, 'Problèmes du ravitaillement dans la région marseillaise', *Revue d'histoire de la deuxièmed guerre mondiale*, 113 (Jan. 1979), 5–43. In the 1946 census it was 646,000 Cf. also F. Pomponi *et.al.*, *Le Mémorial des Corses* (Ajaccio, 1981), vi. p. 480, where 650,000 is the estimate for the population in 1939. The total figure in the 1936 census, 914,000, is an obvious over-statement, probably concocted to outdo Lyon and to support demands for financial and other other assistance from Paris, but that given for the fourth canton — 52,596 — is in line with that of 1931 — 48,865.

5. *MM* 27 Oct. 1933; *MM* 17 May 1939; G. Cazaux, *Quelques vues de Marseille*, (Bordeaux, 1929), pp. 31–34; Louis Blin, *Marselle inconnu* (Avignon, 1941), p. 113.

6. Blin, *op.cit.*, pp. 113–115; André Chagny, *Marseille et ses environs* (Lyon, 1931), p. 32; Anne Sportiello, *Les pêcheurs du Vieux-Port* (Marseille, 1981).

7. Rambert, *op.cit.*, pp. 462–464; P. Guiral, *Libération de Marseille* (Paris, 1974), p. 35; A. Olivesi, in E. Baratier, ed., *Histoire de Marseille* (Toulouse, 1973), pp. 387–420; Stéphane Wlocevski, *L'Installation des Italiens en France* (Paris, 1934), pp. 35, 82; F. Pomponi *et.al.*, *op.cit.*, vi 477; AD M⁶11354, CD to Pref., 14 Jan. 1937; *MM* 3 Sept. 1938; *LPM* 20 April 1933.

8. G. Cazaux, *op.cit.*, p. 28. 'Bachin' was local *argot* for Italian.

9. 1931 census.

10. Pierre MacOrlan, *Quartier réservé* (Paris, 1932), p. 39; Edmond Jaloux, *Marseille* (Paris, 1926), p. 45; cf. also *Jean Dorian, Belles de Lune*. Reportage dans les bas-fonds de Marseille (Paris, 1935).

11. 1936 census (4th. canton, *bureaux de vote* nos. 26, 27, 28); Rambert, *op.cit.*, p. 454 (average 933 per hectare = c.375 per acre) and fig. 48, p. 451; L. Pierrein, 'Marseille depuis 1933', *Etudes rhodaniennes*, XV, 1939, p. 332 (peak of 2,800 per hectare = c.1,100 per acre).

12. Blin, *op.cit.*, pp. 9–10; *LPM* 19 April 1933; see appendix I.

13. From 1936 census (4th. canton, polling stations nos. 26, 28); see appendix I (stations nos. 26, 27, 28). 'Men' denotes all over 14 in 1936.

14. *Ibid* (bureau de vote no.27).

15. Marcel Roncayolo, 'La croissance urbaine de Marseille', Marseille, revue municipale, lvi, July-Sept 1964; Simone Grangier, Naissance et développement de deux quartiers de Marseille: Chapitre-Longchamp et Saint-Charles (Mémoire de maîtrise, Aix-en-Provence, 1954), p. 156; MM 3 Sept. 1935; MM 18 Nov. 1936; M.F. Maraninchi-Attard, *Les associations corses à Marseille, 1920–1960* (thèse de doctorat de troisième cycle, Université de Provence, 1984), p. 71.

16. Blin, *op.cit.*, pp. 64–65; MM 21 April 1934; see appendix I; AD M⁶11785, CD to Pref., 7 Nov. 1934; see appendix ii; the social comparisons are between bureaus nos. 26, 27 and 28 on the one hand and 24 and 25 on the other.

17. MM 2 Nov. 1933; see also *LPM* 21 April 1933, 'La troisième incarnation de Mahmadou'.

18. MM 2, 3, 4, 9, 15 Jan. 1934; MM 19 May 1939; Blin, *op.cit.*, pp. 71–73; AD M⁶8294, *Rapport du capitaine de gendarmerie,* 24 July 1935; Rambert, *op.cit.*, pp. 423–424.

19. MM 26 Jan. 1936; Cazaux, *op.cit.*, pp. 44–45.

20. See appendix I, *bureaux de vote* 115, 119; Rambert, *op.cit.*, p. 451, fig. 48.

21. From reports in AD M⁶IIM³56, CS to Pref., 10 March 1928 and 1 March 1928, and CC to Pref., 14 March 1928; AD M⁶10791, CC to Pref., 5 Feb. 1939; AD M⁶10873, CC to Pref., 24 March 1934; AD

M^610878, CC to Pref., 19 Sept. 1937 and 22 Sept. 1937; AD M^611379, CD to Pref, 26 Dec. 1934.

22. *L'Eclair,* 24 Feb. 1928; *Massalia* 4 May 1929; ML 24 Oct. 1930.

23. From reports of meetings in AD M^610803, CC to Pref., 12 April 1925; MM 28 May 1931, 3 Oct. 1933, 13 March 1933; *Le Radical* 28 June 1925.

24. AD IIIM51, CC to Pref., 9 Oct. 1931.

25. From reports of meetings in AD M^68292, CC to Pref., 23 Dec. 1931; AD M^610803, CC to Pref., 12 April 1925; photo in ML 1 Jan. 1932.

26. AD M^610789, CC to Pref., 24 April 1935; AD M^68294, Pref. to Int., 8 Nov. 1935; AD IIM^360, CD to Pref., 21 April 1936 and CC to Pref., 21 April 1936.

27. From reports of meetings in AD M^614464, *commissaire de police 7ème arrdt.* to CC, 10 April 1935; AD M^610878, CD to Pref., 1 Oct. 1937; AD VM^2284, Pref. to Int., 9 May 1935, CC to Pref., 9 May 1935, and Pref. to Int., 14 May 1935; *LPP* 7 May 1935; AD IIM^356, CC to Pref., 2 May 1928; AD IIIM49, CC to Pref., 21 July 1925.

28. Like those held by *Sabianistes* and socialists in bars in the Place Jules Guesde, cf. *comm. de police 7ème arrdt.* to CC, 10 April 1935.

29. AD M^6IIIM51, police report, 9 Oct. 1931; *MM* 8 Oct. 1934; AD IIM^356, *Comm. de police* to CC, 24 March 1928; AD IIIM53, 22 Sept. 1937; AD IIM^359, CD to Pref., 1 May 1936; AD IIM^356, CC to Pref., 6 March 1928 and 25 Feb. 1928; AD IIM^358, CC to Pref., 16 Oct. 1930; AD M^68287, report of CS, 8 Jan. 1924.

30. AD IIIM53, *Comm. de police* to CC, 1 Oct. 1937, and CC to Pref., 17 Oct. 1937; AD IIIM52, *comm. de police* to CC, 29 Sept. 1934; *LPM* 26 Sept. 1934; AD VM^2268, CC to Pref., 4 May 1929 and 29 April

1929; AD VM^2284, CC to Pref., 26 April 1935.

31. AD IIM^356, CS to Pref., 1 and 10 March 1928; AD IIIM48, Pref. to Int., 16 Aug. 1922; AD M^68292, *comm. de sûreté* to CC, 19 April 1928; *LPM* 7 May 1935 (italics in original); *Candide* 23 Jan. 1930; AD VM^2268, CC to Pref., 7 May 1929; *MM* 25 Oct. 1937; AD IIIM47, *non-lieu* by *Conseil d'Etat*, 31 July 1925; AD IIIM50, CS report, 5 Feb. 1929; AD IIIM49, CC to Pref., 29 Aug. 1924; Michel Bergès, 'Clientélisme et corruption politiques: le cas de deux municipalités françaises des années trente', *Revue occitane,* July 1984.

32. AD IIIM47, *non-lieu* by *Conseil d'Etat*, 31 July 1925; AD M^610816, Pref. to Int., 16 Nov. 1937; MM 11 Oct. 1937; Alban Géronimi, Marseille, 12 Dec. 1983 (interview).

33. AD IIIM53, *Procureur de la République* to *Procureur Général*, 14 Oct. 1937, and *inspecteur de la sûreté* to CC, 11 Oct. 1937; AD IIIM54, *Conseil de Préfecture* ruling, 18 Nov. 1937; AD M^610878, CD to Pref., 11 Oct. 1937; *MM* 7 Dec. 1938, 11 Oct. 1937, 18 Oct. 1937.

34. Alban Géronimi, Marseille, 12 Dec, 1983; AD IIIM47, ruling of *Conseil d'Etat*, 28 Jan. 1921; *L'Echo de Paris*, 14 July 1926; *MM* 15 Oct. 1937.

35. AD M^611355, Pref. to Int., 15 Nov. 1937.

36. *Ibid.*

37. AD VM^2268, *Chef des gardiens* to CC, 26 April 1929; *MM* 2 March 1939.

38. Alban Géronimi, Marseille, 12 Dec. 1983; AD IIIM51, CC to Pref., 9 Oct. 1931; AD IIIM53, CS to Pref., 27 Sept. 1937 and CC to Pref., 9 Oct. 1937; AD IIM^360, CC to *Procureur de la République*, 5 May 1936; AD IIM^358, CC to Pref., 7 Oct. 1930; ADIIM52, *inspecteur de la sûreté* to CC, 11 Oct. 1937.

39. *LPM* 20 Dec. 1929; further details

on numbers and organization of police in AD M^{6}8320; Pref. to Int., 4 Sept. 1921; AD M^{6}11355, Pref. to Int., 22 Jan. 1938; Pref. to Int., 15 Nov. 1937; CD to Pref., 1 Dec. 1935; *L'Echo de Paris* 14 Jan. 1930; AD IIIM53, note of Pref., 3 Oct. 1937.

40. AD IIIM52, Pref. announcement, 25 Sept. 1934; AD M^{6}10803, CC to Pref., 8 Oct. 1925; AD IIIM53, CC to Pref., 4 Oct. 1937; AD IIIM55, CC to Pref., 30 June 1938.

41. AD IIIM50, Pref. to Baret, 5 Feb. 1929; *Le Sémaphore* 30 July 1927; AD IIIM54, *Conseil de Préfecture* ruling, 18 Nov. 1937; AD IIIM53, *Procureur de la République to Procureur Général*, 14 Oct. 1937; AD IIIM55, CD to Pref., 19 April 1939; AD IIIM48, ruling of *Conseil d'Etat*, 14 March 1924.

42. AD M^{6}10878, CD to Pref., 1 Oct. 1937; AD VM^{2}284, Pref. to Int., 14 May 1935; AD IIIM49, Duverger to Pref., 16 July 1925; AD VM^{2}268, CC to Pref., 4 May 1929, *Commissaire de sûreté* to CC, 5 May 1929, and *chef des gardiens* to CC, 26 April 1929; AD IIIM53, CC to Pref., 15 Oct. 1937.

43. Cf. e.g. the complaint filed by Stefani-Martin after his loss to Bon, in AD IIM47, 3 Aug. 1924.

44. Dr. Lucien Fredenucci, Marseille, 11 June 1986 (interview).

45. For the Guerinis see AD M^{6}11946, CD to Pref., 25 Jan. 1940; AD M^{6}10873, CC to Pref., 24 March 1934; AD M^{6}10878, *chef de sûreté* to CC, 25 Oct. 1937; AD IIIM53, CC to Pref., 23 Sept. 1937; for the Renuccis see L'Eclair 7 Feb. 1941; AD IIIM-52, chef de sûreté to CC, 29 Sept. 1934; AD IIIM51, note of Pref., 19 March 1831; AN F^{7}13985, *Enquête [of renseignements généraux] sur les 'gangsters' des Alpes-Maritimes, du Var et des Bouches-du-Rhone*, 24 Nov. 1937; for Carbone and Spirito see e.g. AD M^{6}10791, CC to Pref., 6 Feb. 1939, and p. 00.

46. Candide 23 Jan. 1930.

47. AD M^{6}10930, CD to Pref., 9 Jan. 1940; AD M^{6}11391, Chef de la sûreté to CC, 24 Jan. 1930; pp.

48. Ad 4Msup/51, CD to Pref., 30 Jan. 1930; AD 4M/sup54, Commissaire de police mobile to CD, 10 Nov. 1932.

49. AD VM^{2}268, CC to Pref., 4 April 1929.

50. *Bulletin municipal officiel de la ville de Marseille*, 4 Dec. 1931.

51. *Le Cri de Marseille*, 3 Oct. 1931; *MM* 18 April 1936 and 19 Oct. 1931.

52. *Journal Officiel*, 'Réorganisation administratif de la ville de Marseille', 21 March 1939; AN F^{2}2235, *Réorganisation...Constatations faites à Marseille par les rapporteurs du comité* (n.d., 1939).

53. *Ibid.*

54. AD M^{6}8292: Pref. to Ambrosini, 3 Dec. 1931, 21 Dec. 1921, 27 Nov. 1931, Ambrosini to Pref., 12 May 1931, 9 Feb. 1931; Régis to Pref., 16 Oct. 1931; Pref. to Pollak, 14 Jan. 1931; Tasso to Pref., 16 Dec. 1931; AN F^{7}13985, *Enquête [of renseignements généraux] sur les 'gangsters' des Alpes-Maritimes, du Var et des Bouches-du-Rhone*, 24 Nov. 1937; *L'Echo de Paris*, 14 Jan. 1930; AD M^{6}11353, Ambrosini to Pref., 2 Dec. 1932; AD M^{6}8293, Ambrosini to Pref., 11 June 1934; AD M^{6}11354, Matton to Pref., 19 Oct. 1936; AD M^{6}11412, register of interventions, June to Aug. 1939; AD M^{6}8294; Tasso to Pref., 2 Feb. 1935 and 25 Feb. 1935; Grand to Pref., 24 May 1935 and 21 Feb. 1935; AD M^{6}10794, Pref. to Gouin, Régis to Pref., Vidal to Pref., Bouisson to Pref., all 7 April 1932.

55. Antoine Franceschi, St. Jullien (Marseille), 10 June 1986 (interview).

56. *Bulletin municipal officiel de la ville de Marseille*, 22 March 1935; AD 500U26, case of J. Gro...(see appendix III for a description of this source).

57. AD O⁹53 *Rapport of Court des Comptes*, 1933, and Pref. to Int., Feb. 1939; AN F²2234, *Administrateur délégué des tramways to précepteur des impôts*, 7 Dec. 1938; *Journal Officiel*, 21 March 1939; AN F²2235; AD VM²289, *Conseil de Préfecture* ruling, 4 July 1935.

58. *LPP* 18 March 1928, 20 March 1928; *MM* 3 Oct. 1921; *La vie municipale et préfectorale*, 18 July 1925; *Bulletin municipale*, 22 March 1935. Even if they were not naturalised and did not vote, the Algerian immigrants were a force in the constituency and it would have been imprudent to ignore them.

59. AD M⁶10793, 'Une groupe d'électeurs' to Tasso, 21 June 1935; *MM* 6 Sept. 1935; AD M⁶11353, CC to Pref., 16 Oct. 1933; *MM* 11 Aug. 1931, 23 Nov. 1931, 24 Nov. 1931, 19 Dec. 1931, 3 March 1932, 24 Oct. 1935.

60. *LPM* 28 April 1935; AD 500U237, case of P. Ant . . . (*non-lieu*).

61. *Journal Officiel*, 21 March 1939; AN F²2235, *Réorganisation . . . Constatations faites à Marseille par les rapporteurs*, n.d. 1939; AD 1953: *Rapport of Cour des Comptes*, 1933; *Proc. Gén. près la Cour des Comptes* to Pref., 18 June 1938.

62. AD O³52, *Trésorier payeur central* to Pref., 9 Feb. 1939 and 18 Nov. 1939; *L'Eclair* 27 April 1929; AD O⁹ *Rapport of Cour des Comptes*, 1933; M. Pagnol, *Topaze*, II, iv.

63. AD O⁹, *Rapport of Cour des Comptes*, 1933; *Receveur municipal* to Tasso, 22 Dec. 1939; *Le cri de Marseille*, 23 Aug. 1930; *Journal Officiel* 21 March 1939; AN F²2235, *Réorganisation . . . Constatations faites à Marseille par les rapporteurs*, 1939; A. Olivesi, 'Henri Tasso', *Marseille. Revue municipale*, 100, Jan.-March 1975; A. Olivesi, 'Canavelli', in Jean Maitron, ed., *Dictionnaire biographique du mouvement ouvrier français*, XXI, Paris, 1984.

64. *Le Bavard* 30 Sept. 1922.

65. *MM* 29 Oct. 1938.

66. J.C. Scott, 'Corruption, Machine Politics and Political Change', *American Political Science Review*, lxiii, Dec. 1969; E. Gellner and John Waterbury, eds., *Patrons and Clients in Mediterranean Societies* (London, 1977); J. Lalumia, 'Mafia as a Political Mentality', *Social Theory and Practice*, vii, 1981.

67. Stéphane Wlocevski, *L'Installation des Italiens en France* (Paris, 1934), p. 82; Anne-Marie Faidutti-Rudolph, *L'Immigration italienne dans le sud-est de la France* (Thèse pour le doctorat-ès-lettres, Université de Paris, pub. Gap 1964); AD M⁶10808, report of foreign ministry, 6 Dec, 1928.

68. *MM* 28 Sept. 1931, 1 Jan. 1932; AD M⁶11354, *rapport of Sûreté* on foreigners; D.A.L. Levy, *The Marseille Working Class Movement, 1936–1938* (Oxford University D.Phil. thesis, 1982), p. 26; *LPP* 2 April 1933, 22 May 1933.

69. See appendix I (*bureaux de vote nos* 24 and 28).

70. G. Rambert, *Marseille. La formation d'une grande cité moderne* (Marseille, 1934) pp. 458–459.

71. Appendix I; F. Pomponi *et.al., Le Mémorial des Corses* (Ajaccio, 1981), vi, pp. 453, 477.

72. Paul Bourde, *En Corse* (Paris, 1887), p. 10, Sabiani was born in 1888, Canavelli in 1877.

73. Georges Ravis-Giordani, 'L'Alta pulitica et la bassa pulitica: valeurs et comportements politiques dans les communautés villageoises corses', *Etudes rurales*, lxiii/lxiv 1976; Georges Ravis-Giordani, 'Familles et pouvoir en Corse', *Sociologie du sud-est*, xxi, Oct. 1979; Bourde, *op.cit.*, pp. 109–110.

74. A. Quantin, *La Corse*, Paris 1914, p. 267, pp. 267–273; Bourde, *op.cit.*, p. 83; cf. also F. Pomponi, 'Pouvoir et abus de pouvoir des maires corses au XIX siècle, *Etudes rurales*, lxiii/lxiv 1976.

75. Quantin, *op.cit.*, p. 263; Bourde, *op.cit.*, p. 41.

76. M.F. Maraninchi, *Un exemple de migration dans l'entre-deux guerres: l'ex-*

ode calenzanais (mémoire de maîtrise, Université de Provence, 1977), p. 74 (from oral interviews).

77. *Ibid.*, pp. 61, 80, 82.

78. *Maître* Jacques Luciani (mayor of Casamaccioli, 1947–1977), Casamaccioli, 8 June 1986 (interview).

79. *Re* the Corsican clan see *e.g.* F. Pomponi, 'A la recherche d'un "invariant" historique: la structure clanique dans la société corse', in *Pieve et Paese* (CNRS, 1978); José Gil, 'La puissance d'un peuple', *Revue des temps modernes*, April 1976; Claude Olivesi, 'Le système politique corse: le clan', *Revue cuntrasti*, N°3, 1983; Charles Santoni, 'Les masques du discours politique en Corse', *Revue des temps modernes*, April 1976.

80. Maître Jacques Luciani, Casamaccioli, 8 June 1986 (interview).

81. M.F. Maraninchi-Attard, *Les Associations Corses à Marseille, 1920–1960* (Thèse de doctorat de troisième cycle, Université de Provence, 1984), p. 58.

82. Bourde, *op.cit.*, p. 84; Georges RavisGiordani, *Bergers corses. Les communautés villageoises du Niolu* (Aixen Provence, 1983), pp. 118–119; Alban Géronimi, Marseille, 12 Dec. 1983 (interview); Pierre Guiral and Guy Thuilier, *La vie quotidienne des députés en France, 1870–1914* (Paris, 1980), p. 63; F. Pomponi, 'Pouvoir et abus...', *cit.*p. 157.

83. Louis Barthou, *La Politique* (Paris, 1923), pp. 17–19; A. Tardieu, *La profession parlementaire* (Paris, 1937), p. 41; Etienne Fournol, *Manuel de politique française*, (Paris, 1933), p. 124; Jacques Fourcade, *La République de la province* (Paris, 1936), pp. 134, 156, 194–195; Pierre Guiral and Guy Thuilier, *op.cit.*, p. 63; Pierre de Pressac, *Les forces historiques de la France* (Paris, 1928), p. 160.

84. The Carbones lived in the rue Audimar (in the crowded *quartier des Présentines*), AD M^{6}10813, Pref. to Int., 24 Dec., 1935, and AD

M^{6}11946, CC to Pref., 25 Jan. 1940. Antoine Guerini began has career as the owner of the Bar des Colonies in the rue Bernard-du-Bois, AD M^{6}11946, CD to Pref., 9 Jan. 1940, and Alain Jaubert, *Dossier D... comme drogue* (Paris, 1974), p. 44.

85. *LPM* 1931; AD M^{6}10221, *secrétaire général [Préfecture]* to CC, 3 May 1935; AD M^{6}10789, CD to Pref., 23 April 1936.

86. Like that Tasso sent Sabiani after the latter's electoral victory in 1928 (recollection of Alban Géronimi, Marseille, 12 Dec. 1983).

87. Roger Py (the neighbour), Marseille, 10 June 1986 (interview).

88. AD M^{6}11946, CD to Pref., 9 Jan. 1940.

89. AD IIIM48, Pref. to Int., 16 Aug. 1922; AD VM^{2}268, *Ligue des Marseillais* to Pref., 11 May 1929; AD IIIM49, CC to Pref., 21 July 1925.

90. Voting figures from AD IIIM49, IIIM53, VM^{2}283, VM^{2}289; cortège figures for 1925 from AD IIIM49, CC to Pref., 21 July 1925; for 1937 the only estimate is that of *ML* 24 Oct. 1937, 'plusieurs milliers' — the cortège was forbidden that year but supporters gathered nonetheless on election night; for 1935 the figures are from AD VM^{2}284, Pref. to Int., 9 May 1935, and Pref. to Int., 14 May 1935; for 1939 there are conflicting estimates, one of 4000 in AD M^{6}10792, CD to Pref., 25 Feb. 1939, the other of 1,600 in AD VM^{2}290, CC to Pref., 17 Feb. 1939; the figure given is their average.

91. The periods chosen for comparison here — the first six months of 1926, 1933 and 1934 — are non-electoral ones. 'Open political gathering' here means a public demonstation over a political or social issue, and excludes meetings of single unions over narrow sectorial demands, regularly scheduled party conventions, and 'parapolitical' meetings like those of the *Fédération Nationale Catholique*. For 1926 the meetings

are: an *Action Française* Mass for the victims of the *attentat* of the rue Damrémont, AD M⁶10804, CC to Pref., 11 Jan. 1926; a meeting of the *Parti républicain démocratique et social*, AD M⁶10804, CC to Pref., 18 Jan. 1926; a collective demonstration of *fonctionnaires, LPP* 26 Jan. 1926; an anti-fascist meeting of the *Ligue des droits de l'homme*, AD M⁶10805, CC to Pref., 30 May 1926.

92. Two demonstrations of *fonctionnaires*, LPP 22 Jan. and 21 Feb. 1933; Sabiani–Vidal encounter, AD M⁶11353, CC to Pref., 5 Feb. 1933; *Alliance internationale pour le suffrage et l'action civique des femmes*, AD M⁶11353, CC to Pref., 21 March 1933; *Ligue internationale contre l'antisémtisme*, AD M⁶11353, 22 May 1933.

93. Altogether, seven were collective syndical demonstrations, seven were organized by national parties or *ligues*, one by Sabiani. AD M⁶11381, Pref. to Int., 30 June 1934, gives a list of 67 demonstrations in the Bouches-du-Rhône (of all sizes) during the first six months of the year.

94. AD M⁶10820, note for Pref. on Mayday demonstrations, n.d., 1938; AD M⁶0878, CD to Pref., 21 Feb. 1937; AD M⁶10804, CC to Pref., 8 April 1926; AD M⁶11353, CC to Pref., 15 May 1933 (although the number of participants in the *fête de Jeanne d'Arc* is not given it is clear from the description that it cannot have exceeded 3,000); *LPM* 10 May 1937.

95. AD M⁶11379, CD to Pref., 31 Jan. 1934; D.A.L. Levy, 'The Marseille Working Class Movement' (Oxford University D. Phil. thesis, 1982), appendix viii.

96. AD M⁶11354, CD to Pref., 20 Jan. 1937.

97. AD M⁶11379, CD to Pref., 26 Dec. 1934.

98. Cf. eg incidents reported in AD M⁶10878, CC to Pref., 28 May 1937, and CC to Pref., 31 May

197; AD M⁶10809, CC to Pref., 29 April 1937; AN F⁷14817, *Proc. Gén. près la Cour d'Appel d'Aix* to Min. of Justice, 8 July 1938, and Pref. to Int., 14 Sept. 1937.

99. AD M⁶11354, Cristofol and Matton to Pref., 24 Dec. 1936, and Billoux to Pref., 11 March 1937.

100. Cf. D.A.L. Levy, *op.cit.*, pp. 114, 117; AD M⁶10899, CD to Pref., 19 June 1937; AD M⁶10809, Pref. to Int., 7 April 1936 (report on *Croix-de-feu*, which became the PSF three months later); AD M⁶11354, CD to Pref., 7 June 1937; AD M⁶10878, CC to Pref., 9 Jan. 1937.

101. AD IIM51, AD IIIM53; *Journal Officiel*, 21 March 1939; AD O⁹53, *Rapport of Cour des Comptes*, n.d. 1933; *LPM* 6 April 1925.

Chapter 2

1. *Agathe Sabiani, Marseille, 12 Feb. 1984 and 3 June 1986 (interviews); maître* Jacques Luciani, Casamaccioli, 8 June 1986 (interview); *ML* 3 May 1936 and 12 Sept. 1935; *LPP* 10 Oct. 1916; AD M⁶11381, CS report, 26 Nov. 1918.

2. J.-A. Vaucoret, *Un homme politique contesté: Simon Sabiani (Thése de doctorat de troisième cycle, Université de Provence, 1979)*, pp. 12, 13; AD M⁶11381, CS report, 26 Nov. 1918; AD M⁶10793, CD to Pref., 14 Jan. 1936; AD M⁶10878, CC to Pref., 19 Sept. 1937; AD IIIM48, Pref. to Int., n.d., 1922; *ML* 26 July 1930, 19 Sept. 1930, 12 Dec. 1930, 1 May 1931; *LPM* 3 May 1929; *l'Eclair* 15 Oct. 1931; *MM* 18 Oct. 1937; first quote about Sabiani from Victor Barthélemy, *Du communisme au fascisme. l'Histoire d'un engagement politique* (Paris, 1978), p. 31; second fron *le Charivari*, 2 April 1932.

3. *Roger Py, Marseille, 10 June 1986 (interview); Dr. Lucien Fredenucci, 11 June 1986 (interview); Agathe Sabiani, 12 Feb. 1984 and 10 June 1986 (interviews); Alban Géronimi,*

Marseille, 12 Dec. 1983 (interview); *ML* 2 Oct. 1931, 4 March 1932; AD M⁶10792, poster of Feb. 1939.

4. AD M⁶11381, CS report, 26 Nov. 1918; AD M⁶11380, CS report, 9 and 16 Dec. 1918; AD VM²245, CS report, 1 Dec. 1919; AD VM²250 (1919 election results); Antoine Franceschi, Marseille, 10 June 1986 (interview).

5. D. Moulinard, *Le parti communiste à Marseille. Naissance et débuts.* (Mémoire de maîtrise, Aix-en-Provence, 1971–1972), pp. 16, 47, 49, 52sqq.; A. Kriegel, *Aux origines du communisme français* (Flammarion, 1969), p. 391; AD M⁶8321, CS to Pref., 5 July, 9 Oct., 25 Oct., 16, 20, 22, 29, 30 Nov., 3 Dec. 1920.

6. D. Moulinard, *op.cit.*, p. 69; AD M⁶8321, CS to Pref., 17 Oct. 1920 and 18 Jan. 1921; cf. also A. Kriegel, *op.cit.*, pp. 347–349, and J. Fauvet, *Histoire du parti communiste français*, (Paris, 1964), i. 32, 53, 103, 126, where youth, pacifism and personal temperament appear as motives for joining the PCF; P. Robrieux, *Histoire intérieure du parti communiste français* (Paris, 1980), i. 21 ('la colère des "nés de la guerre", la soif d'action, la volonté de renouvellement . . .') and i. 25 (only 12 of the 68 socialist *élus* left the old party).

7. AD M⁶8321, CS to Pref., 16 Oct. 1920, 11 April 1921, and 18 April 1921; AD M⁶8324, CS to Pref., 21 March 1922, 31 July 1922, and 1 Sept. 1922; AD M⁶III48, CS to Pref., 11 May 1922; AD M⁶8430, Pref. to Int., 14 March 1922.

8. J.-A. Vaucoret, *op.cit.*, p. 30; *Bulletin municipal de la ville de Marseille*, 17 July 1931.

9. AD M⁶8321, CS to Pref., 18b April 1921, 27 March 1922; AD IIIM48 (1922 results).

10. A. Kriegel, *op.cit.*, pp. 347–349; AD M⁶8321, CS to Pref., 18 Dec. 1920.

11. AD M⁶8321, CS to Pref., 22 Dec. 1920 and 8 Dec. 1922; AD M⁶8324, CS to Pref., 25 July 1922, 21 Dec. 1922 and 6 Jan. 1923.

12. AD M⁶8321, CS to Pref., 26 May 1922, 2 June 1922, 16 June 1922; AD M⁶8324, Pref. to Int., 8 Feb. 1922; AD M⁶8410, CS to Pref., 5 Oct. 1923.

13. AD M⁶8321, CS to Pref., 10 Oct. 1922; AD M⁶8324, CS to Pref., 10 Jan. 1923; AD M⁶8410, CS to Pref., 14 March 1923, 19 March 1923, 9 April 1923. Sabiani later claimed that he had left the party after being asked to spy on his country; there is no way of verifying this.

14. AD M⁶8410, CS to Pref., 11 April 1923.

15. AD IIM³56, CC to Pref., 30 Jan. 1928; AN F⁷13.245, Pref. to Int., 13 June 1925; AD M⁶10801, CS to Pref., 16 May 1924, 16 Sept. 1924 and report of *inspecteur*, 14 April 1924; AD M⁶10803, CC to Pref., 28 Dec. 1925 and 8 Oct. 1925; AD M⁶8410, CS to Pref., 16 April 1923, 13 Dec. 1923 and report of CS *adj.*, 1 Aug. 1923; AD M⁶8325, CC to Pref., 27 July 1923; AD M⁶10804, CS report, 19 Oct. 1926; AD M⁶10806, CC to Pref., 16 May 1927; AD M⁶8321, CS report, 30 May 1923.

16. Ad M⁶8325, CS to Pref., 19 May 1923; AD XIVM25/64, CS to Pref., 4 April 1923; origins of *Parti Socialiste-communiste* in J.-P. Brunet, *St-Denis la ville rouge*, 1890–1939 (Paris, 1980), pp. 251–252, AD M⁶10806, CC Arles to *sous-préfet*, 15 May 1927, and in *ML* 10 July 1931.

17. AD M⁶10805, CC to Pref., 20 July 1926.

18. Ad M⁶10811, *dossiers* of 20 Jan. 1923, 2 Feb. 1923; AD XIVM25/26, CS to Pref., 4 April 1923; AD M⁶8321, report of CS adj., 2 June 1922; J.-A. Vaucoret, *op.cit.*, p. 10.

19. Ad M⁶8321, CS to Pref., 18 April 1921, 26 April 1921, 4 Aug. 1921, 30 Sept. 1921; J.-A. Vaucoret, *op. cit.*, pp. 147–148; Alban Géronimi, Marseille 12 Dec. 1983 (interview); Roger Py, Marseille, 10 June 1986 (interview); Jean Bazal, *Le clan des Marseillais* (Paris, 1974), p. 139; *MM* 30 March 1934.

20. AD IIIM49, CC to Pref., 21 July 1925.
21. Results from AD VM^{2}268, AD IIIM^{3}55, AD IIIM49.
22. *Ibid.*; AD IIM^{3}56. In 1924 the communist party won 6 per cent of the city-wide vote, 4.8 per cent in the fourth canton; in the 1925 municipal elections, 4.8 per cent and six per cent; in the first round of the 1928 legislative elections, 8 per cent and 3.5 per cent.
23. AD VM^{2}261, CC to Pref. 15 April 1929.
24. AD M^{6}8410, Pref. to Int., n.d. 1923; AD M^{6}11380, CC to Pref., 19 Dec. 1921; AD IIIM48, Pref. to Int., n.d., 1922, and electoral forecasts, n.d., 1922; AD M^{6}11384, report of *chef de sûreté*, 11 Oct. 1930, and CC to Pref., 26 March 1931. Schurrer was later cleared of the charges against him but doubt persisted, AD M^{6}11946, CD to Gén. Jeanpart, 8 Jan. 1940.
25. AD IIM^{3}55; *Massalia* 27 April 1929; AD VM^{2}268, CC to Pref., 2 April 1929.
26. See eg AD M^{6}10801, report of *inspecteur* Félix, 14 April 1924; AD M^{6}10803, CC to Pref., 28 Dec. 1925.
27. The six deputies were Adrien Artaud, a merchant and president of the Chamber of Commerce, Joseph Régis, an industrialist, Hubert Giraud, a shipbuilder, Joseph Vidal, a merchant, Louis Régis, a doctor, and Raymond Honnorat, employed in commerce; they were elected in 1919, 1924, or 1928. Of the 23 can onal candidates, 9 were in the liberal professions, six were industrialists or merchants, five were office employees or salesmen, three were in other occupations. Of the 29 SFIO cantonal candidates in the same elections (1925, 1928, 1931) 9 were artisans or office employees, 8 were municipal or communal employees, 6 were merchants or industrialists, 4 were in the liberal professions, 2 in others. From biographical information in AD IIIM49, AD IIIM50, AD IIIM51, *LPM* 7 March 1924 and 26 April 1924.
28. AD M^{6}8410, CC to Pref., 27 Nov. 1923.
29. Ad IIIM^{3}56, CC to Pref., 23 Jan. 1928, 7 March 1928, and 15 March 1928; AD IIIM47, report of CS, 13 Dec. 1919; AD VM^{2}268, CC to Pref., 2 April 1929; *l'Eclair* 29 April 1929; Ad M^{6}8410, CC to Pref., 10 Feb. 1924; AD M^{6}8287, report of CS, 25 Jan. 1924; *le Soleil*, 23 April 1929; *MM* 11 May 1931.
30. *LPM* 25 March 1928 (candidates and their committees).
31. *LPM* 28 April 1924 and 21 Jan. 1925; *MM* 18 Dec. 1931, 9 Dec. 1932, and 22 Oct. 1934 (article on the *Grand Cercle*). For the national organisations of the *droite classique*, André Siegfried, *Tableau des partis en France* (Paris, 1930), pp. 172, 179, 180; Malcolm Anderson, *Conservative Politics in France* (London, 1974), pp. 44 *sqq.*; René Rémond, *Les droites en France* (2nd. edn., Paris, 1982), pp. 181–194; mostly for the 1930s alone, W.D. Irvine, *French Conservatism in Crisis* (Baton Rouge and London, 1979), pp. 27–31, 42–44, 50.
32. René Rémond, *op.cit.*, p. 186; AD IIM^{3}55; AD IIM^{3}56, report of CS, 2 March 1928 and CC to Pref., 25 Feb. 1928; *Le Radical* 31 March 1932; AD VM^{2}268, CC to Pref., 29 April 1929; *LPM* 26 Sept. 1934. In 1924 the right took 32.8 per cent of the city-wide vote, 24.8 per cent of that in the fourth canton; in 1925 41.3 per cent in the city, 33 per cent in the fourth canton; from results in AD IIM^{3}55, AD VM^{2}268.
33. The 1924 city-wide lists were elected proportionately to their vote, so that the possibility of the right standing down in the fourth or any other canton did not arise. Results in ADIIM^{3}55, AD IIIM49.
34. In *bureaux de vote* nos. 23, 24, and 115 (*la Joliette* and *Arenc*) Sabiani won 51, 48 and 56 per cent, respectively, of the vote; in the six newly added *bureaux* of the fifth canton he averaged only 29 per cent.
35. Canavelli's vote increased from 4,575 at the first round to 5,690 at

the second; Sabiani's from 4,399 to 5,914. Even allowing for fraud, which was general in any case, Sabiani's increase must have come in large measure from first-round voters of the right. Probably only some of the first-round Communist votes went to him; if all had, Canavelli's increase would have had to have come entirely from the right, which is highly unlikely. The pre-electoral agreement with the right is noted by the CS in AD IIM³56, report of 10 March 1928.

36. *LPM* 12 May 1929, 14 April 1929, 20 April 1929, 30 April 1928.

37. *Le Sémaphore* 8 April 1929 and 13 April 1929; *Le Radical* 2 May 1929; AD VM²268, Pref. to Int., 15 June 1929.

38. *LPM* 13 May 1929.

39. AD 500U115, testimony of Philibert Géraud in Sabiani's trial *in absentia*, 1 Dec. 1945.

40. AD VM²268, CS to *Procureur de la République*, 3 May 1929.

41. AD M⁶11353, CS to Procureur de la République, 3 Feb. 1930.

42. J. Fraissinet, *Au combat à travers deux guerres et quelques révolutions* (Paris, 1968), pp. 68–72; AD M⁶8292, CS to *Procureur de la République*, 20 Nov. 1931; CC to Pref., 23 Dec. 1930; *ML* 6 Sept. 1930; AD M⁶11381, n.d. (1930). poster announcing *MM*.

43. *ML* 11 Jan. 1930, 18 Jan. 1930, 6 Sept. 1930.

44. *MM* 11 May 1931 and 6 June 1931; *ML* 6 Sept. 1930. Sabiani acknowledged receiving support from 'capitalistes' in *ML*, 31 Jan. 1931.

45. *ML* 2 Jan. 1931, pp. 47–48; *re* the PUP cf. J.-P. Brunet, *St Denis la ville rouge* (Paris, 1980), pp. 299–300.

46. *ML* 21 Aug. 1931; *ML* 6 Feb. 1931; *MM* 5 Nov. 1932 and 7 Nov. 1932 (anniversary of *Les Vrais Amis*); AD M⁶8292, CC to Pref., 16 March 1931.

47. *ML* 17 April 1931 and 24 April 1931; Alban Géronimi, Marseille, 12 Dec. 1983 (interview); AD VM²277, Pref. to Int., 23 April 1931 and 27 April

1931; election results in AD VM²277. For the city as a whole Pierre had 45,691 votes to the socialist Roux's 38,180. If Sabiani had supported a candidate of his own or failed to urge his supporters to vote for Pierre, he would have divided the latter's vote and certainly taken the fourth canton away from him, where he won by 3157 votes to Roux's 2078 (and the communist Gabriel Péri's 456).

48. *Le Radical* 19 Oct. 1931; *LPM* 7 May 1935; *re* Ribot's election in the *conseil municipal* see *ML* 8 May 1931 and 15 May 1931, and *MM* 11 May 1931. Sabiani's friend Franceschi recalls seeing Sabiani the night before the vote in the *conseil* and hearing from him that Ribot's election was assured (interview in Marseille, 10 June 1986). Account of Pierre's entry from *l'Eclair* 5 May 1931; Vaucoret, *op.cit.*, p. 280; Alban Géronimi, Marseille, 12 Dec. 1983 (interview).

Chapter 3

1. Sabiani in *Délibérations du conseil municipal de la ville de Marseille*, 9 June 1933; *LPP* 13 May 1931; *LPM* 12 May 1931; *MM* 13 May 1031; Mme. Antoine Morelli, Marseille, 13 Oct. 1986 (interview).

2. *L'Echo de Paris*, 12, 13, 14, 15, 17 and 18 Jan. 1930; *LPM* 26 Nov. 1929, 11 Dec. 1929, and 17 Dec. 1929; *LPP* 17 Dec. 1929; AD M⁶11353, Sabiani to CC, 28 March 1930; *ML* 11 Jan. 1930.

3. *Maître* Jacques Luciani, Casamaccioli, 8 June 1986 (interview); Alban Géronimi, Marseille, 12 Dec. 1983 (interview); J.-A. Vaucoret, *op.cit.*, pp. 239–241; Jean Bazal, *Le clan des Marseillais* (Paris, 1974), pp. 139–144; Roger Peyrefitte, *Manouche* (Paris, 1972), pp. 48 *sqq.*; AD M⁶11380, Pref. to Int., 29 April 1934, and CC to Pref., 30 April 1934; AD M⁶10789, Pref. to Int., 2 April 1934; AN F⁷13024, Pref. to

LPM 29 April 1934; *MM* 7 April 1934 and 20 April 1934; *L'Eclair*, 30 April 1934. Carbone and Spirito had been arrested by the sinister inspecteur Bony during the conseiller Prince affair (a sequel to the Stavisky scandal) when Sabiani made his declarations. Géronimi declared that Sabiani's intervention on behalf of the young Carbone in 1930 was prompted by a request from Carbone's mother which, he said, Sabiani could not possibly refuse.

4. *ML* 27 Oct. 1934; AD M⁶11380, Pref. to Int., 20 Dec. 1934. The municipality, on the other hand, bore heavy responsibility for the death of Barthou, who was left bleeding and unattended during the chaos.

5. In the second half of 1930 the unemployed registered at the *office de placement* amounted to 2.2 per cent of the active population, and to 6.6 per cent in March 1935. The figures are for the *Bouches-du-Rhône* but 90 per cent of the department's unemployed were in Marseille. M. Carenco, *Les problèmes de l'emploi dans les Bouches-du-Rhône entre 1919 et 1939* (Mémoire de maîtrise, Université de Provence, 1975–1976), pp. 84–85; *MM* 10 Aug. 1932, 19 Sept. 1932 and 10 Dec. 1932; *LPM* 29 April 1935; *ML* 5 Aug. 1932 and 16 Dec. 1932; AD M⁶8293, CC to Pref., 25 Nov. 1934.

6. Antoine Leonetti, Ajaccio, 7 June 1986 (interview); *MM* 1 May 1934, 10 July 1932, and 23 Aug. 1932; *ML* 17 April 1935 and 15 July 1932; cf. also Eugène Saccomano, *Bandits à Marseille* (Paris, 1968), pp. 70. sqq.

7. The figures on the membership of the *Parti Socialiste-Communiste* are from *ML*, 28 July 1933 and 23 March 1934. They are given in the small print, as numbers of cards taken per section, and not as propaganda, enhancing their credibility. Information on the various sections and the *commission exécutif fédéral* is from *MM* 17 Nov. 1932, 20 July 1933, 1 May 1933, 11 May 1933, 15 June

1933, 13 March 1933, 11 Nov. 1933, 21 Dec. 1933, 15 Feb. 1934. The frequency of meetings is based on communiqués announcing them in *MM*, 1931 to 1935, eg, in April 1933 there were three in the fourth canton and six in the fifth, in January 1934 three and six respectively, etc. There were consistently fewer in the other cantons.

8. *MM* 5 Nov. 1932, 10 Feb. 1932, 22 Dec. 1933, 9 Nov. 1932, 27 Dec. 1934; *ML* 26 Jan. 1934, 18 Aug. 1933, 27 Feb. 1931. The *Amis'* descriptions of themselves are in *MM* 7 Nov. 1932 and 23 Dec. 1933. Re numbers: the *Amis* claimed 3,000 members in Sept. 1933 (*MM* 3 Sept. 1933), 4,000 in Oct. 1933 (*MM* 5 Oct. 1933), 7,000 in Dec. 1933 (*MM* 13 Dec. 1933), and 8,000 in Jan. 1934 (*ML* 19 Jan. 1934). The estimate of 4,000 of Oct. 1933 was linked to the organisation's twenty-one groups, which would give an average number of about 200 per group; the average was probably closer to 100, for the *amis* of *Trois-Lucs* claimed 170 and the *amis* of *Chave-Mérentié* 135 (*ML* 4 Aug. 1933); those of the seventh canton claimed 170 (*MM* 17 Sept. 1933) and those of the eleventh 50 (*MM* 15 June 1933). An average of 100, or slightly higher, would give a total membership of about 2,000.

9. *ML* 27 Feb. 1931.

10. See Appendix ii, 'The social composition of the *Sabianiste* organisations', for details of this sample. The figures which follow are based on the tables developed in appendix ii or, if they refer to the social composition of the fourth and fifth cantons, to appendix i.

11. *Ibid.*; M.-F. Maraninchi-Attard, *Les associations corses à Marseille de 1920 à 1960* (thèse pour le doctorat de troisième cycle, Université de Provence, 6, 91984), p. 136; *ML* 22 Feb. 1930, 13 March 1931, 11 March 1932, 16 Jan. 1931. 12 Aug. 1932, 3 Feb. 1932, 9 June 1933; AD M⁶11353, Sabiani to Pref., 15 Sept. 1930; AD M⁶8294, CC to Pref., 24 Feb. 1935; Sabiani

in *Délibérations du Conseil Municipal de Marseille*, 4 Dec. 1931. Seventy six of the 167 *fonctionnaires* were Corsican-born.

12. Appendix ii; *MM* 29 Jan. 1935; *ML* 29 April 1932, 17 May 1930, 4 March 1932, 18 Dec. 1932, 7 April 1933, 2 June 1933, 8 Dec. 1933. Ten of the 13 butchers in the sample are from the 1931 electoral committee of the Sabianiste Desoches, the municipal *délégué aux abattoirs*. The sample includes 11 bar owners and four wine merchants.

13. Appendices i and ii. INSEE, in its *Code des catégories socio-professionnelles* (6th. edn., Paris, 1977) makes plumbers and electricians artisans if they are self-employed, skilled workers if they are not — information which in this case is never available.

14. Appendix ii. Re the sailors: AD VM²268, CC to Pref., 5 April 1929; AD M⁶10809, CS *sous-chef* to CD, 24 Feb. 1937; AD M'10789, Pref. to Int., 1 Feb. 1935; AD 500U147, C.J. 3981/ 45, case of T. Sus..., 3 Sept. 1945. Nineteen of the 48 sailors were Corsican-born.

15. Re Sabiani and the dockers: AD M⁶10809, CS to Pref., 14 Aug. 1929; AD M⁶8293, CC to Pref., 18 Oct. 1934; AD 500U11, CJ 1532/44, case of N. Cia..., 29 July 1946. Re the unemployed and the *Amis de Simon Sabiani: MM* 22 Dec. 1933, 3 Feb. 1934, 22 Feb. 1934, 21 Sept. 1934, 27 March 1935.

16. In the fourth canton the lower class was 40.5 per cent, the lower middle 37.5 (both classes as defined above); in the fifth 44.5 and 37.7 per cent respectively. Unskilled industrial workers were 15 per cent in the fourth and 25 per cent in the fifth canton (see appendix i).

17. M. d'Agostino, *L'Implantation socialiste à Marseille sous le Front Populaire* (Mémoire de maîtrise, Université de Provence, 1972), pp. 66 *sqq*. The lower middle class is defined as '... les classes moyennes et les petits commerçants et artisans...' the lower class as 'les prolétaires, ouvriers, manoeuvres, pêcheurs, police [?], auxquels on adjoint les domestiques et les personnels de service'.

18. Appendices i and ii.

19. AD M⁶ 11380, Pref. to Int., 29 April 1934. See also CC to Pref., 30 April 1934.

20. *MM* 30 April 1934.

21. In 1931 Sabiani had candidates (including himself) in five of the six cantons re-electing *conseillers généraux*; they polled 8,687 out of 41,939 votes. Excluding the fourth canton their score would have been even lower — 16.7 per cent. The 1934 figure refers to the elections for the *conseil d'arrondissement*, where Sabiani's candidates won 9,798 out of 46,165; in the cantons electing *conseillers généraux* that year there were no *Sabianistes* at all, although Sabiani gave his support to various candidates of the right and left. AD IIIM51 (results by canton).

22. AD IIIM51; Vaucoret, *op.cit.*, pp. 301–302; *MM* 24 April 1932.

23. Alban Géronimi, Marseille, 12 Dec. 1983. The socialist vote in Sabiani's constituency (fourth and part of the fifth cantons) dropped from 4575 in the first round of the 1928 elections to 3935 in the first round in 1932; Sabiani's increased from 4399 to 6748. Part of his increase must also have come from the right: its candidate had 2362 votes in 1928, 1149 in 1932. ADIIIM³57, AD IIM³59.

24. In 1932 Sabiani had 67 per cent of the vote in *les Présentines* (*bureau* 26, workers and skilled workers 26 per cent) and 37 per cent in St. Lazare-Strasbourg (*bureau* 35, workers and skilled workers 20 per cent); 62 per cent of the vote in la Joliette (*bureaux* 23, 24, artisans 10 per cent in each) and 41 per cent of the vote in le Canetles Crottes (*bureau* 37, artisans 12 per cent); 65 per cent of the vote in the docks of la Joliette (*bureau* 115, office-workers 15 per cent, artisans 7 per cent) and 41 per cent in the *quartier Oddo* (*bureau* 39, office-workers 20 per cent, artisans six per

cent). Calculated from results in AD IIM^{3}59; social composition of *bureaux* from appendix i.

25. *ML* 18 Jan. 1930; *ML* 27 Feb., 5 June, 19 June, 26 June, 31 July, 7 Aug., 2 Oct. and 18 Dec. 1931; *ML* 15 Jan., 11 March, 18 March, 22 April, 17 June and 21 Oct. 1932; *ML* 5 May, 9 June, 16 June, 7 July, 28 July, 1 Dec. and 8 Dec. 1933; *ML* 18 Dec. 1934; AD M^{6}8292, CC to Pref., 3 Aug. 1931.

26. *ML* 2 Oct. 1931, 9 June, 28 July and 8 Dec. 1933; 23 March and 13 July 1934; S. Grossman, 'L'Evolution de Marcel Déat', *Revue d'histoire de la deuxième guerre mondiale,* 97 (Jan. 1975); A. Bergounioux, 'Le néo-socialisme. Marcel Déat: réformisme traditionnel ou esprit des années trente', *Revue historique,* Oct.-Dec. 1978.

27. AD M^{6}8288, CC to Pref., 8 Aug. 1931; AD VM^{2}277, CC to Pref., 19 April 1931; *Le Cri de Marseille* 3 Oct. 1931, 17 Oct. 1931; *Le Sémaphore* 27 April 1932; *LPM* 4 May 1932; *L'Eclair* 15 Oct. 1931.

28. *MM* 5 Oct., 18 Oct., and 30 Dec. 1933; *MM* 17 Jan. and 2 Feb. 1934; *ML* 30 Oct, 1931 and 20 Oct. 1933; AD M^{6}10878, CC to Pref., 22 Sept. 1937 (re Eyssautier); Mangiavacca opposed Sabiani in 1928 but was back in his camp by 1934, see below.

29. *ML* 27 Feb. 1931, 1 April 1932, 14 May 1939.

30. *MM* 25 Sept. 1931, *MM* 14 Aug. 1934; *ML* 24 June 1932, 25 Nov. 1932, 5 May 1933, 19 Jan. 1934, and 29 June 1934.

31. *ML* 22 April 1932, 6 May 1932.

32. Interview in *Le Journal* (Paris), reprinted in *ML*, 21 Nov. 1930.

33. Agathe Sabiani, Marseille, 12 Feb. 1984 and 3 June 1986; Dora Leonetti *née* Sabiani, Ajaccio, 7 June 1986; Antoine Leonetti, Ajaccio 7 June 1986; Roger Py, Marseille, 10 June 1986 (all interviews); *ML* 21 Nov. 1930, 20 Feb. 1931, 31 March 1933. When the Chamber of Deputies was in session Sabiani would be in Paris from Tuesday to Friday. The *Café*

Glacier is today the Air France Office.

Chapter 4

1. AD M^{6}10793, CD to Pref., 28 Nov. 1935; AD M^{6}11353, CD to *Procureur de la République,* 19 April 1933.

2. AD IIIM50, report of CS adj., 28 Sept. 1928, and CC to Pref., 19 Oct. 1928; AD VM^{2}268, CC to Pref., 15 April 1929; AD VM^{2}277, CC to Pref., 19 April 1931; AD IIM^{3}55, *comm. de police* to Pref., 3 May 1924; AD IIM^{3}58, CC to Pref., 5 Oct. 1930; P. Robrieux, *Histoire intérieure du parti communiste* (Paris, 1980), i. 280 *sqq.* The city-wide vote of communist candidates was 6 per cent in 1924, 7 per cent in the cantonal and 4 per cent in the municipal elections of 1925, 8 per cent in the legislative and 5 per cent in the cantonal elections of 1928, six per cent in the municipal elections of 1929, 8 per cent in the cantonal elections of 1931 and 9 per cent in the legislative elections of 1931 and 9 per cent in the legislative elections of 1932.

3. AD M^{6}10804, CS report, 29 May 1926; AD M^{6}11379, CD to Pref., 31 Jan. and 26 Dec. 1934; CS to Pref., 25 Aug. 1932; Int. to Pref., 6 Dec. 1933.

4. AD M^{6}11379, CD to Pref., 26 Dec. 1934; Int. to Pref., 30 Nov. 1935; Int. note, 27 and 31 Dec. 1935; P. Sigal, *Le six février 1934 à Marseille* (mémoire auxiliaire de DES, Aix-en-Provence, 1960); P. Robrieux, *op.cit.,* pp. 456–457; 'François Billoux', in J. Maitron, ed., *Dictionnaire biographique du mouvement ouvrier français* (Paris, 1983), vix., pp. 178–179.

5. AD M^{6}11379, CS to Pref., 25 Aug. 1932 and CD to Pref., 26 Dec. 1934. The Belle-de-Mai had an industrial working class (workers and unskilled workers) of 29 per cent, on the basis of major streets (rue Belle-de-Mai, Boulevard National, rue Clovis-

Hugues) analysed in the 1936 census, fifth canton, *bureaux* nos. 33 and 110; la Cabucelle, in Sabiani's *bureau* 119, had an industrial working class of 51 per cent (see appendix i).

6. From election results in AD IIIM50, AD IIIM51, AD IIIM52.

7. *ML* 14 Feb., 20 April, 22 June, 31 Aug., 14 Sept. and 6 Oct. 1934.

8. AD M[6]11379, CD to Pref., 26 Dec. 1934; AD XIVM25/64, CC to Pref., 1 April 1935.

9. *ML* 14 Feb. 1934.

10. AN F[7]14817, *contrôleur général* to Rotterdam police, 23 July 1930; APP BA 326, *rapports* of 23 Nov. 1930, 16 Nov. 1930, 9 March 1931, 9 March 1932; E. Herriot, *Jadis* (Paris, 1952), ii., 276–277; Paul Chopine, *Six ans avec les Croix-de-Feu* (Paris, 1935), pp. 70–71; numbers from Chopine, *op.cit.*, pp. 55–56.

11. René Rémond, *Les droites en France* (2nd. edn., Paris, 1982), p. 212; Chopine, *op.cit.*, pp. 92–102; Max Beloff, 'The sixth of February', *St Antony's Papers*, 5 (1959), 17; René Rémond, 'Les anciens combatants et la politique', *Revue française de science politique*, 5 (1955); P. Machefer, 'Les Croix-de-Feu', *L'Information historique*, 34(1) (Jan.–Feb. 1972).

12. APP BA 326, *rapports* of 23 July and 4 Aug. 1934, and 10 Jan. 1935; AD M[6]10789, CC to Pref., 23 Feb. 1935; in the mid-1930s their slogan appeared variously as 'Travail, Famille, Nation' (AD M[6]11381, circular from La Rocque, 18 July 1934) or 'Patrie, Famille, Travail' (*MM* 31 Oct. 1935) before assuming its more lasting (Vichy) formulation.

13. AD M[6]10809, CD to Pref., 23 Oct. 1935; *MM* 2 Aug. 1932, 17 June 1934, 10 Nov. 1931. Numbers from *MM* 10 Aug. 1932.

14. *MM* 18 Jan. 1933; numbers are estimates by Arnoult in *MM* 29 Dec. 1934 and in APP BA 326, *rapport* of 29 Jan. 1935.

15. The sample — a list found accidentally by the police and contained in AD M[6]11381, Pref. (*Vaucluse*) to Pref. (*Bouches-du-Rhone*), 6 Sept.

1934 — consists of only 54 members: an 'upper' or 'upper middle' class of 8 landowners, industrialists or merchants, 8 high level office employees (*cadres*), 5 members of the liberal professions; a 'lower middle' class of 7 artisans; 7 lower-level office workers (*employés*), one shopkeeper and two technicians; a 'lower' class of 2 industrial workers, 3 skilled workers, 2 domestic servants and one sailor; and seven other miscellaneous individuals, including four students. The ages — only 3 in the sample are over 35 — suggest it is a group of *Volontaires Nationaux*, the *Croix-de-Feu* youth organisation.

16. AD M[6]19789, CD to Pref., 29 April 1935; APP BA 326, *rapport* of 29 Jan. 1935; Ad M[6]11381, circular from La Rocque, 18 July 1934; *MM* 10 May 1934, 12 Nov. 1932. *Modéré* political candidates who were also in *Croix-de-Feu* at the time included Marc Ambroggi and André Daher.

17. APP BA 327 — (*L'Humanité* 10 March 1936); APP BA 326, *rapports* of 13 and 17 June 1936; P. Chopine, *op.cit.,* p. 175; R. Brasillach, *Notre Avant-Guerre* (Paris, 1966), pp. 161–162; A. Fabre-Luce, *VingtCinq années de liberté* (Paris, 1962), i. 132.

18. *ML* 28 Aug. 1931, 14 Feb. and 27 July 1934, 14 March 1935; Roger Py, Marseille, 10 June 1086 (interview). In 1926 Marseille had 600 *Action Française* members (G. Gaudin, *Le royalisme dans les Bouches-du-Rhône*, thèse de doctorat d'état, Aix-Marseille 1978, p. 901); in 1935 the entire *provençal* section had only 1,500 (table in AD M[6]10806; the *Jeunesses Patriotes* that year had 800, *ibid.*)

19. *ML* 23 March, 20 April, 22 June, 2, 7 and 14 Oct. and 17 Dec. 1934; 17 March, 6, 11 and 20 April and 4 May 1935.

20. A city-wide comparison of *Sabianiste* with communist votes is rendered difficult by the absence of a *Sabianiste* candidate in the fourth sector (second and eighth cantons). Without the fourth sector the *Sabianistes* would

have about 17 per cent of the vote. Results from AD VM^{6}283. In the *Belle-de-Mai* Billoux had 40 per cent of the vote, around the *Boulevard Durbec* 48 per cent (AD VM^{2}284).

21. *ML* 10 May 1935; *LPM* and its friends on the right supported Marc Ambroggi, who stood against Sabiani; *MM* and its friends on the right supported Sabiani in the second round, when he won 48 per cent of the vote in the fourth canton and 31 per cent in the sixth, *MM* 13 May 1935, AD VM^{2}283.

22. AD VM^{2}283.

23. *ML* 1 Jan. 1936 and 22 Sept. 1935; AD 500U258, case of F. Pao...(*non-lieu*).

24. *MM* 28 Sept., 3 Oct. and 22 Dec. 1935; AD M^{6}10793, CD to Pref., 3 and 30 Dec. 1935; AD M^{6}11357, CD to Pref., 6 Dec. 1935; AD M^{6}8294, CD to Pref., 22 Nov. 1935; *LPM* 12 Feb. 1936; A. Olivesi, 'Henri Tasso', *Marseille*, 100 (1975).

25. *ML* 13 May, 14 July, 4 Aug., 1 Sept., 6 Oct., 7 Nov. and 21 Nov. 1935; AD M^{6}8294, Pref. to Int., 29 Aug. 1935; compare treatment of Hitler and Germany in *ML* 27 July 1934, 13 Dec. 1934, *MM* 25 Oct. 1933 with that in *ML* 7 Nov. 1935, 8 March 1936, 2, 5, and 12 April 1936.

26. Numbers for France from APP BA326, *rapports* of 10 July 1935 and 27 May 1936; AN F^{7}13241, note of 3 July 1935; P. Chopine, *op.cit.*, p. 154; P. Machefer, 'Les Croix-de-Feu', *L'Information historique* 34(1) (Jan.–Feb. 1972). Numbers for Marseille from AD M^{6}10809, CD to Pref., 23 Oct. and 19 Nov. 1935, CD to Pref., 23 Jan. 1936, and Pref. to Int., 7 April 1936; AD M^{6}10793, CD to Pref., 28 Oct. 1935; *MM* 12 Dec. 1935.

27. APP BA326 *rapport* of 10 July 1935; AD M^{6}10809, Pref. to Int., 7 April 1936, CD to Pref., 22 Feb. 1936; AD M^{6}11357, CS to CD, 30 May 1936; *inspecteur principal* to CS, 15 Dec. 1935; *MM* 8 and 13 Feb. 1936.

28. APP BA326, *rapports* of 28 Jan. 1936

and 11 Dec. 1935; APP BA327, *rapport* of 25 Dec. 1935; AD M^{6}10793, CD to Pref., 27 Nov. 1935; AD M^{6}10809, CD to Pref., 23 April 1936; *MM* 29 Jan. 1936.

29. *ML* 28 July, 29 Aug., 17 Nov. and 12 Dec. 1935, 20 Feb. 1936 (and 18 Dec. 1934 re *Sabianiste* support for the dissolution of the *ligues*).

30. *ML* 15 May, 27 June and 11 Aug. 1935, 12, 19, 23 Jan. and 23 April 1936. Sabiani did once call Sarraut, at the time *Président du Conseil*, the 'prisonnier des loges maçonniques' in *ML* 5 March 1936.

31. AD IIM^{3}60, CD to Pref., 30 March, 17 April, 1 May 1936; AD M^{6}10789, CD to Pref., 23 April 1936; AD IIM^{3}59, CD to Pref., 30 Jan. 1936; *MM* 27 April 1936; *ML* 12 April, 19 April 1936.

32. AD IIM^{3}60, CD to Pref., 21 April 1936 and CC to Pref., 21 April 1936 — the former estimated the crowd at 15,000, the latter at 6,000; *ML* 23 April 1936; Antoine Leonetti, Ajaccio, 7 June 1986 (interview).

33. AD IIM^{3}62.

34. In the fifth canton Billoux had an average of 42 per cent in the first round; in 1935 at the first round he had won 32 per cent, see p. 105. In la Madrague, which was 45 per cent skilled and unskilled workers (see appendix i, *bureau* 119) he had 47 per cent of the vote in the first round in 1936. The Communists had 29 per cent city-wide (AD IIM^{3}62).

35. Marie-Paul Delisle, *Etude éléctorale et sociologique du quartier Saint-Pierre de 1880 à 1971* (Mémoire de maîtrise, Aix-en-Provence, 1971); Dominique Bianchi, *Etude socio-politique des quartiers de Bonneveine et de Montredon* (Mémoire de maîtrise, Aix-en-Provence, 1971), p. 143.

36. In the Lazaret and Arenc, which had 28 per cent skilled and unskilled workers (see appendix i, *bureau* 23), Sabiani had 43 per cent of the vote in the first round; in 1931 he had had 59 per cent there (AD IIIM51), in 1932 60 per cent (AD IIM^{3}58), in

1935 48 per cent (AD VM²283). Billoux had 26 per cent, higher than his fourth canton average of 22 per cent. In la Joliette skilled and unskilled workers were 21 per cent in *bureau* 24, 22 per cent in *bureau* 25; in the Boulevard des Dames 21 per cent (*bureau* 27) — it had also an unusually high percentage (6 per cent) of upper level employees (*cadres*). See appendix i.

At the second round Sabiani had 58 per cent of the fourth canton vote to Billoux's 42 per cent; in the fifth canton (where there were 2,000 more voters), 37 per cent to Billoux's 60 per cent (AD IIM³62).

37. *ML* 3 and 17 May, 21 and 25 June, 2 and 6 July 1936; *MM* 6 May and 21 June 1936; AD M⁶10817, CD to Pref., 8 and 29 July 1936. Carbone's brother François was the one arrested.

38. APP BA327 *rapports* of 15 June, 17 June and 12 July 1936; *Le Flambeau* 27 June 1936; Pozzo di Borgo and other 'durs' left the *Croix-de-Feu* after La Rocque's failure to defy the dissolution.

39. AD M⁶10793, report to CD, n.d., July 1936; AD M⁶10809, CD to Pref., 25 July 1936. According to the CC there were 30,000 in attendance.

40. *ML* 2 July 1936, 26 July 1936.

Chapter 5

1. Antoine Franceschi, Marseille, 10 June 1986 (interview).
2. *ML* 30 Jan. 1931; Victor Barthélemy, *Du communisme au fascisme. L'histoire d'un engagement politique* (Paris, 1978), pp. 385 *sqq.*; AD 500U115, testimony of Philibert Géraud in Sabiani's trial *in absentia*, 1 Dec. 1945.
3. J.-P. Brunet, *Jacques Doriot. Du communisme au fascisme* (Paris, 1986), pp. 166, 215; G. Allardyce, 'The Political Transition of Jacques Doriot', *Journal of Contemporary History*, I,i (1966); D. Wolf, *Doriot. Du communisme à la collaboration* (Paris, 1969, tr. of *Die Doriot Bewegung*, Stuttgart, 1967), pp. 136–137, 425–426; J.-P. Brunet, 'Réflexions sur la scission de Doriot, février-juin 1934', *Le mouvement social*, 70 (1970).

4. *ML* 15 June 1934, 24 Oct. 1935, 23 Feb. 1936.
5. V. Barthélemy, *op.cit.*, p. 102; J.-P. Brunet, *Doriot* (*op.cit.*), pp. 201, 230–231; *EN* 4 July 1936; D. Wolf, *op.cit.*, pp. 163–171; A. Fabre-Luce, *Vingtcinque années de liberté*, i, *Le grand jeu, 1936–1939* (Paris, 1962), p. 156. The estimate of 100,000 members is that of J.-P. Brunet, *Doriot* (*op.cit.*), p. 229; D. Wolf, in *Doriot* (*op.cit.*,) p.223, arrives at an estimate of 50 to 60,000, with about another 300,000 falling within its 'influence'; the party's official estimates are completely unreliable.

6. *EN* 1 Aug. 1936; *ML* 30 July 1936; AD M⁶10809, CD to Pref., 27 July 1936; AD M⁶10793, Pref. to Int., 28 July 1936.

7. AD M⁶11354, CD to Pref., 23 and 27 Sept. 1936; AD M⁶10809, CC to Pref., 19 Sept. 1936; AD M⁶10878, CC to Pref., 19 Sept. 1937.

8. AD M⁶11354, CD to Pref., 7 June 1937, 4 May 1937, and PPF circular, April 1937; AD M⁶10874, CC to Pref., 25 Feb. 1937 and CD to Pref., 9 April 1937; AD M⁶10809, CS *souschef* to CD, 24 Feb. 1937; AD M⁶10814, CD to Pref., 21 Dec. 1938; AD M⁶10888, CD to *Sûreté Nationale*, 23 May 1939; AD M⁶10899, CD to Pref., 19 June 1937 (*re* PPF strategy); *ML* 24 Jan., 14 March, and 5 Dec. 1937.

9. *MM* 21 May 1937; *EN* 21 July 1939.
10. AD M⁶11354, CD to Pref., 5 April 1937 (PPF circular) and 7 June 1937.
11. *ML* 10 Sept. 1936; *EN* 15 Aug. 1936, 25 Feb. 1938, 16 June 1939.
12. AD M⁶10809, CC to Pref., 18 Sept. 1936; AD M⁶10792, CD to *Sûreté Nationale*, 28 March 1939; AD M⁶10877, CD to Pref., 12 July 1937; AD M⁶10882, CC to Pref., 27 June 1938; *MM* 6 Dec. 1936; *ML* 13 March 1938 and 12 March 1939; *EN* 15

Aug. and 24 Oct. 1936, 26 Aug. 1938, 22 Dec. 1939.

13. *ML* 27 Aug. 1936, 28 March 1937, 6 March 1938, 20 March 1938, 7 Aug. 1938, 4 Dec. 1938; *EN* 12 Aug. 1938, 25 Nov. 1938.

14. AD M^{6}10878, CD to Pref., 31 July 1937; AD M^{6}10790, 28 Oct. 1936 (poster); AD M^{6}11354, CD to Pref., 18 Sept. 1936; Ad M^{6}10899, CC to Pref., 28 Aug. 1936 (PPF leaflet); *ML* 6 Aug., 5 Nov. and 6 Dec. 1936, 7 Jan. 1937, 20 March 1938.

15. AD M^{6}10790, Pref. to Int., 2 Dec. 1938 (poster); *ML* 13 Sept. 1936, 30 May and 5 Dec. 1937, 27 Feb., 13 March, 20 March, 18 Sept., 2 Oct., and 9 Oct. 1938; *EN* 23 Sept., 30 Sept. and 7 Oct. 1938.

16. AD M^{6}10877, CC to Pref., 29 Oct. 1937; AD M^{6}10878, CD to Pref., 1 Oct. 1937; *ML* 25 Sept. 1939, *EN* 1 Sept. 1939.

17. AD M^{6}11354, *Le Jour*, 20 Dec. 1936; *ML* 14 March and 19 Dec. 1937.

18. AD M^{6}10877, CC to Pref., 3 July 1977; AD M^{6}10809, CC to Pref., (PPF leaflet); AD M^{6}10879, CC to Pref., 28 May 1938; *ML* 10 Sept. 1936, 20 March, 31 July and 7 Aug. 1938; *EN* 17 July 1937, 28 Jan., 19 March, 1 and 19 July 1938; R. Girardet, *Mythes et mythologies politiques* (Paris, 1986), 'La Conspiration', pp. 25–62; T.W. Adorno *et.al.*, *The Authoritarian Personality* (New York, 1950), chapter xvi, esp. 'The Functional Character of Antisemitism', pp. 609–612 (p. 609, the 'infantile fear of the strange') and 'The Imaginary Foe', pp. 612–617.

19. R. Giradet, *op.cit.*, pp. 57–62.

20. AD M^{6}10809, CC to Pref., 19 Oct. 1936; AD M^{6}110809 *bis*, CC to Pref., 25 April 1938; AD M^{6}11354, CD to Pref., 18 Sept. 1936; AD M^{6}10874, CC to Pref., 7 Feb. 1937; photo in *L'Epoque*, 18 Oct. 1937; *ML* 20 Sept., 11 Oct., 15 Nov. and 27 Dec. 1936, 13 June 1937, and 26 Feb. 1939; *EN* 27 March and 17 July 1937, 19 March 1938.

21. *ML* 2 Aug. 1936; there are no defections on record. The idealistic Henri

Toti had already left the *Sabianistes*, cf. A. Olivesi, 'Henri Toti', *Marseille*, 1982.

22. *ML* 2 Aug. 1936; the *bureau* secretaries remaining in place were Sottano (2nd. canton), Albertini (3rd), Valentini (4th), Stoeffels (5th), Capelle (6th), Mussa (7th), Vaissade (8th), Martini (9th), Campana (10th); for the first, eleventh and twelfth cantons the data are incomplete but there is nothing to suggest that they differed from the other cantons in retaining their secretaries. From *communiqués* in *MM* 9 to 30 Aug. 1936 and earlier *Sabianiste* list.

23. AD M^6 10809, CD to Pref., 6 Aug. 1936; AD M^{6}11354, CD to Pref., 27 Sept. 1936 and 11 June 1937; AD M^{6}10874, CD to Pref., 14 Jan. and 24 Feb. 1937; AD M^{6}10816, CD to Pref., 19 Jan. 1938; AD M^{6}10888, CD to *Sûreté Nationale*, 27 May 1939; *MM* 4 and 5 Dec. 1936; *ML* 14 Jan. 1937; *EN* 22 May 1937; SFIO and PCF membership figures from D.A.L. Levy, 'The Marseille Working Class Movement' (Oxford University D. Phil. thesis, 1982), p. 114, app. viii.

24. See appendix ii, and appendix iii for details on the post-Liberation source.

25. *EN* 22 May 1937; appendix ii; *supra*, p. 67; the PPF rank and file come from the post-Liberation trials and investigations.

26. AD 500U series, *liasses*: 19, case of J. Fa...; 92, case of P. Rey...; 109, S. Tou...; 186, M. Ama...; 263, E. Pel...; 90, L. San...

27. See appendix ii.

28. AD 500U series, *liasses*: 3, case of B. Bak...; 210, L. Cin...; 34, P. Luc...; 109, A. Mel...; 22, G. Fra...; 62, H. Rou...; 37, P. Ma...; 117, F. Ro...; 42, P. Oc...

29. The three cases of private interest or motivation not given above are AD 500U49, case of S. Ros...; AD 500U73, case of L. Teo...; AD 500U11, N. Cia... — the last a borderline case of a syndicalist docker.

30. See appendix ii.
31. AD 500U series, *liasses*: 72, case of J. Tam...; 80, case of L. Ric...; 103, F. Cha...; 275, J. Chi...; 57, P. Mor...; 102, V. Pad...; 139, G. Gal... and R. Gal...; these eight are the only artisans, shopkeepers, or office-workers giving motives (all but one personal and private).
32. Appendix ii; *supra*, p. 65; AD M⁶10809 bis, CD to Pref., 12 Feb. 1938; Journal Officiel 21 March 1939.
33. AD 500U series, *liasses*: 18, case of E. Du...; 254, A. Ris...; 44, E. Per...; 23, F. Gar...; 204, J. Luc ...; 49, D. Rom...; 80, J. Lan...; 277, D. Acq...; 59, B. Vio...; 76, A. Gia...; 39, F. Mes...
34. AD 500U series, *liasses*: 128, case of A. Man...; 148, P. Mor...; 58, A. Vai...; 109, T. Ma...; 130, L. Fra...
35. The cases of private interest not cited above are in AD 500U *liasses*: 59, A. Vis...; 150, A. Alb...; 280, L. Cas. and R. Com...; 155, A. Car...; 4, S. Bas...; 276, A. Fil... ('solidarité corse'); 100, F. Bre...; 104, F. Po ...; the two cases of conviction not cited above are in AD 500U38, R. Me... and AD 500U195, B. Fig... Four remaining cases — AD 500U: 100, L. Man...; 27, A. Gug...; 45, A. Pie...; 102, T. Ris... — are on the borderline between private interest and public conviction.
36. AD 500U237, case of P. Ant...; AD 500U51, case of F. San...; AD 500U278, case of A. Fre...; AD M⁶11354, CS report of 26 Nov. 1936 and *commissaire* to CC, 4 May 1937; Ad M⁶11355, Pref. to Int., 15 Nov. 1937; AD M⁶10899, CS *auxiliaire* to CD, 26 Nov. 1936; cf. references to bar owners in AD 500U59, case of B. Vio... and AD 500U114, case of P. Gui...
37. See appendix ii; of 224 lower and lower middle class members in the sample, 39 are from the fourth and 52 from the seventh, the best represented cantons. Of 78 *bourgeois* or upper middle class members, only

three are from the fourth and eight from the seventh cantons; 20 are from the sixth and ten from the second, the best represented of cantons. Of 101 upper middle class members, five were Corsican (87 of the other 307); 33 were from Provence (42 of the 307 others); 24 were under 35 compared to 40 of 81 lower class and 76 of 206 lower middle class members.
38. AD 500U series, *liasses*: 48, case of L. Reb...; 26, case of E. Gon...; 185, P. Deh...; 104, C. Ma...; 98, G. Be...; 8, M. Bo...; 231, H. Ren...; 234, J. Reb...; 53, E. Sic ...; 36, P. Mar... The case of private motivation (friendship) not mentioned above is in AD 500U28, J. Hum... The cases of conviction not given above are in AD 500U: 237, L. Ric...; 9, I. Cac...; 48, A. Re...; 51, M. Sa...; 78, A. Gi...; 188, J. Alb... — the last three present a private and personal element as well.
39. In addition to the 83 individual motives itemised above, 12 members whose profession, if any, is unclear also give motives. Seven are girls or women (AD 500U: 160, H. Deg...; 67, M. Bal...; 59, Y. Vil...; 51, D. Sa...; 70, M. Val...; 117, M. Th ...; 3, P. Bal...) of whom only one, a schoolgirl, joins out of conviction (160, H. Deg...). Of the remaining five cases (AD 500U: 142, J. Jou...; 102, C.Pa...; 190, N. Alf ...; 126, A. To...; 170, M. Cro...), two are *lycéens* who join for fun, one a crippled and blind adolescent who joins for work, like the two remaining men. With these, there are only 22 cases of conviction alone among the 95 motives available in the sample.
40. AD M⁶10816, CD to Pref., 26 Dec. 1938; AD M⁶10888, CD to *Sûreté Nationale*, 27 May 1939; AD M⁶10895, CC to Pref., 11 Dec. 1938; AD VM²290, CC to Pref., 17 Feb. 1939; AD M⁶11354, CD to Pref., 4 May 1937; AD M⁶10874, CD to Pref., 7 Jan. 1937; *EN* 16 July 1938;

ML 19 Sept. 1937; Roger Py, Marseille, 10 June 1986 (interview).

41. AD M[6]10809, CC to Pref., 18 Sept. 1936; D. Wolf, *Doriot. Du communisme à la collaboration* (Paris, 1969, tr. from German edn., Stuttgart 1967), pp. 213–215; J.-P. Brunet, *Doriot. Du communisme au fascisme* (Paris, 1986), pp. 238–240; J.-A. Vaucoret, *Simon Sabiani. Un homme politique contesté* (thèse pour le doctorat de troisième cycle, Université de Provence, 1979), pp. 414–415. Vaucoret does not give a source for his statement that the *Casa d'Italia* gave the PPF money 'de la main à la main'.

42. *ML* 10 Sept. 1936; D. Wolf, *op.cit.*, p. 212; J.-P. Brunet, *op.cit.*, pp. 235–236; Alban Géronimi, Marseille, 12 Dec. 1983 (interview); AD 500U, case of P. Deh...; AD 500U115, testimony of P. Géraud in Sabiani's trial *in absentia*.

43. AD M[6]11354, CD to Pref., 5 April 1937; AD M[6]10877, CD to Pref., 29 Oct. 1937.

44. *ML* 13 June 1937; AD M[6]10816, CD to Pref., 19 Jan. 1938; AD M[6]10877, CC to Pref., 21 and 25 June 1937, and CD to Pref., 21 and 25 June 1937 and 24 Jan. 1938; AD M[6]10809, CD to Pref., 1 May 1937; AD M[6]10878, CD to Pref., 16 Sept. 1937; AD M[6]10874, CC to Pref., 19 April 1937; AD IIIM53, CD to Pref., 10 Sept. 1937; *ML* 13 Feb. 1938; *EN* 27 Aug. 1937; P. Machefer, 'L'Union des droites. Le PSF et le Front de la Liberté, 1936–1937', *Revue d'histoire moderne et contemporaine*, Jan.-March 1970.

45. AD IIIM53; around the Boulevard des Dames (for social composition see appendix i, *bureau* 27) Sabiani had 56 per cent of the vote in the first round; in Arenc and the Lazaret (for social composition see appendix i, *bureau* 23) 40 per cent. Neither the PSF nor the other parties of the right presented candidates in the fourth canton.

46. Comparison of results in AD IIIM54 and AD IIM51. In 1931 as in 1937 there were *Sabianiste* candidates in five of the six cantons involved, making the comparison possible.

47. In 1936 the communists had 39,196 out of 136,758, or 29 per cent, in 1937 31,504 out of 124,924 (including the elections for the *conseil d'arrondissement*) or 25 per cent; S. Berstein, 'Le Parti Radical-Socialiste, arbitre du jeu politique français' in R. Rémond and J. Bourdin, eds., *La France et les Français en 1938–1939* (Paris, 1978), esp. pp. 288–291; A. Olivesi, 'La situation sociale en province — Marseille et le Sud-Est' in R. Rémond and J. Bourdin, eds., *Edouard Daladier, chef de gouvernement* (Paris, 1977); AD M[6]10888, CD to Pref., 2 May 1939; AD M[6]10789, CD to Pref., 21 Sept. 1938; AD M[6]10792, CD to Pref., 25 Feb. 1939; AD M[6]10790, CD to Pref., 27 and 30 Oct. 1938; AD M[6]10874, CD to Pref., 11 March 1937; *EN* 23 Sept. 1938 and 16 June 1939; *ML* 26 March and 18 June 1939.

48. *ML* 30 Oct. 1938 and 9 April 1939; only two municipal sectors (the fourth, with the second and eighth cantons, and the third, with the fourth and sixth) were involved, and the Communists at the first round had only 4,874 out of 30,987 votes, or 16 per cent — AD VM[2]290; *EN* 29 Sept. and 6 Oct. 1939, *ML* 25 Sept. 1939.

49. *ML* 2 July and 11 Oct. 1936.

50. P. Allum, *Politics and Society in Postwar Naples* (Cambridge, 1973), p. 167. J. Cutler, *"Honey Fitz": Three Steps to the White House* (New York, 1962), p. 46 (quote from Martin Lomasney, the 'Ward Eight Mahatma').

51. The apparent paradox — of an anti-modern movement employing modern methods — surfaces repeatedly in the controversy over fascism and modernisation in Germany and Italy. See H.A. Turner, 'Fascism and Modernization', *World Politics 24/4* (July 1972); A. James Gregor, 'Fascism and the Counter-modernization of Consciousness',

and 'Fascism and Modernization: Some Addenda', *Comparative Political Studies, 10/2* (July, 1977); A.J. Joes, 'On the Modernity of Fascism. Notes from Two Worlds', *ibid*; A.L. Greil, 'The Modernization of Consciousness and the Appeal of Fascism' and 'What does it mean when I call you a Fascist? Reply to Gregor and Joes', *ibid*. The 'modernization' of K.J. Muller's 'French Fascism and Modernization', *Journal of Contemporary History* 11/4 (1976), has to do largely with the interests of some businessmen.

52. In which frustration or deprivation are obsessively blamed on an external source, cf. G. Allport, *The Nature of Prejudice*, (2nd edn., New York, 1958), p. 396.

53. *EN* 6 Jan., 29 Sept., and 6 Oct. 1939; *ML* 18 June and 25 Sept. 1939.

54. Cf. eg H. Brugmans, 'Pourquoi le fascisme n'a-t-il pas "pris" en France', *Res publica — Revue de l'Institut Belge de Science Politique, 7* (1965); R. Rémond, *op.cit.*, pp. 218–223, and Z. Sternhell, 'Strands of French Fascism', in S. Larsen, B. Hagtvet, and J. Myklebust, eds., *Who were the Fascists* (Oslo, 1980), p. 498.

Chapter 6

1. AD M⁶10932, CD to Pref., 17 and 18 June 1940; AD M⁶11055/11055 bis, *Commissaire de contrôle des postes intêrieures*, 18 Aug., weeks of 25–31 Aug., 8–15 Sept., and 15–22 Sept. 1940.

2. AD M⁶10932, CD to Pref., 22 June 1940.

3. Henri Frenay, *La nuit finira, i, Mémoires de résistance, 1940–1943* (Paris, 1973), p. 38.

4. AD M⁶10930, CD to Pref., 31 Jan. 1940; AD M⁶10927, CD to Pref., 29 Dec. 1939; AD M⁶11055/11055 bis, Commissaire de contrôle des postes intérieures to Pref., 3 and 4 Aug., 20 Oct., 10 Nov. 1940; J.-P. Beauquier, 'Problèmes de ravitaillement dans la

région marseillaise (1940–1944)', *Revue d'histoire de la deuxième guerre mondiale*, 113 (Jan. 1979).

5. J.-M. Guiraud, 'La vie intellectuelle et artistique à Marseille au temps du Maréchal Pétain', *Revue d'histoire de la deuxième guerre mondiale*, 113 (Jan. 1979); Henri de Montherlant, *Le solstice de juin* (Paris, 1941), p. 00.

6. AN^F1CIII1200, *Rapport sur la situation administrative de la ville de Marseille, du département des Bouches-du-Rhône et de la région de Marseille*, Aug. 1942, pp. 3, 4, 19, 20; prefectoral report, Oct. 1942.

7. From a prefectoral report in AD M⁶11040 (n.d., c.June 1941) on the *cadres* of the *Légion*. The full breakdown was: *sans étiquette: 172; modérés et nationaux: 66;* Action Française *militants et sympathisants: 17; conservateurs symapthisants: 16; progrès Social Français militants: 17; Comité de Défense Paysanne: 9; SF10 militants et sympathisants: 8; Républicains de Gauche militants et sympathisants: 6; Union Socialiste Républicaine: 5; Parti Démocrate Populaire militants: 4; Radical-Socialiste militants et sympathisants: 3; PPF: 2.* A survey by the *police administrative* in AN F⁷15304 (n.d., c. Nov. 1940) of 44 local *Légion* presidents in the *Bouches-du-Rhône* shows similar proportions, with the *modérés* and the PSF most numerous (of those who have a political past). The leader in Marseille, Jean-Marie Arnould, was a doctor, a member of the *Légion d'Honneur*, the father of six children, and the prewar local head of the *Parti Démocrate Populaire* (AD M⁶11040, *secrétaire-général* to Pref., 16 Sept. 1941).

8. AD M⁶11039, Bouyala (*Bouches-du-Rhône* head) to Pref., 28 Dec. 1940; Arnould to Pref., 18 Feb., 20 March, and 19 April 1941, 28 Jan. and 4 March 1942; AD M⁶10978, CD to police, 9 Jan. 1941; AN F⁷15304, report of *renseignements généraux de la Légion*, 17 March 1941; AN F¹CIII1143, prefectoral report for May 1942; N. Brashover, *Les partis nationaux devant le gouvernement de*

Vichy et devant la collaboration à Marseille de 1939 à 1944 (Mémoire de maîtrise, Aix-en-Provence, 1971), pp. 34, 83, 100–101. Including the subsidiary non-veterans organisation, the *Amis de la Légion*, total membership was 45,000 in July 1941, AD M[6]11040, Pref. to Int., 4 July 1941.

9. M. Baudoin, *Témoins de la résistance en région 2. Intérêt du témoignage en histoire contemporaine (Thèse pour le doctorat d'état*, Université de Provence Aix-Marseille, 1977), i, pp. 31, 36, 43; AN F[1CIII] 1143, prefectoral reports for Dec. 1941 and April 1942; A. Olivesi, 'Henri Tasso', *Marseille,* 100 (1975).

10. AN F[1CIII] 1143, prefectoral reports of Feb. and March 1942; AD M[6]11055/11055 *bis, Commissaire de contrôle des postes intérieures* to Pref., 10 Nov. 1940; *cf.* also P. Machefer, 'Sur quelques aspects de l'activité du Colonel de la Rocque et du "Progrès Social Français" pendant la seconde guerre mondiale', *Revue d'histoire de la deuxième guerre mondiale*, 58 (April 1965).

11. AD 500U198, case of H. Ripert (*nonlieu*); AD M[6]10985, Pref. to Int., 11 July 1942; Emile Régis, 'La Chambre de Commerce de Marseille pendant l'occupation allemande', *Provence historique* 19 (April/June 1969) (Régis was en poste from 1940.).

12. AD M[6]10930, CD to Pref., 2 Jan. 1940; AD M[6]10927, CD to Pref., 28 Dec. 1939; AD M[6]10929, CD to Pref., 9 Oct. 1939.

13. AD M[6]11292, CD to Pref, n.d., report on arrests for Oct. 1940; M. Baudoin, *op.cit.*, i, pp. 56, 119, 164–165, and iii, p. 365; H. Kedward, *Resistance in Vichy France* (2nd. edn., Oxford, 1983), pp. 273–275.

14. *ML* 28 July 1940, 19/26 May 1940.

15. J.-A. Vaucoret, *Un homme politique contesté: Simon Sabiani* (thèse de doctorat de troisième cycle, Université de Provence, 1979), pp. 476–481; Agathe Sabiani, Marseille, 12 Feb. 1984 and Alban Géronimi, Mar-

seille, 12 Dec. 1983 (interviews); the uncle of Sabiani's neighbour Roger Py happened by chance to be in Port Vendres; when he encountered François on the point of leaving he sent a telegram to Sabiani: 'Demain trop tard. Arrivez ce soir' — Agathe Sabiani, Roger Py, Marseille 10 June 1986 (interviews).

16. *ML* 30 June/7 July 1940, 14/21 July 1940, 1 Sept. 1940.

17. *ML* 18 Aug., 8, 22 and 29 Sept., 13 and 20 Oct. 1940; *EN* 31 Aug. 1940; AD M[6]11038, Pref. to Int., 28 Aug. 1940.

18. *ML* 28 July, 14/21 July, 25 Aug., 29 Sept., 17 Nov. 1940; *EN* 17 Aug. 1940.

19. AN F[7]15280, report of *renseignements généraux* (Vichy) on the PPF in the south-east, 31 Jan. 1942 (esp. historical review in section II); *EN* 9 Nov. 1940, 14 Dec. 1940, 15 March 1941; *ML* 1 Dec. 1940.

20. *EN* 5 Aug. 1940, 28 Dec. 1940; *ML* 13, 20 and 27 Oct. 1940, 22 Dec. 1940, 23 Feb. 1941; N. Brashover, *Les partis nationaux devant le gouvernement de Vichy et le Maréchal Pétain à Marseille de 1939 à 1944* (Mémoire de maître, Aix-en-Provence, 1971), p. 43.

21. *EN* 17 Aug. 1940.

22. Cf. J.-P. Brunet, *Doriot, op.cit.*, pp. 309–327; *ML* 1 Dec. 1940, 8 Dec. 1940, 23 Feb. 1941; Sabiani in *Cahiers de l'Emancipation Nationale*, Dec. 1941 (in AD 500U99, case of M. Cic ...); M.-Y. Sicard (a.k.a. Saint-Paulien), *Histoire de la collaboration* (Paris, 1964), p. 226.

23. AD M[6]10973, *Inspecteur Général des Services de Police Administrative* to Pref., 20 March 1941; AD M[6]11055-bis, *notes d'écoute* of 28 June 1941; AN F[7]15280, report of *renseignements généraux* (Vichy), 31 Jan. 1942 (section II).

24. *ML* 16/23 June 1940, 30 June/7 July 1940, 22 and 29 Sept. 1940, 3 and 17 Nov. 1940; *EN* 21 Sept. 1940.

25. *EN* 17 Aug. 1940, 2 and 23 Nov. 1940, 14 Dec. 1940, 1 and 22 Feb. 1941.

26. *ML* 25 May 1941.
27. Cf. Owen Antony Davey, 'The origins of the LVF', *Journal of Contemporary History*, 6 (1971); J.-P. Brunet, *Doriot, op.cit.*, pp. 362–364.
28. AN F⁷15301, *renseignements généraux* (Vichy) report of 29 July 1941; *EN* 9 Aug. 1941; AN F⁷15280, *renseignements généraux* (Vichy) report on PPF in south-east (31 Jan. 1942, section II); An F¹ᶜᴵᴵᴵ 1143, prefectoral reports for October, November and December 1941; *ML* 11 Oct. 1941; *EN* 26 July and 19 Dec. 1941; AD M⁶11038, *notes d'écoute* of 8 Nov. 1941 (Sabiani to 'X').
29. *ML* 29 June and 27 July 1941; AD M⁶11038, *notes d'écoute of 24 July 1941* (Sabiani to Carbuccia) and 26 Jan. 1942 (Sabiani to Lebrun); AN f⁷15280, Vichy *renseignements généraux* report, 31 Jan. 1942 (section II).
30. *ML* 27 Dec. 1941 and 4 April 1942; *EN* 14 Feb. 1942, AD M⁶11038, *notes d'écoute* of 23 Aug. 1940.
31. AN F⁷14956, *séance* of LVF *comité* of 5 May 1942; Ad M⁶11038, *notes d'écoute* of 9 Sept. 1941 (Lebrun to 'X') and 9 Dec. 1941 (Pietri to 'X'). Re the German attitude to the LVF cf. Owen Antony Davey, *art. cit.*, and J. Delarue, *Trafics et crimes sous l'occupation* (Paris, 1968), p. 228.
32. Cf. R. Paxton, *Vichy France. Old Guard and New Order, 1940–1944* (2nd, edn., New York, 1982), p. 254n.
33. AN F⁷15280, Vichy *renseignements généraux* report, 31 Jan. 1942, (section II); *ML* 7 Sept. 1941; AD M⁶11038, *notes d'écoute* of 18 April 1942 (Sabiani to Frasson).
34. AD M⁶11038, *notes d'écoute* of 26 Jan. 1942 (Géraud to Sabiani) and 7 March 1942 (Lebrun to Roussel at *Ministère de l'Information); ML* 2 May 1942, 19 Dec. 1942; R. Paxton *op.cit.*, p. 254; AN F¹ᶜᴵᴵᴵ 1200, prefectoral report for Aug. 1942; on 27 Oct. 1942 the cheque from the Ministry of Information to the PPF in Marseille for publication expenses was Frs. 60,000.00 for the three month period Oct.-Dec. It was ad-

dressed to 'Simon Sabiani, journaliste' — cf. intercept in AD M⁶11038.
35. AD M⁶11038, *notes d'écoute* of 1 (also *re* Sabiani's reaction to Mangiavacca's arrest) and 11 Sept. 1942; accounts of the 14th July demostration and its aftermath in: AD M⁶10985, Pref. to Int., n.d. (July 1942); AD M⁶11254, *Comm. de police administrative* to CC, 19 and 31 July 1942; AD F¹ᶜᴵᴵᴵ 1143, prefectoral report for July 1942; F¹ᶜᴵᴵᴵ 1200, prefectoral report for August 1942; AD 500U70, case of A. Ben..., 13 Feb. 1945.
36. AD M⁶11038, notes d'écoute of 17 April 1942 (Sabiani to Jean Gaillard).
37. AN F¹ᶜᴵᴵᴵ 1143, prefectoral reports for Oct. and Nov. 1941, March, April, May, June, August, and September 1942; *ML* 18 July 1942; AD M⁶10971, Pref. to Int., 27 May 1941. Already in early August 1940 Sabiani and Géraud were receiving hâte mail at *Marseille-Libre*.
38. ie. the party had 1,500 members in each of these years. J.-A. Vaucoret, *op.cit.*, p. 489, does not give a source for his statement that in July 1940 police estimated the membership of the PPF in Marseille at 1400; in July 1941 the police thought it was 1500, AD M⁶10980, Pref. to police, 18 July 1941; B.M. Gordon, *Collaborationism in France during the Second World War* (Ithaca and London, 1980), p. 237, states that in the *Bouches-du-Rhône* in 1942 the party had 1,700 members.
39. The civil courts tried or investigated 530 members of the PPF in all; of these, at least 167 were already members when the Germans occupied the southern zone in November 1942; at least 254 joined between then and the Liberation in August 1944; for 109 no entry date was available. All of the statistical statements about the PPF in this chapter, unless otherwise noted, refer to the 167 known to have been in the party before November 1942; those in the next chapter, unless otherwise noted, refer to the 254 known to

have joined after November 1942; see also appendix ii; an aggregate social analysis, including also all those whose entry date is unknown, is given in appendix iv. The samples thus defined are the basis for the more general affirmations in the text. Personal descriptions and quotations are taken from the members ·themselves or witnesses (in the pre-trial *instructions*).

40. See appendix ii. Thirty-seven per cent of the *fonctionnaires* — 13 of 35 — were born in Corsica.

41. Canton of residence is available for 140 of the 167 in the sample; 29 were from the fourth, 26 from the fifth, 21 from the seventh, 14 from the second, nine from the sixth.

42. 112, or 71%, of the 157 for whom such information is available had already joined before the war. Some of them give reasons for joining originally, see chapter V, but only ten give reasons for staying in the party during the war.

43. AD 500U series, *liasses*: 49, case of D. Ro..., 11 July 1945; 44, case of J. Pe..., 28 Aug. 1945; 18, E. Du..., 1 Feb. 1945; 73, L. Teo..., 21 March 1945; 27, J. Gr..., 11 April 1945.

44. Of the 45 in the sample known to have joined between June 1940 and November 1942 and for whom such information is available, 11 joined to cross the demarcation line, nine with the hope or promise of employment, six under pressure from family or friends, four out of conviction, one believing he could obtain the release of a prisoner in Germany, and two, former prisoners themselves, fearing being sent back. Ten joined for miscellaneous other motives, sometimes several at once.

45. AD 500U series, *liasses*: 74, case of P. Bar..., 18 April 1945; 56, L. Tra..., 31 Jan. 1946; 67, M. Boi..., 10 Jan. 1945; 119, M. Sal..., 9 Feb. 1946; 3, P. Bal..., 8 May 1945; 101, C. Mar..., 16 Nov. 1944; 259, J.-B. Bel... (*non-lieu*); 123, J. Ga..., 11 April 1946;

94, R. Syl..., 5 June 1946.

46. AD 500U series, *liasses*: 126, J. Mi..., 1 June 1946; 58, L. Ve..., 27 June 1945; 95, E. Ca..., 25 June 1946; 173, G. Ga..., 10 July 1946; 233, R. Ay... (*non-lieu*); 244, P. Bar... (*non-lieu*); 38, A. Ma..., 22 Dec. 1945; 54, M. Su..., 31 May 1945; 20, J. Fil..., 3 Oct. 1945.

47. *ML* 28 Feb. 1942, 14 Feb. 1942.

48. AD 500U79, F. To..., 8 Aug. 1945; J. Fra..., 19 July 1945; in the pre November 1942 sample there are four cases of conviction, all but one of them mixed with other motives as well.

49. Eight of the 111 for whom such information is available took part in such activites; of the 68 members of pre-war vintage for whom such information is available, 27 had no activity and 22 went to a few meetings only. Of the 43 joining after 1940 for whom such information is available 20 had no activity and six went to a few meetings only.

50. AD M^{6}11038, A. Stoeffels to Sabiani, 15 Oct. 1942; AD M^{6}10871, Pref. to Int., 1 July 1941; AD M^{6}11055 *bis, note d'écoute* of 28 June 1941.

51. AD VIT 7/6, Géraud to Paul Marion, 13 August 1941; AD 500U25, case of A. Gio..., 1 March 1945; see p. 113, n.2. Five resigned before 1940 (AD 500U: 234, J. Re... (*non-lieu*); 53, E. Sic..., 2 May 1945, 237, L. Ri..., (*non-lieu*); 48, A. Re..., 14 March 1945; 188, J. Alb... (*non-lieu*), four resigned in 1940 (AD 500U: 263, E. Pe... (*non-lieu*); 231, H. Ren... (*non-lieu*); 109, T. Ma..., 19 May 1945; 185, P. Deh... (*non-lieu*) and four resigned between 1940 and 1944 (AD 500U: 42, P.Oc..., 24 Oct. 1945; 26, E. Gon...; 8, M. Bo..., 11 July 1945; 128, A. Ma..., 6 June 1946).

52. AD M^{6}10980, Pref. to Int., 18 July 1941; AD M^{6}11038, interception of 17 Oct. 1941.

53. AD 500U: 44, J. Pe..., 28 Aug. 1945; 73, L. Teo..., 21 March 1945; 74, P. Bar..., 18 April 1945; Alban

Géronimi, Marseille, 12 Dec. 1983 (interview).

54. AD 500U: 275, case of F. Air... (non-lieu); 237, P. Ma..., 27 Dec. 1944; 109, M. Ma..., 1 June 1945.

55. V. Barthélémy, *Du communisme au fascisme, l'histoire d'un engagement politique* (Paris, 1978), p.   ; AD 500U-115, testimony of P. Géraud in trial of Sabiani *in absentia*, 1 Dec. 1945.

56. AD 500U281, A. Man... (non-lieu)

57. Three unemployed among the 106 who joined before the war, six among the 29 who joined after (among those for whom such information is available).

58. AD M⁶11038, Pref. to Int., 28 Aug. 1940; *EN* 15 March 1941.

59. AD 500U 174 *bis*, cases of M. La..., L. Gui..., J. Ge..., Y. Mo..., 25 July 1946.

60. Here and elsewhere 'collaborationism' and 'collaborationist' denote the theory and its theorist, 'collaboration' and 'collaborator' the practice and its practicant; AD M⁶13300, CD to Pref., 21 Sept. 1944; AD 500U86, case of M. Pin..., 15 Jan. 1946; Ad M⁶10809, CD to Pref., 2 April and 18 May 1936; AN F¹ᶜᴵᴵᴵ 1143, prefectoral report of Oct./Nov. 1942.

61. AD 500U268 (non-lieu); du Porzic's remark, attributed to him by a witness, tends to confirm R. Paxton's view that after the summer of 1942 Vichy officials had at least a confused idea of the fate awaiting the deportees, see R. Paxton and M. Marrus, *Vichy France and the Jews* (New York, 1982), p. 352. Of the 17 officials (all employed before Nov. 1942; see chapter VIII, p. 258, for the 1940–1944 figures), one was convicted but absolved for services to the resistance, and ten, after an investigation, had the charges dropped without a trial (non-lieu).

62. AD 500U169, case of F. RO..., 12 June 1946; Ad 500U102, A. Ped..., 9 Dec. 1944.

63. AD M⁶10978, CD to *Directeur des Services Administrative de Police*, 9 Jan. 1941; N. Brashover, *op.cit.*,

p. 46; AD 500U series, *liasses*: 40, case of G. Mo..., 27 June 1945; 71, E. Spi..., 6 Feb. 1945; 5, A. Be..., 25 Oct. 1945; 11, F. Ci..., 11 Jan. 1945.

64. AD M⁶11039, Pref. to Bouyala, 6 Aug. 1942, and Bouyala to Pref., 27 April 1942; Ad 500U series, *liasses*: 126, M. Jou... 16 May 1944; 74, L. Cl..., 23 April 1945; 80, G. Dag..., 14 Aug. 1945.

65. J. Delperrie de Bayac, *Histoire de la Milice, 1918 à 1945* (Paris, 1945) pp. 96–97, 104–105, 116–117, 129–130; AD 500U *liasses*: 122, case of E. Br... 28 March 1946, E. Po...4 April 1946, and L. Bu...28 March 1946; 28 J. He...25 Oct. 1945; 55, J. Tar...31 Jan. 1946; 65, G. Tri..., 18 Dec. 1944; 75, G. Gui...15 May 1945; 75, L. Auz...28 March 1945; 33, L. Le...3 May 1945.

66. Of 431 members of the SOL investigated or brought to trial, 157 were known to have joined before November 1942 and 27 to have joined after; for 276 no entry date was available. Incorporating those for whom no entry date was available into the pre-November 1942 recruits (permissible here because the SOL only had until March 1943 to live), sixty-two, or 44%, of the 142 for whom information on motives is available joined from the *Légion*. Entry motives of those joining after November 1942 are given in chapter VIII, p. 259.

67. AD 500U series, *liasses*: 3, case of A. Ba...17 July 1945; 11, C. Ci...7 Feb. 1945; 2, R. d'A...10 Jan. 1945; 15, M. De...20 June 1945; 11, P. Cha...22 Feb. 1945; 62, J. Tou...17 Oct. 1944; 37, A. Ma...28 March 1945. 29 of the 142 (incorporating those for whom no entry date is available into the pre-November 1942 recruits) or 20 per cent for whom such information is available joined out of some form of conviction.

68. Twenty-three, or 5.6%, of the 411 members joining before November 1942 (incorporating those for whom

no entry date is available into the pre-November 1942 recruits) for whom such information is available were unemployed, or had no steady job. Information on the social background of those known to have joined after Novmeber 1942 is given in chapter VIII, p. 122 and n. 4; an aggregate social analysis is given in appendix iv.

69. After the Liberation none gave work as a motive for joining; AD 500U52, case of I. Se..., 7 Fcb. 1945.

70. One hundred and three, or 25%, of the 411 (incorporating those for whom no entry is available into the pre-November 1942 recruits) for whom such information is available were industrialists, merchants, or members of the liberal professions; see appendix ii; of 11 SOL officials (for the duration of its existence) tried after the Liberation, four were from the upper middle class, four from the lower middle, and three were *fonctionnaires*.

71. AD 500U49, case of F. Ric...3 May 1945.

72. AN F[1CIII] 1143, prefectoral report of Oct./Nov. 1942.

73. AD 500U series, *liasses*: 62, case of P. Mi..., 16 Oct. 1944; 11, N. Cha...3 Jan. 1945; 48, A. Rem...8 Feb. 1945; AN F[1CIII] 1143, prefectoral reports of June/July and Fen./March 1942; N. Brashover, *op.cit.*, pp. 72–73; French Basic Handbook (London, Foreign Office, 1943/1944), p. 152.

74. B. Gordon, in *Collaborationism in France during the Second World War* (Ithaca and London, 1980), puts their number at 600 for the *Bouches-du-Rhône* in 1942. 146 were tried or investigated after the Liberation; 85 of these had joined before November 1942; 20 joined after; for 41 no entry date is available.

75. Thirty-three, or 40%, of the 83 for whom such information is available (before November 1942) were from the upper middle class. Twelve were from the liberal professions (includ-

ing teachers). Information on the motives and backgrounds of those joining after November 1942 is given in chapter VIII, pp. 127–8 and n. 18; an aggregate social analysis is given in appendix iv.

76. Seventeen, or 25%, of the 69 for whom such information is available (before November 1942) joined out of cultural curiosity; AD 500U69, D. Las..., 7 Feb. 1945; 32, E. Lab ..., 14 March 1945; 20, L. Fop..., 20 Dec. 1944; 13, A. Cr..., 29 Aug. 1945; 28, A. Hug..., 11 Jan. 1945; 49, J. Ro..., 27 June 1945.

77. AD M[6]11038, *note d'écoute* of 24 March 1942.

78. AD 500U110, L. Po...28 June 1945; 62, P. Mi...16 Oct. 1944.

79. AN F[1CIII] 1200, prefectoral report for June 1942; AD 500U72, Y. Fa...19 March 1945.

80. Seventy-six were found by the post-Liberation courts to have volunteered before November 1942 for Germany and 48 to have volunteered after; for 32 no entry date is available. Among those known to have volunteered before November 1942, 14, or 33 per cent, of the 43 for whom motives are available went in search of work. Information on the motives of post-November 1942 volunteers is given in chapter VIII, p. 128 and n. 20; 27 of 83 (33%) in all for whom motives are available gave work as their motive.

81. Sixteen, or 22 per cent, of 74 known pre-November 1942 volunteers (for whom such information is available) were unemployed or had no steady employment when they volunteered; information on the social background of post-November 1942 volunteers is given in chapter VIII, p. 128 and n. 20; an aggregate social analysis is given in appendix iv; AD 500U series, *liasses*: 35, V. Ma...10 Jan. 1946; 500U54, E. Sp...19 Sept. 1945; 57, J. Tre...31 Jan. 1946; 41, F. Ne...14 Nov. 1945; 44, P. Pe... 11 July 1945.

82. Of the 11 (among the known pre-November 1942 volunteers) who

gave the release of a prisoner as a motive, none obtained satisfaction. Out of the 74 for whom such information is available, 37, or 50 per cent, were from the lower or working class (industrial workers, sailors, dockers, servants and service personnel) in addition to the 16 unemployed.

83. Ad 500U series, *liasses*: 128, A. Cro...6 June 1946; 53, M. Sis...30 Aug. 1945; 96, M. Du...2 July 1946; 185, J. Ber... (*non-lieu*); 125, E. Br...9 May 1946; 94, M. Ar...12 June 1946.

84. Most of those convicted received the minimum sentence of five years' loss of civic rights.

85. After the Liberation 89 LVF volunteers were tried. 39 had joined before November 1942; 31 after; for 19 there was no entry date. Information on the motives and backgrounds of those joining after November 1942 is given in chapter VIII, pp. 128–9 and n. 21; an aggregate social analysis is given in appendix iv. Seventeen out of 36 known pre-November 1942 recruits (for whom such information is available) were unemployed or had no steady job; another seven were from the working class; AD 500U series, *liasses*: 108, J. Ar...28 April 1945; 123, J. So...12 April 1946; 82, G. No... 19 Oct. 1945.

86. AD M⁶11038, *note d'écoute* of 14 Oct. 1941.

87. AD 500U159, case of J. Be... (*non-lieu*); Sabiani's son may also have felt unable to stay out of the LVF while his father urged others of his age to enlist. Other cases of (claimed) conviction; AD 500U157, P. Sa...30 Jan. 1946; E. Gio...5 Feb. 1946.

88. The LVF with its 47 per cent unemployed and 20 per cent working class inverts the *relève* proportions (22 and 50 per cent respectively).

89. AD M⁶ 11038, *notes d'écoute* of 9 and 16 Sept. 1941; cf. also that of 13 Sept. 1941: '. . . pas mal se sont perdus dans les décors à peine passé la ligne de démarcation' (Vanor). Julius West-

rick, representing the German embassy on the LVF *Comité Directeur* in Paris, said that of 1039 volunteers between January and April 1942, 544 had been accepted and 105 of these had subsequently been expelled for disciplinary reasons, AN F⁷14956, *Comité Directeur* session of 16 April 1942.

90. Fifteen of the 39 known to have signed up before November 1942 already had criminal records. Their real number is almost certainly higher — but after the Liberation a fire at police headquarters in the *rue de l'Evêché* destroyed most prewar criminal records.

91. AD 500U series, *liasses*: 6, case of C. Bi...31 Oct. 1945; 46, H. Pro...21 Nov. 1945 and M.P...7 Feb. 1946.

92. AN F⁷15301, *renseignements généraux* reports of 7 and 12 Jan. 1942 (giving reports of the forced march); 123, J. So...12 April 1946; 154, G. Ale... 18 Dec. 1945; 156, R. Buo...17 Jan. 1946; 79, R. Ca...9 April 1946; 82, G. Nou...19 Oct. 1945; 108, J. Ar...28 April 1945; 94, P. Gia...11 June 1946; 75, L. Fi...29 May 1945; 28, C. He...29 July 1946.

93. AD 500U154, G. Ale...18 Dec. 1945. Albert Merglen, in 'Soldats français sous uniformes allemands', *Revue d'histoire de la deuxième guerre mondiale*, 27 (Oct. 1977) affirms that until Feb. 1942, 3641 left France for the east, and that between 1941 and 1944 the LVF never had more than 2300 men in the field at any one time. J. Delarue, in *Trafics et crimes sous l'occupation* (Paris, 1968), declares that there were 2,600 men at Deba in October 1941, p. 176. Owen Antony Davey, 'The Origins of the LVF', *Journal of Contemporary History*, 6 (1971), uses German sources to arrive at a figure of 3641 *légionnaires* from September 1941 to February 1942. There is no reliable estimate of the number from Marseille; after the Liberation 89 *marseillais* were tried by the civil courts for membership in the LVF; more were tried by the military tribunals; and many never returned.

94. *ML* 27 June 1942; AD 500U115, trial of Sabiani *in absentia*, 1 Dec. 1945, testimony of P. Géraud and M. Ro . . .; Agathe Sabiani and Roger Py, Marseille, 10 June 1986 (interviews).

95. An undated German Foreign Ministry note, probably from 1941, makes Sabiani Doriot's strongman in southern France: 'In Lyon und Marseille sind die Hauptstütepunkte, wo der Vertrauensmann Doriots, Simon Sabiani, äuserst aktiv ist und sich gerade im Süden Frankreichs eine starke Stellung verschafft hat' — AN F⁷15145.

96. AN F¹ᶜᴵᴵᴵ 1,200, prefectoral report of July 1942; AD VIT7/6, *notes d' ecoute* of 15 July (intercepts 3,994 and 4,023), 5 August (4,397), 10 August (4,473), 3 and 11 September (Sabiani letter and intercept 5,076) — all 1942.

Chapter 7

1. Cf. eg *LP*, 12 Nov. 1942; A. Négis, *Marseille sous l'occupation* (Paris and Marseille, 1947), pp. 18–19; A. Sauvageot, *Marseille dans la tourmente* (Paris, 1949), p. 186.

2. AD M⁶ 11046, report of *Directeur du service régional de liaison*, 29 Nov. 1943; AN F¹ᶜᴵᴵᴵ 1143, prefectoral report of Feb.–April 1944. Fischer was replaced by *Generalmajor* Myło at the beginning of 1943, Mylo by *Generalmajor* Elster in March 1943, Elster by *Generalmajor* Huhnermann in the spring of 1944.

3. Strictly speaking, the Gestapo did not operate outside of territories directly administered by the Reich. In 1939 the *Sicherheitspolizei* (SIPO) and *Sicherheitsdienst* (SD) were combined into the *Reichssicherheitshauptamt* (RSHA), in which Amt IV (the Gestapo) was responsible for counterespionage inside, and Amt VI for counterespionage outside, the Reich and its territories. The office at 425 *rue Paradis* was thus an office of Amt VI of the SD or RSHA. Cf. report of *Service de documentation extérieure et de contre-espionnage* (SDECE), 12 Dec. 1946, on German police organisation in France, in AN 393 M13, microfilm copy of R70 Frankreich series, Bundesarchiv, Koblenz: *archives des services spéciaux de la police allemande en France, 1940–44*.

4. Cf. A. Négis, *op.cit.*, p. 18: 'Les marseillais, pour la plupart, n'avaient jamais vu qu'au cinéma les uniformes feldgrau'.

5. A. Ducasse, *Quard ma ville ne riait plusou Mars et les marseillais* (Marseille, 1946), p. 218.

6. L. Gaillard, *Marseille sous l'occupation* (Rennes, 1982), p. 23; A. Sauvageot, *op.cit.*, pp. 186, 190, 222; A. Négis, *op.cit.*, pp. 20, 24, 25; AN F¹ᶜᴵᴵᴵ 1143, prefectoral report of Oct.–Nov. 1942.

7. A. Sauvageot, *op.cit.*, pp. 196–198; A. Ducasse, *op.cit.*, p. 222; A. Négis, *op.cit.*, pp. 90, 101.

8. AN F¹ᶜᴵᴵᴵ 1143, prefectoral report of Oct.–Nov. 1942; A. Négis, *op.cit.*, pp. 25, 28, 47; recollection of Pierre Guiral.

9. The reasons behind the German decision have never been fully elucidated. At the time there were rumours of shady construction interests. Jacques Delarue, in *Trafics et crimes sous l'occupation* (Paris, 1968), pp. 248–249, stresses the rivalry between the SS and the Wehrmacht, the latter trying to pre-empt the former. P. Guiral, in *Libération de Marseille* (Paris, 1974), pp. 55–56, concludes that for lack of better evidence, Hitler's (reported) hatred of Marseille was the main reason — a view supported by the German Consul, von Spiegel, in his postwar interrogation, when he declared that Marseille had a very bad reputation and that the order for the operation came from 'une très haute personalité allemande' — AD 500U242 (*affaire du Vieux-Port*).

10. See letters of protest and cheques for evacuees in AD M⁶ 11019; AN F¹ᶜᴵᴵᴵ 1143, prefectoral reports of Dec. 1942–Jan. 1943, Feb.–March 1943, Dec. 1943–Feb. 1944; AN F¹ᶜᴵᴵᴵ

1200, reports of 12 Feb. 1943, 13 March 1943, 8 July 1943.

11. Possibly the American raid was a feint, designed to draw German attention away from the impending Normandy landings — it had been preceded by raids on Toulon and Nice and was accompanied that day by raids on Avignon, Nîmes, Montpellier; cf. also P. Guiral, *op.cit.*, p. 27; AD 500U16, case of L. Dos...8 Feb. 1945; AD 500U61, case of A. Ay...9 Oct. 1944.

12. Cf. J. Evrard, *La déportation des travailleurs français dans le III Reich* (Paris, 1972), and also the summary of the reléve and the STO in M. Gratier de Saint-Louis, 'Les réquisitions de main-d'oeuvre pour l'Allemagne dans le Rhône', *Revue d'histoire de la deuxième guerre mondiale*, 125 (Jan. 1982); AN F^{1CIII} 1143, prefectoral report of Dec. 1942–Jan. 1943; AN F^{1CIII} 1200, prefectoral reports of 8 June 1942, 7 and 12 August 1943; A. Ducasse, *op.cit.*, p. 242; A Négis, *op.cit.*, p. 116.

13. The regional prefect, in his report of 9 Sept. 1943, AN F^{1CIII}1200, states that 15,500 had left by Sept. 1943; A. Négis, *op.cit.*, p. 260, says that 23,000 left during the occupation, a figure repeated by L. Gaillard in *Marseille sous l'occupation* (Rennes, 1982), p. 37; A. Sauvageot, *op.cit.*, p. 282, puts the number at 18,000; the number finally proclaimed by the plaque in the rue Honnorat is 16,000. Part of the confusion arises from the blurring of the local (marseillais) conscripts with regional (provençaux) ones, although Marseille, because of its industrial concentration, provided the lion's share. The figure of 2,000 is from P. Guiral, *op.cit.*, p. 58, and A. Négis, *op.cit.*, p. 120.

14. J. Kupfer, *Les Juifs à Marseille de 1939 à 1945* (Mémoire de maîtrise, Université de Provence, Aix-Marseille, n.d.), pp. 6, 9, 23.

15. *Ibid.*, pp. 23, 26; of the 22,000–25,000 evacuated, 6,000 were arrested, cf. AD M^{6}11019; the re-

gional prefect's report to Laval on 29 July 1943, AD M^{6}11046, makes it clear that at least 1019 of these subsequently arrived in the camp of Compiègne, including foreign Jews whom the Germans refused to release.

16. AN F^{1CIII}1143, prefectoral reports of Oct.–Nov. 1942 and Dec. 1942–Jan. 1943; A. Négis, *op.cit.*, p. 51; figures on *attentats* from P. Guiral, *op.cit.*, p. 70. *Re* the arrests of April 1943 see M. Baudoin, *Témoins de la résistance en région 2* (Thèse pour le doctorat d'état, Université de Provence, Aix-Marseille), 1977, i, 67 *sqq.*

17. M. Baudoin, *op.cit.*, ii, 315, *témoignage* of Col. Simon, regional head of the FFI; P. Guiral, *op.cit.*, p. 87; A Négis, *op.cit.*, p. 260: the numbers in all accounts roughly converge.

18. AN AJ^{40}545, *Beurteilung vom 13 juni 1944 durch die Feldkommandantur 497, Marseille* (report on Maljean); J.-P. Beauquier, 'Répétition ou démonstration? L'agitation ouvrière dans la région marseillaise au printemps 1944', *Provence historique, XXIX, 117* (summer 1977); Emile Régis, 'La chambre de Commerce de Marseille pendant l'occupation allemande (12 novembre 1942–23 août 1944)', *Provence historique, XIX, 76*, (spring 1969).

19. A. Sauvageot, *op.cit.*, p. 164; AD M^{6}10985, pref. to Int., n.d., July 1942; AN F^{1CIII}1143, prefectoral reports of Aug.–Sept. 1942, April–May, Aug.–Sept., and Oct.–Dec. 1943, Dec. 1943–Feb. 1944; AN F^{1CIII}1200, prefectoral report of Aug. 1942 and 13 March 1943.

20. AN F^{1CIII}1143, prefectoral report of Dec. 1942–Jan. 1943; AN F^{1CIII}1143, prefectoral report of Dec. 1942–Jan. 1943; AN F^{1CIII}1200, perfectoral reports of 10 Oct. 1943, 12 Nov. 1943.

21. See pp. 163–164; *EN* 24 July 1943.

22. AD 500U series, *liasses*: 279, case of J. Me...(*non-lieu*); 12, B. Cla..., 27 June 1945; 120, L. Jun...28 Feb. 1946; 130, M. Cha..., 20 June 1946; 150, P. Don...16 Oct. 1945;

206   NOTES TO PP. 93–119

Int., 2 April 1934 and 23 April 1934; 72, A. Pet. . .13 March 1945; 58, H. Var. . ., 27 June 1945.

23. AD 500U series, *liasses*: 6, case of M. Bi. . ., 27 Sept. 1945; 149, P. Sal. . ., 24 Sept. 1945; 22, J. Fra. . ., 13 June 1945.

24. AD 500U series, *liasses*: 6, case of M. Bi. . ., 27 Sept. 1945; 149, P. .Sal. . ., 24 Sept. 1945; 22, J. Fra. . ., 13 June 1945; 26, M. Go. . ., 31 May 1945; 114, A. Du. . ., 23 Nov. 1945.

25. Recollection of A. Fin. . ., Marseille, 15 Oct. 1986 (interview with the arrested *résistant*, who requested anonymity); J.-A. Vaucoret, *Simon Sabiani. Un homme politique contesté* (thèse pour le doctorat de troisième cycle, Aix-en-Provence, 1979), p. 571; AD 500U4, case of R. Ba. . ., 29 Jan. 1945; 34, P. Luc. . ., 7 March 1945; 185, case of L. Go. . . (*non-lieu*).

26. Cf. *ML* 13 March and 2 Oct. 1943, 26 Feb. 1944, *EN* 10 and 14 April, 5 June, 3 July 1943.

27. AD 500U series, *liasses*: 142, case of J. Er. . ., 23 May 1945; 131, J. Cir. . ., 22 June 1946; 157, G. Man. . ., 6 Feb. 1946.

28. *EN* 22 May 1943; AD 500U 114, A. Du. . ., 23 Nov. 1945; AD 500U67, A. Bal. . ., 16 Jan. 1945; recollection of Pierre Guiral (interview).

29. See appendix ii (an aggregate social analysis of the PPF, over the entire war, including those whose entry date is unknown, is given in appendix iv). 18 of the 254 known to have joined after Nov. 1942 had been born in Corsica; 150, or 60 per cent, in Marseille, 56, or 22 per cent elsewhere in France. 53, or 20 per cent, of the 254 lived in the fourth or fifth cantons; the others came from the other cantons in no very marked pattern. 33, or 13 per cent, had been born before 1900 (against 68, or 40 per cent, in the pre-November 1942 sample, reflecting the weight of the prewar members still in the party), 39, or 15 per cent, between 1900 and 1910 (against 32 earlier), 60, or 24 per cent, between 1910 and 1916 (against 28 per cent earlier).

30. Twenty-one of the 254 were found to have attended a few meetings; for a further 65 not even that could be proved. For 106 the level of activity is unclear.

31. AD 500U153, case of L. Ch. . ., 22 Nov. 1945.

32. *ML* 6 March, 5 June 1943, 8 April 1944, *EN* 24 April, 22 May, 10 July 1943 (photo); AN F^{1CIII}1143, prefectoral report of Dec. 1943–Feb. 1944.

33. AN F^{1CIII}1200, prefectoral reports of Oct. and Nov. 1943; EN 8 June 1944; AD 500U225, case of P. Tr. . . (*non-lieu*).

34. AD 500U99, case of L. La. . . (*non-lieu*); AD 500U50, case of R. Ra. . ., 17 May 1945; J.-P. Beauquier, 'Répétition ou démonstration? L'agitation ouvrière dans la région marseillaise au printemps 1944', *Provence historique* 29 (summer 1979).

35. Fifty-four out of 99 members with low levels of activity (for whom such information is available) joined to avoid the STO.

36. AD 500U series, *liasses*: 157, case of G. Man. . ., 6 Feb. 1946; 62, L. Ro. . ., 9 Oct.1944; 51, V. Sal. . ., 20 Dec. 1944; R. Du. . .3 March 1945; J. Vi. . ., 3 March 1945; G. Sal. . ., 20 Dec. 1944; 131, J. Cir. . ., 22 June 1946; 53, S. Sor. . ., 7 Feb. 1945; 11 M. Cir. . ., 15 June 1945; 49, A. Rug . . ., 11 April 1945; 22, G. Fu. . .; M. Ago. . .21 Feb. 1945.

37. AD 500U series, *liasses*: 1, case of P. Ago. . ., 8 Feb. 1945; 51, J. San. . ., 3 May 1945; 56, B. Tor. . ., 18 Jan. 1945; 40, H. Mou. . ., 10 Jan. 1945; 36, P. Mar. . ., 18 Jan. 1945; 17, A. Du. . .6 June 1945.

38. 20 out of 84 joining to avoid the STO (for whom such information is available) were unemployed, 31 were working class. Two were *fonctionnaires*: they may have felt threatened in spite of their theoretical exemption, or have wanted added insurance. In the party at large *fonctionnaires* were now only six per cent (see appendix ii).

39. AD 500U40, case of N. Mus..., 8 March 1945 (psychologist's report).
40. Only eight, or three per cent, of the 254 from after November 1942.
41. AD 500U series, *liasses*: 70, case of P. Cl..., 13 Dec. 1945; 105, A. Mar..., 3 Feb. 1945; 196, A. Ber... (*non-lieu*); 79, G. Cha..., 8 Aug. 1945; 119, M. Sal..., 9 Feb. 1946.
42. AN F^{7}15280, report of *renseignements généraux* (Vichy), 31 Jan. 1942; An F^{1CIII}1143, prefectoral reports of Nov. 1941, Feb.–March 1942; AD M^{6}10971, Pref. to Int., 27 June 1941; AD M^{6}11038, *notes d'écoute* of 5 Feb. 1942; AD 500U series, *liasses*: 43, J. Pan..., 6 Sept. 1945; 153, R. Sa..., 28 Nov. 1945; *EN* 9 May 1942, 15 June 1944.
43. Of 18 members of the JPF with little activity in the organisation, eight had joined to avoid the STO. Twelve of the 39 in the post- November 1942 sample (who are elsewhere included in the 254 PPF members) had joined to avoid the STO; 18 of the 39, being under the age of 18, were not liable for the STO.
44. Five of seven known clerical and service personnel had been unemployed when they joined the PPF.
45. See appendix ii; there were many more unemployed in the PPF sample (17 of 69 for whom such information was available) than in the JPF (1 of 18); 7 of 93 had been born in Corsica; 52 of the 93, or 56 per cent, had been born after 1916, about the same as for the party as a whole (see p. 214).
46. Thirty-three out of 75 joining after Nov. 1942 for whom such information is available had demonstrated their sympathies for 'the other side'. Six of them had provided help to *réfractaires* and eleven in some way helped or later joined the resistance or the *maquis*.
47. AD 500U series, *liasses*: 131, case of V. Can..., 27 Jun 1946; 17, P. Duc..., 27 Feb. 1945; 194, P. Ma... (*non-lieu*); 225, P. Tr... (*non-lieu*); 256, J. Rig... (*non-lieu*); 36, P. Mar..., 6 Dec. 1944 (etc.); 6, J. Bia..., 2 March 1945.

48. The text of Dunker's last appeal for clemency, which may have been drafted by his lawyer Maître Garci, is given in M. Baudoin, *Témoins de la résistance en région 2* (Thèse pour le doctorat d'état, Université de Provence, Aix-Marseille, 1977), iii, 793–794.
49. AD 500U285, *Affaire Delage* (interrogation of 11 May 1945; Dunker was tried by a military court, which sentenced him to death on 22 Jan. 1947, but copies of hs testimony are kept in the dossiers of the civil cases. He was executed in 1950); M. Baudoin, *op.cit.*, iii, 790–791.
50. AN 393 MI3, SDECE report, Paris, 12 March 1946, in microfilm of R70 Frankreich, Bundesarchiv, Koblenz: *archives des services spéciaux de la police allemande en France, 1940–1944*.
51. AD 500U285, *Affaire Delage*; M. Baudoin, *op.cit.*, ii, pp. 65–66.
52. *Ibid*: thirteen different *procès-verbaux* in the *affaire Delage* alone incriminate him in brutality, torture, and murder.
53. M. Baudoin, *op. cit.*, ii, 66; AD 500U155, case of R. Dov...and R. Las..., 8 Jan. 1946 (testimony of Delage).
54. AD 500U119, case of M. Sal..., 9 Feb. 1946 (testimony of H. Stadelhofer); AD 500U285, *affaire Delage*.
55. AD 500U285 (*affaire Delage*); M. Baudoin, *op.cit.*, iii, 793 (from *recours en grâce*).
56. AD 500U285, *affairs Delage* and *rapport Flora*; AD 500U402, G. Da..., 27 June 1956. Five of the 122 arrested in the *Flora* sweep of April 1943 were doubled.
57. AD 500U series, *liasses*: 117, M. Fra..., 4 Jan. 1946 (list of French agents); 119, M. Me..., 15 Feb. 1946 (plot on Delage); 402, G. Daveau, 5 Sept. 1946; 126, Blanche di Meglio, 30 May 1946; 285 (*affaire Delage*); M. Baudoin, *op.cit.*, i, 46, and iii, 794; names used because of prior mention in Baudoin.
58. The four were Thomas Ricci, Charles Oliveiri, André Mariani, and Pierre Cassagnes; the trials of the first

three are missing but information on them is available in AD 500U117, case of M. Fra..., 4 Jan. 1946; AD 500U120, L. Jun..., 28 Feb. 1946; AD 500U168; M. Baudoin, *op. cit.*, iii, 794; Cassagnes' trial *in absentia* is in AD 500U168 (CJ 2717), 11 June 1946. Another PPF SD agent, Charles Palmieri, did not work for Delage and is covered below, pp. 241–245.

59. After the Liberation agents of the *Direction de la Surveillance du Territoire* (DST) conducted an investigation into 'Albert' — see DST report of 16 Nov. 1945 in AD 500U168, case of E. Cor..., 12 June 1946; also details on him in AD 500U133, cases of J. Gue... and J. Pi..., 18 July 1946.

60. AD 500U: *liasses*: 133, J. Gue... and J. Pi..., 18 July 1946; 121, J. And... and J. Ca..., 15 March 1946; 82, R. Ma..., 16 Oct. 1945; 76, R. Ro..., 18 June 1945.

61. AD M⁶11576, extensive report of 24 Sept. 1945 of *renseignements généraux* on PPF intelligence gathering operations for the Germans; J.-P. Brunet, *Doriot. Du communisme au fascisme* (Paris, 1986), pp. 432–434.

62. AD M⁶11576, *renseignements généraux* report of 24 Sept. 1945; AD 500U113, G. Mez... and G. Co..., 5 Oct. 1945; AD 500U174 *bis*, R, Li..., M, Li..., M, Pa..., L. Bi ..., 31 July 1946. 'Réné Page' was Roger Peter, who answered the phone at *l'Emancipation Nationale* as such, of AD M⁶11038, *notes d'écoute* of 6 and 22 Nov. 1941, 2 May 1942, etc. The turning of the OSS agent was the subject of a special post-war investigation by the US Seventh Army, a copy of which is in AD 500U288.

63. AD M⁶11576, *renseignements généraux* report of 24 Sept. 1945 on PPF intelligence work for the Germans; AD 500U174, case of R. Mi..., 11 July 1946; 500U174 *bis*, cases of M. Pa..., R. and M. Li..., L. Bi..., 31 July 1946; AD 500U168, case of E. Cor..., 12 June 1946. From the outset Doriot had worked with

Nosek of the SD as well as Reile of the Abwehr.

64. AD 500U167, A. Da..., 6 June 1946; AD 500U162, E. Ma..., 2 May 1946; AD 500U168, E. Cor..., 12 June 1946.

65. AD 500U167, A. Da..., 6 June 1946; Ad 500U162, E. Ma..., 2 May 1946; AD 500U168, E. Cor..., 12 June 1946.

66. The twelve *Légion Brandenbourg* recruits tried by the civil courts are: AD 500U119, C. Gu..., 16 Feb. 1946; 127, G. Ca...24 May 1946; 157, Y. Ma..., 7 Feb. 1946; 163, J. Fe..., 9 May 1946; 164, H. Oha ..., 15 May 1946; 73, R Fr..., 27 March 1946; 78, H. La..., 4 July 1945; 88, A. Som..., 11 March 1946; 90, J. Go..., 2 Apr. 1946 and C. Ri..., 14 March 1945; 98, G. Per... and E. Bl..., 22 July 1946.

67. J.-P. Brunet, *Doriot. Du communisme au fascisme.* (Paris, 1986), p. 455.

68. The precise number of PPF working as anti-resistance agents and informers is unknowable. Many disappeared or were killed at the Liberation, the activities of others were never proved; the numbers above are taken from the trials in front of civil courts, but many, for this sort of charge, were brought before military courts. The only conclusion permissilble here is that the PPF was the only organised presence among such collaborators; see chapter VIII, pp. 124–5 for the role of the Milice in this connection.

69. AD M⁶13301, *renseignements généraux* report of 5 Oct. 1944; AD 500U: 85, C. Ri..., 7 March 1946; 119, J. Bat... 15 Feb. 1946; 61, B. Mo..., 20 Oct. 1944; 74, A. Bou..., 24 April 1945. Documents found at the SD after the Liberation indicated that 292 people worked for Section III, but these would have included many working not at the Hôtel Californie but at the OPA on the rue Beauvau; on the other hand, as many as 120 PPF members may have worked at the *Californie*, cf. below.

70. AD M⁶13301, *renseignements généraux* report of 5 Oct. 1944; AD 500U97, J. Pag..., 9 July 1946; 85, C. Ri..., 7 March 1946; 134, J. Da..., n.d.; the police report of 5 Oct. 1944 in AD M⁶13301 says that the Battesti brigade consisted of six teams of eight to ten men each, but an agent who had infiltrated the brigade said in the trial of A. Mel..., AD 500U109, 15 June 1945, that it had 120.

71. AD 500U90, L. San..., 8 April 1946; AD 500U134, J. Da...(report of infiltrator), n.d.

72. AD 500U: 143, O. Pet..., 18 May 1946; 91, V. Ai..., 30 April 1946; 97, J. Pag..., 9 July 1946 and J. Zoc..., 9 July 1946; 146, P. Fal..., 31 July 1945.

73. In fact 249 were tried but activities could only be determined for 197. This figure includes all those working for the Hôtel Californie or the *Office de Placement Allemand*, whether they were known to be PPF or not. Eleven were known to be members of the Milice — for the activity of the Milice in this connection, see chapter VIII, p. 126; it is not always clear from the trial material whether the individual was in PPF/Battesti brigade or not, but, by all accounts, that brigade was the largest element in the *réfractaire* — hunting network. For the 70 mentioned the activity was proved; for the others the activity, though highly probable in some cases, could not be proved.

74. AD 500U: , ..., ; 97, J. Alz ..., 9 July 1946; 125, A. Cap..., 10 May 1946; 97, J. Zoc...9 July 1946; 97, J. Pag..., 9 July 1946; 91, V. Ai..., 30 April 1946; 165, G. Da ..., 28 May 1946.

75. AD 500U99, J. De..., 22 Sept. 1944; the numbers refer to all working in the STO organisation, whether they were known to arrest *réfractaires* or not — of the 28 who had helped the resistance in some way, 14 had worked for the OPA but refused to arrest *réfractaires*.

76. Of the 249 (including some not knwon to be members of the PPF) tried for working for the OPA or the Hôtel Californie, professions were available for 236 (see appendix iv): 126, or 54 per cent, were unemployed or from the working class. Of the 249, 12, or 5 per cent, were born between 1865 and 1890, 64, or 26 per cent, between 1891 and 1905, 81 or 33 per cent, were born between 1906 and 1916, 92, or 37 per cent, after 1916. Ninety-nine, or 40 per cent, were born in Marseille, 13, or 5 per cent, in Corsica, 69, or 28, elsewhere in France; there was an important Italian element of 27, or 11 per cent, among those convicted — many sent there by the *Casa d'Italia* which had extracted oaths of loyalty to the fascist régime at the time of the Italian armistice in Sept. 1943, see AD 500U256, A. Bol...(*non-lieu*).

77. AD 500U404, case of Charles Palmieri; AD 500U86, case of Victor Palmieri, 29 Jan. 1946; AD 500U225, case of R. Br...(*non-lieu*); *MM* 8 Sept. 1937.

78. AD 500U404, case of Charles Palmieri; AD 500U145, case of Jacqueline Palmieri *née* Payeur, 24 July 1945.

79. AD 500U404, case of Charles Palmieri, AD 500U255, case of R. Br...(*non-lieu*); AD 500U92, F. He..., 22 May 1946.

80. AD 500U404, case of Charles Palmieri; AD 500U86, case of Victor Palmieri, 29 Jan. 1946; AD 500U145, case of Jacqueline Palmieri *née* Payeur, 24 July 1945; the descriptions of Charles and Alfred are from R. Br ..., the probable D.G.E.R. agent who infiltrated the group; the phrase 'le truand à l'état pur' is applied to him by P. Guiral in *Libération de Marseille* (Paris, 1974), p. 146.

81. AD 500U92, case of J. Qui..., 22 May 1946; AD 500U256, R. Bal... (*non-lieu*); AD 500U93, R. Don...27 May 1946.

82. Of the thirteen, six were unemployed or had no steady job, four

were working class, two lower middle, one upper middle; five were born in Marseille, four elsewhere in metropolitan France, two in Corsica, one in Italy, one (Armenian) in Turkey.

83. AD 500U 97, J. Zoc..., 9 July 1946; 81 J. Pa..., 1 Oct. 1945; 146, P. Fal ...31 July 1945; 86, V. Palmieri..., ·29 Jan. 1946.

84. AD 500U125, L. Ric..., 10 May 1946; 99, J. Cos..., n.d. Oct. 1944; AD 500U91, F. He..., 22 May 1946; 165, E. and A. Alb..., J. Vil..., L. Don..., Kal..., 21 May 1946; 99, J. De..., 22 Sept. 1944.

85. 25 of the 78 employed by the *Hotel Californie* (who were tried by the civil courts); for 53 no judicial record was available.

86. André Ducasse, *Quand ma ville ne riait plus ou Mars et les marseillais* (Marseille, 1946), p. 259; instances of German disciplinary action in AD 500U91, V. Ai..., 30 April 1946; 161, J. Co..., 11 April 1946; 97, J. Alz..., 9 July 1946.

87. Paul Paillole, *Services spéciaux 1935– 1945* (Geneva, 1978), and Paul Paillole, letter to M. Baudoin in her *Témoins de la résistance en région 2, op. cit.*, iii, 243, source of the quotation above. In 1939 Paillole was a captain in the *deuxième bureau*, in 1942 the head of counter-espionage, all the while working with London and later Algiers; AD M⁶11576, *rapport of Service départemental des renseignements généraux* on the PPF/German intelligence links, 24 Sept. 1945; AD 500U120, P. Dar..., 9 March 1946; AD 500U81, J. Pas..., 1 Oct. 1945; AD 500U119, C. Gu..., 16 Feb. 1946; Undôcumented accounts of Carbone (Paul Buonaventure Carbone, the senior brother, often known as Venture) and Spirito appear in R. Peyrefitte, *Manouche* (Paris, 1972), pp. 80 ff.; J. Bazal, *Le clan des marseillais* (Paris, 1974), pp. 165 ff.; and E. Saccomano, *Bandits à Marseille* (Paris, 1968), pp. 92 ff.

88. AD 500U: 161, J. Co..., 11 April 1946 (re Battesti); 252, information on Renucci brothers; 119, J. Renucci (*non-lieu*); 98, A. Ca..., 22 July 1946; 84, E. Pi..., 10 Dec. 1945; P. Paillole, *op. cit.*, pp. 101–103; M. Baudoin, *op. cit.*, ii, p. 528.

89. From references and descriptions in AD 500U: 133, J. Gue...and J. Pi..., 18 July 1946, and J. Ca..., 25 Jan. 1946; 159, A. Gh..., 12 March 1946; 143, H. pa..., 13 June 1944; 119, M. Me..., 15 Feb. 1946; 126, J. Ac..., 23 May 1946; 142, H. Ob..., 30 May 1945; 124 G. Bl..., 2 May 1946; 152, L. Vo..., 13 Nov. 1945; 48, L. Reb..., 16 May 1945; 94, P. Gia..., 11 June 1946; 90, L. San..., 8 April 1946; 92, P. Di..., 22 May 1946; 93, R. Don..., 27 May 1945; 62, R. Se..., 11 Oct. 1944; 100, I. Do..., 12 Oct. 1944. There are many other references to these and other establishments of the *quartier* in the 500U series.

90. AD 500U114, P. Gu..., 19 Oct. 1945.

91. They are probably somewhere between ten and twenty per cent of all PPF between November 1942 and August 1944. 28, or 11 per cent, of the 254 members of the PPF known to have joined between those dates took part in such activities; if those for whom no entry date is known are added the total would be 46 and the percentage 18. But there are, in addition, those in the PPF-affiliated organisations, like the *Bureau Merle*, who were not officially members of the party, and those, like Antoine Tortora, who disappeared before they could brought to trial (a particularly likely fate for those given to these activities), and those whose membership in the party was unknown at the time of their trial. If all the employees of the Hôtel Californie and the OPA are included, for example, minus the *miliciens* but including those of uncertain affiliation, the percentage would be 22 per cent instead of 11.

92. At least eight on a list of twelve section leaders in AD 500U121, R. de F..., 14 March 1946, were *en*

poste before the war. But the list is undated, and may well be from the very end of the war.

93. AD M⁶11576, report of *Service départemental des renseignements généraux* on PPF-German intelligence links, 24 Sept. 1945; AD 500U98, G. Be..., 16 July 1946.

94. *ML* 2 Oct. 1943, *EN* 8 and 15 Jan. 1944.

95. AD 500U: 73, R. Fr..., 27 March 1945 and J. So..., 9 April 1945; Sabiani was said to have gone on the Simiane expedition but the nature of his participation is unclear, AD 500U: 54, A. Mag..., 21 Feb. 1945; 105, F. Fa..., 9 Feb. 1945; 115, Simon Sabiani, 1 Dec. 1945. J.-A. Vaucoret, *Simon Sabiani, op.cit.*, does not give a source for his statement, p. 566, that Delage had Sabiani's apartment searched, but the action is plausible: he had intervened (unsuccessfully) to have Antoine Zattara, the police chief arrested in Delage's Catilina operation, released, see AD 500U285, *affaire Delage*.

96. AD 500U: 94, C. Ma..., 18 June 1946; 155, A. Ca..., 13 July 1945 and R. Am..., 5 Oct. 1945; 61, B. Mo..., 20. Sept. 1944.

97. AD 500U: 115, Simon Sabiani, 1 Dec. 1945; 170, M. Cro..., 18 June 1946; 86, V. Palmieir, 29 Jan. 1946; 165, E. Alb..., 21 May 1946; 148, P. Mor..., 11 Sept. 1945. V. Barthélémy, in *Du communisme au fascisme. L'histoire d'un engagement politique* (Paris, 1978), pp. 385 ff., says that Sabiani created the Battesti operation at the suggestion of Sauckel and in defiance of Doriot, a claim which J.-A. Vaucoret, Simon Sabiani, *op.cit.*, p. 567–569, convincingly disputes.

98. AD 500U404, C. Palmieri; AD 500U255, R. Br... (*non-lieu*); AD 500U72, A. Pet...13 March 1945.

99. AD 500U115, Simon Sabiani, 1 Dec. 1945; ML 12 Feb. and 29 April 1944. For as active and important a figure as Sabiani, the evidence against him at his trial *in absentia* is extraordin-

arily thin. The evidence of his anti-resistance activity is given above, apart from one isolated account alleging that he organised two expeditions against the *maquis* late in July. He had a file card at the SD, which only proves that he, like other approved public figures, had some German protection including the *Ausweiss* (cf. testimony of H. Stadelhofer in AD 500U 119, case of M. Sal..., 9 Feb. 1946). He also sent some job applicants to work as prison guards at the *Baumettes*, where some of the prisoners were 'terrorists'. In general, apart from the incidents mentioned above, the most damaging case against him arguably rests on his own speeches and articles.

Chapter 8

1. ML 26 Feb. 1944; AD M⁶11038, *note d'écoute* of 11 Sept. 1942 (Peter to Dédé).

2. AD 500U series, *liasses*: 47, B. Ram ...27 June 1945; 405, R. Ri...n.d.; 95, M. Reg...25 June 1946; J. Ser ...18 April 1945; 192, F. Pr... (*non-lieu*); 194, J. Co... (*non-lieu*); 197, R. Go ... (*non-lieu*); 197, R. Go... (*non-lieu*). Of 49 Vichy officials tried or investigated at the Liberation, charges were dropped for 24, 2 were acquitted, 6 given the minimum sentence of *dégradation nationale*.

3. AN F¹ᶜᴵᴵᴵ1200, prefectoral report of 12 Nov. 1943; AD M⁶11040, Pref. to Laval, 8 Dec. 1943.

4. AD 500U: 101, M. Fat..., 17 Nov. 1944; 74, P. Gal..., 23 April 1945; 62, J. Tou..., 17 Oct. 1944; 15, M. Dej..., 20 June 1945; 10, A. Cau... n.d.; 2, M. Au...25 Oct. 1945. The numbers are small and can only hint at social change: of 27 known to have joined the SOL after November 1942, 3 (11 per cent) were unemployed, compared to 5.6 per cent earlier, see p. 87; 8, or 30 per cent, were from the working class, compared to 20 per cent earlier (calcula-

tions as in ch. 6, n. 68 and n. 70) 6, or 22 per cent from the lower middle, unchanged from before, and six, or 22 per cent, from the upper middle, almost unchanged from before (25 per cent).

5. AN F^{7}15300, note of *Service de Documentation*, 23 July 1945 (re Knipping); J. Delperrie de Bayac, *Histoire de la Milice, 1918–1945* (Paris, 1969), pp. 184, 200, 245; AD M^{6}110141, note of Pref., 23 Oct. 1943, Laval to Pref., 5 May 1943, Pref. to Laval, 11 and 28 May 1943, *Secrétaire général du gouvernment* too Pref., 17 Feb. 1943; N. Brashover, *Les partis nationaux devant le gouvernement de Vichy et la collaboration à Marseille de 1939 à 1944* (mémoire de maîtrise, Aix-en-Provence, 1971), pp. 131–133; AD 500U234, R. Pe... (*non-lieu*); 115, P. Dur...1 Dec. 1945; 50, R. Ro ...8 Feb. 1945.

6. AN FF^{1CIII}1143, prefectoral reports of April–May 1943, Oct.–Dec. 1943; AD M^{6}11041, Knipping to Pref., 24 Nov. 1943, Pef. to Knipping 26 June 1944; AN F^{7}15301, Pref. to Police (Vichy), 28 March 1943.

7. See appendix iv. The comparison is with the social composition of members known to have joined the PPF after Nov. 1942, ie with the table in appendix ii. Two other regional studies suggest a stronger lower middle class base, see M. Luirard, 'La Milice française dans la Loire', *Revue d'histoire de la deuxième guerre mondiale*, 92 (July 1973), and M. Chanal, 'La Milice française dans l'Isère', *ibidem*, 127b (July 1982). 711 *miliciens* were tried at the Liberation, 530 members of the PPF. It seems likely that a higher proportion of *miliciens* than PPF members were brought to trial: a list of 130 members of the PPF in Marseille was found, while a list of 467 *miliciens* was found; also the *Milice* seems to have kept better of its members (see AD 500U290). The figure of 1,000 is little more than a guess, however. In Lyon, a city of comparable size, the *Milice* had

about 1200 members, AN F^{7}15301, *renseignements généraux* note of 23 June 1944.

8. 101, or 14 per cent, of the 711 tried joined from the SOL, but for 256 no entry motive was available: if these are excluded the percentage joining from the SOL would be 22. In the Isère the percentage may have been as high as 50, see M. Chanal, *art.cit.*

9. 155 out of the 711 (22 per cent) joined to avoid the STO; deducting the 256 for whom no entry motive is available, the 155 would amount to 34 per cent. AD 500U: 120, M. Sa...8 March 1946; 100, R. Tou..., 13 Oct 1944; 136, G. di...20 Feb. 1945; 137, M. Gui...15 March 1945; 94, G. Bo...11 June 1946; 39, S. Me ...7 March 1945; 62, G. Ba...16 Oct. 1944.

10. Of the 455 *miliciens* providing entry motives (of the total of 711), only 20, or 4 per cent, attributed their membership to conviction — but allowance must be made for the danger of such avowals after the Liberation; 41 or 9 per cent, joined for work, money or priivieleges; 29, or 6 per cent, under pressure from friends or relatives. AD500U: 15, R. de...18 April 1945; 126, A. Mad ...31 May 1946; 91, C. Dou...14 May 1946.

11. AD500U205, M. Gu...21 June 1946 (testimony of *milicien* G. Bo ...); AD500U29, E. Jac...11 April 1945.

12. AD M^{6}11041, Vaugelas to Pref., 17 and 28 June 1943; N. Brashover, *op. cit.*, p. 133; AD 500U:124, P. Fus... 26 April 1946; 155, A. Las...8 Jan. 1946; 130, R. Li...20 June 1946; 168, P. Chi...11 June 1946; 162, P. Ph...8 May 1946; 18, A. El...16 Aug. 1945. Of the 711 *miliciens* tried, 126 (18 per cent) had worked in such occupations, but after excluding the 229 *miliciens* whose activities are unknown their percentage would rise to 26.

13. J. Delperrie de Bayac, *Histoire de la Milice 1918–1945* (Paris, 1969), p. 234 (interview in *Paris-Soir*, 7 Jan.

1944); AD 500U: 168, E. Cor...28 Oct. 1946; 111, P. Gan...20 July 1945; 86, J. Nov...29 Jan. 1946; 87, H. Du... 20 Feb. 1946; 164, B. Fa ...16 May 1946; 168, P. Chi...n.d; 116, J. Bo... 15 Dec. 1944; 71, E. Pey...27 Feb. 1945; 166, P. Ven... 11 June 1946.

14. AD 500U44, C. Pel...20 Sept. 1945; of the 443 *miliciens* excluding the *francs-gardes* for whom information on activities is available, 86 or 19 per cent took part in anti-*maquis* operations. Of the 39 known *francs-gardes* tried, information on activities is available for 31: 17, or 55 per cent, had taken part in anti-*maquis* operations. Among the Prefect's 143 recruits on whom socio-professional information is available (AD M⁶11041, Pref. to Laval, 11 and 28 May 1943), 40 were from the working class, 72 were from the lower middle class, 17 from the upper middle; 7 were *fonctionnaires* and two were unclassifiable. Professions are available for all of the 39 known *francs-gardes* tried, and 7, or 18 per cent, were unemployed.

15. AD 500U: 117, A. Pi...4 Jan. 1946 (quote from H. Du...); 130, R. Li...20 June 1946; 103, L. Ma... 12 Jan. 1945. Out of the 482 miliciens for whom such information is available, 157, or 33 per cent, had minimal activity. Information on the mobilisation of late May and early June is very incomplete, but only 164 of the 711 were clearly mobilised: many of the others managed to escape, but how many is unclear.

16. AD 500U: 121, J. Ga...9 March 1946; 33, A. Le...5 Sept. 1945; 129, F. Pit...13 June 1946; 76, A. Sav... 4 June 1945; 101, O. Ser...25 Nov. 1944; 76, M. ben...18 June 1945; 106, M. Ca...24 Feb. 1945. Re the Ringo brigade: AD 500U: 73, F. La ...9 April 1945; 75, L. Ame...14 May 1945; 76, R. Fe...5 June 1945; 85, Charles Ringo (*contumace*)...7 July 1946; 88, C. Mat...13 March 1946 — only the last was clearly in the *Milice* while also in the Ringo bri-

gade. Quote from AN F⁷15300, note of *renseignements généraux* (Vichy), 3 May 1943.

17. With so much destroyed in the post-Liberation fire at police headquarters, evidence on criminal records was scanty. But 44 of 711 *miliciens* had criminal records when they joined: 90 out of 530 PPF members had criminal records when they joined. 25 of the 711 *miliciens* were found to have robbed, blackmailed, or murdered while in the *Milice*: 41 of the 530 members of the PPF were found to have done so while in PPF.

18. AD 500U: 58, M. Ve...18 Jan. 1945; 15, H. Del...22 Feb. 1945; 49, J. Rib...7 March 1945; 59, O. We...8 Feb. 1945; 46, O. Qui...17 Jan. 1945; 189, E. Le...(*non-lieu*); 194, E. Bo...(*non-lieu*). There is only one mention after Nov. 1942 of the *Groupe* in the prefects' reports, AN F¹ᶜᴵᴵᴵ1143, report of April/May 1943. Of 146 members of the *Groupe* tried, 85 were known to have joined in the first year of its existence, Nov. 1941–Nov. 1942, only twenty from Nov. 1942–Aug. 1944. Those twenty were socially more heterogeneous than the earlier members (see p. 88–9): three unemployed, one working class, nine lower middle, two *fonctionnaires*, three upper middle, two unclassifiable. 37 were signed up without their knowledge, most in 1943 (they are excluded from the 146 members who joined voluntarily). Of 48 members known to have reigned from the *Groupe*, 31 did so after Nov. 1942.

2. AD 500U: 62, P. Mi...16 Oct. 1944; 139, J. Cr...27 March 1945; 78, J. Mar...16 July 1945; 50, S. Ro ...8 March 1945; G. Tou...30 May 1945; 100, M. Du...13 Oct. 1944; 253, J. Sa...6 Oct. 1945 — the last put the *Jeunesses* at 'une trentaine': 24 were tried.

19. AN F¹ᶜᴵᴵᴵ1143, prefectoral reports of April/May 1943, Dec. 1943–Feb. 1944; AD M⁶13300, note of *renseignements généraux*, 5 Sept. 1944; AD500U: 10, P. Ch...12 Dec. 1945

and following eleven cases; 71, P. Vi...6 March 1945.

20. Of the 29 known to have volunteered after Nov. 1942 (for whom such information is available) seven did so for work and seven to escape a personal or domestic quarrel; the others left for a wide variety of individual motives. Of 44 for whom such information is available, 18 were unemployed, 15 from the working class, the others scattered across the social spectrum. AD 500U: 12, M. Co...31 Jan. 1946; 72, J. Vi... 12 March 1945; 79, M. Lep...1 Aug. 1945; 68, A. Va...29 Jan. 1945.

21. AD 500U: R. d'U...14 May 1946; 152, L. Dr...15 Nov. 1945 (re recruitment offices). See appendix iv for comparison of LVF 141–44 with Waffen-SS. Of the 31 LVF volunteers known to have joined after Nov. 1942, 10, or 32 per cent were unemployed, 9, or 29 per cent, working class (32 and 18 per cent respectively in the Waffen-SS, were appendix iv). Among those for whom entry motives are available: of 19 post-Nov. 1942 LVF volunteers, six (33 per cent) joined to escape from domestic troubles (12 of 49 for all LVF 1941–44) against four (18 per cent) of 22 Waffen-SS; three (16 per cent) of the 19 post-Nov. 1942 LVF volunteers joined for money and an occupation (ten of 49, or 20 per cent, for all LVF 1941–44) against only one Waffen-SS volunteers; one post-Nov. 1942 LVF volunteer joined under pressure from family or friends (two for all LVF 1941–44) against three Waffen-SS (14 per cent). See pp. 90–91 for backgrounds and motives of the earlier LVF volunteers.

22. AD 500U:163, R. d'U...14 May 1946; 125, P. At...3 May 1946; 89, G. Ca...26 March 1946; 153, R. Gir...27 Nov. 1945, and J. Pi...29 Nov. 1945; 152, L. Dra...15 Nov. 1945; 158, L. Mo...28 Feb. 1946; 156, J. Fa...16 Jan. 1946; 91, F. Gu

...9 April 1946; 120, G. Pe...8 March 1946.

23. Fritz Todt, killed in a plane crash in 1942, was Albert Speer's predecessor at the Ministry of Arms and Munitions. The figure of a half-million is from David Pryce-Jones, Paris in the Third Reich (New York, 1981), p. 36: he does not give a source. Re the Organisation Todt in Marseille cf. André Négis, Marseille sous l'occupation (Paris and Marseille, 1947), p. 116.

24. For the social composition of the Organisation Todt see appendix iv. Of 163 tried for their membership in the Organistaion Todt, entry motives are available for 88. 32 (36 per cent) joined for the job, 26 (30 per cent) under pressure from the Germans, 13 (15 per cent) to avoid the STO, the others for a variety of motives, including escaped prisoners or requis fearing an enforced return to Germany. AD 500U: 76, J. Ya...18 June 1945; 44, A. Per...25 Jan. 1945; 69, A. Mo...5 Feb. 1945; 85, M. Sol...8 Jan. 1946; 86, G. Cl... 21 Jan. 1946; 119, M. Ada...16 Feb. 1946; 2, L. Al...26 July 1945; 122, P. Hat...4 April 1946; 13, E. Co... 17 May 1945; 72, E. Le...20 March 1945; 75, R. Lec...4 June 1945; 106, P. Cu...9 March 1945; 54, R. Tak ...29 July 1946; 114, G. Au...10 Nov. 1945.

25. See appendix iv; 26 of 49 interpreters (tried after the Liberation) who had worked for the Germans (Organisation Todt, Kriegsmarine, SD, Kommandantur and general administration, German industry in France) were from Alsace or Lorraine. AD 500U: 46, J. Po...11 April 1945; 61, R. Sch...4 Oct. 1944; 197, J. Bar... (non-lieu); 219, M. Co...(non-lieu); 226, J. Fre...(non-lieu); 229, G. Ju... (non-lieu); 106, r. Wag...3 March 1945; 170, F. Ma...25 June 1946.

26. The word 'contractor' is used to encompass anyone owning a business undertaking regular work for the Germans. After the Liberation 85

were tried or investigated, of whom 60 provide motives (for social composition see appendix iv): 35 (58 per cent) were coerced by the Germans, 13 (22 per cent) by the French. The others had a variety of motives, including simple commercial gain. After the Liberation charges were dropped against 51 of the 85; a further 8 were tried and acquitted. AD 500U: 213, J. Pa...; 190, P. Tos...; 194, M. Du...; 198, J. Bol ...; 197, M. Del...(all *non-lieux*); 79, J. Ne...and M. Ne...3 Aug. 1945; 20, P. Fi...29 July 1946; 118, P. Ca...1 Feb. 1946; 15, M. Del... 20 Nov. 1945; 136, J. Ro...22 Feb. 1945.

27. Cf. AN F$^{1C III}$1200, prefectoral report of Oct. 1943.

28. AN F$^{1C III}$1200, prefectoral report of July 1943; of the 711 members of the *Milice* tried, 30 were women; of the 530 members of the PPF, 32 were women (mostly members of the Jeunesses Féminines Françaises); of the 163 employees of the *Organisation Todt*, ten; of the 146 volunteers in Germany, 25; of the 54 employed by the *Kommandantur* and Hôtel Splendide, 26; of the 58 at the SD, 11; of the 146 members of the Groupe Collaboration, 38.

29. 17 of the 65 tried were maids; 16 were unemployed; 14 were secretaries. AD 500U: 3, F. Ba...24 Jan. 1945; 51, Y. Sal...27 Feb. 1945; 43, M. Pad...26 Jan. 1945; 8, H. Bru ...25 Sept. 1945; 6, C. Be...14 Jan. 1945; 143, Y. Sa...14 June 1945; 1, R. Ag...15 Nov. 1945; 57, P. Tr ...10 Jan. 1946; 10, S. Ri...16 May 1945. Cf. discussions of *la collaboration horizontale* in R. Cobb, *French and Germans, Germans and French* (Hanover and London, 1983), pp. 104–196, and in H. Amouroux, *La grande histoire des Français sous l'occupation* (Paris, 1978), iii, 436–438.

30. AD 500U: 197, A. Be...(*non-lieu*); 78, M. Co...17 July 1945; 110, A. Kes...22 June 1945; 151, E. Mil... and following 5 cases, 27 July 1945;

13, R. Cou...24 Jan. 1945; 106, R. Wag...3 March 1945.

31. Of 162 denunciations, 46 were political without any apparent personal tie, 25 involved neighbours, landlords, or tenants, 20 involved relatives or lovers, 16 involved business colleagues, 15 involved employers or employees. AD 500U: 125, E. Bar ...10 May 1946; 151, P. Ch... /M. Sch...24 Oct. 1945 and M. Sa ...17 Oct. 1945; 135, H. Bel...26 July 1946; 137, L. Hai...15 March 1945; 140, M. Vad...25 April 1945; 143, J. Fi...19 June 1945; 163, M. Ja .../J. Ja...9 May 1946; 167, A. Fri ...22 Aug. 1945; 65, G. Leo...12 Dec. 1944; 72, B. Fra...19 March 1945; 71, M. Lu.../E. Ba...6 Feb. 1945; 61, R. Sco...2 Oct. 1944. The girl who denounced her father was found by a psychologist to be 'instable' and 'sans grande défense aux entrainements mauvais.

32. The evidence suggests that the PPF had more *corbeaux* proportionately speaking than the *Milice* — at least 19 of 530 members of the PPF (for 1940–44) had denounced one or more people, compared to 24 of 711 *miliciens*). AD 500U: 61, M. Fo...2 Oct. 1944; 139, N. Ha...28 March 1945; 145, A. Ac...24 July 1945; 73, V. Si...27 March 1945; 121, J. De...14 March 1946 — the last two involve men identified as 'PPF', almost certainly Palmieri's. *Re* Palmieri's. *Re* Palmieri's informers, see p. 221.

33. Taking the loosest definition of 'collaborator' — anyone who voluntarily served the occupant in some way, even so coerced as to leave only a razor's edge of choice and as to merit, often, acquittal or *non-lieu* — 2835 investigated or tried by the Marseille civil courts may be said to have 'collaborated'. Doubling this to allow for the dead, the lucky, and those found guilty by the military tribunals (613 for all the Bouches-du-Rhone) still gives a figure of under 7,000, or less than 1% of the popu-

lation of perhaps 700,000. (The statistics compiled by L. Gaillard ('Les étrangers et l'épuration dans les Bouches-du-Rhone', *Revue d'histoire de la deuxième guerre mondiale*, 113 (1979) show that 3175, from the entire department, were convicted of some act of collaboration; 1192 were acquitted.) A much narrower measure — known membership in a collaborationist party — yields a figure of 0.2 per cent for Amiens (D. Duverlie, 'Amiens sous l'occupation allemande', *Revue d'histoire de la deuxième guerre mondiale*, 44 (Jan.– March 1982) and 0.33 per cent for Dijon (P. Gounand, 'Les groupements de collaboration dans une ville française occupée: Dijon', idem, 91 (July 1973) and 0.27 per cent for Marseille. For the Nord the figures are equally diminutive (cf. M. Etienne Dejonghe 'Aspects du régime d'occupation dans le Nord et le Pas-de-Calais durant la seconde guerre mondiale', Revue du Nord, 53 (1971) and D. Laurent 'Statistique de la répression des faits de collaboration dans le département du Nord 1941– 1948, idem). If numbers are the measure of importance then collaboration, like resistance, would merit no attention at all.

34. J.-P. Brunet, *Doriot, op.cit.*, pp. 437–438; Marc Sueur, 'La collaboration politique dans le département du Nord', *Revue d'histoire de la deuxième guerre mondiale*, 135 (July, 1984); P. Gounand, 'Les groupements de collaboration dans une ville française occupée: Dijon', *idem*, 91 (July, 1973); D. Duverlie, 'Amiens sous l'occupation allemande', *idem*, 252 (Jan/March 1982).

35. AN F⁷14897, *Procureur général près Cour d'Appel de Riom* to Minister of Justice, 1 Aug. 1944; Préfet de l'Eure to Int. and *Maintien de l'ordre*, 28 June 1944; *Préfet d'Indre-et-Loire* to *Préfet régional* (Angers); M.-Y. Sicard, a.k.a. Saint-Paulien, *Histoire de la collaboration* (Paris, 1964), pp. 433–434.

36. AN F⁷14897, police note on meet-

ing of 15ᵉᵐᵉ section (Paris), 13 May 1944; Knipping (*délégué du Maintien de l'Ordre en zone* nord) to Oberg, 20 May 1944; *Préfet* des Vosges to Int., 4 Oct. 1943; J.-P. Brunet, *op.cit.*, p. 452 (quote from Darnand); Proc. Gén. (Riom) to Min. of Justice, 1 Aug. 1944; J.-M. Guillon, 'Les mouvements de collaboration dans le Var', Revue d'histoire de la deuxième guerre mondiale, 113 (Jan. 1979).

Chapter 9

1. EN 10 Aug. 1944; AD 500U: 115, S. Sabiani, 1 Dec. 1945; 167, A. Da . . .6 June 1946; 153, R. Sa. . .28 Nov. 1945.

2. Of the 530 members of the PPF tried by the civil courts, only 32 had gone to Germany at the Liberation. Even allowing for those who never returned and those who escaped prosecution, their actual number cannot have exceeded 100.

3. Of the 32 tried who had gone to Germany at the Liberation, 19 had worked for the SD, the Abwehr, or the Hôtel Californie; five had led active official party lives; only three had clearly done very little as members of the party. J.-A. Vaucoret, *Simon Sabiani, op.cit.*, p. 584, that 800 stayed behind. He does not give a source, but the number is plausible if the total membership in the summer of 1944 is taken to be about 1000. AD 500U113, A. Ca. . .6 Oct. 1945; AD 500U87, J. Sab. . .6 Feb. 1946.

4. of 711 *miliciens* tried, 157 had gone to Germant at the Liberation. AD 500U: 120, M. Da. . .1 March 1946; 129, L. Por. . .14 June 1946; 159, F. Bi. . .19 March 1946; 164, C. Ey. . . 16 May 1946; 54, E. Sto. . .10 Jan. 1946; 89, C. Ger. . .20 March 1946.

5. J.-P. Brunet, *Doriot, op.cit.*, pp. 462, 468–469; K.-D. Bracher, *The German Dictatorship*, tr. Jean Steinberg, London, 1980, p. 511; Agathe Sabi-

ani, Marseille, 12 Feb. 1984 and 3 June 1986 (interviews). Cf. also the memoirs of Jean Hérold Paquis, *Des illusions... désillusions (15 août 1944–15 août 1945)* (Paris, 1948).

6. J.-P. Brunet, *Doriot, op.cit.*, p. 473; *re* Doriot's resistance to moving to Sigmaringen and his other dealings with the Germans, Archives of German Foreign Ministry (US National Archives) microfilm series, T120 2129: Struve to foreign ministry, 9 and 11 Sept. 1944; Doriot to Struve, 9 Sept. 1944 Abetz to Ribbentrop, 29 Sept. 1944.

7. AD 500U: 94, H. Ri... 5 June 1946; 160, H. Deg... 20 March 1946; 153, J. Tom... 27 Nov. 1945 and R. Sa ... 28 Nov. 1945; 88, R. Ne... 4 March 1946; 98, G. Be... 16 July 1946; of the 32 members of the PPF tried who had gone to Germany, 19, while there, worked in some way at some time for German intelligence or the PPF network (including the schools).

8. Archives of the German Foreign Ministry (US National Archives, Washington), microfilm series, T120 2129, Struve to foreign ministry, 11 Sept. 1944, where he says that 15 agents were already at work, and foreign ministry note (Sonnenhol) of 15 Sept. 1944; information *re* Wiesbaden and Reutlingen from the exhaustive report on the PPF intelligence and sabotage schools and operations in AD M⁶11576, *Commissaire principal, service départemental des renseignements généraux to commissaire divisionaire, service régionale des renseignements généraux*, 24 Sept. 1945. Re 'Page' see pp. 232, 257.

9. AD M⁶11576, report of *renseignements généraux*, 24 Sept. 1945.

10. AD 500U88, H. Ve... 11 March 1946; AD 500U 90, L. San... (testimony of M. Tom...), 8 April 1946; L.-F. Céline, *D'un château l'autre* (Paris, 1969), pp. 368–369. J.-P. Brunet, in *Doriot, op.cit.*, quotes the same passage, pp. 487–488.

11. V. Barthélémy, *Du communisme au fascisme. L'histoire d'un engagement politique* (Paris, 1978), p. 472; AD 500U 167, A. Da... 6 June 1946; Agathe Sabiani, Marseille, 3 June 1986 (interview) and Alban Géronimi, Marseille, 12 Dec. 1983 (interview).

12. J. Delperrie de Bayac, *Histoire de la Milice, 1918–1945* (Paris, 1969), p. 533; of 122 *miliciens* for whom such information is available, 31 worked in *Milice* camps, 27 worked for German employers, and 11 worked in Pétain's entourage at Vichy; AD 500U: 120, M. Sa... 8 March 1946; 90, P. La... 3 April 1946; 124, G. Ge... 3 May 1946; E. Po... 26 Feb. 1946; 95, M. Cha... 1 July 1946; 122, R. Alb... 29 March 1946.

13. Of the 122 *miliciens* for whom such information is available, 25 had joined the *Division Charlemagne*; A. Merglen, 'Soldats français sous uniformes allemands, 1941–1945: LVF et "Waffen-SS" français', *Revue d'histoire de la deuxième guerre mondiale*, 108 (Oct. 1977); J. Delperrie de Bayac, *op.cit.*, p. 575, 577, says that 4,000 *miliciens* were sent to the *Division Charlemagne*, of whom 2,500 actually entered; quotes from the memoirs of the *Waffen-SS* volunteer Christian de la Mazière, *Le rêveur casqué* (Paris, 1976), pp. 43, 56.

14. Of the 85 men tried for belonging to the *Division Charlemagne*, 25, or 29 per cent, came from the *Milice*, 51, or 60 per cent, from the LVF or the *Stürmbrigade*, 2 from the PPF, 4 from the *Organisation Todt* or the *Kriegsmarine*, 3 from the volunteer workers in Germany; AD 500U: 123, E. Pi... 26 April 1946; 125, A. Gui... 9 May 1946; 123, A. Be... 6 April 1946; C. de la Mazière, *op.cit.*, pp. 71–72, says that many, including himself, managed to avoid the tatooing, out of prudence or distaste.

15. AD 500U: 117, G. Go... 18 Jan. 1946; 122, M. Da... 5 April 1946; 125, A. Gui... 9 May 1946; 128, S. Bas... 1 June 1946; 157, P. Do... 12 Feb. 1946; 164, G. Deg... 14 May 1946; B. Co... 17 July 1946; 152, A.

Ma...8 Nov. 1945; 93, C. Gu...4 June 1946 and E. Fa...3 June 1946; 89, G. Ca...26 March 1946; 95, G. Pa...25 June 1946.

16. AD 500U: 44, H. Pe...21 Nov. 1945; 46, H. Pro...21 Nov. 1945; cf. also 123, V. Noc...11 April 1946; 6, C. Bi...31 Oct. 1945.

17. Cf. P. Guiral, *Libération de Marseille* (Paris, 1974), and L. Gaillard, *Marseille sous l'occupation* (Rennes, 1982).

18. AD M⁶13300, *renseignements généraux* reports of 28 Aug. 1944, 29 Aug. 1944, 1, 7, and 8 Sept. 1944.

19. AD 500U128, J. Pad...31 May 1946; AD M⁶13300, *renseignements généraux* reports of 1 Sept. 1944, 8 Sept. 1944, 15 Sept. 1944; AD M⁶13301, *renseignements généraux* report of 14 Oct. 1944.

20. AD M⁶13301, *renseignements généraux* report of 26 Sept. 1944; Ad M⁶13300, *renseignements généraux* reports of 2, 4, 5, 7, 9 and 19 Sept. 1944 (multiple reports on all days).

21. AD M⁶13300, *renseignements généraux* reports of 6 Sept. 1944, 12 Sept. 1944 (multiple reports). AD 500U61, D. Tch...11 Sept. 1944.

22. The statistics for the cases judged the three *Cours de justice* in Marseille between their creation on 11 Sept. 1944 and their dissolution on 31 July 1946 are: death sentences: PPF:55, Milice:44, other:67; life imprisonment: PPF:16, Milice:24, other:27; 10–25 years' imprisonment: PPF:22, Milice:41, other:74; 5–10 years' imprisonment: PPF: 18, Milice: 45, other:42; 1–5 years' imprisonment: PPF:76, Milice:164, other:165; less than a year's imprisonment: PPF:37, Milice:89, other:82; loss of civic rights (for any duration): PPF:174, Milice:193; other:394.

23. AD 500U276, Georges Ribot (*non-lieu*); AD 500U000, Gustave Chipponi (*non-lieu*); E. Saccomano, *Bandits à Marseille* (Paris, 1968), pp. 94–96; AD M⁶13705, *renseignements généraux* report of 21 Nov. 1944; J.-A. Vaucoret, *Simon Sabiani, op.cit.*, p. 586; AD 500U100, L. Mangiavacca, 14 Oct. 1944.

24. AD 500U404, Charles Palmieri; AD 500U86, Victor Palmieri, 29 Jan. 1946; AD M⁶13302, *renseignements généraux* report of 11 Jan. 1945.

25. AD 500U168, E. Cor...12 June 1946 (DST inquiries).

26. A. Négis, *Marseille sous l'occupation* (Paris and Marseille, 1947), pp. 44–46; L. Gaillard, *Marseille sous l'occupation* (Rennes, 1982), p. 59; M. Baudoin, *Témoins de la résistance en région 2* (Thèse pour le doctorat d'état, Université de Provence Aix-Marseille I, 1977), i, 60–65.

28. AD 500U115, Simon Sabiani, 1 Dec. 1945; AD M⁶13300, *renseignements généraux* reports of 8 and 23 Sept. 1944; AD M⁶13705, *renseignements généraux* report of 2 Dec. 1944; *France-Soir, 5 Sept. 1945 (from AN F⁷15303); J.-A. Vaucoret, Simon Sabiani, op. cit.*, pp. 597–598.

29. J.-A. Vaucoret, *Simon Sabiani, op.cit.*, pp. 597–598; J. Bazal, *Le clan des marseillais* (Paris, 1974), pp. 174–175; AN F⁷15303, *Sûreté nationale* note of 8 July 1948; Agathe Sabiani, Marseille, 12 Feb. 1984 and 3 June 1986 (interviews).

30. Agathe Sabiani, 3 June 1986, and Madame Antoine Morelli, 13 Oct. 1986, Marseille (interviews).

Conclusion

1. According to J.-A. Vaucoret, *op. cit.* — he does not give a source.

2. Daniel Vernet in *Le Monde*, 20 March 1985.

3. See D. Bell, 'Politics in Marseille since World War II with special reference to the role fo Gaston Defferre' (Oxford Univ. D. Phil. thesis, 1978), pp. 297, 299–307, 315, 339.

4. Agathe Sabiani, Marseille, 3 June 1986 (interview).

SOURCES

A. Unpublished Sources

I. Primary Unpublished Source (archival sources)

Archives Nationales (Paris)

The following cartons in the F^7 series each include varying amounts of material as indicated on Marseille:

$F^7$12950 Action Française/Jeunesses Patriotes/Faisceau

$F^7$12976 Daily reports, CD to Pref., Marseille, 1936

$F^7$13024 Weekly reports, BDR Pref. to Int, 1934

$F^7$13032 Monthly reports, Pref. and CS., BDR and Marseille, Feb. and March 1931, Nov. 1936.

$F^7$13200, 13201, 13202 Action Française, 1928–1932

$F^7$13209 Le Faisceau, first half 1926

$F^7$13210 Le Faisceau, second half 1926

$F^7$13219 and 13221 Fédération Nationale Catholique, 1926

$F^7$13222 and 13224 Fédération Nationale Catholique, 1927

$F^7$13232 Jeunesses Patriotes

$F^7$13233 and 13234 Jeunesses Patriotes, 1926 and 1927

$F^7$13235 Jeunesses Patriotes, 1928–1932

$F^7$13237 Ligue Républicaine Nationale, 1926–1927

$F^7$13238 and 13239 Solidarité Française, 1933–1935

$F^7$13241 Francistes, Croix-de-Feu, 1935

$F^7$13245, 13246, 13247 Fascisme, 1925–1928

$F^7$13308 Sixth Feb. 1934 — telegrams from Pref. to Int.

$F^7$13313 Demonstrations, including Marseille, Feb. 1925.

$F^7$13102 Parti Communiste, 1923–1924

$F^7$13104 Parti Communiste, 1926

$F^7$13106 Parti Communiste, 1926

$F^7$13108 Parti Communiste, 1927

$F^7$13115 Parti Communiste, 1929

$F^7$13120 Parti Communiste, 1930

F^{7}13081 Parti Socialiste 1926–1932
F^{7}14817 PSF and PPF, 1936–1939
F^{7}14897 Activities of authorised parties, 1943–1944
F^{7}15300 Milice, 1943–1944
F^{7}15301 LVF and Milice
F^{7}15302 Gestapo Français, 1940–44
F^{7}15303 Gestapo Français, 1940–44
F^{7}15304 Légion Française des Combattants, Waffen-SS, LVF
F^{7}15279 PPF 1940–1944
F^{7}14961 Milice
F^{7}14956 LVF
F^{7}14957 LVF
F^{7}15280 PPF (1940–1944)
F^{7}14833, 14836 and 14856 Narcotics and white slavery, 1923–1939
F^{7}13983 Various parties, 1936
F^{7}13985 Various, including 'gangsterism' in Provence, 1937

Cartons in the Archives Nationales devoted entirely to Marseille:

F^{2}2234 Finances and administration: 1932–1940
F^{2}2235 Administrative reorganisation of Marseille, 1938–1939
(*Constatations faites à Marseille par les rapporteurs du comité*)
F^{1CIII}1143 Prefects' reports, 1940–1944
F^{1CIII}1200 Regional prefects' reports, 1942–1944.

German archives in the Archives Nationales with material on Marseille:

AJ^{40}545 Reports of *Feldkommandantur* on Prefects and prefectoral personnel, 13 June 1944)
393M13 Microfilm of R70 Frankreich in Bundesarchiv (Koblenz): *archives des services spéciaux de la police allemande en France*, 1940–1944
F^{7}15150 'Livre d'ordre de la SD de Marseille, avril 1943–mars 1944'.
F^{7}15151 'Archives de la Geheime Feld Polizei'

Archives de la Préfecture de Police (Paris)
(*série provisoire*)

BA 326 Croix-de-Feu 1931–1936
BA 327 Croix-de-Feu and PSF, 1936–1938
BA 328 Jeunesses Patriotes and Parti National Populaire, 1925–1936
BA 329 Parti Républicain National et Social, 1930–1939
BA 337 PPF, 1936–1939 (newspaper cuttings)
BA 341 PPF, 1936–1941 (newspaper cuttings).

National Archives, Washington D.C.

T120 2129 (microfilm) Telegrams of German foreign ministry, Sept. and Oct. 1944 (re Sabiani and Doriot in exile).

Archives départementales des Bouches-du-Rhône (Marseille)

Police and prefectoral reports, 1918–1930:

M^{6}8320 Diverse police matters including *banditisme* (1921–1923)
M^{6}8321 Communist party, 1921
M^{6}8324 Communist party and unions, 1921
M^{6}8325 Communist party and unions, 1921–1923
M^{6}10811 Communist party, 1922–1923
14M25/64 Communist unions, 1923 (re Sabiani)
M^{6}10865 Political reports, 1921–1924, esp. on Communist party
M^{6}8430 Various reports, 1922
M^{6}8410 Monthly reports, 1923–1924
M^{6}10801 Political reports, 1923–1924
M^{6}8287 Varied reports. mostly
M^{6}10802 Political reports, 1925
M^{6}10803 Political reports, 1925
M^{6}10804 Political reports, 1926
M^{6}10805 Political reports, 1926
M^{6}10819 May Day demonstrations, 1926–1932
M^{6}10806 Political reports, 1927
M^{6}11779 General police, 1927–1930
M^{6}10869 Neighbourhood complaints about crime, 1927
M^{6}10807 Political reports, 1928
M^{6}10808 Political reports, 1929
M^{6}19818 1 Aug. demonstrations, 1929–1931
AMsup/49 *Police judiciaire* report on *affaire des bandits* derrière la Bourse (1928)
M^{6}11391 *Affaire des bandits de derrière de derrière la Bourse* (1929–1930)
— newspaper cuttings
IIIM47 Cantonal elections, 1919
IIIM48 Cantonal elections, 1921–1922
IIIM49 Cantonal elections, 1923–1925
IIIM50 Cantonal elections, 1928
VM^{2}245 Municipal elections, 1919
VM^{2}250 Municipal elections, 1919 (results)
VM^{2}261 Municipal elections, 1925
VM^{2}268 Municipal elections, 1929
VM^{2}275 and 276 Municipal elections, 1929 (results)
IIM^{2}55 Legislative elections, 1924

IIM^{2}56 Legislative elections, 1928
IIM^{2}57 Legislative elections, 1928 (results)

Police and prefectoral reports, 1931–1939:

M^{6}8292 Prefectoral correspondence, mostly politics (1931)
M^{6}8288 Varied reports, including Croix-de-Feu and Jeunesses Pat-
riotes, 1933
M^{6}11353 Political parties and demonstrations, 1930–1933 (includ-
ing newspaper cuttings)
4M/sup51 False identity papers ring, 1930 (*police judiciaire*)
4Msup/54 White slavery ring, 1932 (*police judiciaire*)
M^{6}11384 *Affaire Schurrer* and others, early 1930's
M^{6}8293 Prefectoral correspondence, mostly political (1934)
M^{6}8294 Prefectoral correspondence, mostly political (1935)
M^{6}10221 Reports on cantonal and municipal elections, 1934–1935
M^{6}10809 Political reports, 1934–1935
M^{6}10789, 10790, 10791, 10702 Daily, weekly and monthly reports
of CD, CC and Pref., 1934–1939 (some missing).
M^{6}10793 Political reports, 1932–1939
M^{6}10794 Political reports, 1932–1939
M^{6}10795 Press, including banned papers, 1933–1939
M^{6}10817 Political reports, 1935–1936
M^{6}11354 Political parties and demonstrations (including PPF), 1936;
daily reports, 1936–1937
M^{6}11355 Parties and demonstrations, 1936–1937; reports about the
police, 1935–1937
M^{6}11357 Dockers' strike, 1935–1936
M^{6}11945 Narcotics trade, 1934–1940
M^{6}11785 General police including crime, 1934
14M 25/74 Political meetings, 1934–1935 (including Sabiani)
M^{6}11379 Communist party, 1932–1939
M^{6}10809bis Political reports, 1936–1939
M^{6}10812, 10813, 10814 Surveillance of 'extremists'. c. 1936–1938
M^{6}10816 Political reports, 1936–1939
M^{6}10873, 10879, 10883, 10884, 10885 Daily reports, June 1936–Jan.
1939
M^{6}10899 Parties and Spanish war, 1936–1939
M^{6}10823 Political reports, 1936 (incl. dissolution of *ligues*)
M^{6}10874 Prefectoral corespondance, 1937, mostly political
M^{6}10877 Various political and social reports, June-Dec. 1937
M^{6}10878 Various political and social reports, June-Dec. 1937
M^{6}10882 Various political and social reports, 1938
M^{6}10886 Scandals, 1938–1939

0^{9}52 and 0^{9}53 Prefectoral correspondence regarding financial irregularities: *rapport of Cour des Comptes*, 1933
M^{6}10976 Press cuttings on *Nouvelles Galeries* fire (1938)
14M25/149 *Inscrits maritimes* rivalries, 1938–1939 (re PPF)
M^{6}10820 May Day demonstrations, 1938–1939
M^{6}10887 and 10888 Prefectoral correspondence, Jan.–Sept. 1939 (including press and public opinion)
M^{6}11412, 11413, and 11414 Interventions by *élus* on behalf of constituents or protégés, 1937, 139, 1940
M^{6}11257 Daily reports, late 1939
IIIM51 Cantonal elections, 1931
IIIM52 Cantonal elections, 1934
IIIM53 Cantonal elections, 1937
IIIM54 Cantonal elections, 1937
IIIM55 Cantonal bye-election, 1938
VM^{2}277 Municipal bye-elections, 1931
VM^{2}283 Municipal elections, 1935
VM^{2}284 Municipal elections, 1935 (Press cuttings)
VM^{2}289 Resignations and contestested results, 1937–40
VM^{9}290 Municipal bye-election, 1939
IIM^{2}58 Legislative bye-election, 1930, and elections, 1932
IIM^{2}59 Legislative elections, 1932
IIM^{2}60 Legislative elections, 1936
IIM^{2}61 Legislative elections, 1936
IIM^{2}62 Legislative elections, 1936; bye-election, 1939

Police and prefectoral reports, 1918–1939:

M^{6}114463 Demonstrations, 1925, 1934
M^{6}14464 Varied political meetings, 1919–1936
M^{6}11380 and 11381 Varied political reports, 1918–1938, including Socialist party, *Croix-de-Feu*, etc.
M^{6}11382 Posters, 1924–1936
M^{6}10895 Italian inititatives and repercussions, 1925–1938

Police and prefectoral reports, 1939/40–1945

M^{6}10927, 10929, 10930, 10931, 10932 Police reports on politics and public opinion, Oct. 1939–June 1940
M^{6}11292 Report on political arrests, Dec. 1939–Oct. 1941
M^{6}11786 and 11794 Communist party and unions, 1939–1940
M^{6}11946 Prefectoral correspondence, Jan.–July 1940
M^{6}11055 and 11055bis Telephone intercepts of *services téléphoniques*, Aug. 1940–June 1941

6T 7/22 Telephone intercepts, 1941

M⁶11038 Telephone intercepts, 1941–1942

M⁶10970, 10971, 10973, 10974, 10977, 10978, 10979, 10980 Prefectoral correspondence, Feb. 1941–Nov. 1942

M⁶10985 and 10986 Prefectoral reports, 1942, esp. demonstration of 14 July.

M⁶11254 Prefectoral correspondence, esp. re Communists, 1939–1941, and incidents of 14 July 1942

M⁶11018, 11019, 11020 Varied prefectoral correspondence 1940–1944, including political incidents and evacuation of Vieux-Port

M⁶11039 Légion Française des Combattants, 1940–1942

M⁶11040 Légion Française des Combattants, 1941–1943

M⁶11041 Some prefectoral correspondence with Légion, LVF, Milice, COSI, 1943–4

M⁶10988–10998 Some prefectoral correspondence, March 1943–Aug. 1944

M⁶11046 Evacuees of Vieux-Port; liaisn with occupants

M⁶11576 *Renseignements généraux* report (1945) on PPF seceret service

M⁶11788 and 11789 Some reports on foreigners and on crime, 1939–19456

M⁶13300 *Renseignements généraux* reports, Aug–Sept. 1944

M⁶13301 *Renseignements généraux* reports, Oct. 1944

M⁶13705 *Renseignements généraux* reports, Nov.–Dec. 1944

M⁶13302 *Renseignements généraux* reports, Jan.–Feb.1945

M⁶13303 *Reneseignements généraux* April–Oct., 1945

6T 7/5 Prefectoral relations with press, 1939–1944

6T 7/6 Banned papers, 1941–1944

6T 7/7 Various press affairs, 1940–1944

Judicial records, 1944–1946

500U:

Libasses 1–60 (number 31 missing): Chambre civique, December 1944 to July 1946 (869 cases)

Liasses 61–98 *Cour de justice* section A, October 1944 to July 1946 (505 cases)

Liasses 99–135: *Cour de justice* section B, October 1944–July 1946 (545 cases)

Liasses 136–174 bis: *Cour de justice* section C, February 1945 to July 1946 (426 cases)

Liasses 185–273: *non-lieux* (1199)

Liasses 274–289: *Enquêtes divers* (including *affaires classées sans suite*)

Liasse 290: *Milice* expeditions

Liasses 291–296 bis: *répertoires divers* (including some partial membership lists); statistics
Liasses 296ter–299: other *non-lieux*
Liasses 400–405: additional cases (16 cases)
Archives communales de Marseille
Listes electorales (1931, 1933, 1935, 1937, 1939)
Recensement (1936)

II. Secondary unpublished sources (theses)

M. d'Agostino *L'implantation socialiste à Marseille sous le Front Populaire* (mémoire de maîtrise, Université de Provence, 1972)

M. Baudoin *Témoins de la résistance en région 2. Intérêt du témoignage en histoire contemporaine* (thèse pour le doctorat d'état, Université de Provence Aix-Marseille, 1977)

D. Bianchi *Etude socio-politique des quartiers de Bonneveine et de Montredon* (mémoire de maîtrise, Aix-en-Provence, 1971)

N. Brashover *Les partis nationaux devant le gouvernement de Vichy et devant la collaboration à Marseille de 1939 à 1944* (Mémoire de maîtrise, Aix-en-Provence, 1971)

M. Carenco *Les problèmes de l'emploi dans les Bouches-du-Rhône entre 1919 et 1939* (mémoire de maîtrise, Université de Provence, 1975–1976

M.-P. Delisle *Etude électorale et sociologique du quartier Saint-Pierre de 1880 à 1971* (mémoire de maîtrise, Aix-en-Provence, 1971)

G. Gaudin *Le royalisme dans les Bouches-du-Rhône* (thèse de doctorat d'état, Aix-Marseille, 1978)

S. Grangier *Naissance at développement de deux quartiers de Marseille: Chapitre-Longchamp et Saint-Charles* (mémoire de maîtrise, Aix-en-Provence, 1954)

J. Kupfer *Les juifs à Marseille de 1939 à 1945* (mémoire de maîtrise, Univesité de Provence Aix-Marseille, n.d.) M.-F. Maraninchi-Attard *Un exemple de migration dans l'entre-deux guerres: l'exode calenzanais* (mémoire de maîtrise, Université de Provence, 1977)

M.-F. Maraninchi-Attard *Les associations corses à Marseille de 1920 à 1960* (thèse de doctorat de troisième cycle, Université de Provence, 1984)

D. Moulinard *Le parti communiste à Marseille. Naissance et débuts* (mémoire de maîtrise, Aix-en-Provence, 1971–1972)

P. Sigal *Le six février 1934 à Marseille* (mémoire auxiliaire de DES, Aix-en-Provence, 1960)

J. A. Vaucoret *Un homme politique contesté: Simon Sabiani* (these de doctorat de troisième cycle, Université de Provence, 1979)

B. Printed Sources

1. Primary printed sources
Marseille-Matin (daily; 1931–1940)
Le Petit Marseillais (daily; 1919–1940)
Le Petit Provençal (daily; 1919–1940)
Marseille-Libre (later *Midi-Libre*) (weekly; 1930–1944)
l'Emancipation Nationale (weekly; 1936–1944)
Journal Officiel (1938, 1939 — *réorganisation administrative de Marseille*)
Bulletin municipal officiel de la ville de Marseille (1930–3939)
French Basic Handbook (London, Foreign Office, 1943/1944)

2. Secondary printed sources
(Works referred to in the footnotes)
T.W. Adorno *et al, The Authoritarian Personality* (New York, 1950)
G. Allardyce 'The political transition of Jacques Doriot', *Journal of Contemporary History* I,i. (1966)
P. Allum *Politics and Society in Postwar Naples* (Cambridge, 1977)
H. Amouroux *La grande histoire ds Français sous l'occupation*, iii (Paris, 1978)
M. Anderson *Conservative politics in France* (London, 1974)
Raymond Aron in L'Express 4 Feb. 1983 (review of 2. Sternhell)
Robert Aron *Histoire de l'épuration*, ii (Paris, 1969)
E. Baratier, ed. *Histoire de Marseille* (Toulouse, 1973)
V. Barthélémy *Du communisme au fascisme. L'histoire d'un engagement politique* (Paris, 1978)
L. Barthou *La politique* (Paris, 1923)
M. Baudoin *Histoire des Groupes Frances (M.U.R.) des Bouches-du-Rhône de septembre 1943 à la Libération* (Paris, 1962)
J. Bazal *Le clan des marseillais* (Paris, 1974)
J.-P. Beauquier 'Répétition ou démonstration? L'agitation ouvriére

dans la région marseillaise au printemps 1944', *Provence historique*, XXIX, 117 (summer 1977)

J.-P. Beauquier 'Problèmes du ravitaillement dans la région marseillaise', *Revue d'histoire de la deuxième guerre mondiale*, 113 (Jan. 1979)

D. Bell *Politics in Marseille since World War II with special reference to the role of Gaston Defferre* (Oxford University D. Phil. thesis, 1978)

M. Bergès 'Clientélisme et corruption politiques: le cas de deux municipalités françaises des annees trente', *Revue occitane*, July 1984

A. Bergounioux 'Le néo-socialisme. Marcel Déat: réformisme traditionnel ou esprit des années trente', *Revue historique*, Oct.–Dec. 1978

Louis Blin *Marseille inconnu* (Avignon, 1941)

Paul Bourde *En Corse* (Paris, 1887)

J. Bourdin and R. Rémond, eds., *La France et les français en 1938–1939* (Paris, 1978)

J. Bourdin and R. Rémond, eds. *Edouard Daladier, chef de gouvernement, 1938–1939* (Paris, 1977)

P. Bourdrel *La cagoule* (Paris, 1970)

K.D. Bracher *The German Dictatorship*, tr. Jean Steinberg (London, 1980)

R. Brasillach *Notre avant-guerre* (Paris, 1941)

H. Brugmans 'Pourquoi le fascisme n'a-t-il pas "pris" en France', *Res publica — revue de l'Institut Belge de Science Politique*, 7 (1965)

J.-P. Brunet 'Réflexions sur la scission de Doriot, février-juin 1934', *Le mouvement social*, 70 (1970)

J.-P. Brunet *St Denis la ville rouge* (Paris, 1980)

J.-P. Brunet *Jacques Doriot. Du communisme au fascisme* (Paris, 1986)

P. Burrin 'La France dans le champ magnétique du fascisme', *Le Débat* 32 (Nov. 1984)

P. Burrin *La dérive fasciste. Doriot, Déat, Bergery, 1933–1945* (Paris, 1986)

G. Cazaux *Quelques vues de Marseille* (Bordeaux, 1929)

L.-F. Céline *D'un château l'autre* (Paris, 1969)

André Chagny, *Marseille et ses environs* (Lyon, 1931)

M. Chanal 'La Milice française dans l'Isère', *Revue d'histoire de la deuxième guerre mondiale, 127* (July 1982)

P. Chopine *Six ans avec les Croix-de-feu* (Paris, 1935)

R. Cobb *French and Germans. Germans and French* (Hanover and London, 1983)

G. Comte *Le Monde Diplomatique*, March 1985

H. Coston *Partis, journaux et hommes politiques d'hier et d'aujoud'hui* (Paris, 1960)

J. Cutler '"Honey Fitz": Three Steps to the White House' (New York, 1962)

Owen Antony Davey 'The Origins of the LVF', *Journal of Contemporary History* 6 (1971)

J. Delarue *Trafics et crimes sous l'occupation* (Paris, 1968)

J. Delperrie de Bayac *Histoire de la Milice, 1918 à 1945* (Paris, 1945)

M. Dejonghe 'Aspects du régime d'occupation dans le Nord et le Pas-de-Calais durant la seconde guerre mondiale', *Revue du Nord*, 53 (1971)

P.-M. Dioudonnat, *Je Suis Partout, 1930–1944. Les Maurrassiens 'devant la tentation fasciste* (Paris, 1973)

J.-M. Domenach Letter to *Esprit* (Aug.–Sept. 1983)

J. Dorian *Belles de lune. Reportage dans les bas-fonds de Marseille* (Paris, 1935)

A. Ducasse *Quand ma ville ne riait plus ou Mars et les marseillais* (Marseille, 1946)

D. Duverlie 'Amiens sous l'occupation allemande', *Revue d'histoire de la deuxième guerre mondiale*, 44 (Jan.–March 1982)

J.-P. Enthoven, 'Fascistes, si vous saviez', *Le nouvel observateur*, 18 Feb. 1983

J. Evrard *La déportation des travailleurs français dans le II-reich* (Paris, 1972)

A. Fabre-Luce *Vingt-cinq années de liberté, i, Le grand jeu* (Paris, 1972)

J. Fauvet *Histoire du parti communiste français, i,* (Paris, 1964)

A.-M. Faidutti-Rudolph *L'immigration italienne dans le sud-est de la France* (these pour le doctorat-ès-lettres. Université de Paris, pub. Gap, 1964)

R. de Felice *Fascism. An informal introduction to its theory and practice* (New Brunswick, 1976)

J. Fourcade *La république de la province* (Paris, 1936)

E. Fournol *Manuel de politique française* (Paris, 1933)

Henri Frenay *La Nuit Finira, i, Mémoires de résistance, 1940–1943* (Paris, 1973)

L. Gaillard 'Les étrangers et l'épuration dans les Bouches-du-Rhône', *Revue d'histoire de la deuxième guerre mondiale*, 113 (1979)

L. Gaillard *Marseille sous l'occupation* (Rennes, 1982)

E. Gellner and J. Waterbury, eds. *Patrons and Clients in Mediterranean Societies* (London, 1977)

R. Girardet 'Notes sur l'esprit d'un fascisme français, 1934–1939', *Revue française de science politique*, 5 (1955)

J. Gil 'La puissance d'un peuple', *Revue des temps modernes*, April 1976

R. Girardet *Mythes et mythologies politiques* (Paris, 1986)

B. Gordon *Collaborationism in France during the Second World War* (Ithaca and London, 1980)

P. Gounand 'Les groupements de collaboration dans une ville française occupée: Dijon', *Revue d'histoire de la deuxième guerre mondiale*, 91 (July 1973)

A. James Gregor 'Fascism and the Counter-mondernization of Consciousness', *Comparative Political Studies* 10/2, (July, 1977)

A. James Gregor. 'Fascism and Modernization: Some Addenda', *Compharative Political Studies*, 10/2 (July 1977)

A. L. Greil 'The Modernization of Consciousness and the Appeal of Fascism', *Comparative Political Studies* 10/2 (July 1977)

A. L. Greil 'What does it mean when I call you a Fascist?', *Comparative Political Studies*, 10/2 (July 1977)

M. Gratier de Saint-Louis 'Les réquisitions de main-d'oeuvre pour l'Allemagne dans le Rhône', *Revue d'histoire de la deuxième guerre mondiale*, 125 (Jan. 1982)

S. Grossman 'L'évolution de Marcel Déat', *Revue d'histoire de la deuxième guerre mondialei*, 97 (Jan. 1975)

Y. Guchet *Georges Valois* (Paris, 1975)

J.-M. Guillon 'Les mouvements de collaboration dans le Var', *Revue d'histoire de la deuxiéme guerre mondiale*, 113 (Jan. 1979)

P. Guiral *Libération de Marseille* (Paris, 1974)

P. Guiral and G. Thuilier *La vie quotidienne des députés en France, 1870–1914* (Paris, 1980)

J.–M. Guiraud 'La vie intellectuelle et artistique à Marseille au temps du Maréchal Pétain', *Revue d'histoire de la deuxième guerre mondiale*, 113 (Jan. 1979)

E. Herriot *Jadis*, ii, (Paris, 1952)

A. Jacomet 'Les chefs du francisme: M. Bucard et Paul Guiraud', *Revue d'histoire de la deuxième guerre mondiale*, 97 (Jan. 1975)

E. Jaloux *Marseille* (Paris, 1926)

A. Jaubert *Dossier D...comme drogue* (Paris, 1974)

A.J. Joes 'On the Modernity of Fascism. Notes from Two Worlds', *Comparative Political Studies* 10/2 (July 1977)

J. Julliard 'Sur un fascisme imaginaire — à propos d'un livre des Zeev Sternhell', *Annales ESC*, March 1985

H. Kedward *Resistance in Vichy France* (2nd. edn., Oxford, 1983)

A. Kriegel *Aux origines du communisme français* (2nd. ed., Paris, 1969)

J. Lalumia 'Mafia as a Political Mentality', *Social Theory and Practice* vii, 1981

D. Laurent 'Statistique de la répression des faits de collaboration dans le département du Nord, 1941–1948', *Revue du Nord*, 53 (1971)

D. Levy, *The Marseille Working Class Movement, 1936–1938* (Oxford University D. Phil. thesis, 1982)

J. Levey 'Georges Valois and the Faisceau: the making and breaking of a fascist', *French Historical Studies* 8 (1973)

H. Lottman *The People's Anger* (London, 1986)

M. Luirard 'La milice française dans la Loire', *Revue d'histoire de la deuxième guerre mondiale*, 91 (July 1973)

Pierre MacOrlan *Quartier réservé* (Paris, 1932)

230   COMMUNISM AND COLLABORATION

J. Maitron, *ed. Dictionnaire biographique du mouvement ouvrier français*, XXI, Paris, 1984

M. Marrus and R. Paxton, *Vichy France and the Jews* (New York, 1982)

P. Machefer 'Sur quelques aspects de l'activité du Colonel de la Rocque et du "Progrès Social Français" pendant la seconde guerre mondiale', *Revue d'histoire de la deuxième guerre mondiale*, 58 (April 1965)

P.ʹMachefer 'L'union des droites. Le PSF et le Front de la liberté, 1936–1937', *Revue d'histoire moderne et contemporaine*, Jan.–March 1970

P. Machefer, 'Les Croix-de-feu', *L'information historique* 34 (1) (Jan.–Feb. 1972)

Christian de la Mazière *Le rêveur casqué* (Paris, 1976)

A., Merglen 'Soldats français sous uniformes allemands', *Revue d'histoire de la deuxiéme guerre mondiale*, 27 (Oct. 1977)

Henri de Montherlant, *Le solstice de juin* (Paris, 1941)

P. Milza *Les fascismes* (Paris, 1985)

K. Muller 'French Fascism and Modernization', *Journal of Contemporay History* 11/4 (1976)

A. Négis Marseille sous l'occupation (Paris and Marseille, 1947)

E. Nolte *Three Faces of Fascism* (2nd. edn., New York, 1969, tr. from German edn., Munich, 1963)

P. Novick *The Resistance versus Vichy. The Purge of Collaborators in Liberated France* (New York, 1968)

A. Olives: Le situation sociale en province' in R. Rimend and J. Bourdin, eds., *La France et les Frengis en 1938–1939* (Paris, 1978)

A. Olivesi in E. Borotior, ed. Histoire de Mosoille (Toulense, 1973)

A. Olivesi 'Henri Tasso', *Marseille, revue municipale*, 100

A. Olivesi 'Henri Toti'. *Marseille, revue municipale*, 1982 (Jan.–March 1975)

C. Olivesi 'Le système politique corse: le clan', *Revue cuntrasti*, 3, (1983)

M. Pagnol *Topaze*

P. Paillole *Services spéciaux 1939–1945* (Geneva, 1978)

J.-H. Paquis, *Des illusions...désillusions (15 août 1944–15 août 1945) (Paris 1948)*

R. Paxton *Vichy France. Old Guard and New Order, 1940–1944* (2nd. edn., New York, 1982)

R. Peyrefitte *Manouche* (Paris, 1972)

L. Pierrein 'Marseille depuis 1933', *Etudes rhodaniennes*, XV, 1939, p. 332

J. Plumyène and R. Lasierra *Les fascismes français, 1923–1963* (Paris, 1962)

F. Pomponi 'A la recherche d'un "invariant" historique: la structure clanique dans la société corse', in *Pieve et Paese* (Paris, 1978)

F. Pomponi 'Pouvoir et abus de pouvoir des maires corses au XIX-siècle', *Etudes rurales lxiii/lxiv* (1976)

F. Pomponi *et al Le mémorial des corses* (Ajaccio, 1981)

P. de Pressac *Les forces historiques de la France* (Paris, 1928)

D. Pryce-Jones *Paris in the Third Reich* (New York, 1981)

A. Quantin *La Corse* (Paris, 1914)

G. Rambert, *Marseille. La formation d'une grande cite moderne* (Marseille, 1934)

G. Ravis-Giordani 'L'alta pulitica et la bassa pulitica: valeurs et comportements politiques dans les communautés villageoises corses', *Etudes rurales*, lxiii/lxiv (1976)

G. Ravis-Giordani 'Familles et pouvir en Corse', *Sociologie du sud-est*, xxi, (Oct. 1979)

G. Ravis-Giordani *Bergers corses. Les communautés villageoises du Niolu* (Aix-en-Provence, 1983)

E. Régis, 'La Chambre de Commerce de Marseille pendant l'occupation allemande', *Provence historique 19* (April/June 1969)

R. Rémond *Les droites en France* (2nd. edn., Paris, 1982)

P. Robrieux *Histoire intérieure du parti communiste français, i.* (Paris, 1980)

M. Roncayolo 'La croissance urbaine de Marseille', *Marseille, revue municipale*, lvi (July–Sept. 1964)

E. Saccomano *Bandits à Marseille* (Paris, 1968)

Shlomo Sand 'L'idéologie fasciste en France', *Esprit* Aug.–Sept. 1983

A. Sauvageot *Marseille dans la tourmente* (Paris, 1949)

I. Shahak 'The Life of Death', *New York Review of Books*, 29 February 1987

M.-Y. Sicard (a.k.a. Saint-Paulien) *Histoire de la collaboration* (Paris, 1964)

A. Siegfried *Tableau des partis en France* (Paris, 1930)

R. Soucy 'The nature of fascism in France', *Journal of Contemporary History*, I, i. (1956)

R. Soucy 'Centrist fascism: the Jeunesses Patriotes', *Journal of Contemporary History*, 16/2 (April 1981)

R. Soucy *French Fascism: The First Wave, 1924–1933* (New Haven and London, 1986)

Anne Sportiello *Les pêcheurs du Vieux-Port* (Marseille, 1981)

Z. Sternhell 'Anatomie d'un mouvement fasciste en France. Le Faisceau de Georges Valois', *Revue française de science politique*, xxvi, 1 (Feb. 1976)

Z. Sternhell 'Strands of French Fascism' in S. Larsen, B. Hagtvet, and J. Myklebust, eds., *Who Were the Fascists?* (Oslo, 1980)

Z. Sternhell 'Socialisme nationale n'égale pas national socialisme', *Le monde* 11–12 March 1984

Z. Sternhell 'Sur le fascisme et sa variante française', *Le Débat*, 32 (Nov. 1984)

Z. Sternhell 'Emmanuel Mounier et la contestation de la démocratie libérale dans la France des années trente', *Revue française de science politique*, 6 (Dec. 1984)

M. Sueur 'La collaboration politique dans le départment du Nord', *Revue d'histoire de la deuxième guerre mondiale*, 135 (July, 1984)

A. Tardieu *La profession parlementaire* (Paris, 1937)

J.-R. Tournoux *L'histoire secrète* (Paris, 1962)

H. A. Turner 'Fascism and Modernization', *World Politics* 24/4 (July 1972)

E. Weber 'Nationalism, Socialism and National-Socialism in France', *French Historical Studies*, 2 (spring 1962)

M. Winock 'Fascisme à la française ou fascisme introuvable?', *Le Débat* 25 (May 1983)

D. Wolf Doriot. *Du communisme à la collaboration* (Paris, 1969, tr. of *Die Doriot Bewegung*, Stuttgart, 1967)

S. Wlocevski, *L'installation des Italiens en France* (Paris 1934)

C. Interviews

M. and Mme. L. Fin...Marseille, 14 Oct. 1986

M. Antoine Franceschi, St. Julien (Maresille), 10 June 1986

Dr. Lucien Fredenucci, Marseille, 11 June 1986

M. Alban Géronimi, Marseille, 12 Dec. 1983

Mlle. Agathe Sabiani, Marseille, 12 Feb. 1984 and 3 June 1986

M. Antoine Léonetti, Ajaccio, 7 June 1986

Mme. Dora Léonetti née Sabiani, Ajaccio, 7 June 1986

Maître Jacques Luciani, Casamaccioli, Corsica, 8 June 1986

Mme. Antoine Morelli, Marseille, 13 Oct. 1986

M. Roger Py, Marseille. 10 June 1986

INDEX